Shonen Note: Boy Soprano 1 is a work of fiction. Names, characters, places, and incidents are the products of the author's imagination or are used fictitiously. Any resemblance to actual events, locales, or persons, living or dead, is entirely coincidental.

A Kodansha Trade Paperback Original

Published in the United States by
Kodansha USA Publishing, LLC, New York.

Publication rights for this English edition arranged through
Kodansha Ltd., Tokyo.

First published in Japan in 2011 by Kodansha Ltd., Tokyo.

ISBN 978-1-64651-501-1

Printed in the United States of America.

9 8 7 6 5 4 3 2 1

Translation: Rose Padgett
Lettering: Sara Linsley
Editing: Tiff Joshua TJ Ferentini
Kodansha USA Publishing edition cover design by Abigail Blackman

Publisher: Kiichiro Sugawara

Director of Publishing Services: Ben Applegate
Director of Publishing Operations: Dave Barrett
Associate Director of Operations: Stephen Pakula
Publishing Services Managing Editors: Alanna Ruse, Madison Salters
Senior Production Manager: Angela Zurlo

KODANSHA.US

KODANSHA

PERFECT WORLD

Rie Aruga

A TOUCHING NEW SERIES ABOUT LOVE AND COPING WITH DISABILITY

An office party reunites Tsugumi with her high school crush Itsuki. He's realized his dream of becoming an architect, but along the way, he experienced a spinal injury that put him in a wheelchair. Now Tsugumi's rekindled feelings will butt up against prejudices she never considered — and Itsuki will have to decide if he's ready to let someone into his heart...

"Depicts with great delicacy and courage the difficulties some with disabilities experience getting involved in romantic relationships... Rie Aruga refuses to romanticize, pushing her heroine to face the reality of disability. She invites her readers to the same tasks of empathy, knowledge and recognition."
—Slate.fr

"An important entry [in manga romance]... The emotional core of both plot and characters indicates thoughtfulness... [Aruga's] research is readily apparent in the text and artwork, making this feel like a real story."
—Anime News Network

KC
KODANSHA
COMICS

SHONEN NOTE

Boy Soprano

YUHKI KAMATANI

1

CONTENTS

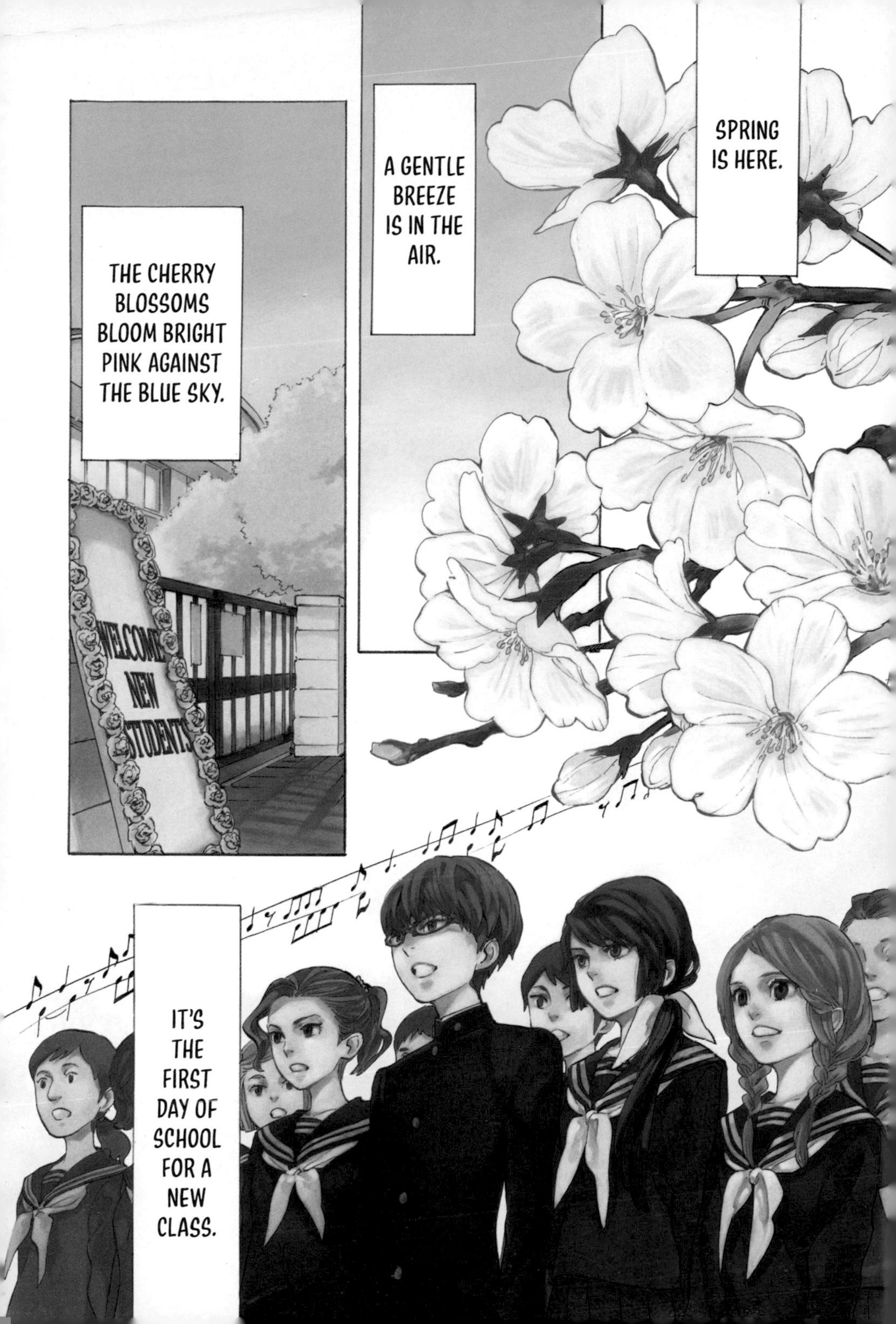
SPRING IS HERE.
A GENTLE BREEZE IS IN THE AIR.
THE CHERRY BLOSSOMS BLOOM BRIGHT PINK AGAINST THE BLUE SKY.
WELCOME NEW STUDENTS
IT'S THE FIRST DAY OF SCHOOL FOR A NEW CLASS.

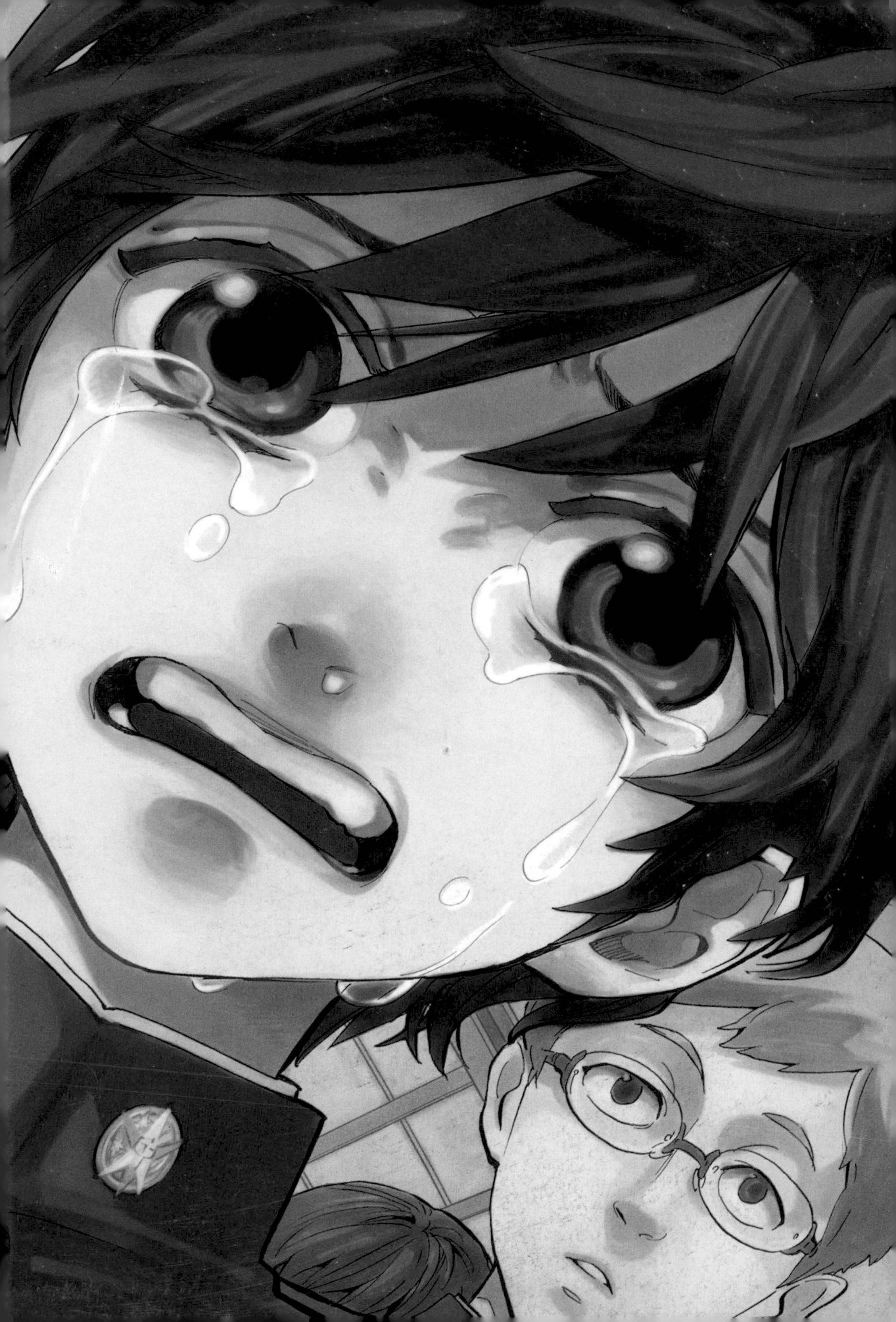

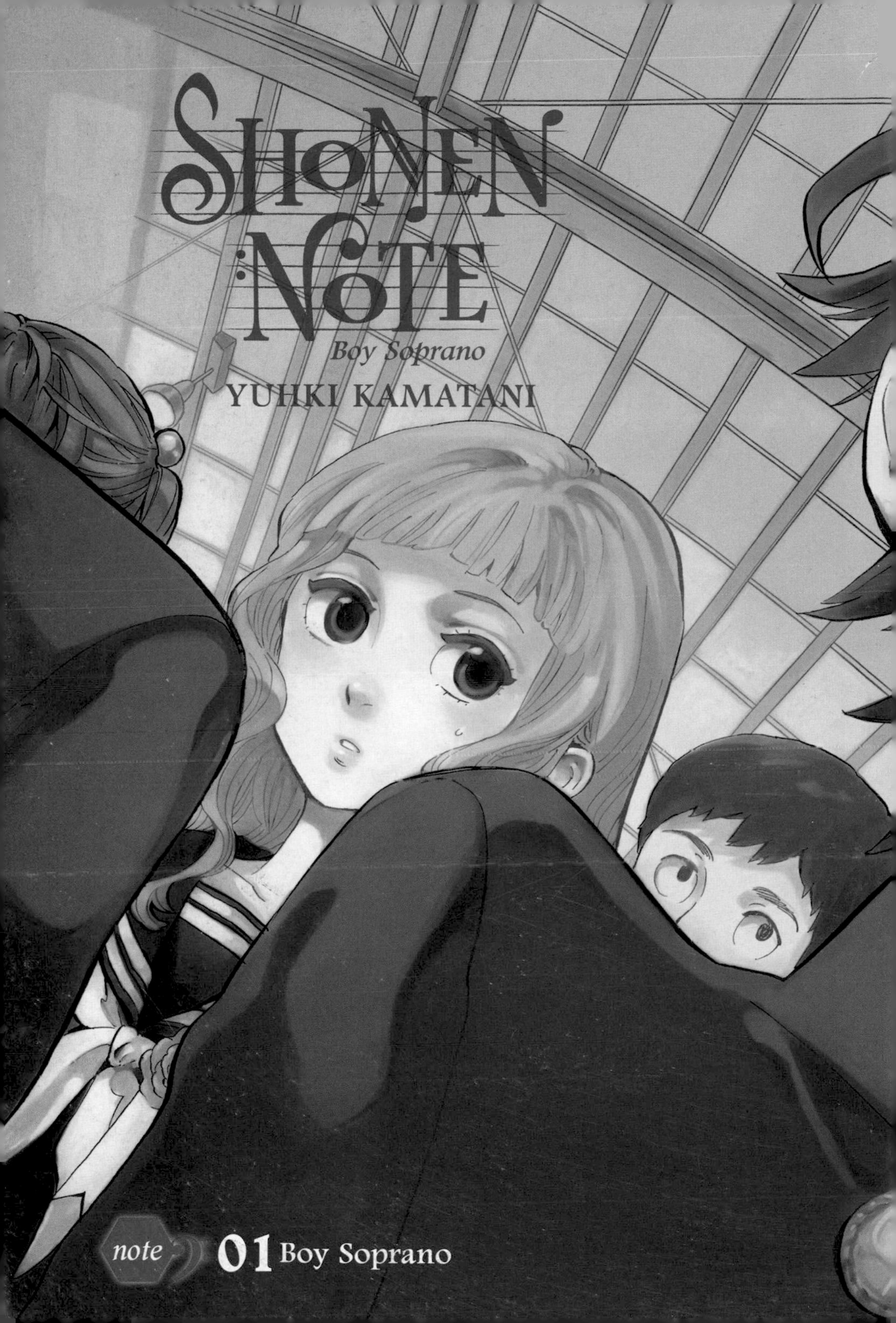
SHONEN NOTE
Boy Soprano
YUHKI KAMATANI
note 01 Boy Soprano

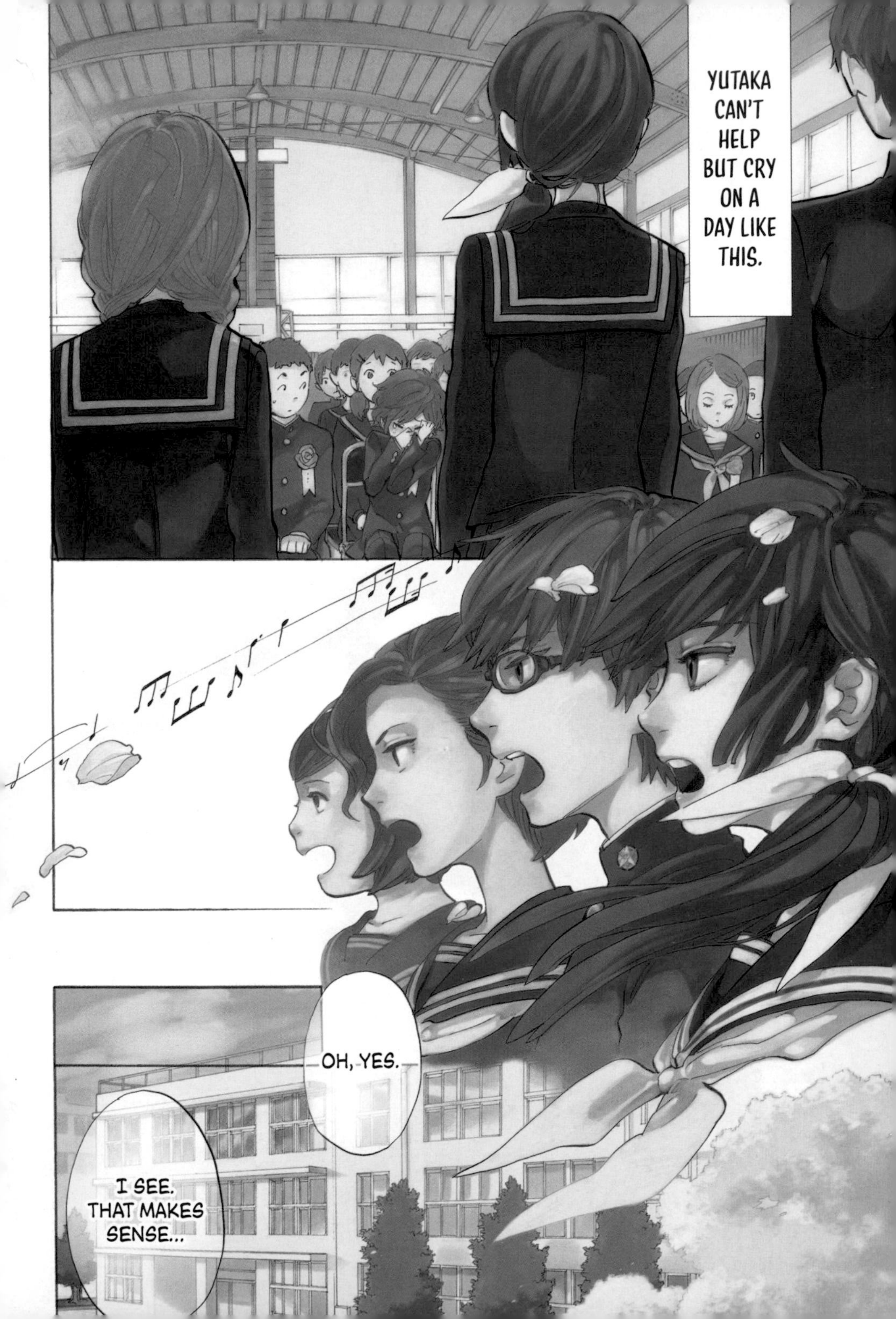
YUTAKA CAN'T HELP BUT CRY ON A DAY LIKE THIS.
OH, YES.
I SEE. THAT MAKES SENSE...

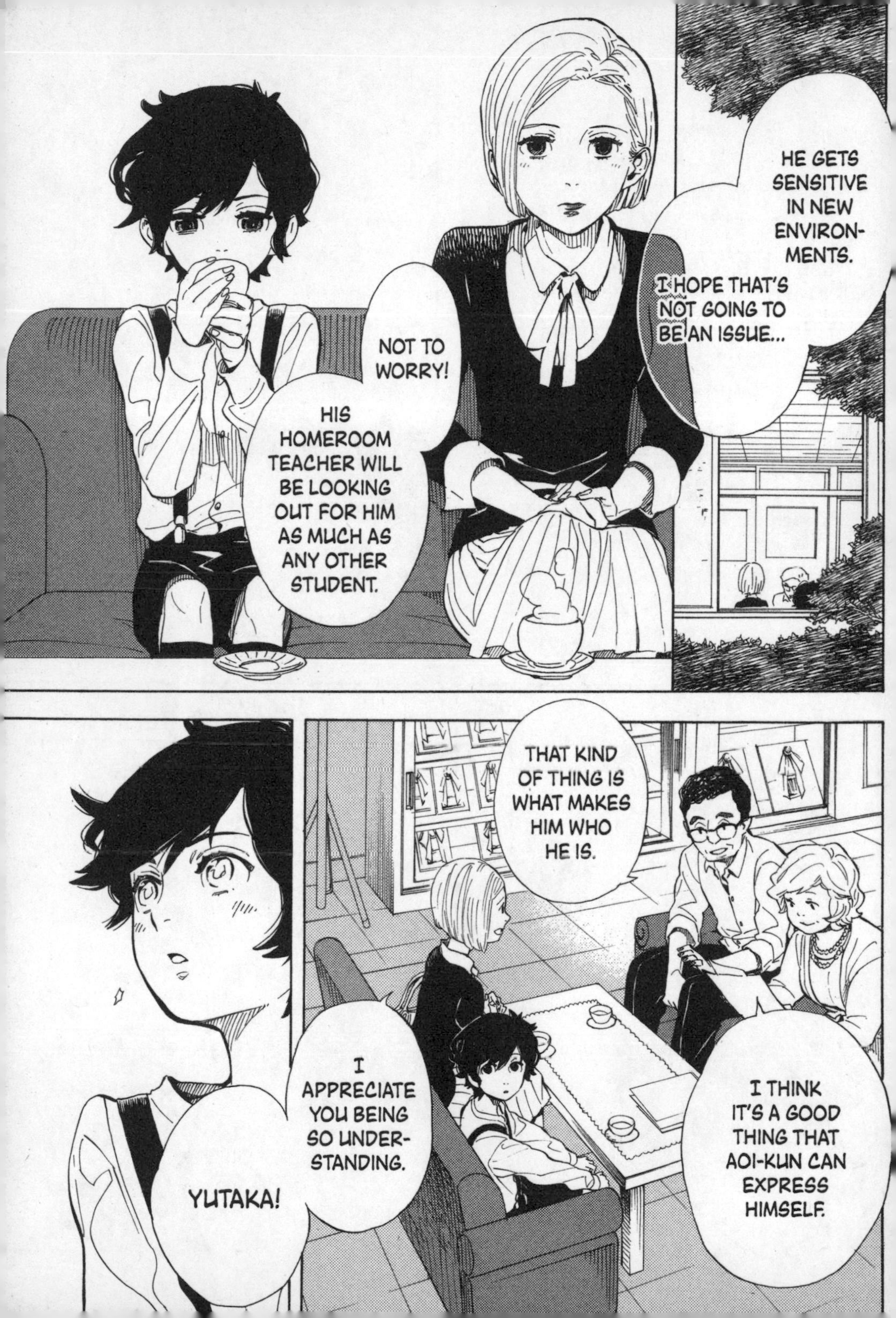
HE GETS SENSITIVE IN NEW ENVIRON-MENTS.
I HOPE THAT'S NOT GOING TO BE AN ISSUE...
NOT TO WORRY!
HIS HOMEROOM TEACHER WILL BE LOOKING OUT FOR HIM AS MUCH AS ANY OTHER STUDENT.
THAT KIND OF THING IS WHAT MAKES HIM WHO HE IS.
I THINK IT'S A GOOD THING THAT AOI-KUN CAN EXPRESS HIMSELF.
I APPRECIATE YOU BEING SO UNDER-STANDING.
YUTAKA!

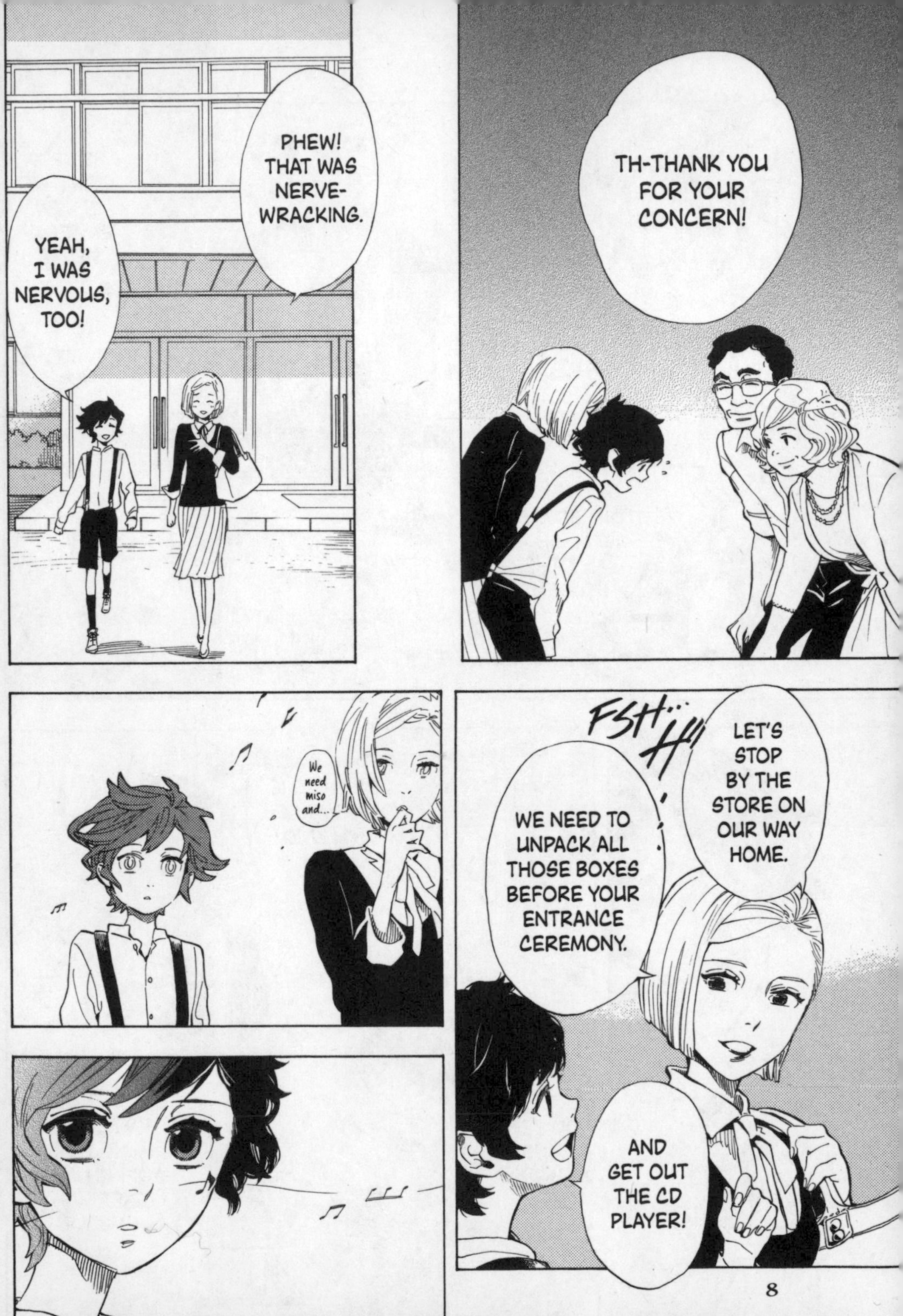
TH-THANK YOU FOR YOUR CONCERN!
PHEW! THAT WAS NERVE-WRACKING.
YEAH, I WAS NERVOUS, TOO!
FSH... H!!
LET'S STOP BY THE STORE ON OUR WAY HOME.
WE NEED TO UNPACK ALL THOSE BOXES BEFORE YOUR ENTRANCE CEREMONY.
AND GET OUT THE CD PLAYER!
We need miso and...

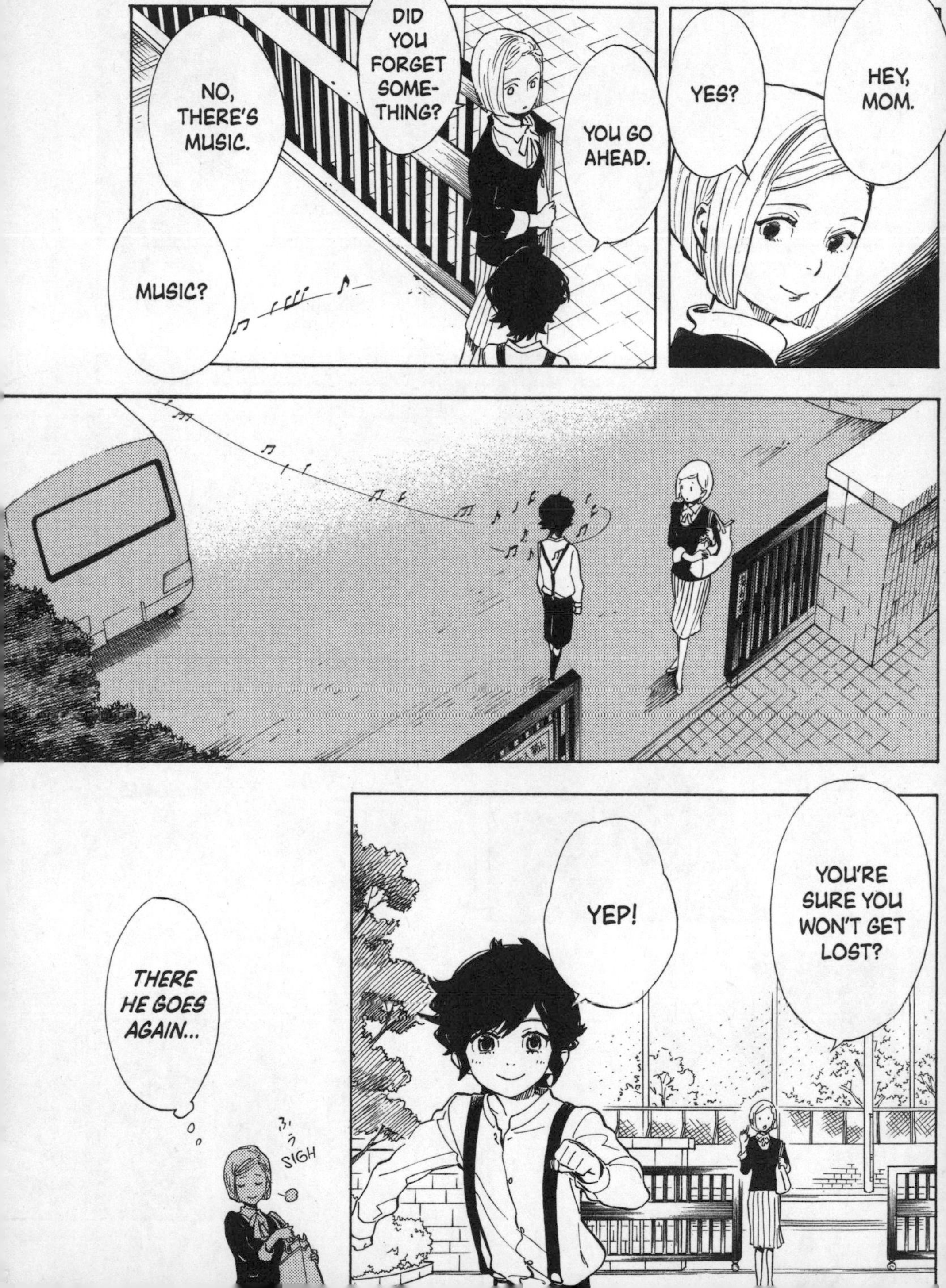
HEY, MOM.
YES?
YOU GO AHEAD.
DID YOU FORGET SOME-THING?
NO, THERE'S MUSIC.
MUSIC?
YOU'RE SURE YOU WON'T GET LOST?
YEP!
THERE HE GOES AGAIN...
ふぅ
SIGH

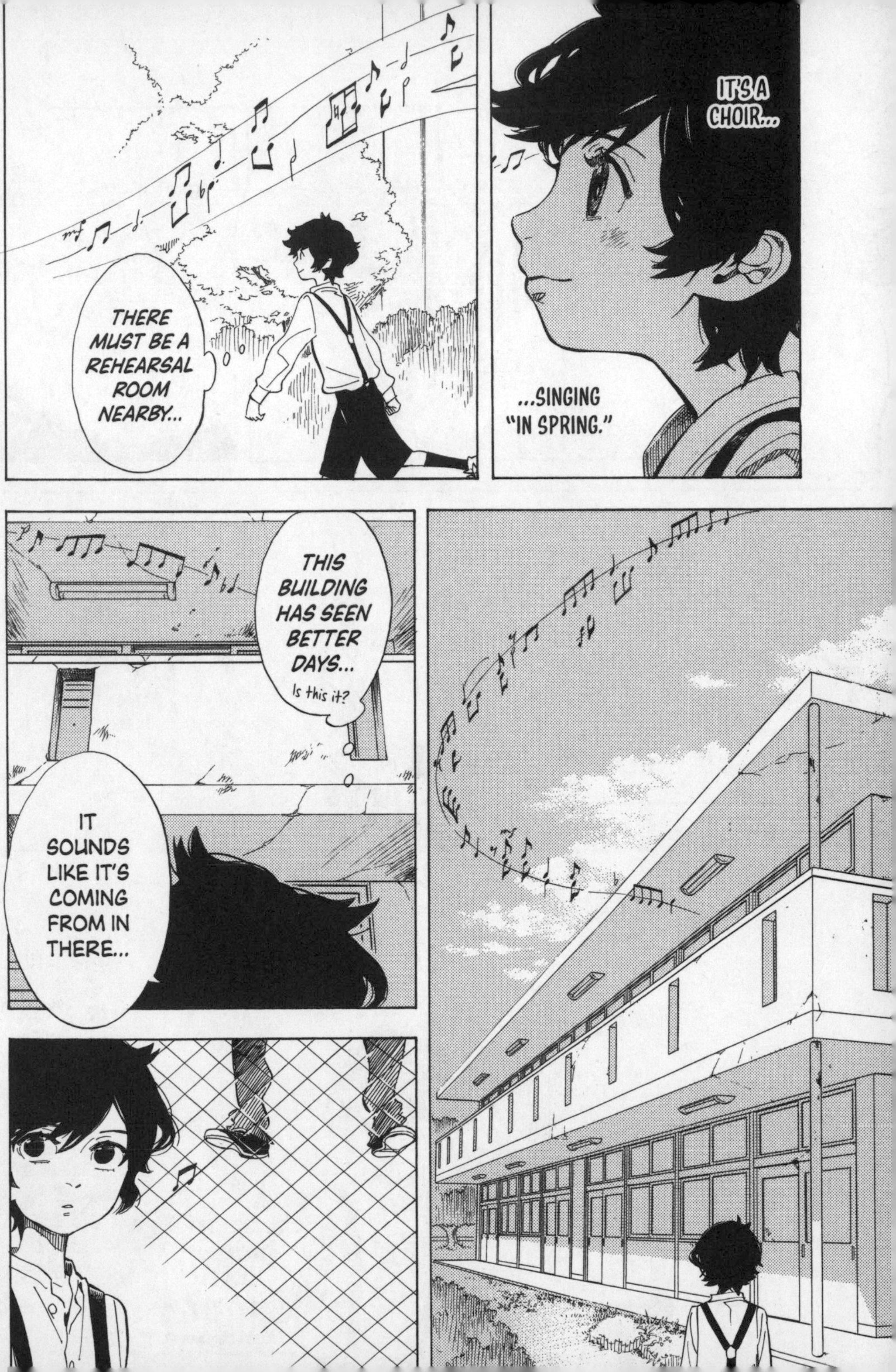
IT'S A CHOIR...
...SINGING "IN SPRING."
THERE MUST BE A REHEARSAL ROOM NEARBY...
THIS BUILDING HAS SEEN BETTER DAYS...
Is this it?
IT SOUNDS LIKE IT'S COMING FROM IN THERE...

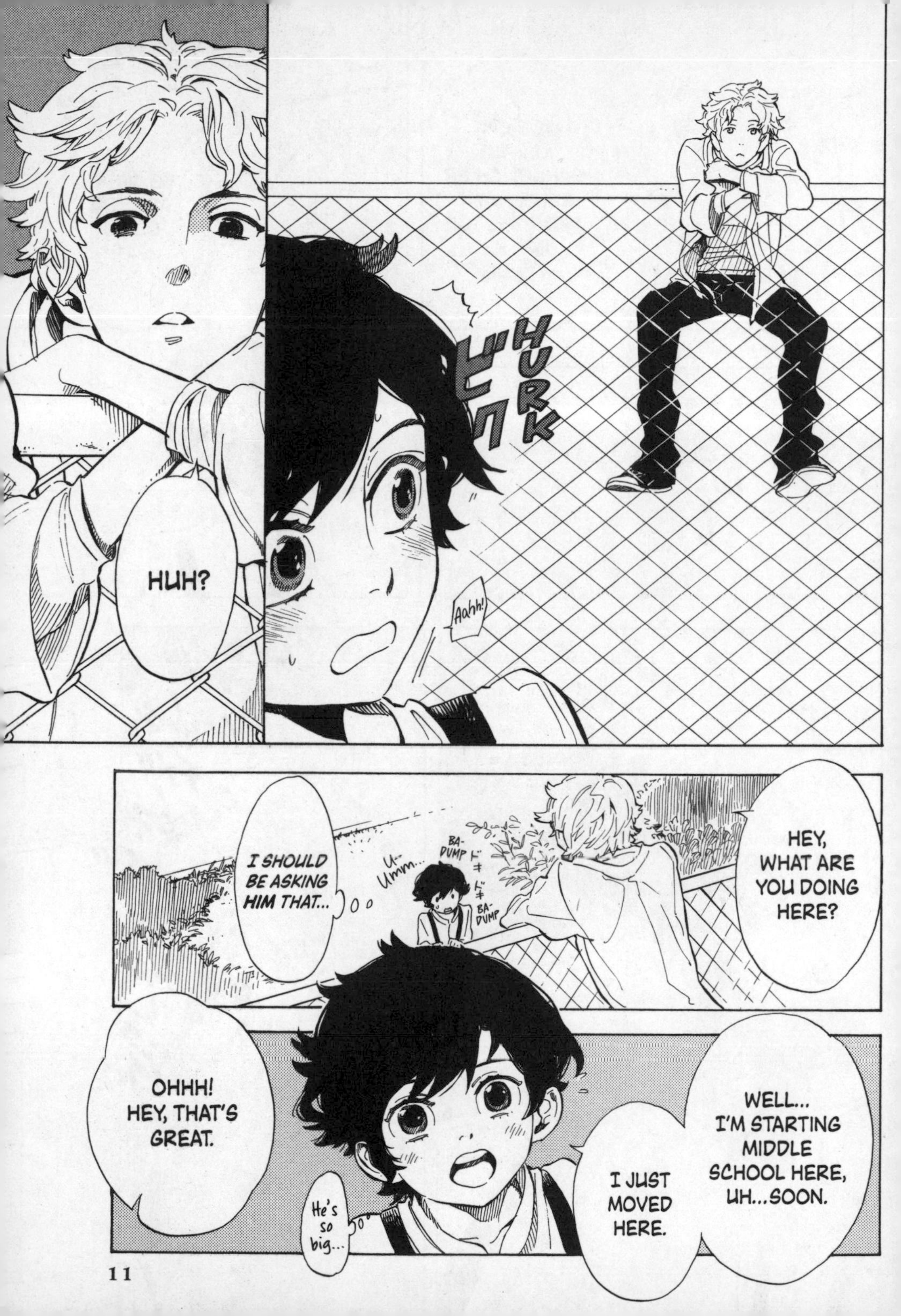
ビク HURK
Aahh!
HUH?
HEY, WHAT ARE YOU DOING HERE?
BA-DUMP ドキ
ドキ BA-DUMP
U-Umm...
I SHOULD BE ASKING HIM THAT...
WELL... I'M STARTING MIDDLE SCHOOL HERE, UH...SOON.
I JUST MOVED HERE.
He's so big...
OHHH! HEY, THAT'S GREAT.

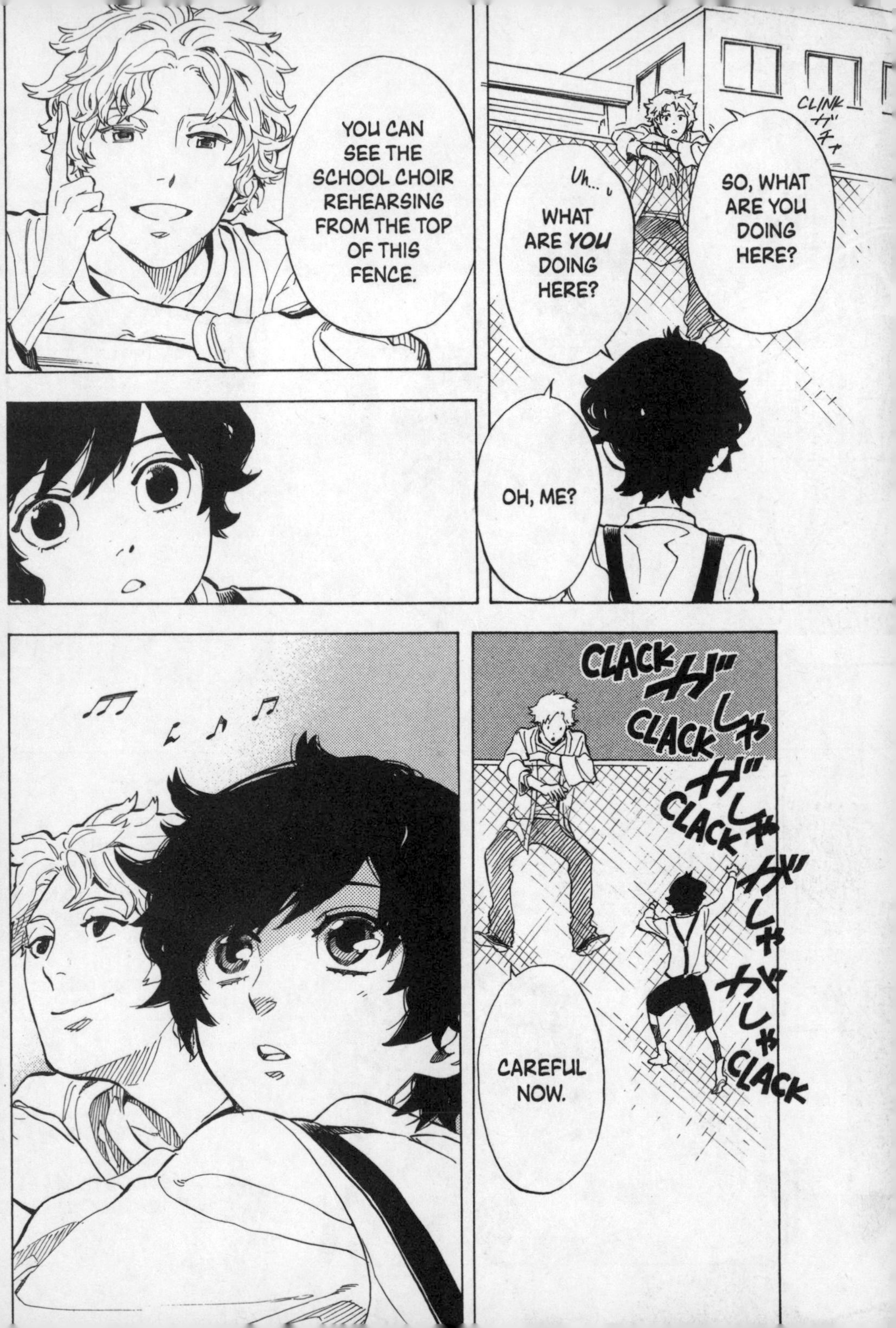
CLINK ガチャ
SO, WHAT ARE YOU DOING HERE?
Uh...
WHAT ARE YOU DOING HERE?
OH, ME?
YOU CAN SEE THE SCHOOL CHOIR REHEARSING FROM THE TOP OF THIS FENCE.
CLACK がしゃ
CLACK がしゃ
CLACK がしゃ
がしゃ CLACK
CAREFUL NOW.

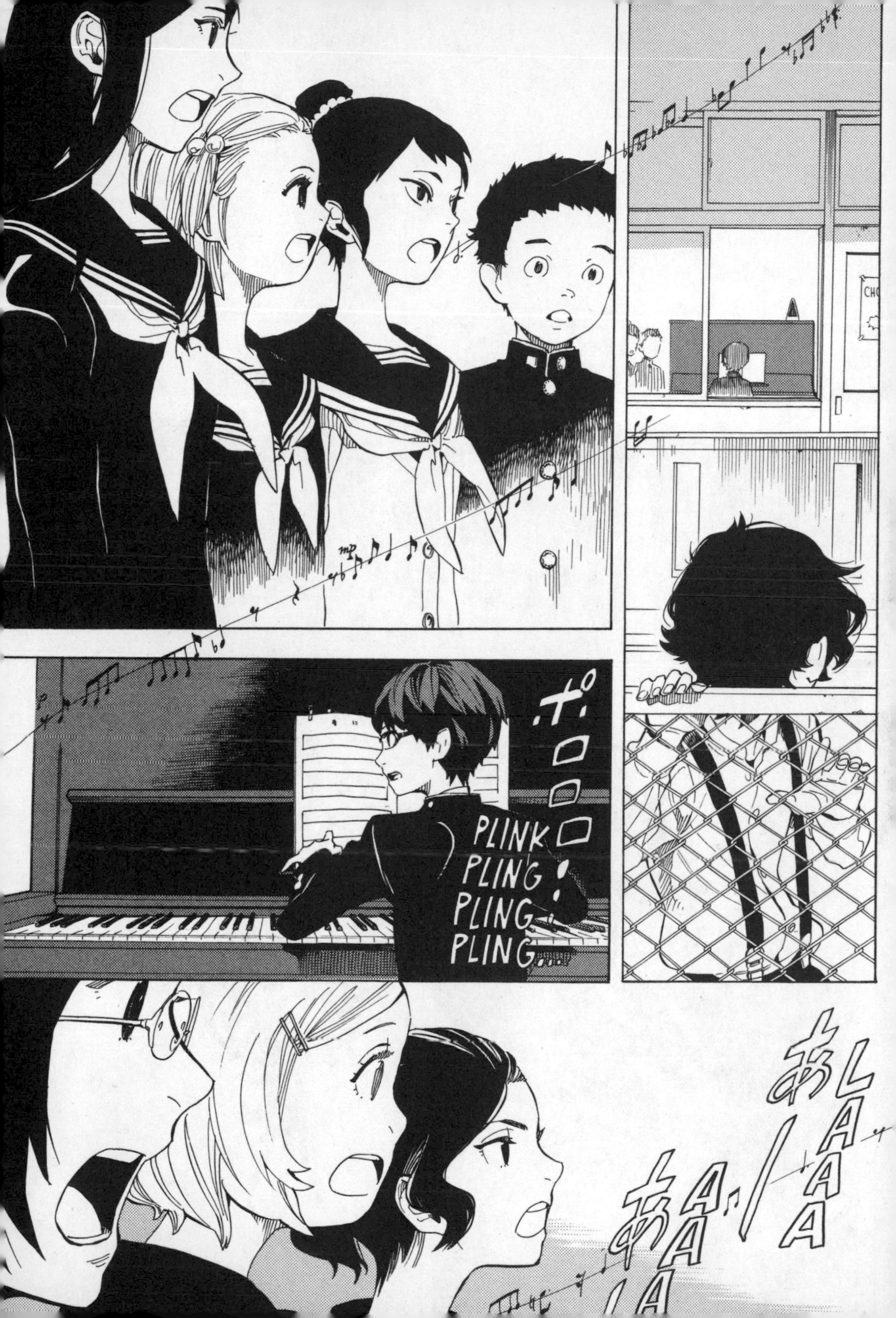
ポロロロロ…!
PLINK
PLING
PLING
PLING…
あ〜
LAAA
あ
AAA

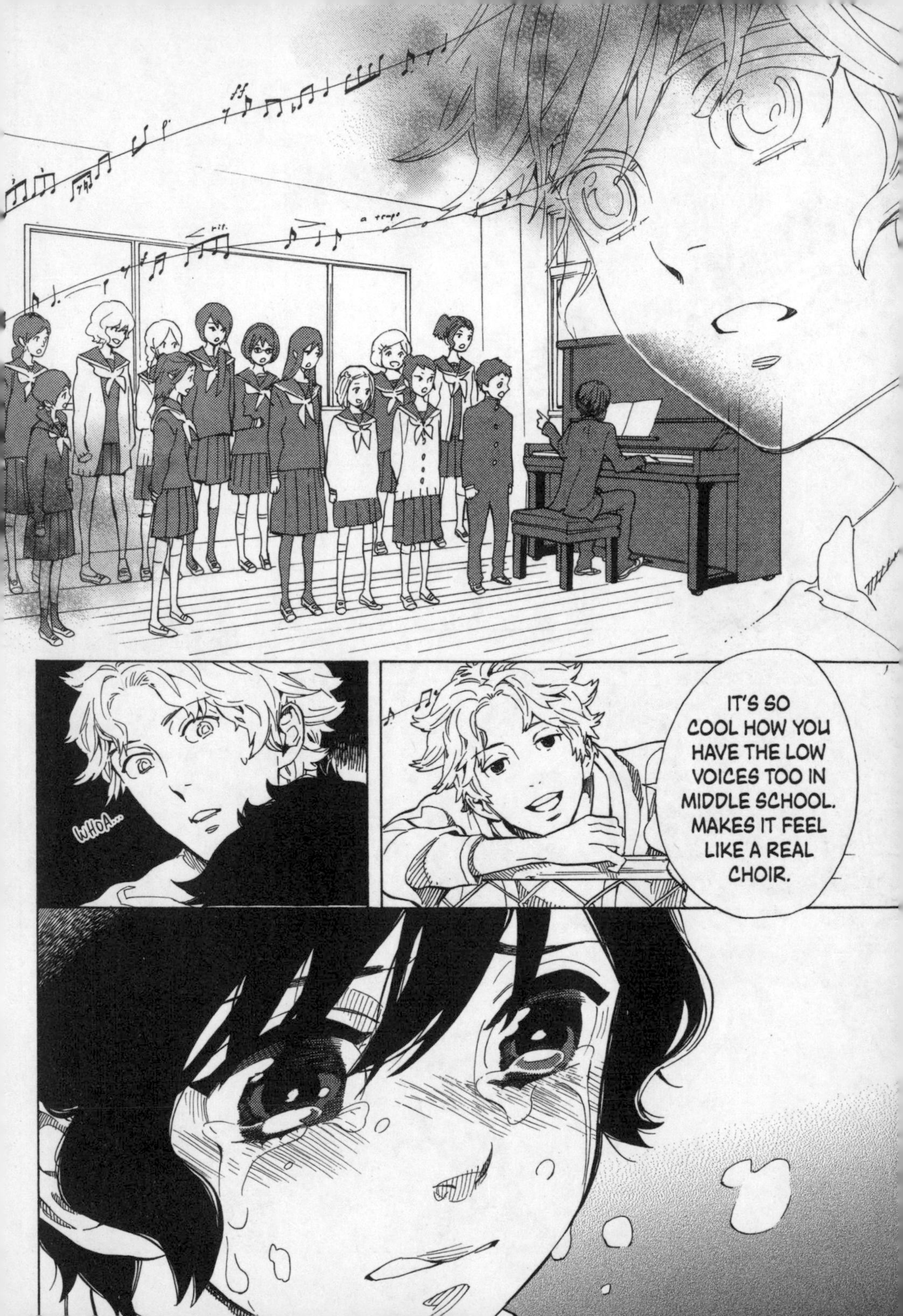
rit.
a tempo
IT'S SO COOL HOW YOU HAVE THE LOW VOICES TOO IN MIDDLE SCHOOL. MAKES IT FEEL LIKE A REAL CHOIR.
WHOA...

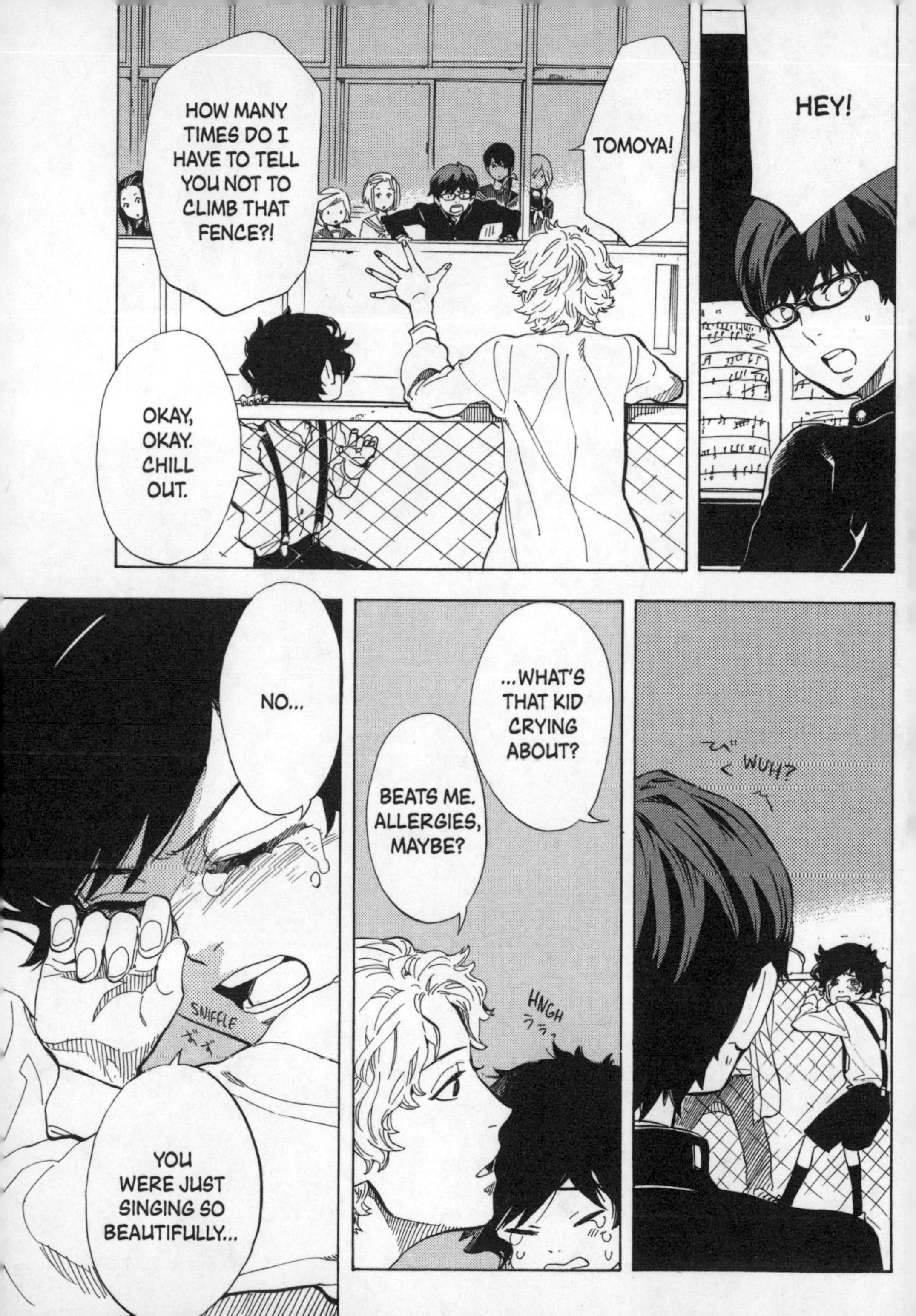
HEY!
TOMOYA!
HOW MANY TIMES DO I HAVE TO TELL YOU NOT TO CLIMB THAT FENCE?!
OKAY, OKAY. CHILL OUT.
WUH?
...WHAT'S THAT KID CRYING ABOUT?
BEATS ME. ALLERGIES, MAYBE?
HNGH
NO...
SNIFFLE
YOU WERE JUST SINGING SO BEAUTIFULLY...

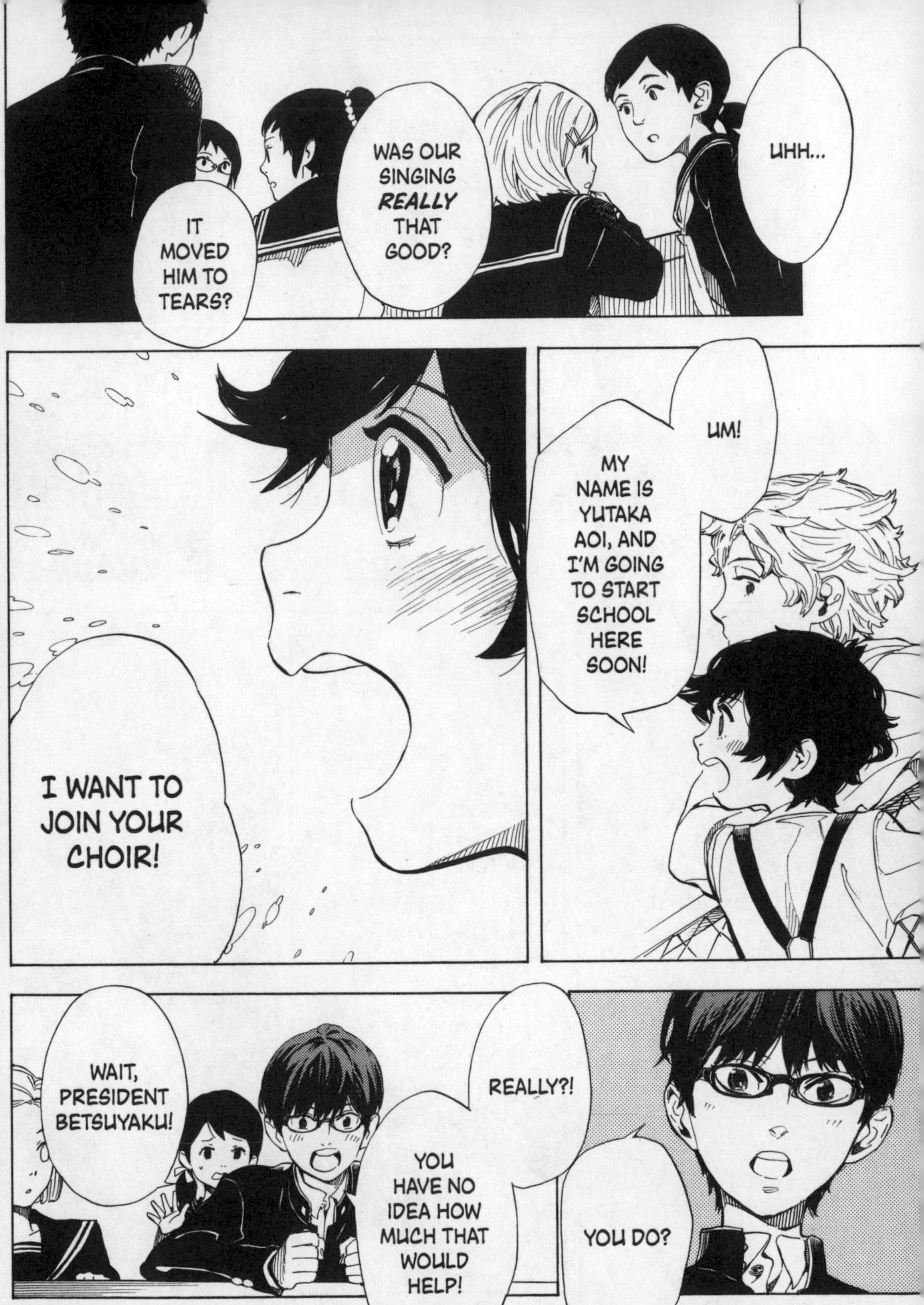
UHH...
WAS OUR SINGING *REALLY* THAT GOOD?
IT MOVED HIM TO TEARS?
UM!
MY NAME IS YUTAKA AOI, AND I'M GOING TO START SCHOOL HERE SOON!
I WANT TO JOIN YOUR CHOIR!
YOU DO?
REALLY?!
YOU HAVE NO IDEA HOW MUCH THAT WOULD HELP!
WAIT, PRESIDENT BETSUYAKU!

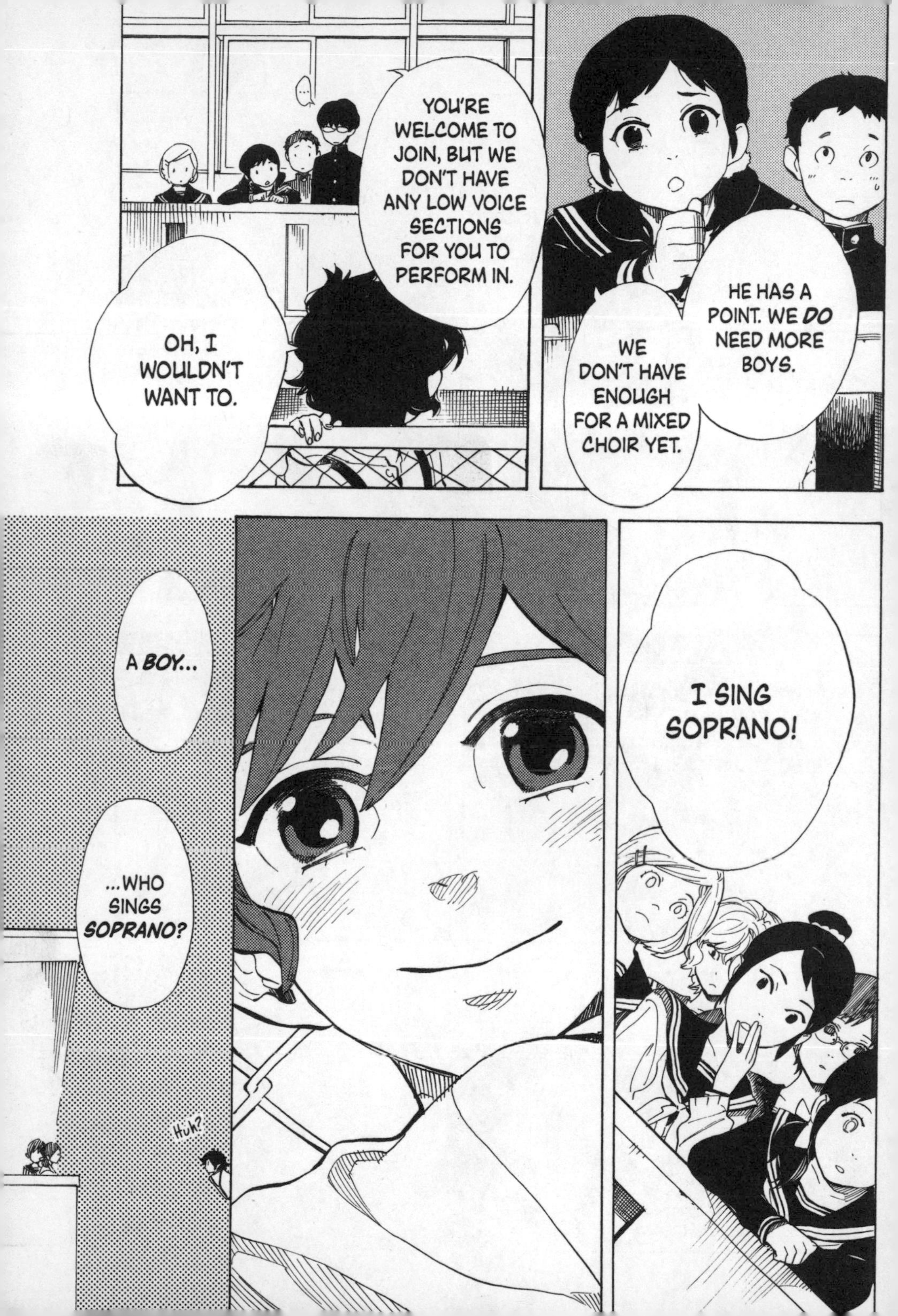
HE HAS A POINT. WE DO NEED MORE BOYS.
WE DON'T HAVE ENOUGH FOR A MIXED CHOIR YET.
...
YOU'RE WELCOME TO JOIN, BUT WE DON'T HAVE ANY LOW VOICE SECTIONS FOR YOU TO PERFORM IN.
OH, I WOULDN'T WANT TO.
I SING SOPRANO!
A BOY...
...WHO SINGS SOPRANO?
Huh?

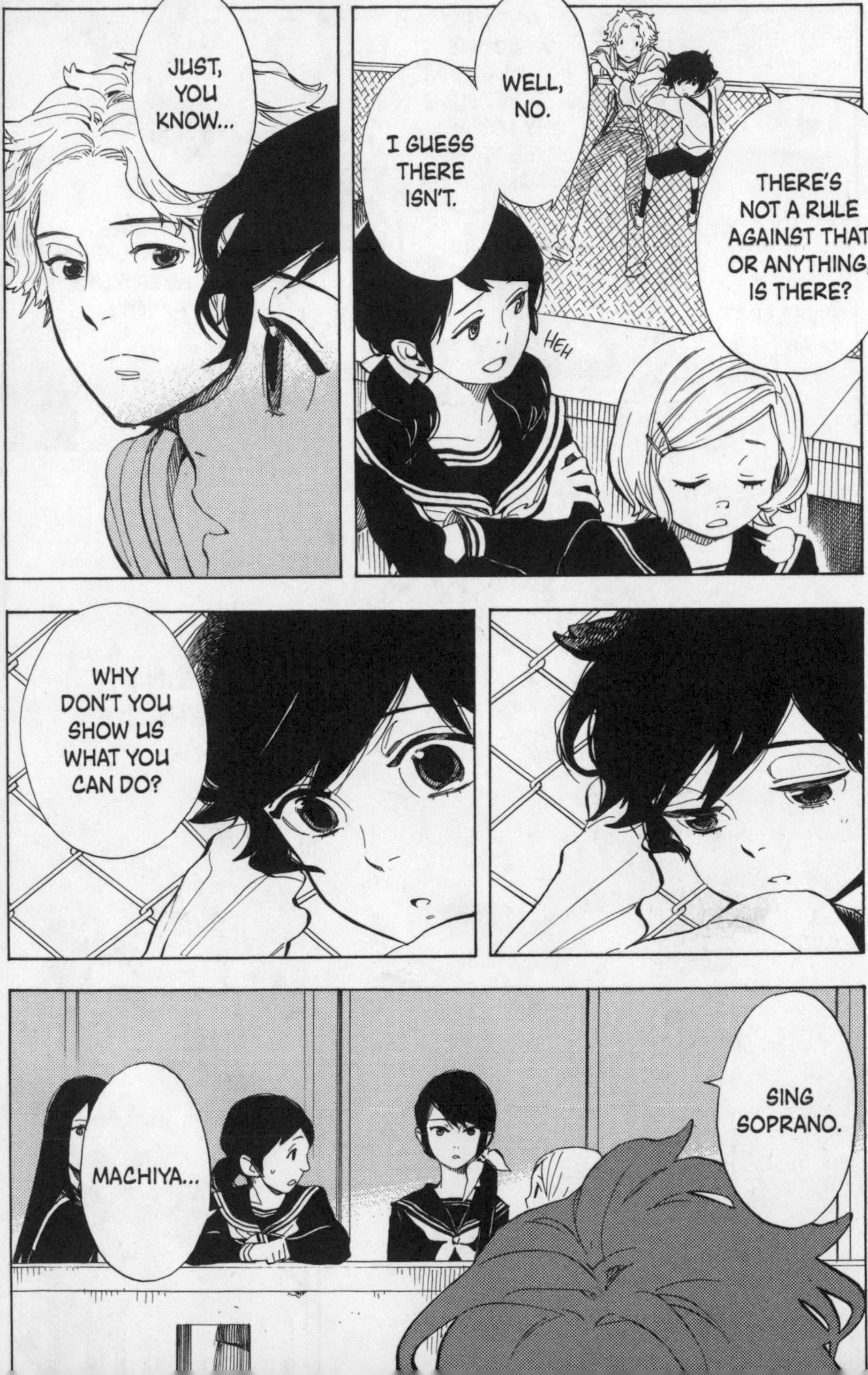
THERE'S NOT A RULE AGAINST THAT OR ANYTHING, IS THERE?
WELL, NO.
I GUESS THERE ISN'T.
HEH
JUST, YOU KNOW...
WHY DON'T YOU SHOW US WHAT YOU CAN DO?
SING SOPRANO.
MACHIYA...

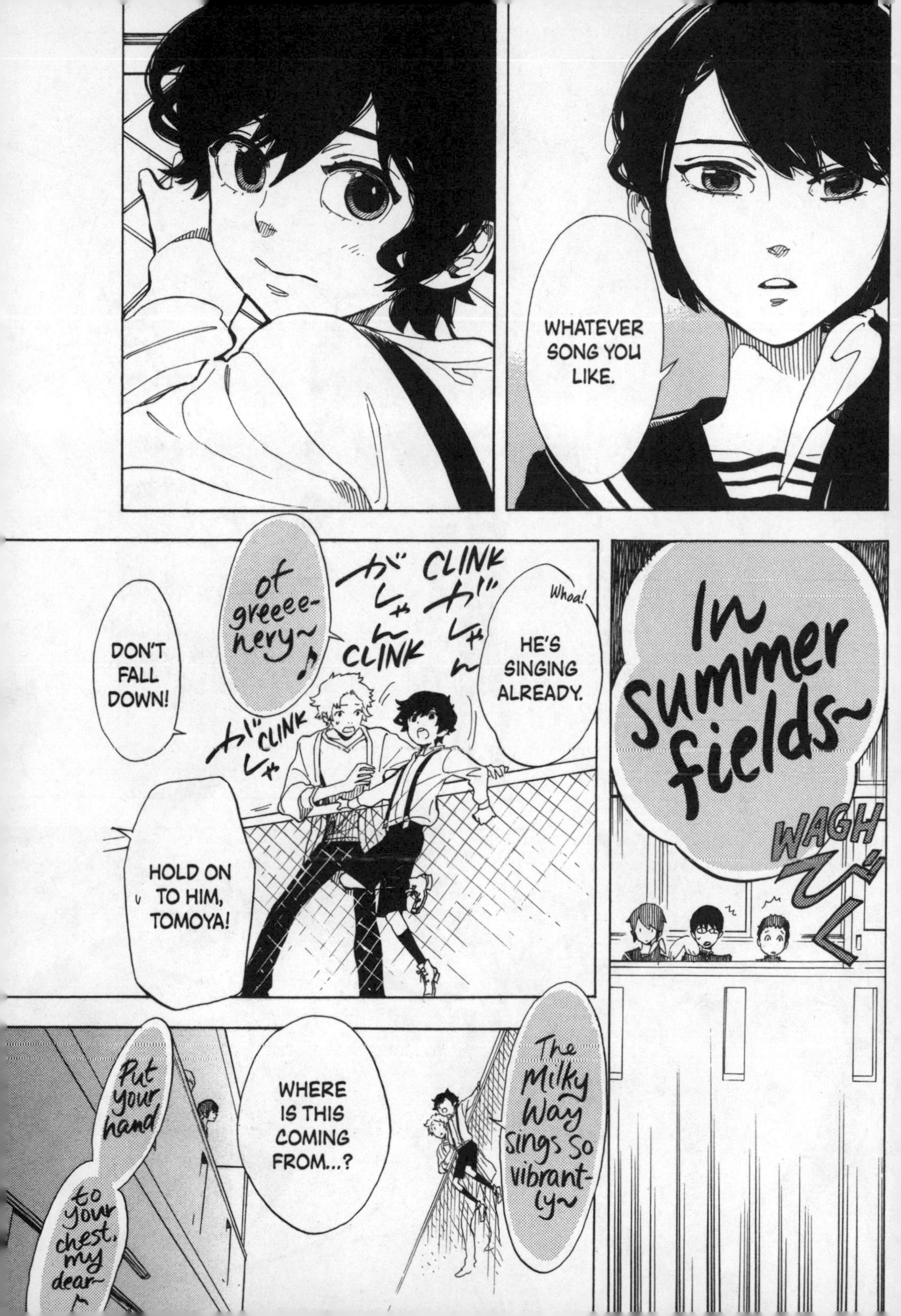
WHATEVER SONG YOU LIKE.
In summer fields~
WAGH
Whoa!
HE'S SINGING ALREADY.
CLINK
CLINK
CLINK
of greeee-nery~
DON'T FALL DOWN!
HOLD ON TO HIM, TOMOYA!
The Milky Way sings so vibrant-ly~
WHERE IS THIS COMING FROM...?
Put your hand to your chest, my dear~

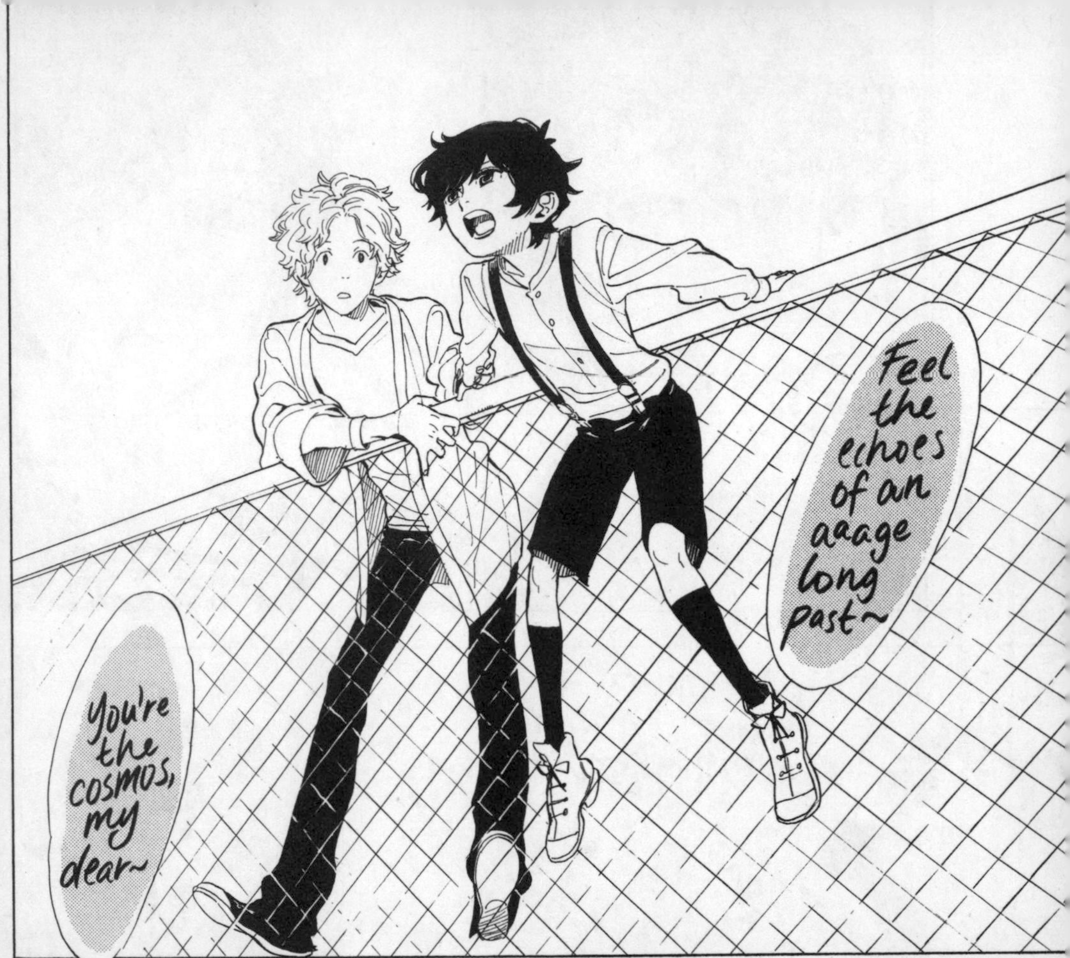
Feel the echoes of an aaage long past~
You're the cosmos, my dear~
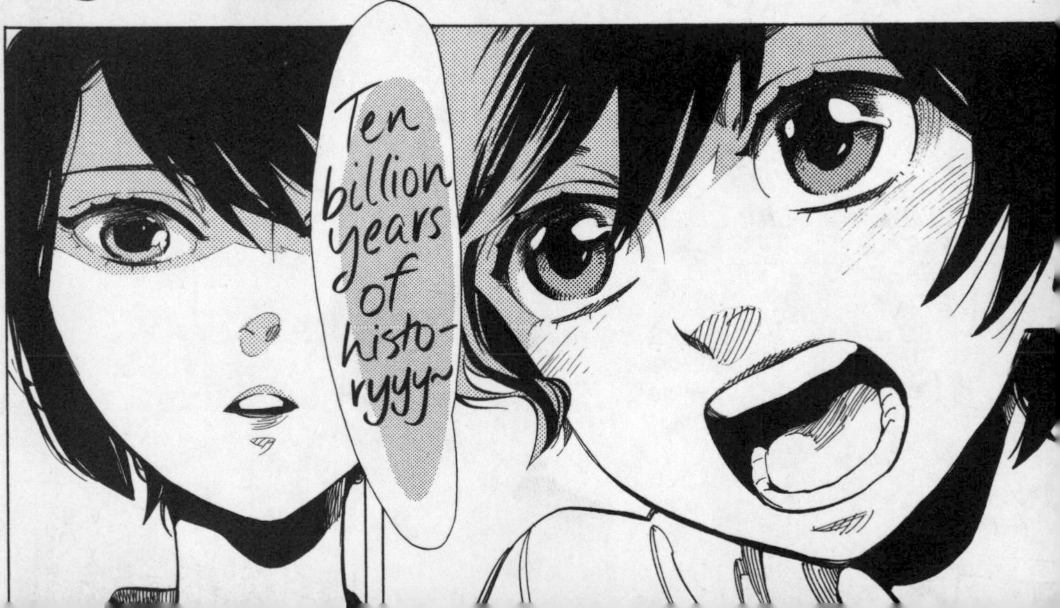
Ten billion years of histo-ryyy~

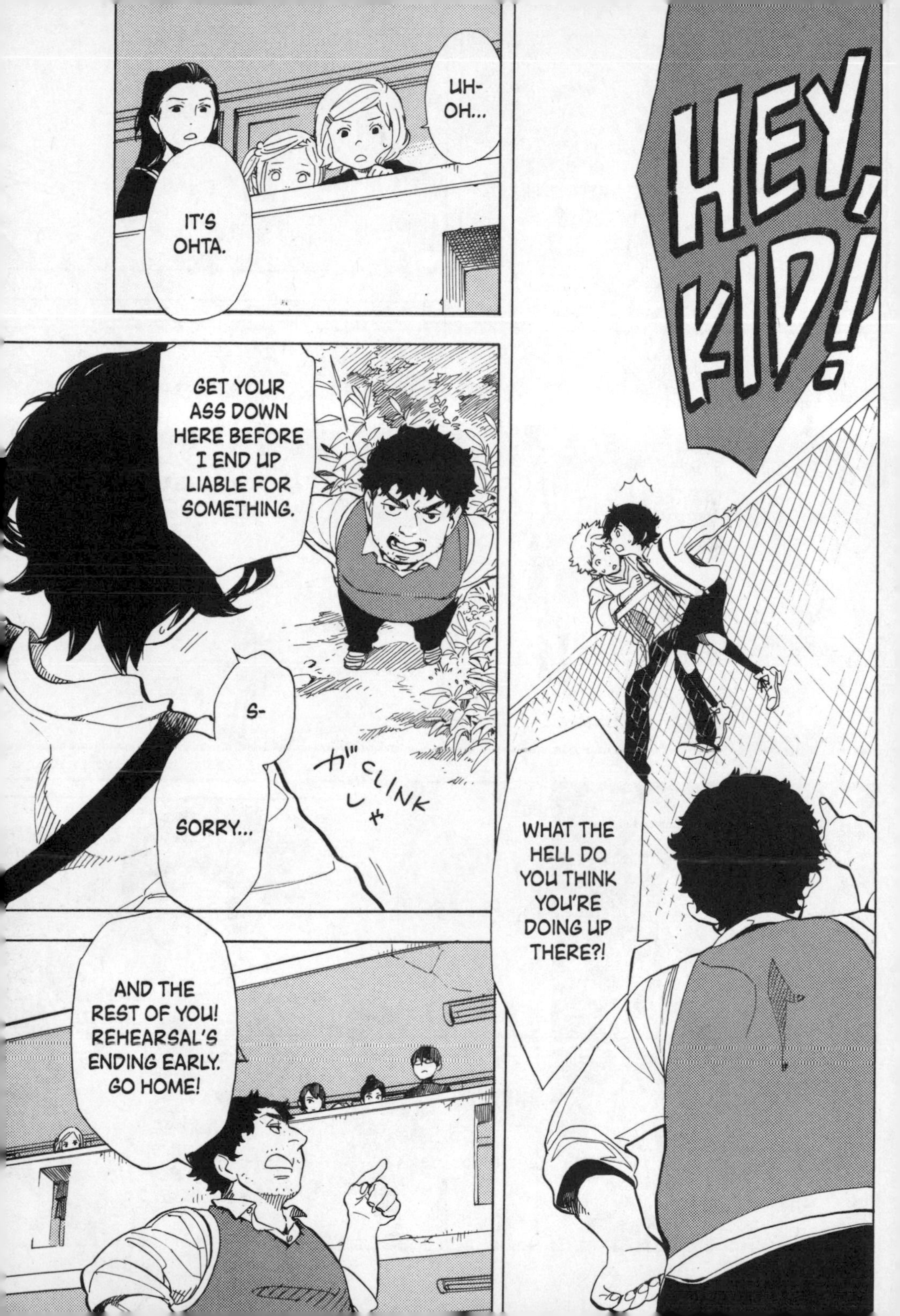
HEY, KID!
WHAT THE HELL DO YOU THINK YOU'RE DOING UP THERE?!
UH-OH...
IT'S OHTA.
GET YOUR ASS DOWN HERE BEFORE I END UP LIABLE FOR SOMETHING.
S-
SORRY...
ガシャ CLINK
AND THE REST OF YOU! REHEARSAL'S ENDING EARLY. GO HOME!

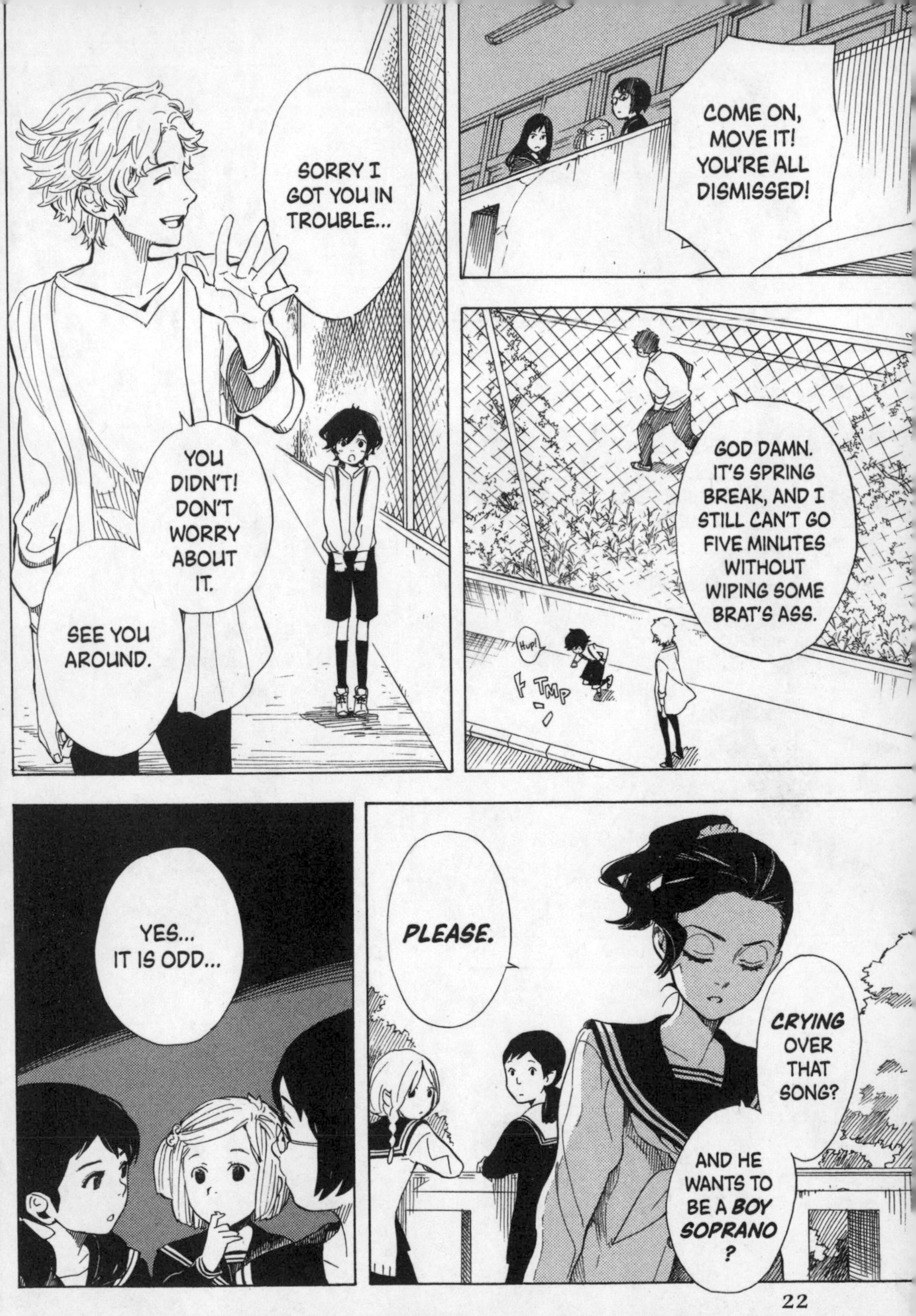
COME ON, MOVE IT! YOU'RE ALL DISMISSED!
GOD DAMN. IT'S SPRING BREAK, AND I STILL CAN'T GO FIVE MINUTES WITHOUT WIPING SOME BRAT'S ASS.
Hup!
TMP
SORRY I GOT YOU IN TROUBLE...
YOU DIDN'T! DON'T WORRY ABOUT IT.
SEE YOU AROUND.
CRYING OVER THAT SONG?
AND HE WANTS TO BE A BOY SOPRANO?
PLEASE.
YES... IT IS ODD...

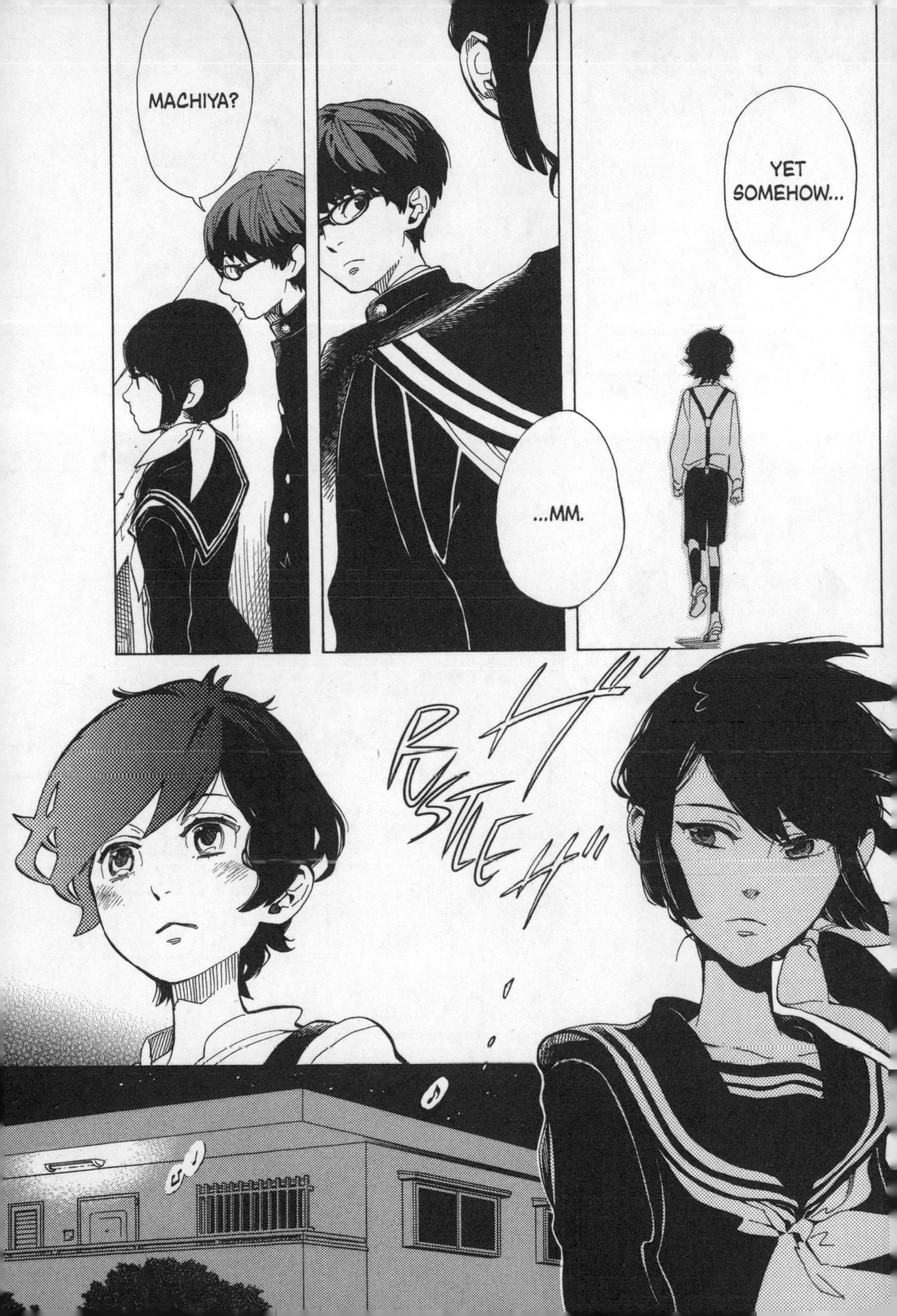
YET SOMEHOW...
...MM.
MACHIYA?
RUSTLE

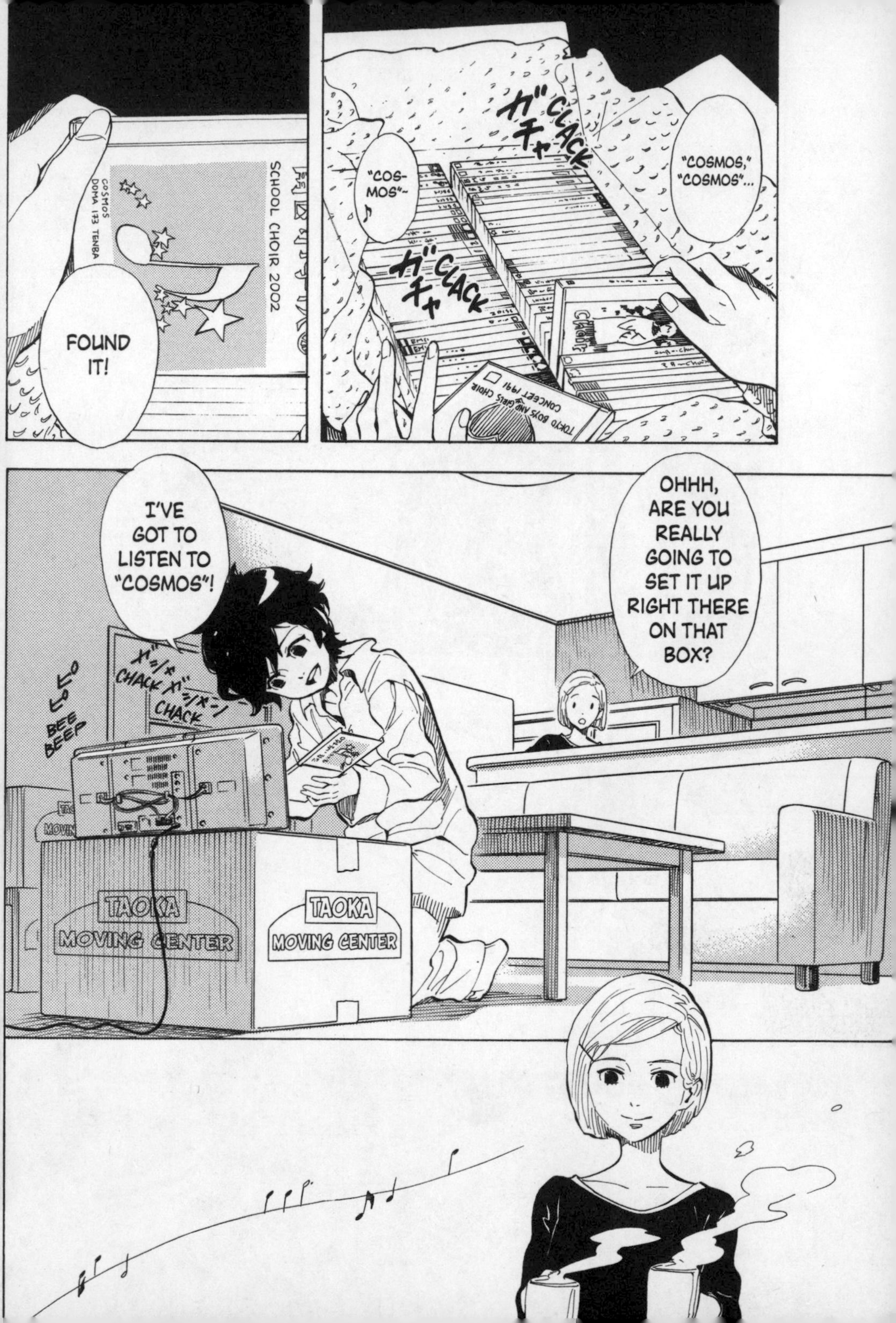

"COSMOS," "COSMOS"...
ガチャ CLACK
"COS-MOS"~♪
ガチャ CLACK
TOKYO BOYS AND GIRLS CHOIR CONCERT 1991
SCHOOL CHOIR 2002
COSMOS DOMA 173 TENBA
FOUND IT!
OHHH, ARE YOU REALLY GOING TO SET IT UP RIGHT THERE ON THAT BOX?
I'VE GOT TO LISTEN TO "COSMOS"!
CHACK
CHACK
BEE BEEP
TAOKA MOVING CENTER
TAOKA MOVING CENTER

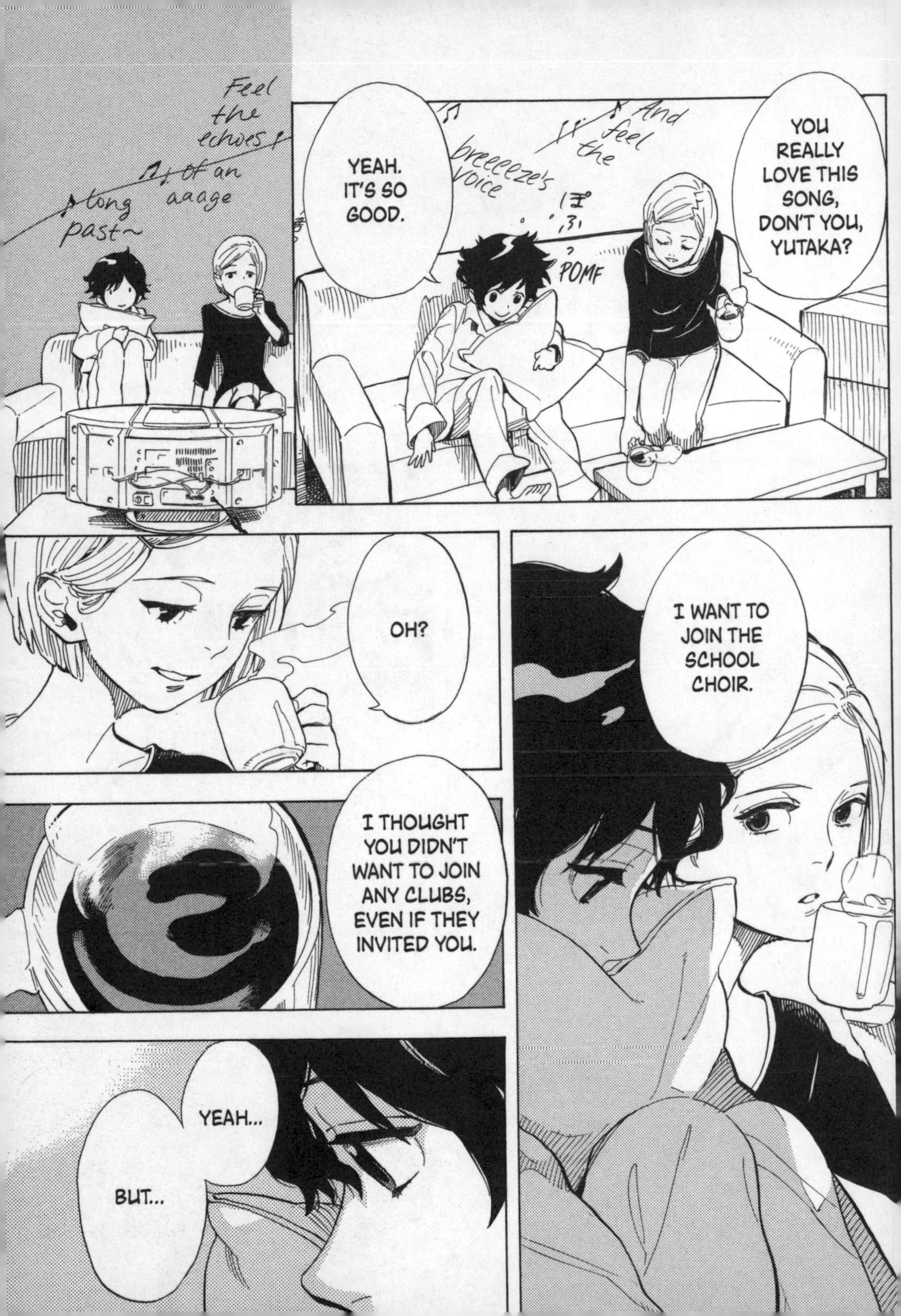
YOU REALLY LOVE THIS SONG, DON'T YOU, YUTAKA?
And feel the breeeeze's voice
YEAH. IT'S SO GOOD.
POMF
Feel the echoes of an aaage long past~
I WANT TO JOIN THE SCHOOL CHOIR.
OH?
I THOUGHT YOU DIDN'T WANT TO JOIN ANY CLUBS, EVEN IF THEY INVITED YOU.
YEAH...
BUT...

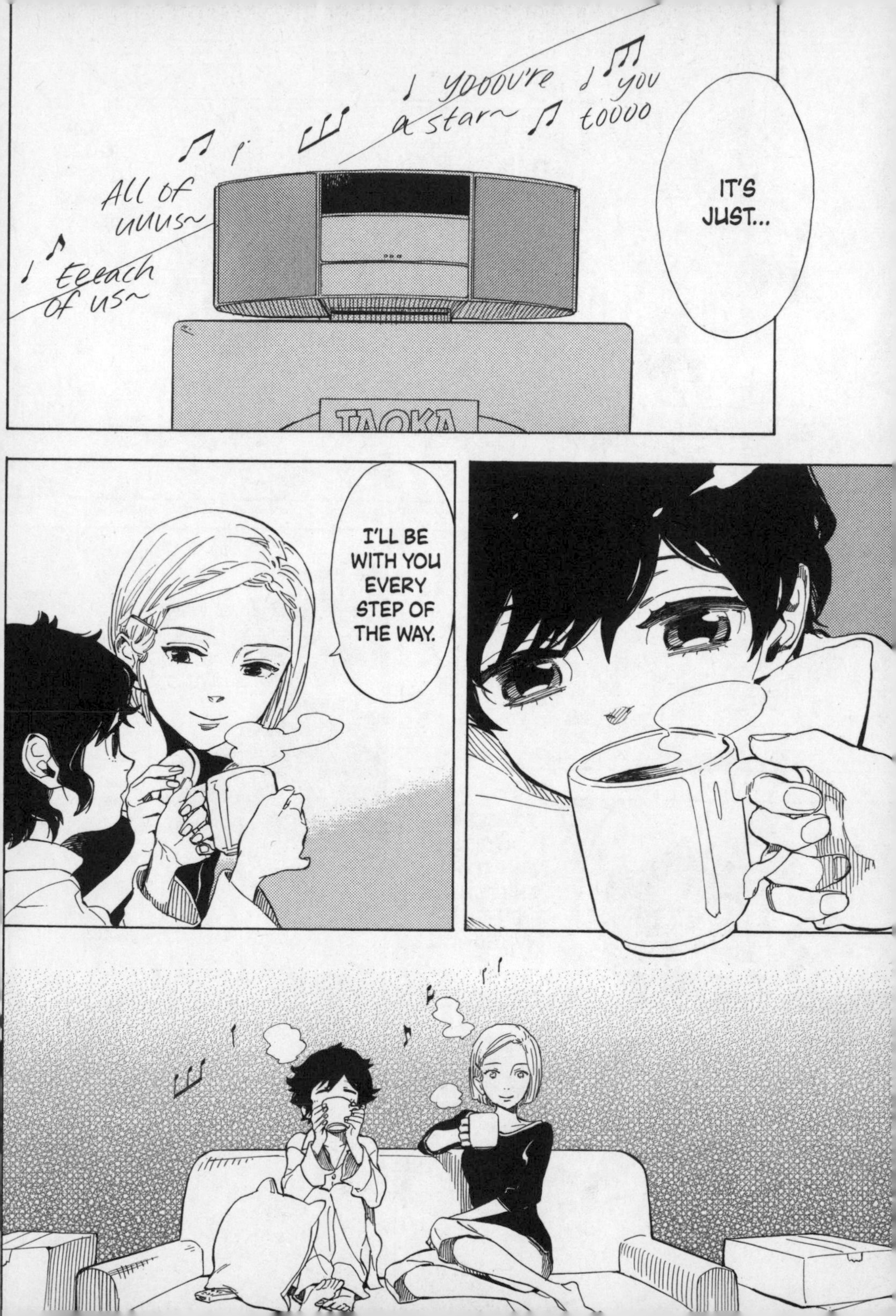
IT'S JUST...
Eeeach of us~
All of uuus~
Yooou're a star~
you toooo
TAOKA
I'LL BE WITH YOU EVERY STEP OF THE WAY.

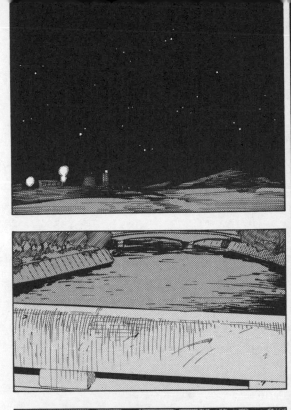

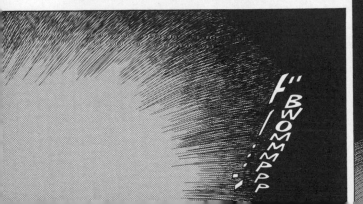

ド"
BWOMMMMPPP

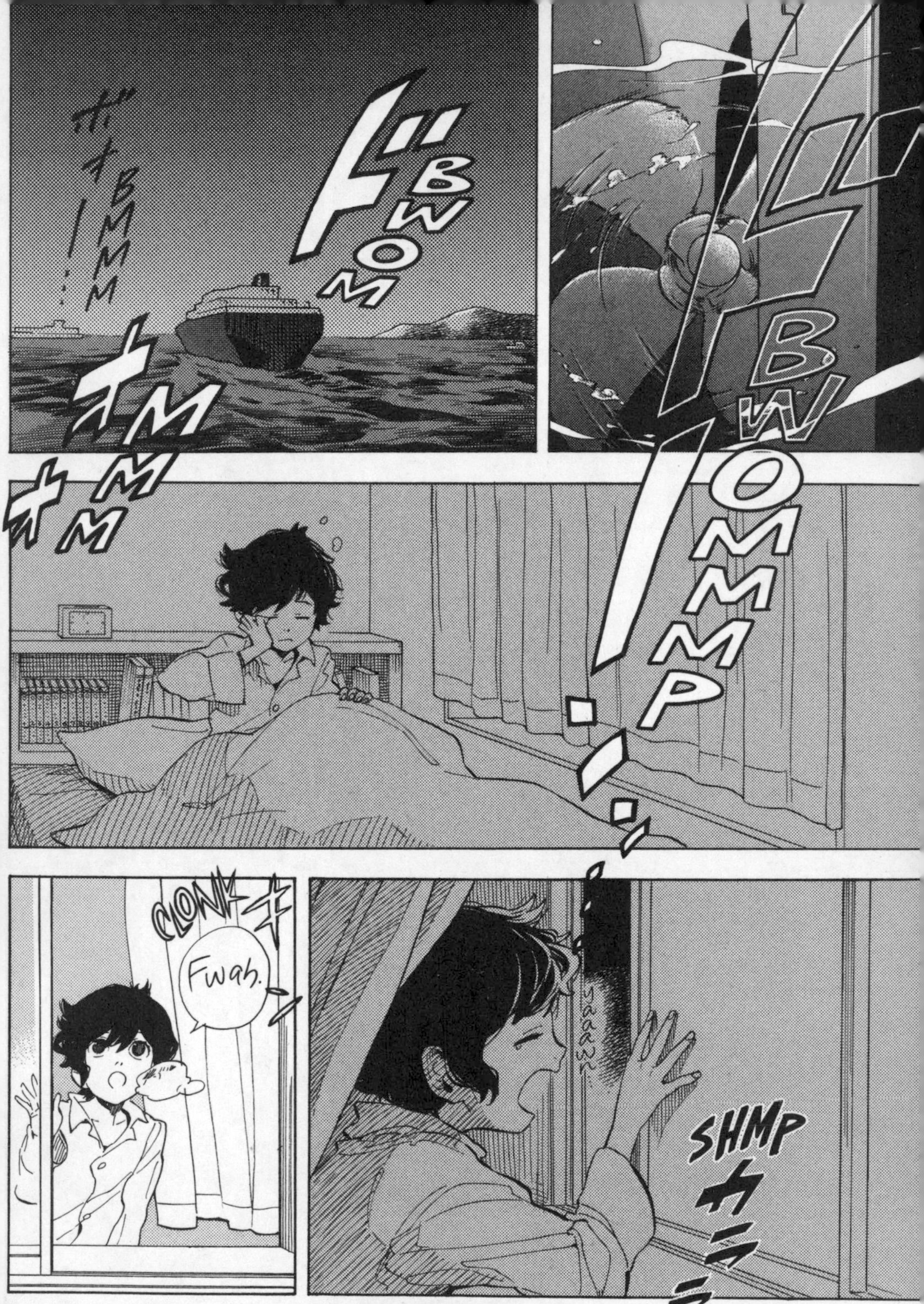
BWOMMMP
BWOM
BMMMM
MMM
yaaawn
SHMP
CLONK
Fwah.

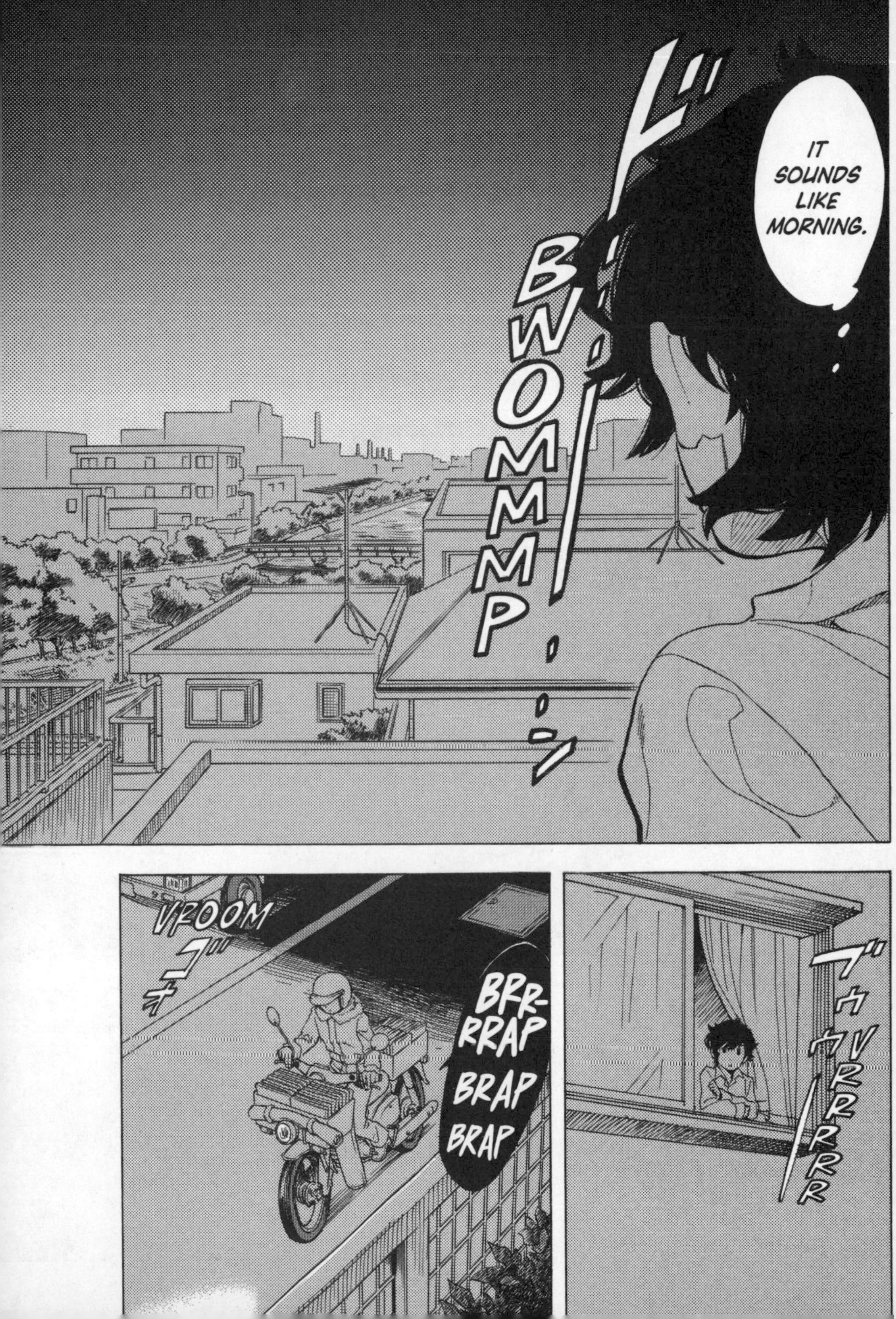
IT SOUNDS LIKE MORNING.
BWOMMMP
VRRRRRRR
VROOM
BRR-RRAP BRAP BRAP

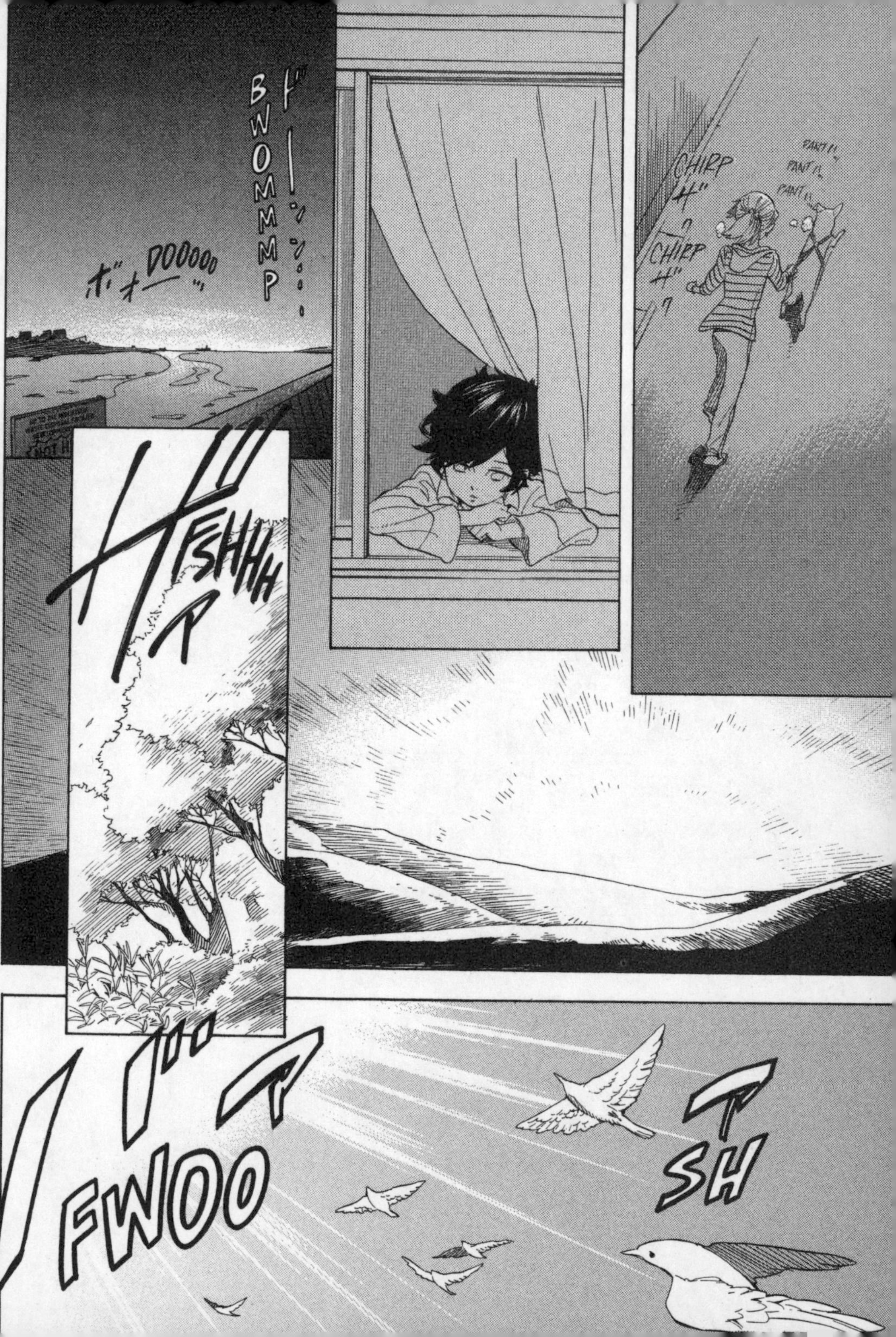
CHIRP
CHIRP
PANT!!
PANT!!
PANT!!
BWOMMMP
DOOOOO
HFSHHHH
FWOO
SH

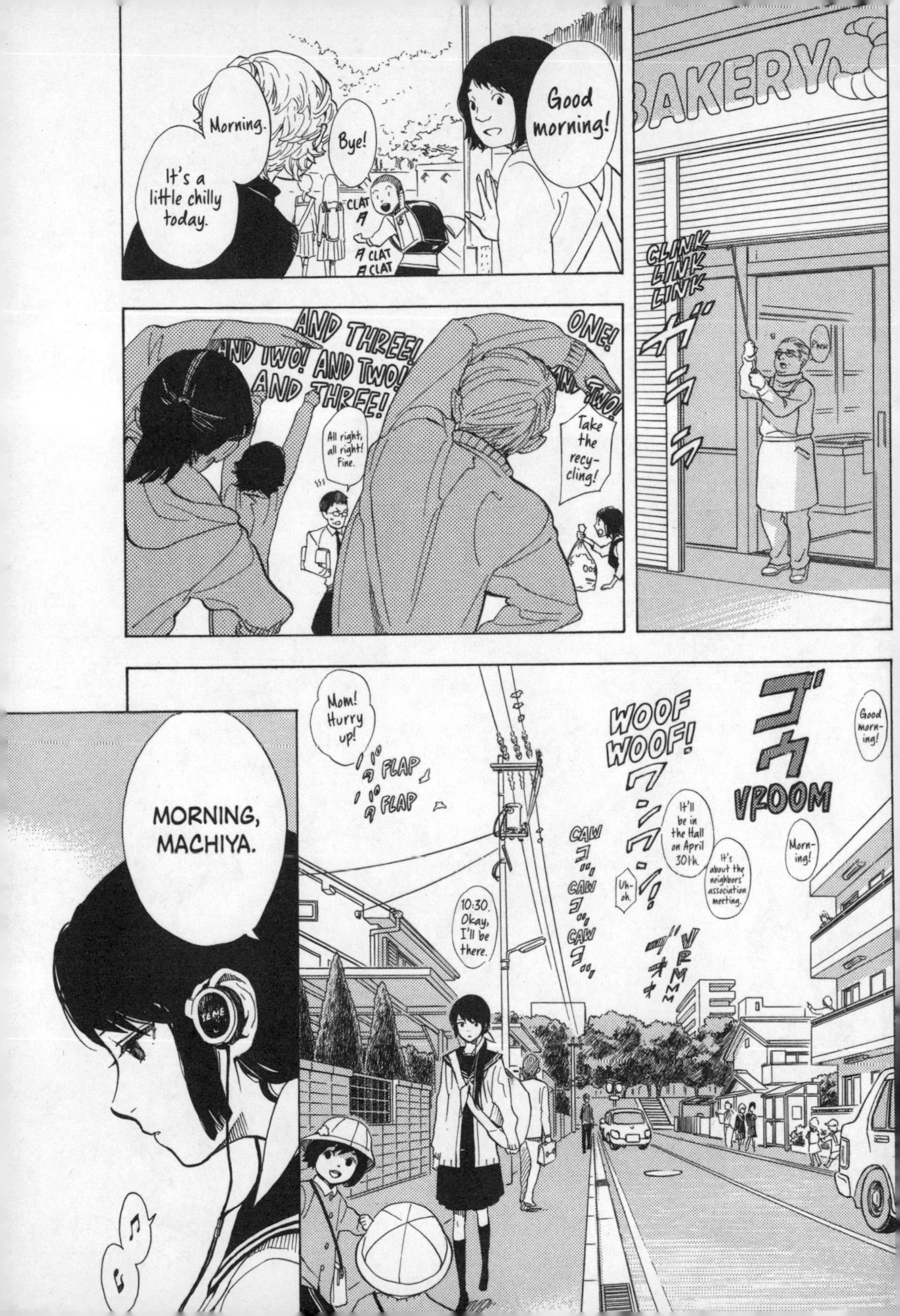
BAKERY
CLINK LINK LINK
Phew
Good morning!
Bye!
Morning.
It's a little chilly today.
CLAT CLAT CLAT
ONE! TWO!
AND THREE! AND TWO! AND THREE!
AND TWO!
Take the recycling!
All right, all right! Fine.
Good morning!
VROOM
Morning!
WOOF WOOF!
It'll be in the Hall on April 30th.
It's about the neighbors' association meeting.
Uh-oh.
VRMM
CAW CAW CAW
10:30. Okay, I'll be there.
Mom! Hurry up!
FLAP FLAP
MORNING, MACHIYA.

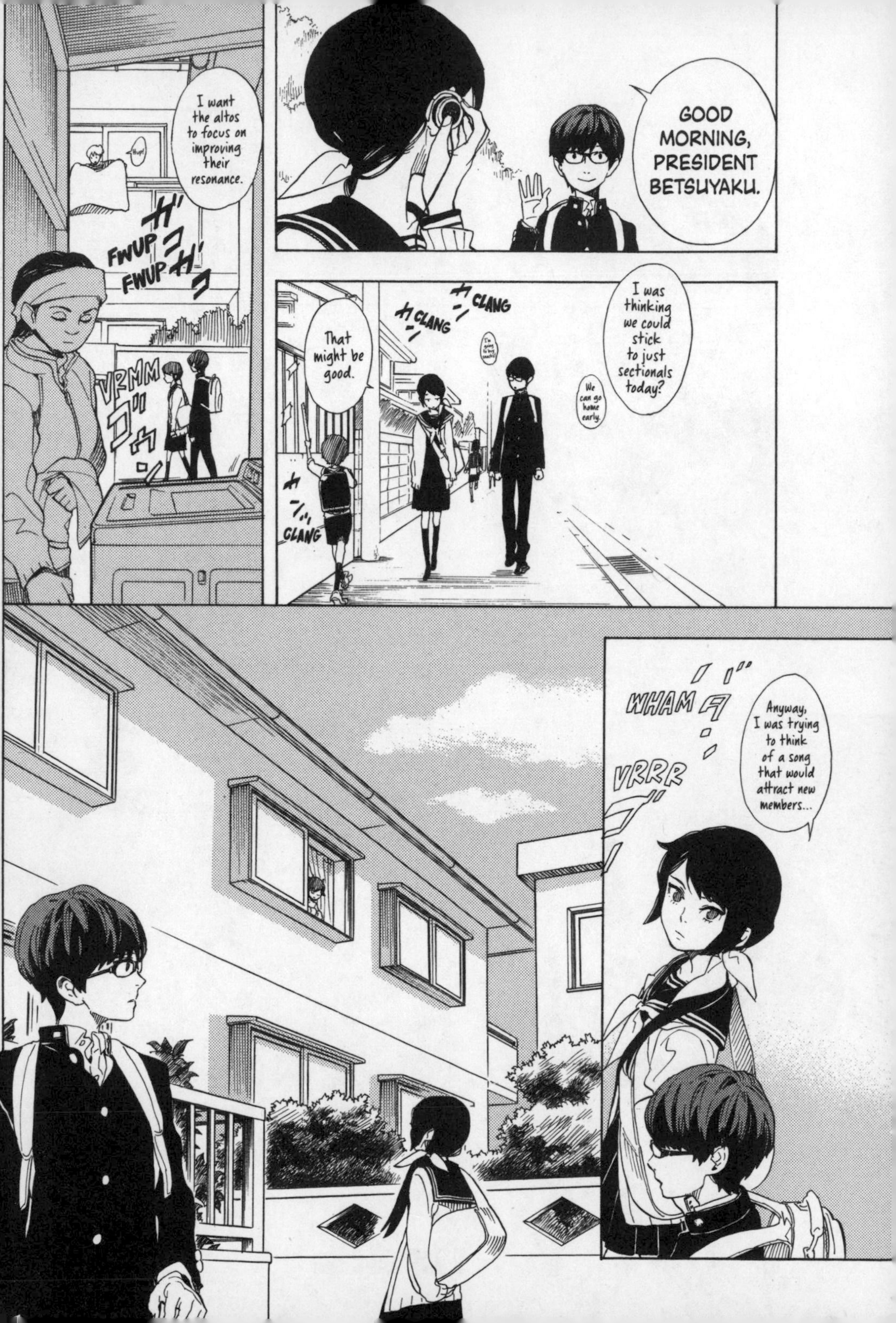
GOOD MORNING, PRESIDENT BETSUYAKU.
I was thinking we could stick to just sectionals today?
We can go home early.
CLANG
CLANG
I'm going to buy snacks!
That might be good.
CLANG
I want the altos to focus on improving their resonance.
Hup!
FWUP
FWUP
VRMM
WHAM
VRRR
Anyway, I was trying to think of a song that would attract new members...

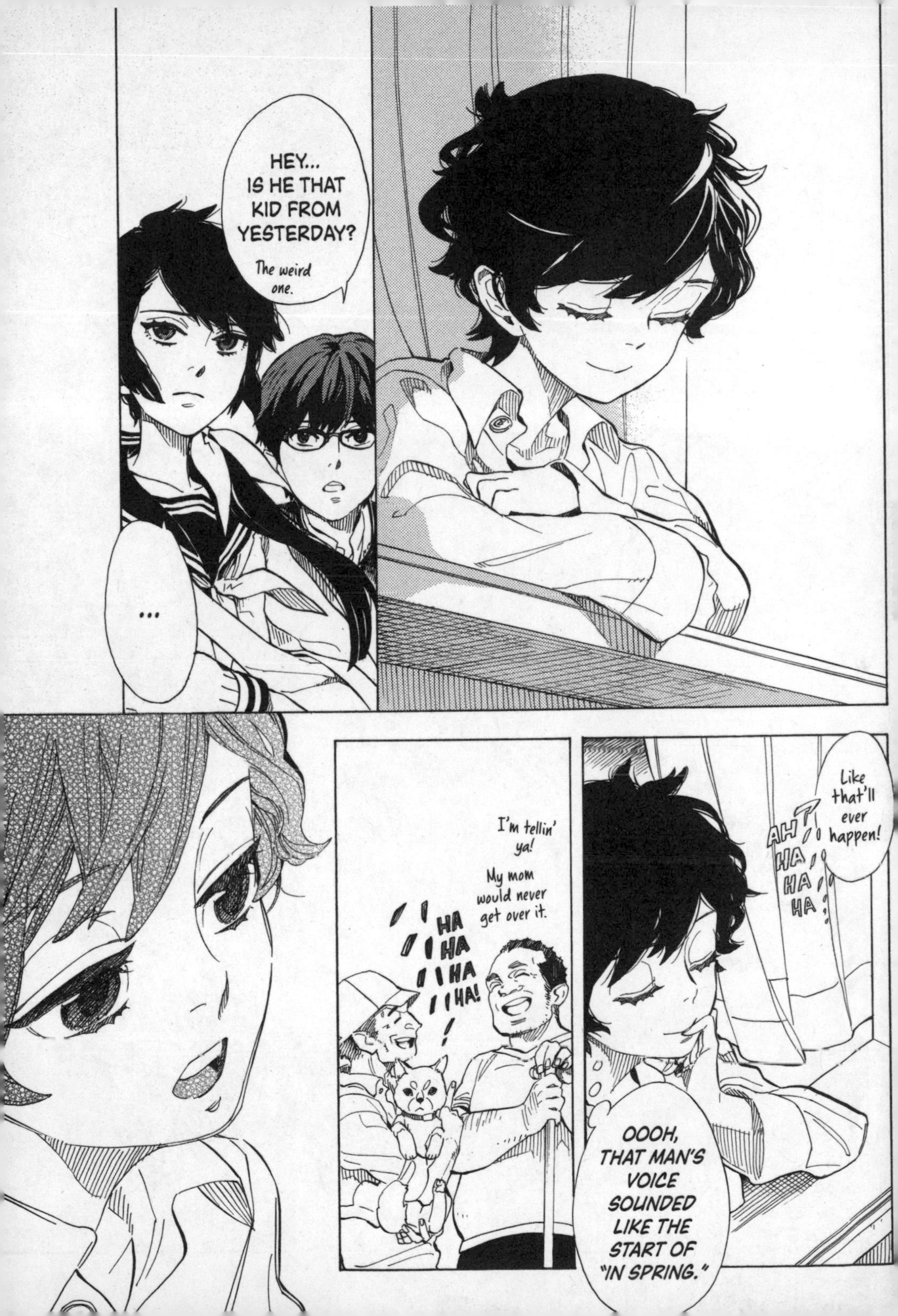
HEY... IS HE THAT KID FROM YESTERDAY?
The weird one.
...
Like that'll ever happen!
AH HA HA HA
OOOH, THAT MAN'S VOICE SOUNDED LIKE THE START OF "IN SPRING."
I'm tellin' ya!
My mom would never get over it.
HA HA HA HA!

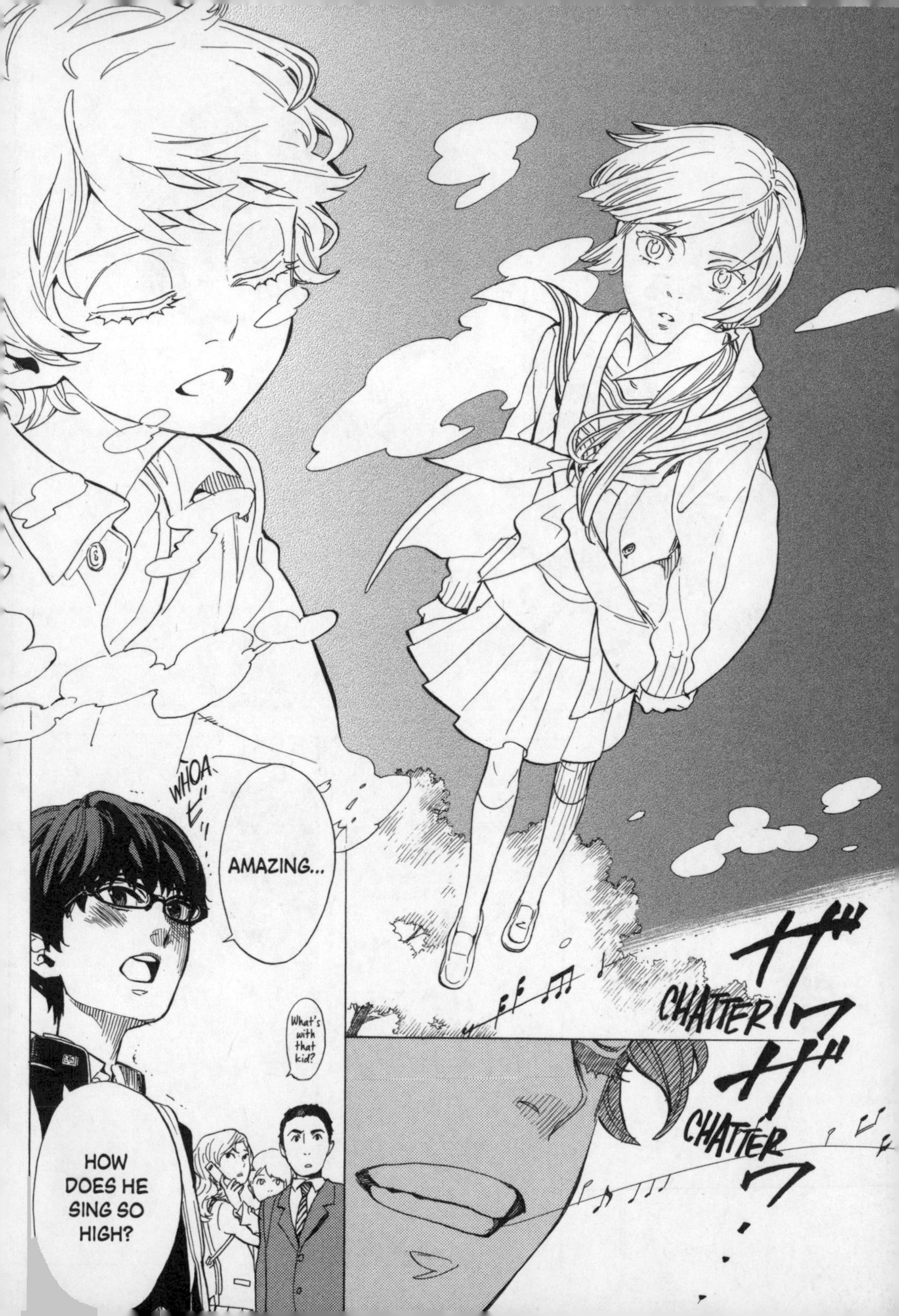
CHATTER
CHATTER
WHOA
AMAZING...
What's with that kid?
HOW DOES HE SING SO HIGH?

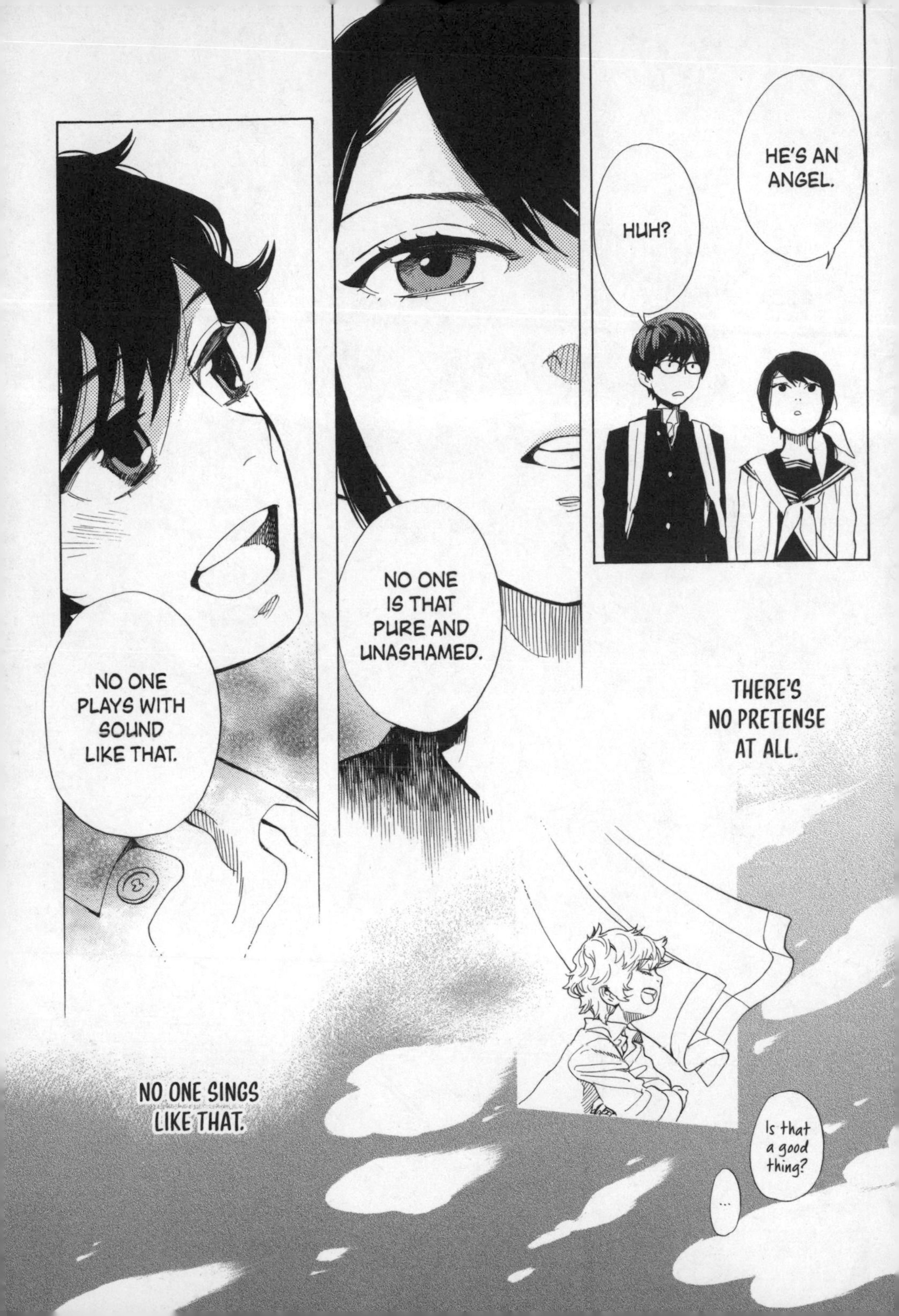

HE'S AN ANGEL.
HUH?
NO ONE IS THAT PURE AND UNASHAMED.
NO ONE PLAYS WITH SOUND LIKE THAT.
THERE'S NO PRETENSE AT ALL.
NO ONE SINGS LIKE THAT.
Is that a good thing?
...

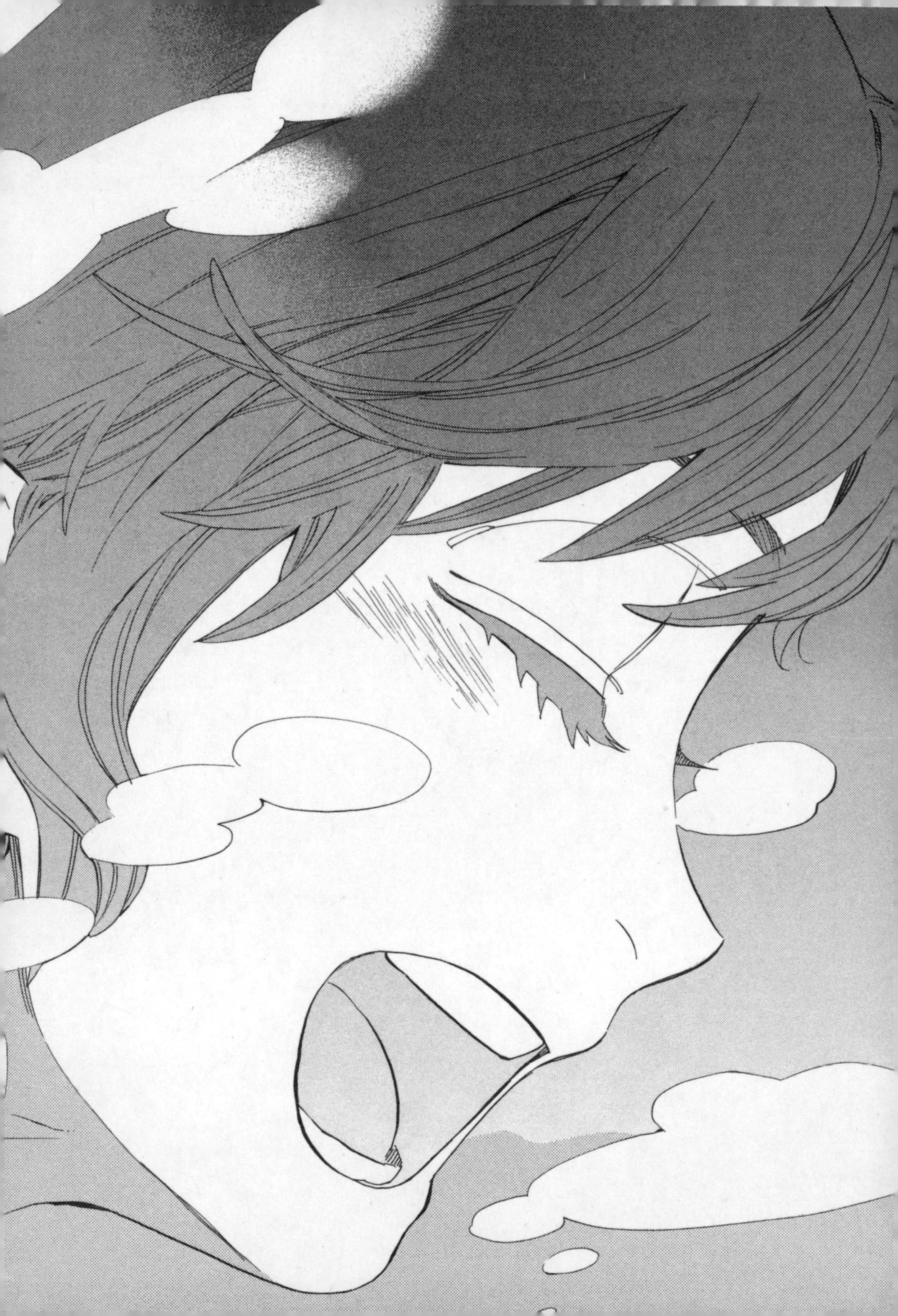

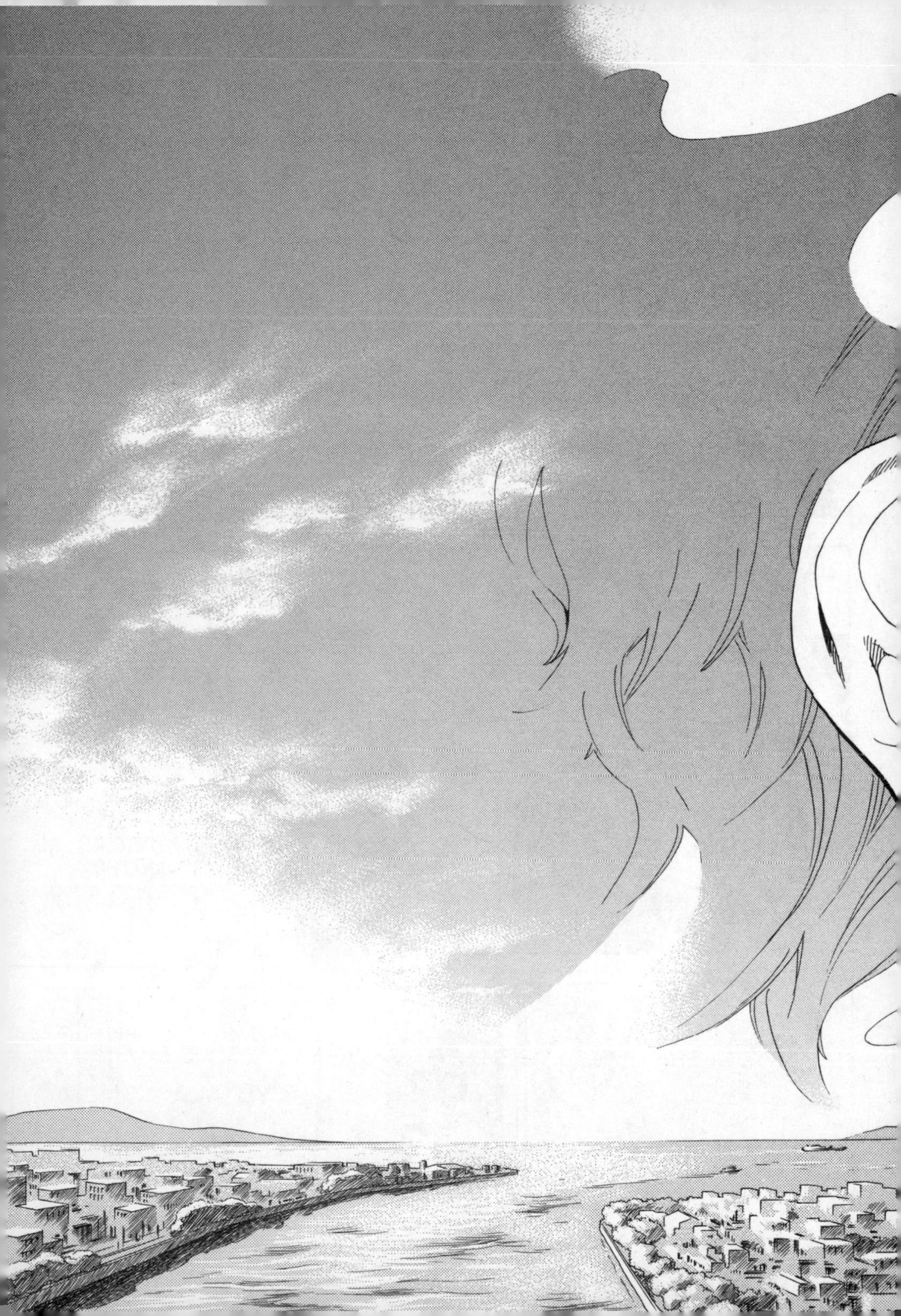

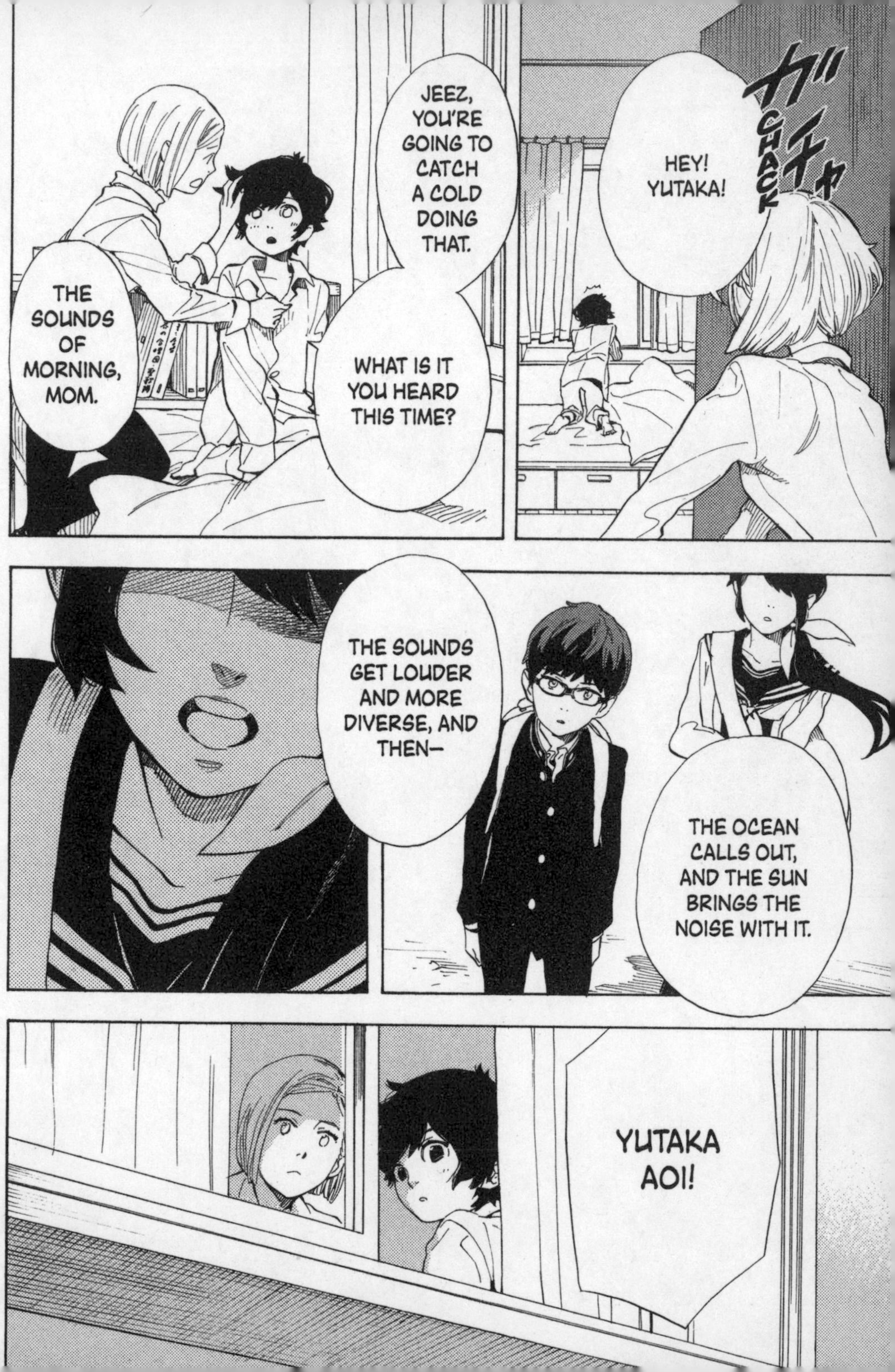
CHACK
HEY! YUTAKA!
JEEZ, YOU'RE GOING TO CATCH A COLD DOING THAT.
WHAT IS IT YOU HEARD THIS TIME?
THE SOUNDS OF MORNING, MOM.
THE SOUNDS GET LOUDER AND MORE DIVERSE, AND THEN—
THE OCEAN CALLS OUT, AND THE SUN BRINGS THE NOISE WITH IT.
YUTAKA AOI!

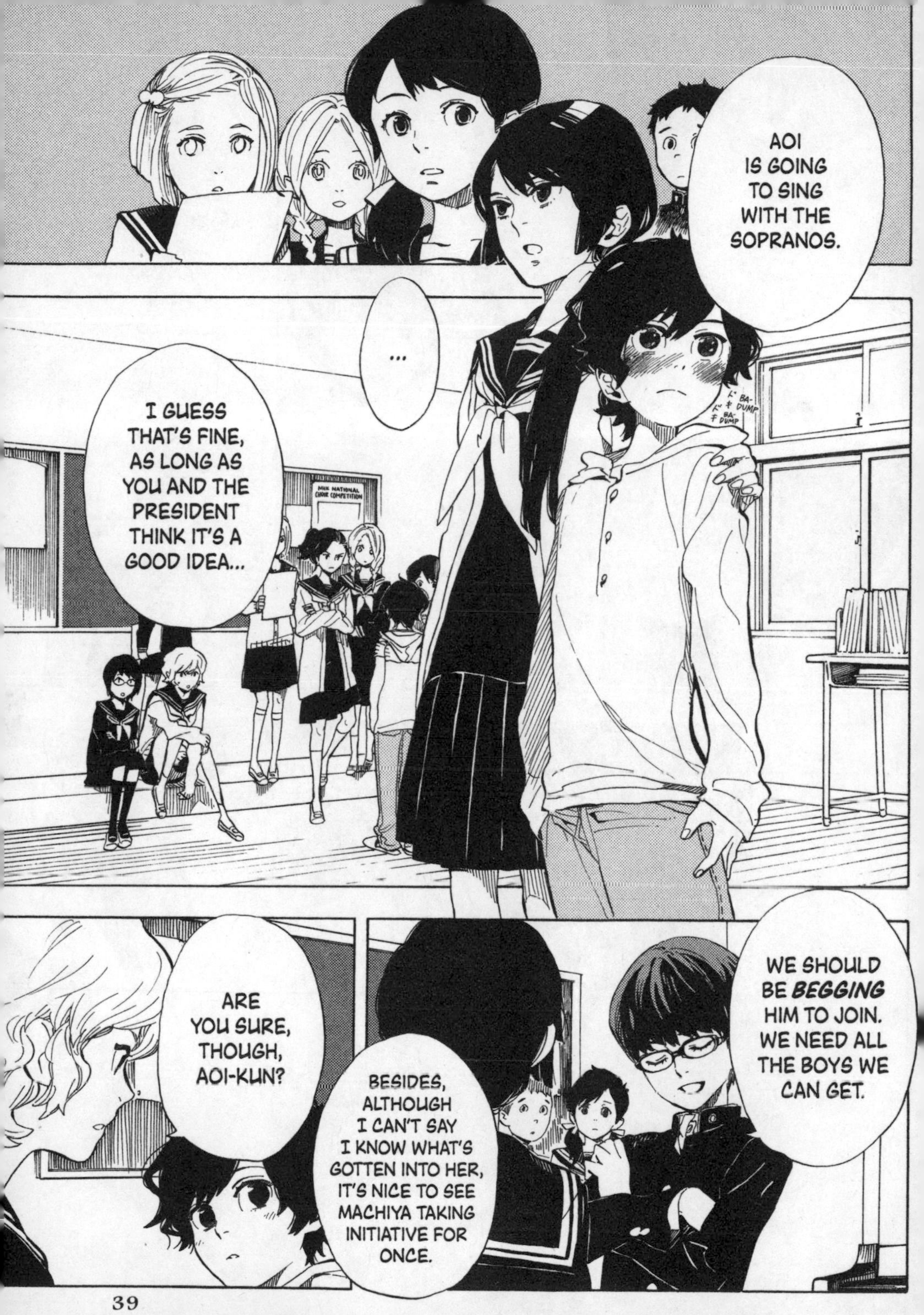
AOI IS GOING TO SING WITH THE SOPRANOS.
BA-DUMP BA-DUMP
...
I GUESS THAT'S FINE, AS LONG AS YOU AND THE PRESIDENT THINK IT'S A GOOD IDEA...
NHK NATIONAL CHOIR COMPETITION
WE SHOULD BE ***BEGGING*** HIM TO JOIN. WE NEED ALL THE BOYS WE CAN GET.
BESIDES, ALTHOUGH I CAN'T SAY I KNOW WHAT'S GOTTEN INTO HER, IT'S NICE TO SEE MACHIYA TAKING INITIATIVE FOR ONCE.
ARE YOU SURE, THOUGH, AOI-KUN?

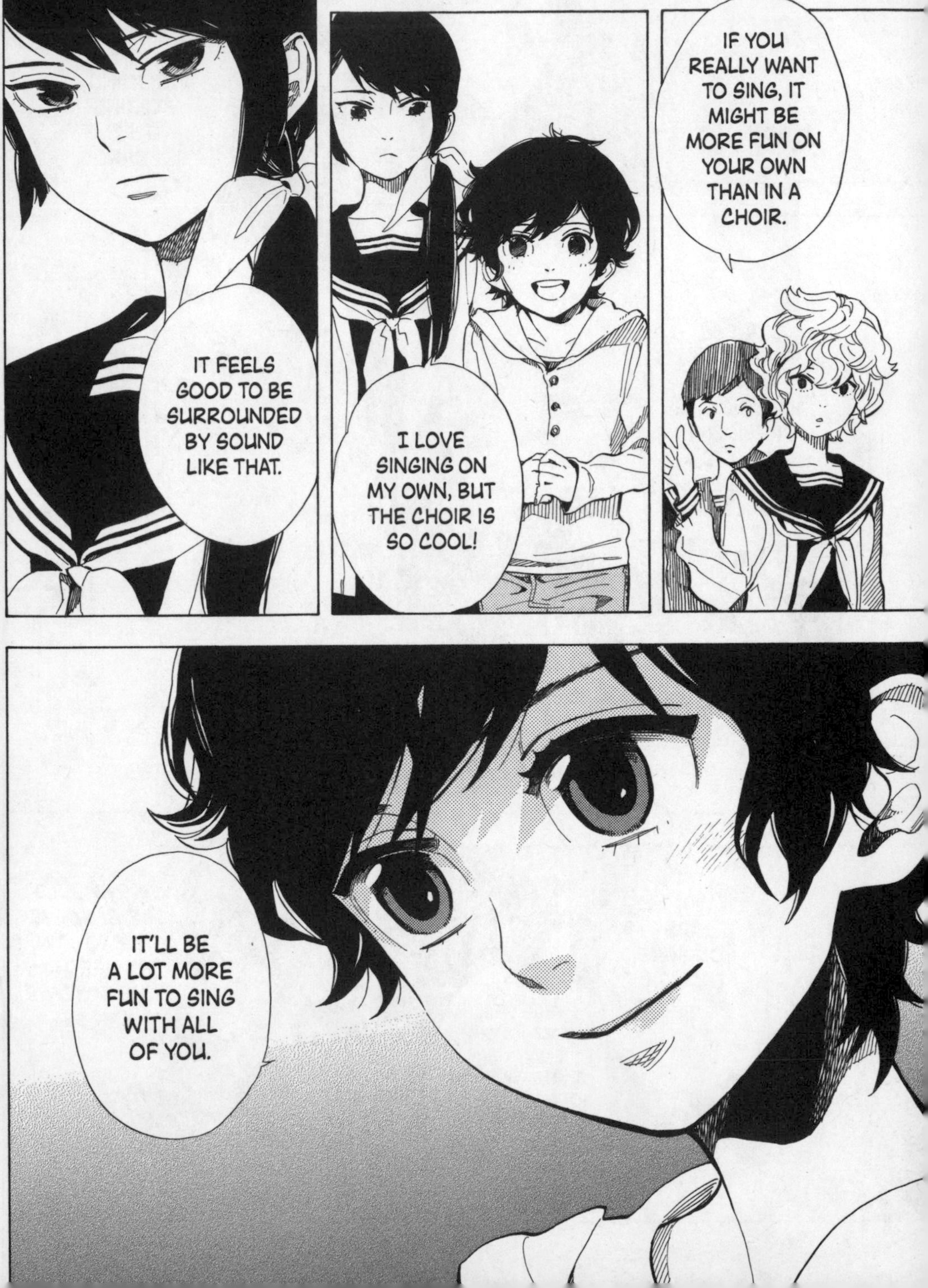
IF YOU REALLY WANT TO SING, IT MIGHT BE MORE FUN ON YOUR OWN THAN IN A CHOIR.
I LOVE SINGING ON MY OWN, BUT THE CHOIR IS SO COOL!
IT FEELS GOOD TO BE SURROUNDED BY SOUND LIKE THAT.
IT'LL BE A LOT MORE FUN TO SING WITH ALL OF YOU.

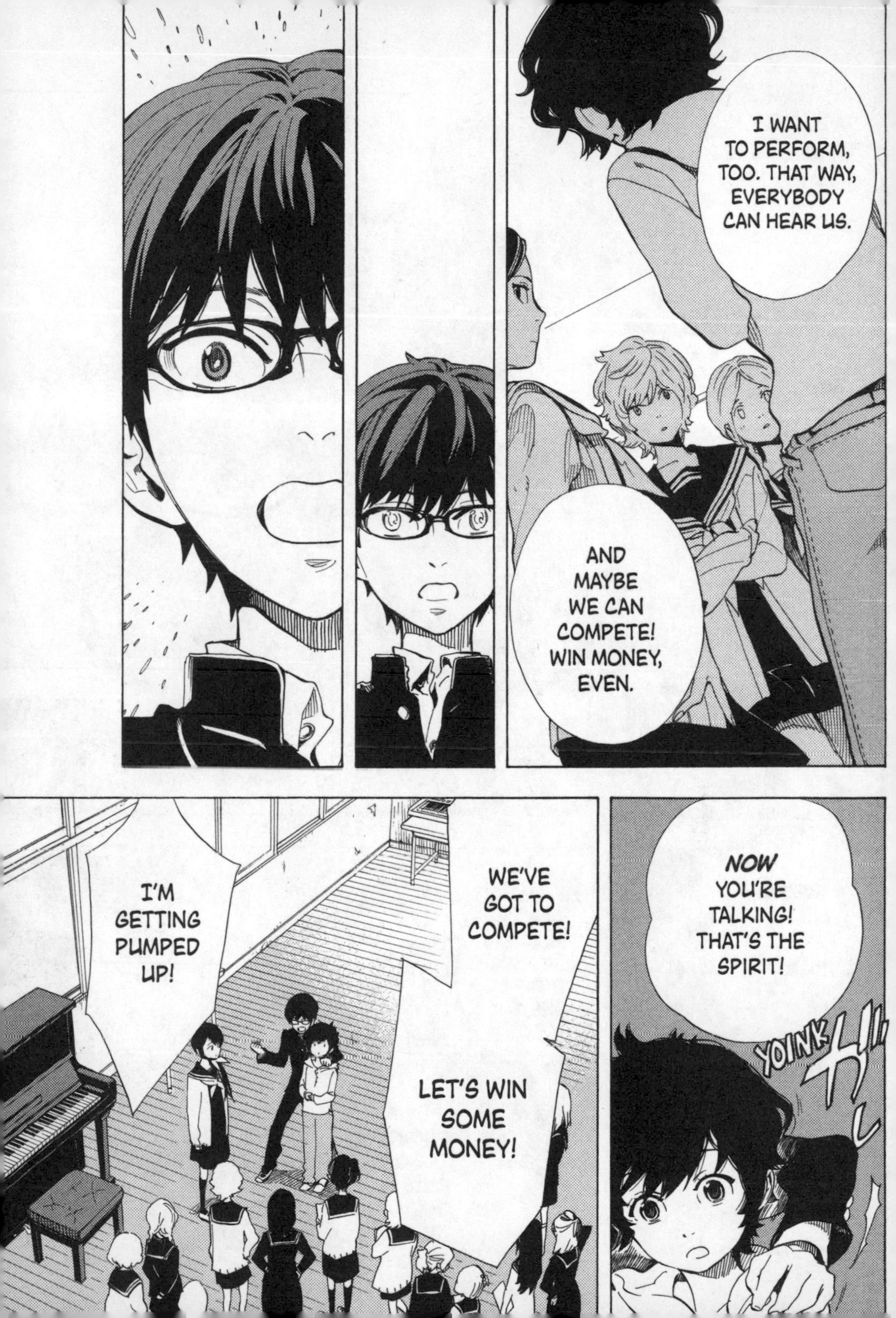
I WANT TO PERFORM, TOO. THAT WAY, EVERYBODY CAN HEAR US.
AND MAYBE WE CAN COMPETE! WIN MONEY, EVEN.
NOW YOU'RE TALKING! THAT'S THE SPIRIT!
YOINK
WE'VE GOT TO COMPETE!
I'M GETTING PUMPED UP!
LET'S WIN SOME MONEY!

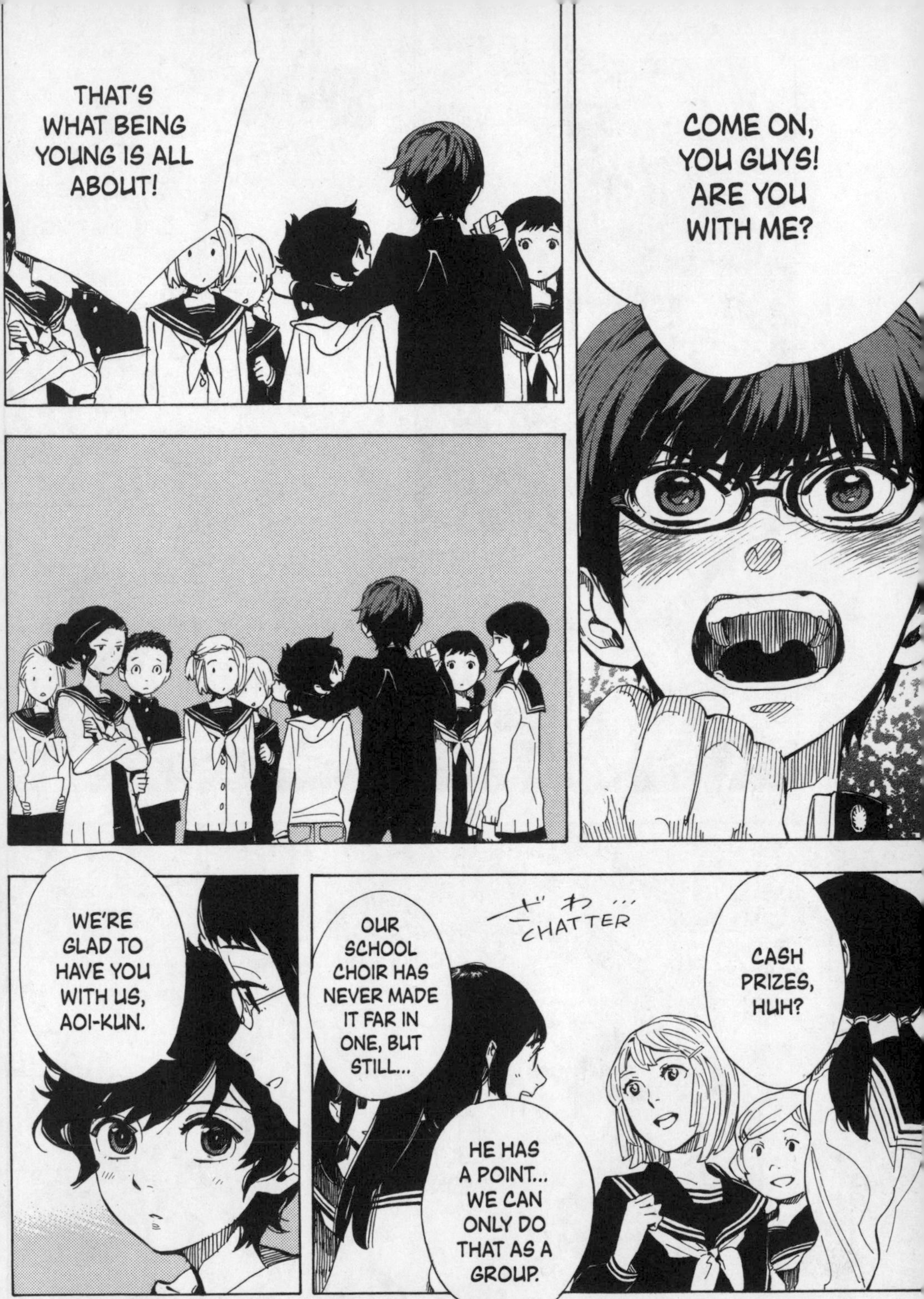
COME ON, YOU GUYS! ARE YOU WITH ME?
THAT'S WHAT BEING YOUNG IS ALL ABOUT!
CASH PRIZES, HUH?
ざわ… CHATTER
OUR SCHOOL CHOIR HAS NEVER MADE IT FAR IN ONE, BUT STILL...
HE HAS A POINT... WE CAN ONLY DO THAT AS A GROUP.
WE'RE GLAD TO HAVE YOU WITH US, AOI-KUN.

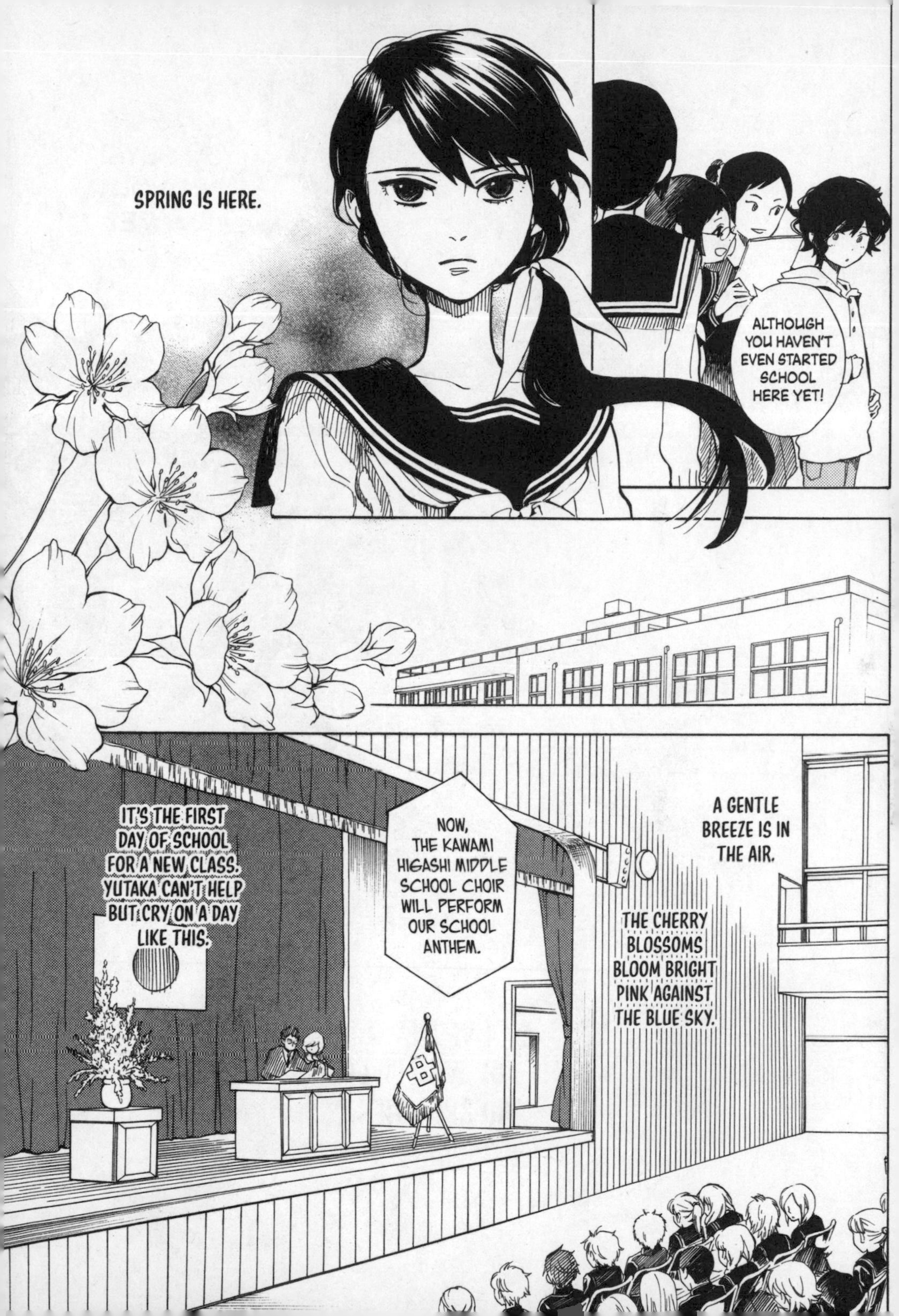
ALTHOUGH YOU HAVEN'T EVEN STARTED SCHOOL HERE YET!
SPRING IS HERE.
A GENTLE BREEZE IS IN THE AIR.
THE CHERRY BLOSSOMS BLOOM BRIGHT PINK AGAINST THE BLUE SKY.
NOW, THE KAWAMI HIGASHI MIDDLE SCHOOL CHOIR WILL PERFORM OUR SCHOOL ANTHEM.
IT'S THE FIRST DAY OF SCHOOL FOR A NEW CLASS. YUTAKA CAN'T HELP BUT CRY ON A DAY LIKE THIS.

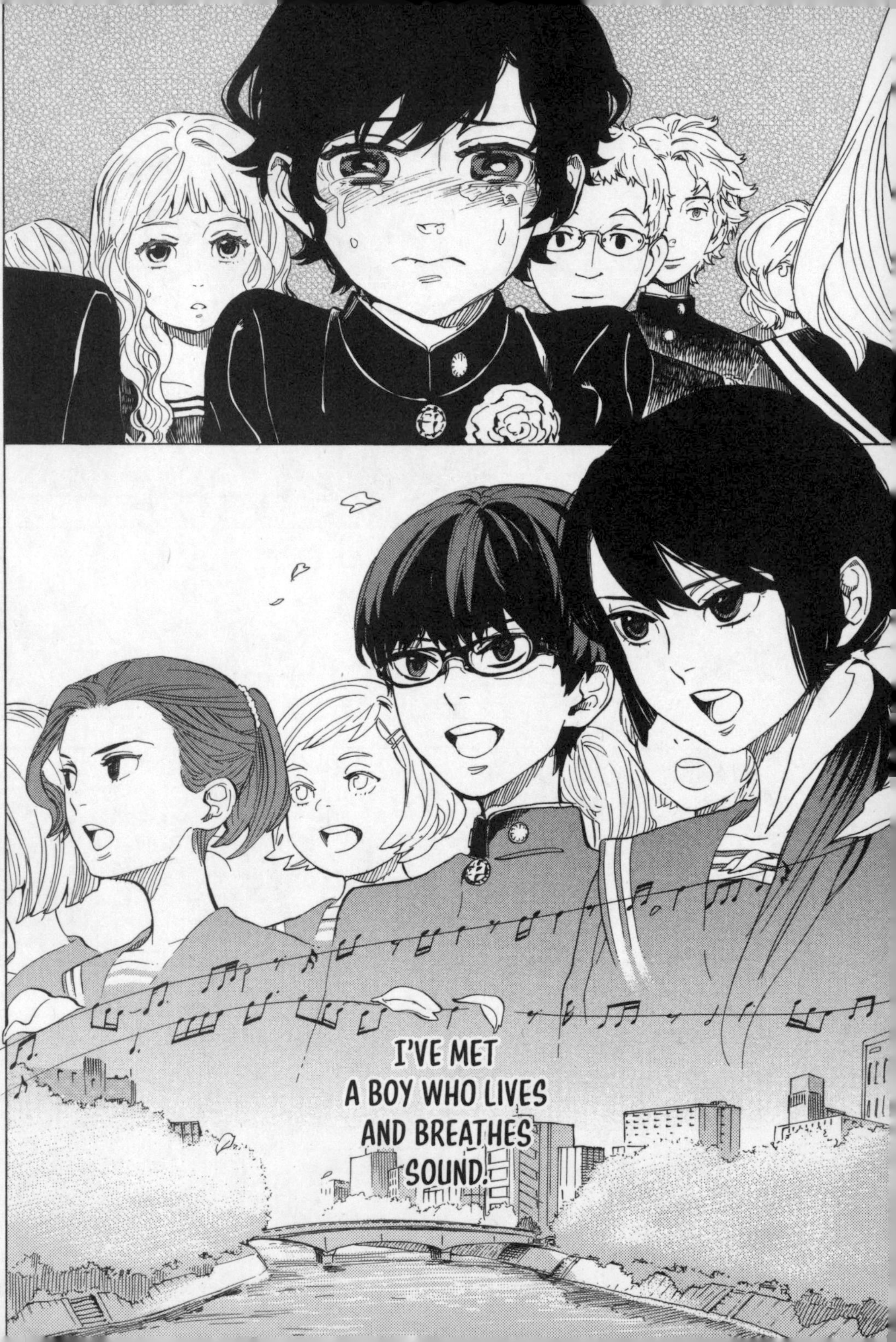
I'VE MET
A BOY WHO LIVES
AND BREATHES
SOUND.

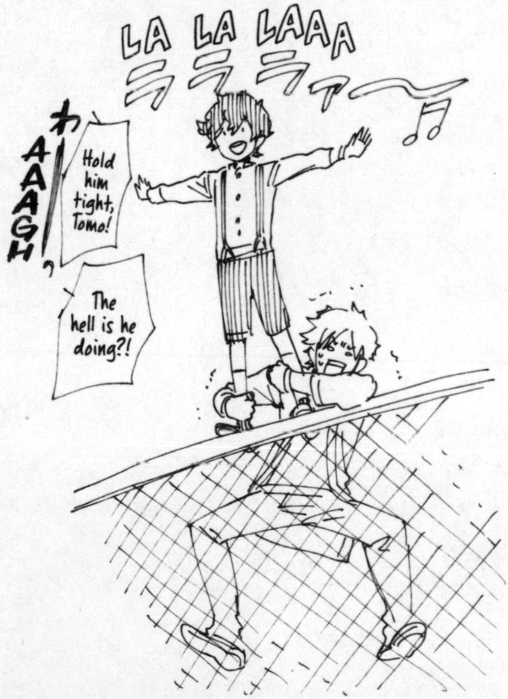
LA LA LAAA
ラララァ〜
わ
AAAAGH
Hold him tight, Tomo!
The hell is he doing?!

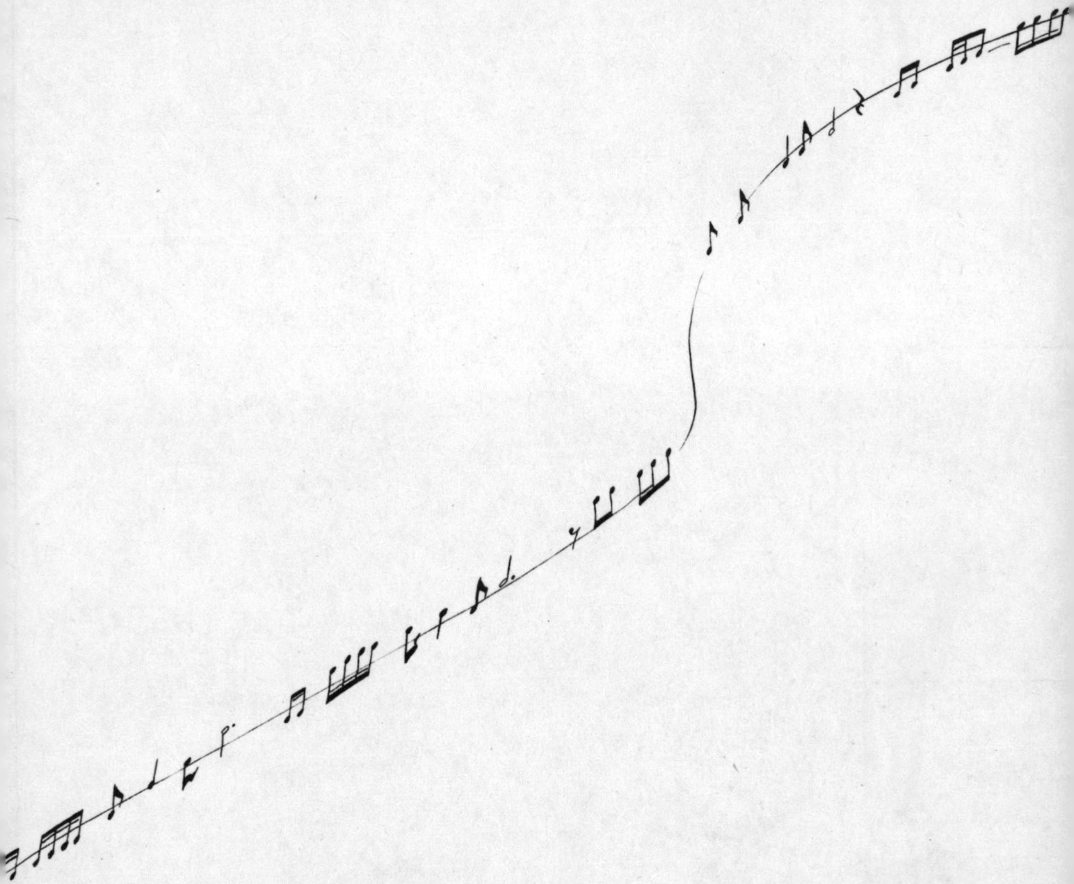

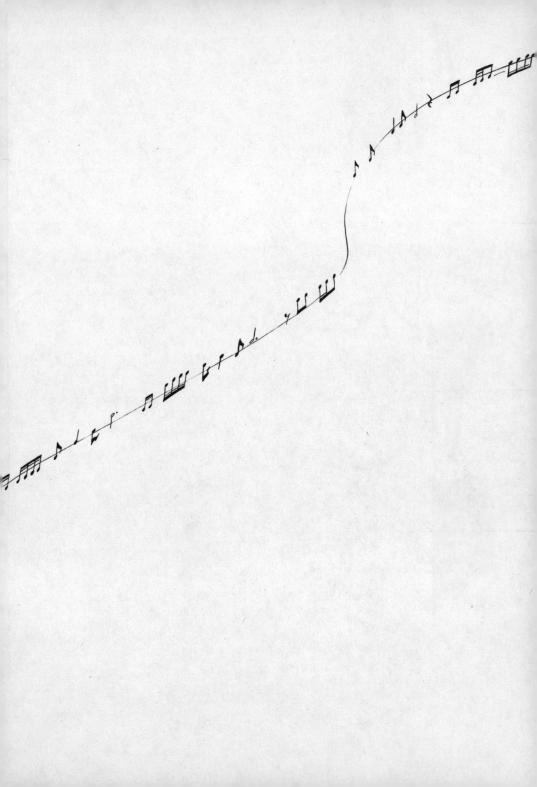

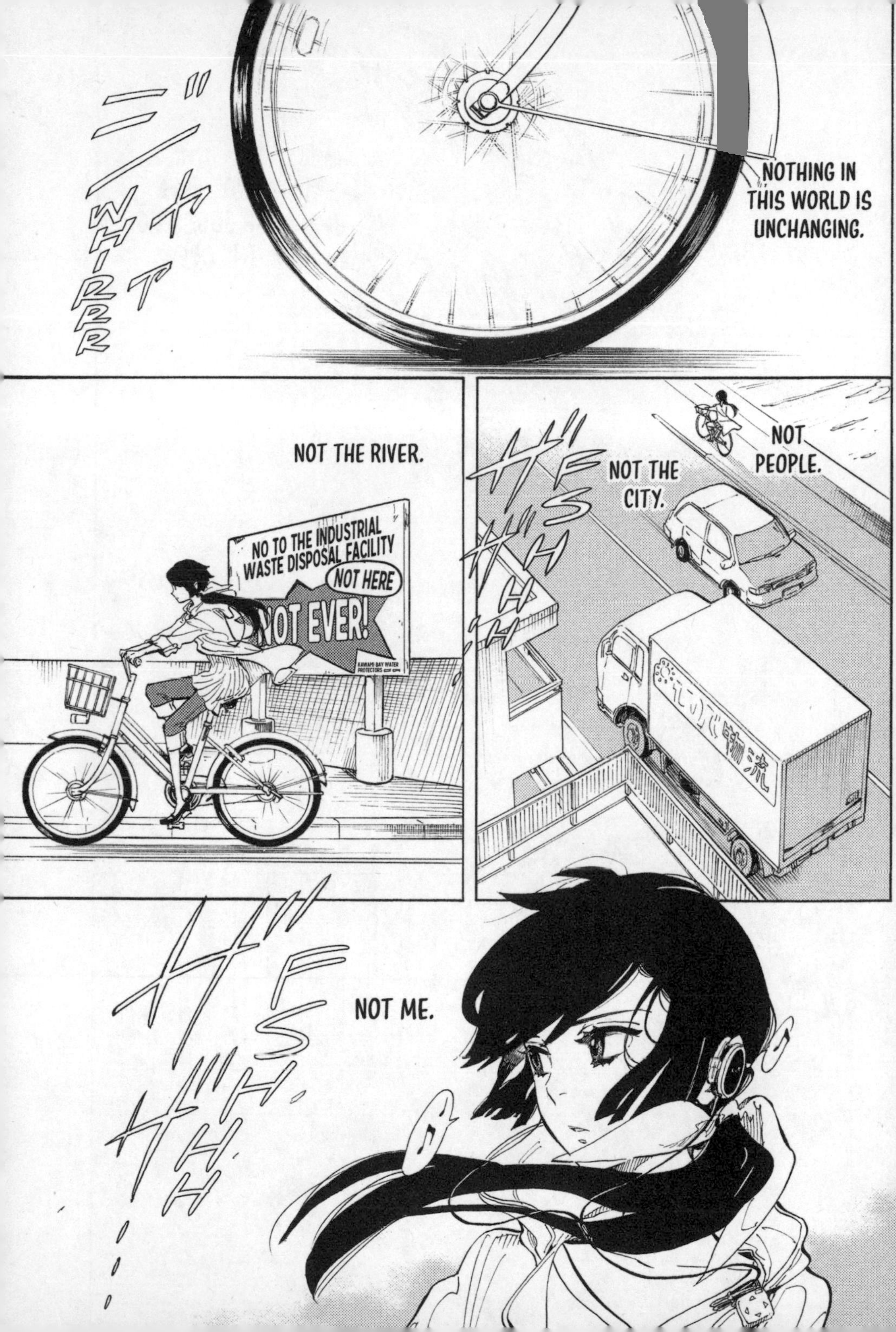
WHIRRR
NOTHING IN THIS WORLD IS UNCHANGING.
NOT PEOPLE.
NOT THE CITY.
FSHHH
NOT THE RIVER.
NO TO THE INDUSTRIAL WASTE DISPOSAL FACILITY
NOT HERE
NOT EVER!
FSHHHH
NOT ME.

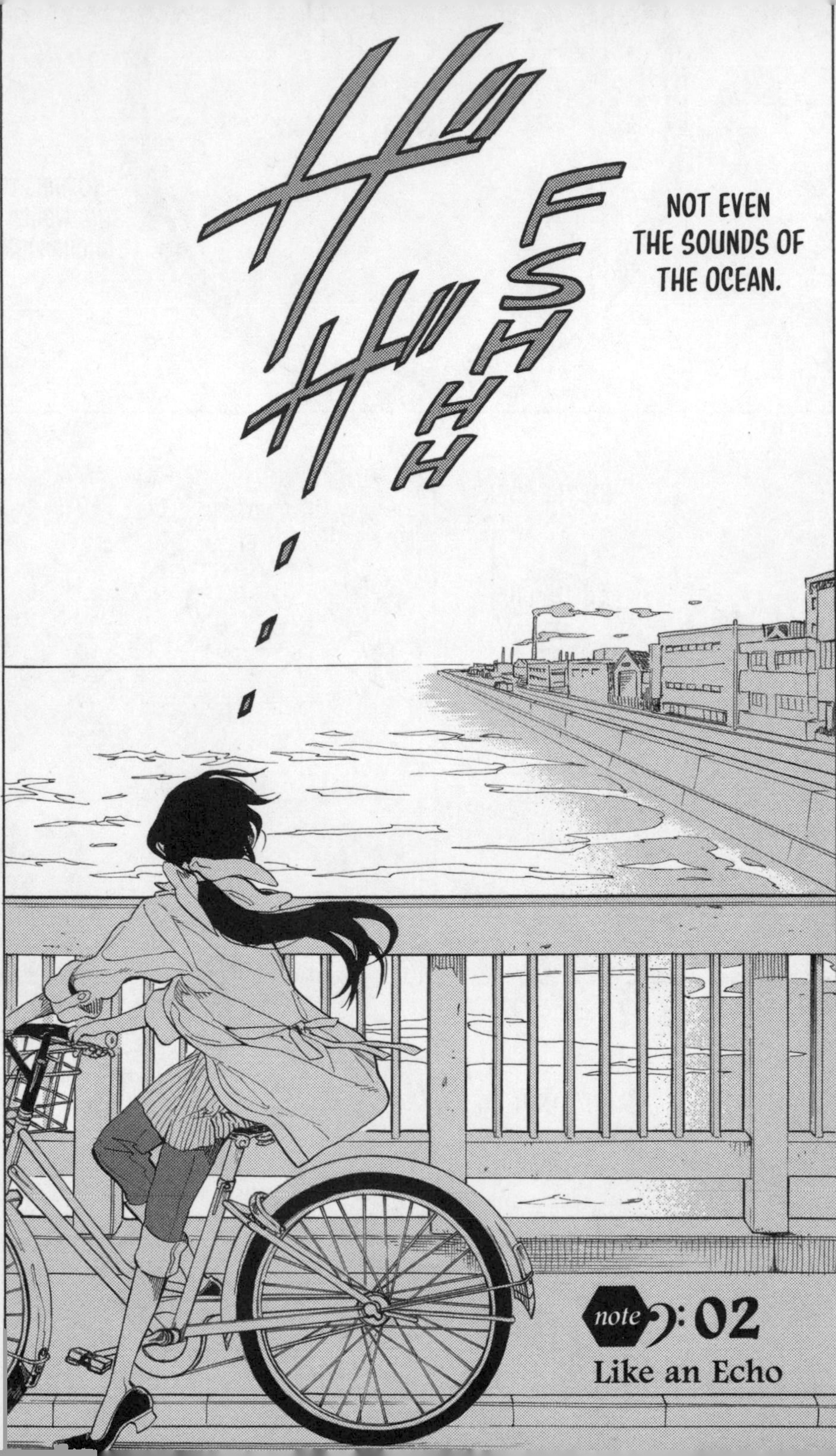
FSHHH
NOT EVEN THE SOUNDS OF THE OCEAN.
note: 02
Like an Echo

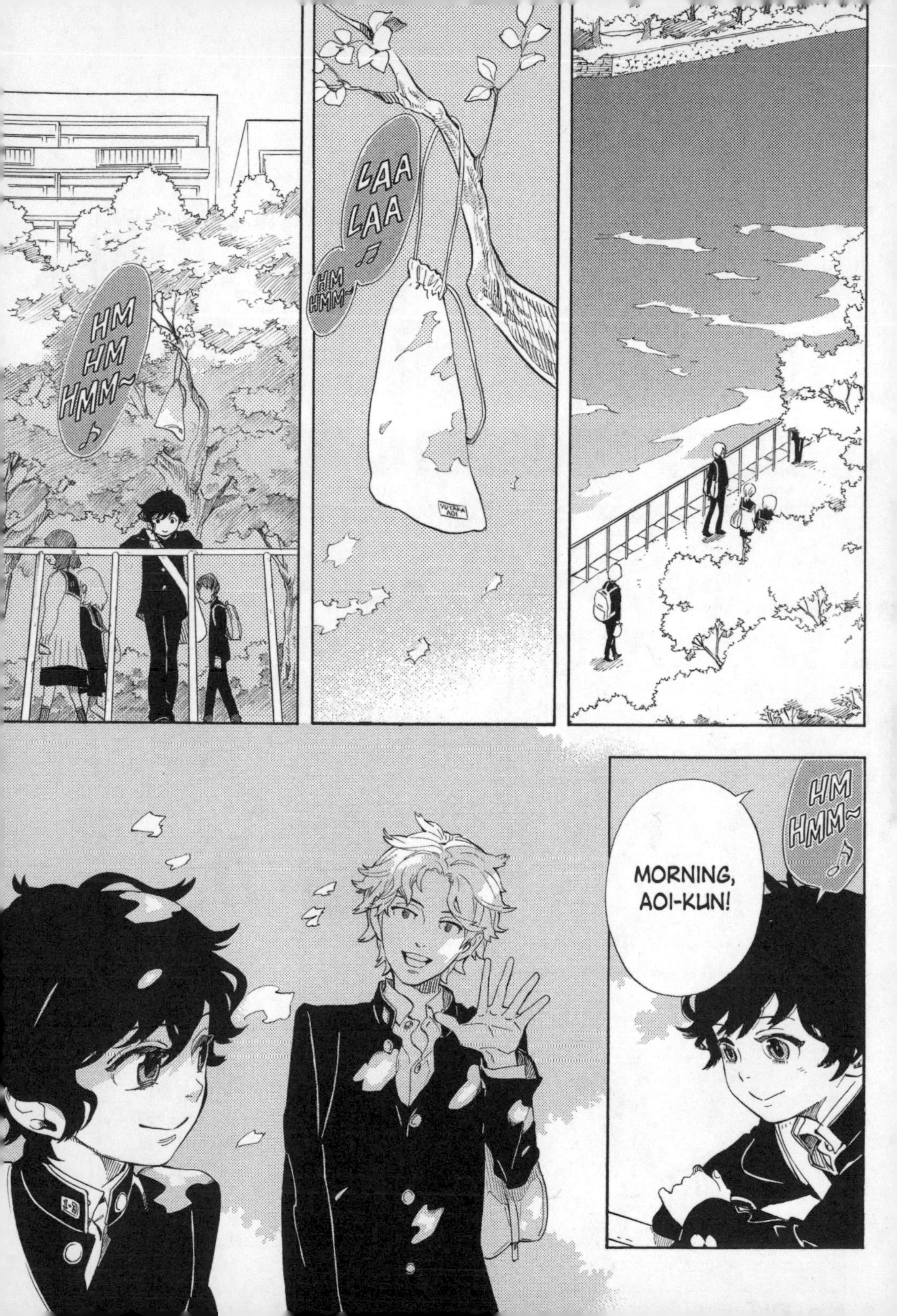
LAA LAA ♪
HM HMM~
YUTAKA AOI
HM HM HMM~ ♪
HM HMM~ ♪
MORNING, AOI-KUN!

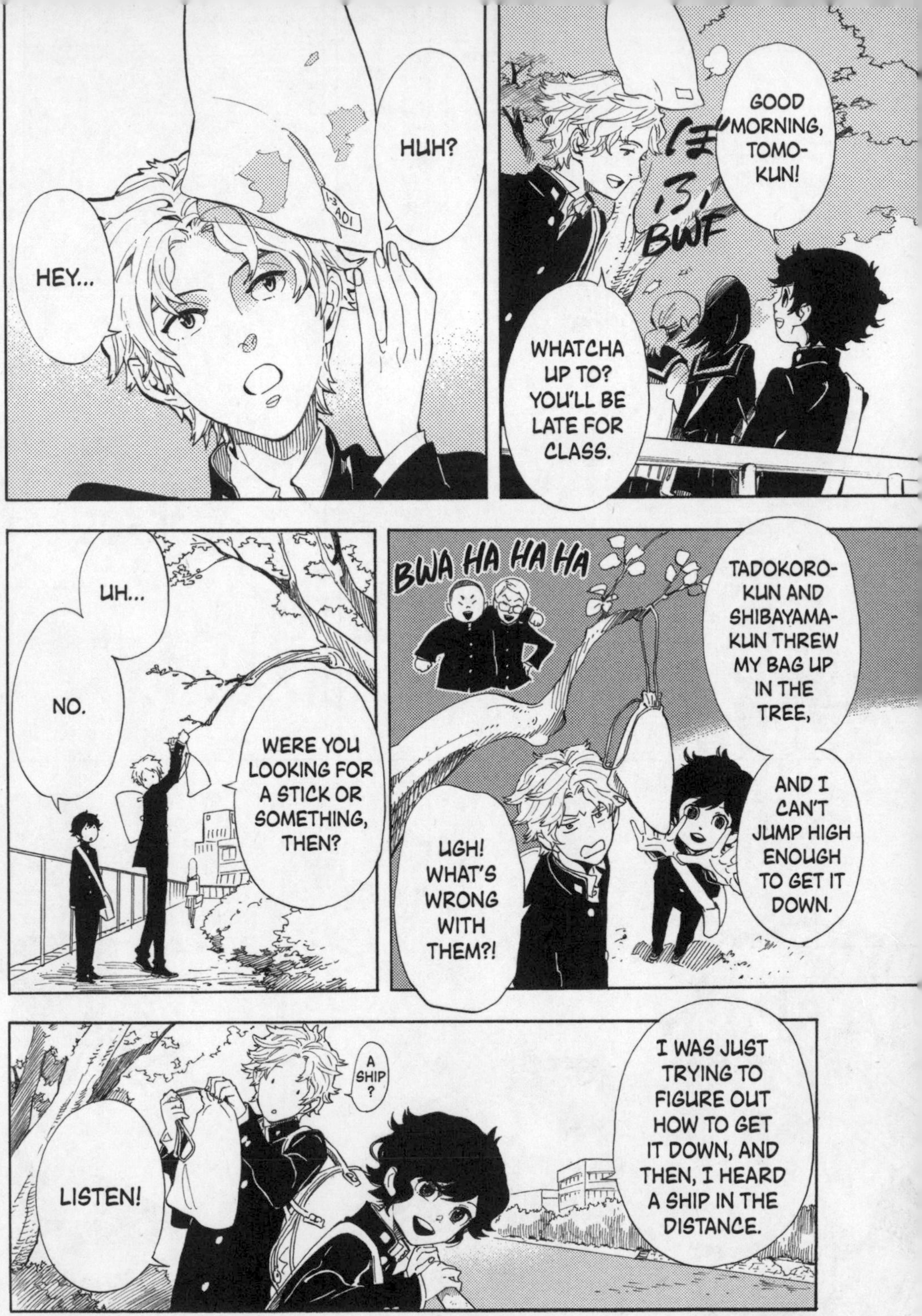
GOOD MORNING, TOMO-KUN!
ぼふ
BWF
WHATCHA UP TO? YOU'LL BE LATE FOR CLASS.
HUH?
1-3 AOI
HEY...
BWA HA HA HA
TADOKORO-KUN AND SHIBAYAMA-KUN THREW MY BAG UP IN THE TREE,
AND I CAN'T JUMP HIGH ENOUGH TO GET IT DOWN.
UGH! WHAT'S WRONG WITH THEM?!
WERE YOU LOOKING FOR A STICK OR SOMETHING, THEN?
UH...
NO.
I WAS JUST TRYING TO FIGURE OUT HOW TO GET IT DOWN, AND THEN, I HEARD A SHIP IN THE DISTANCE.
A SHIP?
LISTEN!

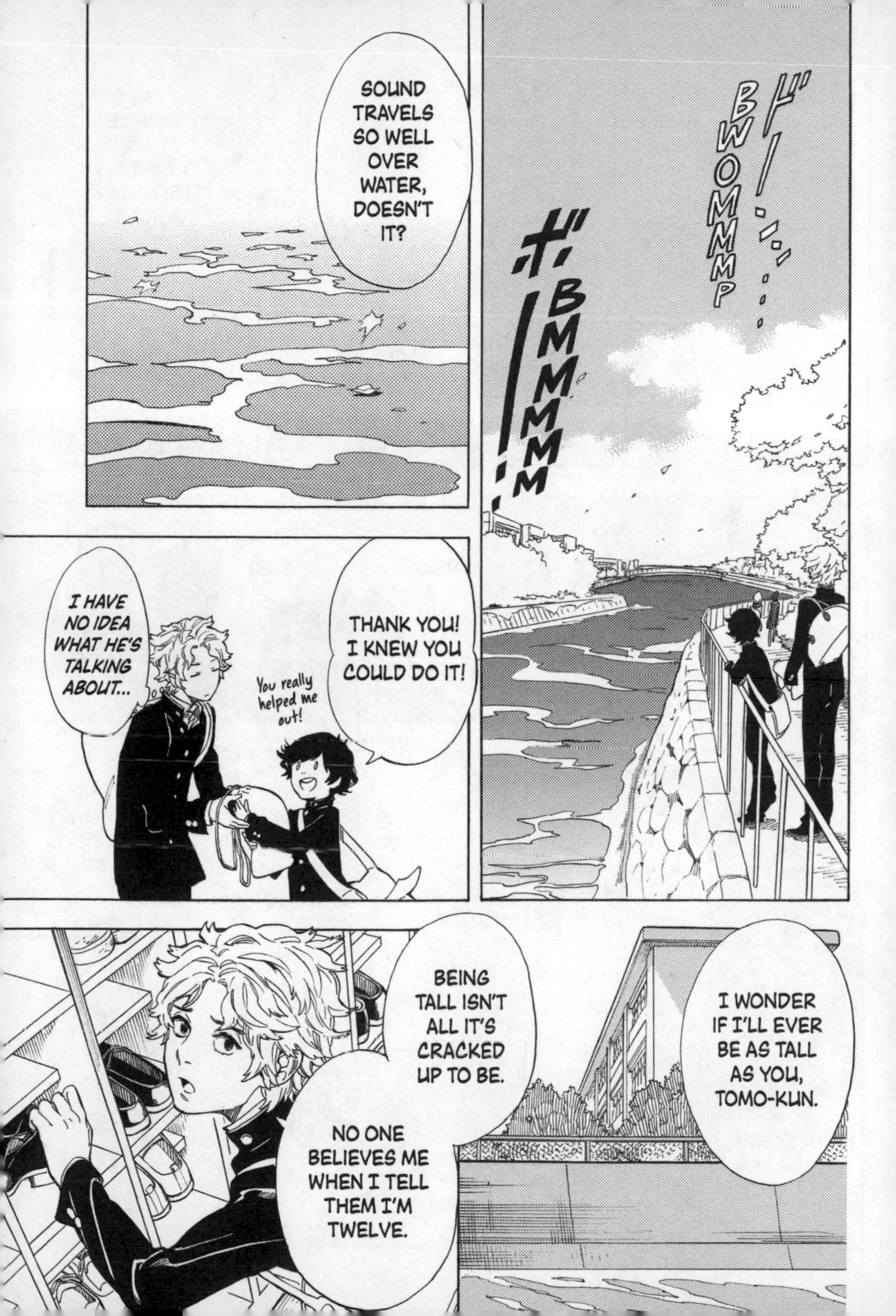
BWOMMMP
BMMMMM
SOUND TRAVELS SO WELL OVER WATER, DOESN'T IT?
THANK YOU! I KNEW YOU COULD DO IT!
You really helped me out!
I HAVE NO IDEA WHAT HE'S TALKING ABOUT...
I WONDER IF I'LL EVER BE AS TALL AS YOU, TOMO-KUN.
BEING TALL ISN'T ALL IT'S CRACKED UP TO BE.
NO ONE BELIEVES ME WHEN I TELL THEM I'M TWELVE.

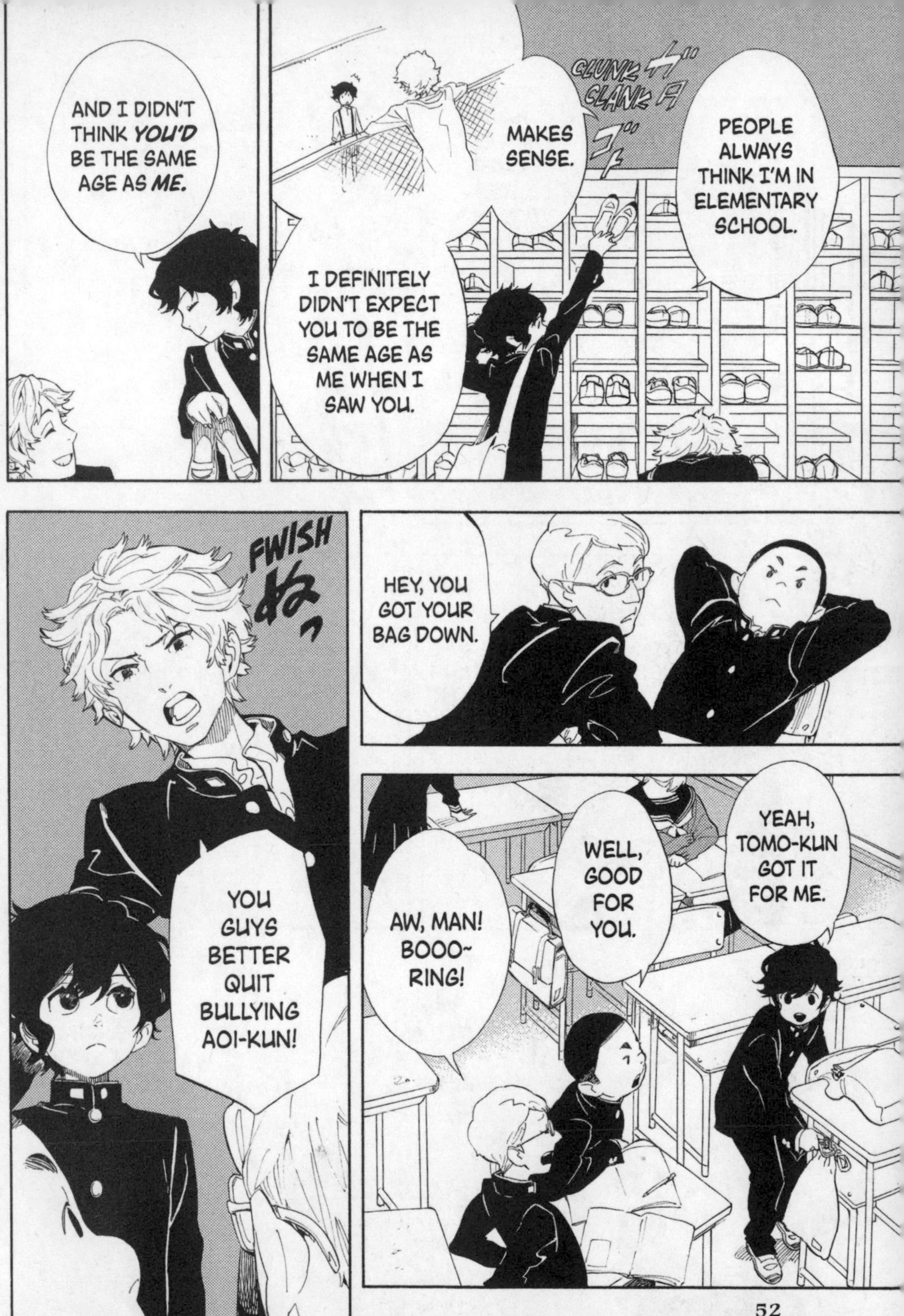

PEOPLE ALWAYS THINK I'M IN ELEMENTARY SCHOOL.
GLUNK
GLANK
MAKES SENSE.
I DEFINITELY DIDN'T EXPECT YOU TO BE THE SAME AGE AS ME WHEN I SAW YOU.
AND I DIDN'T THINK *YOU'D* BE THE SAME AGE AS *ME.*
HEY, YOU GOT YOUR BAG DOWN.
YEAH, TOMO-KUN GOT IT FOR ME.
WELL, GOOD FOR YOU.
AW, MAN! BOOO~RING!
FWISH
ぬっ
YOU GUYS BETTER QUIT BULLYING AOI-KUN!

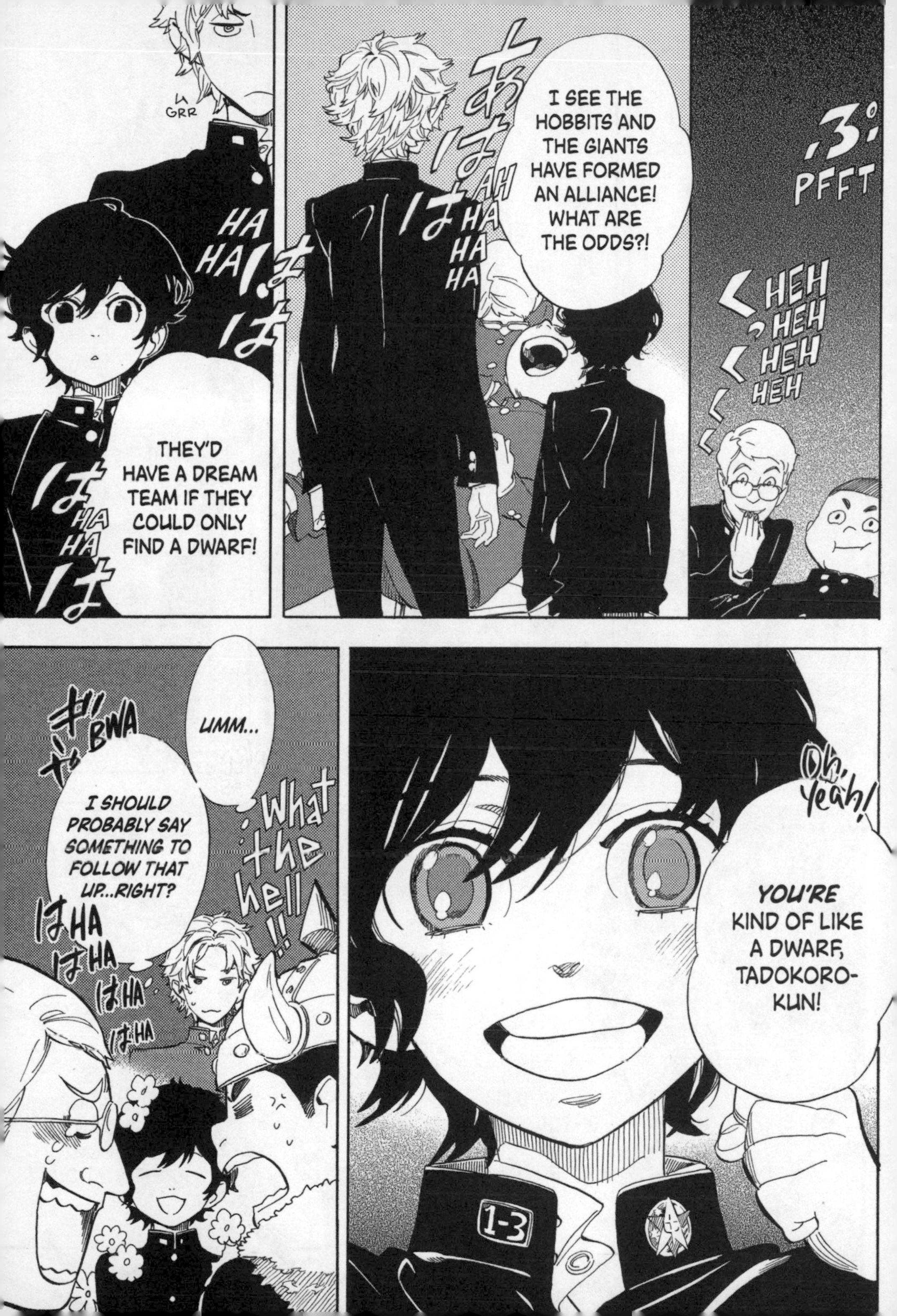

PFFT
HEH HEH HEH HEH
I SEE THE HOBBITS AND THE GIANTS HAVE FORMED AN ALLIANCE! WHAT ARE THE ODDS?!
AH HA HA HA HA
GRR
HA HA
THEY'D HAVE A DREAM TEAM IF THEY COULD ONLY FIND A DWARF!
HA HA
Oh, yeah!
YOU'RE KIND OF LIKE A DWARF, TADOKORO-KUN!
UMM...
What the hell!!
BWA
I SHOULD PROBABLY SAY SOMETHING TO FOLLOW THAT UP...RIGHT?
HA HA HA HA

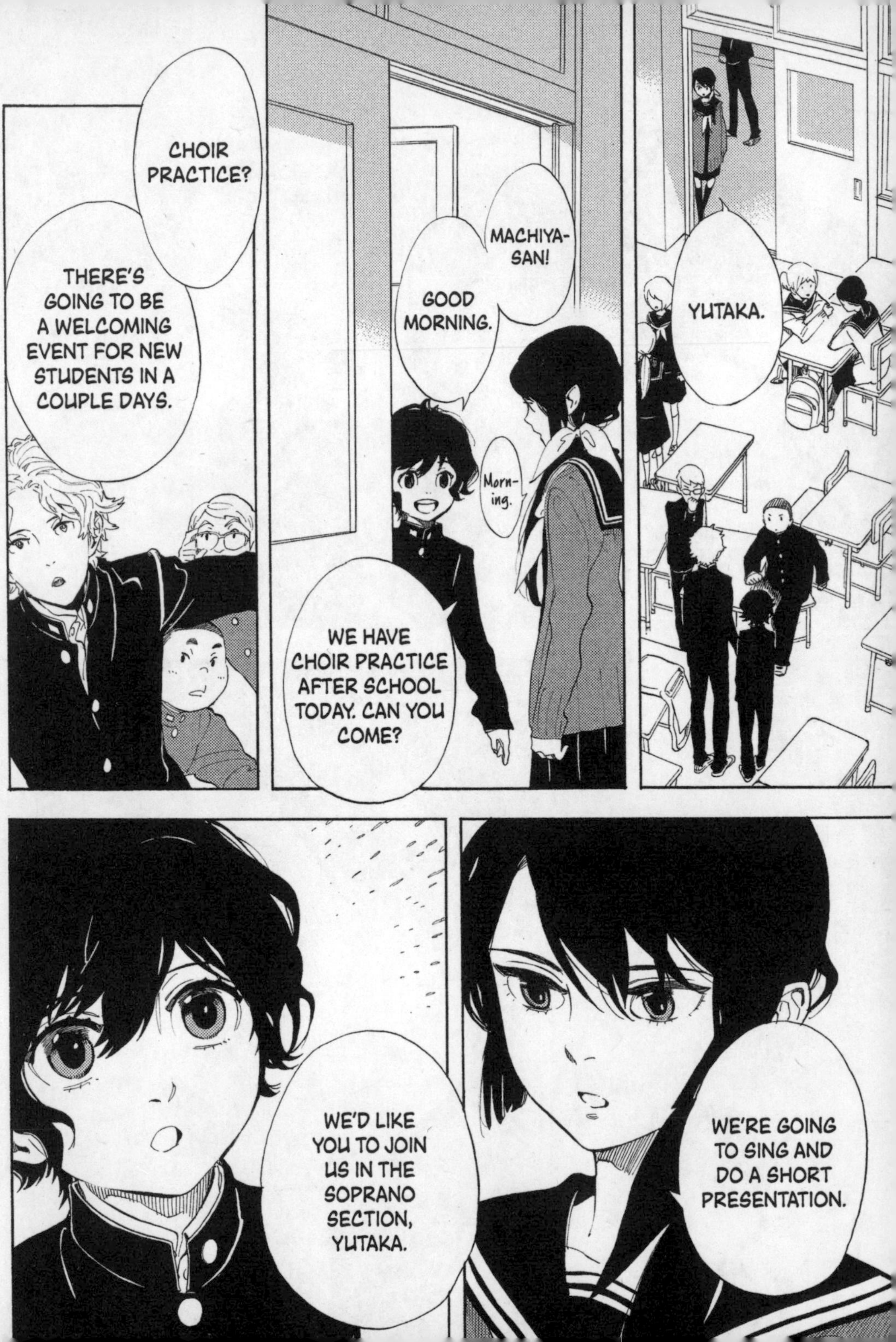
YUTAKA.
MACHIYA-SAN!
GOOD MORNING.
Morning.
WE HAVE CHOIR PRACTICE AFTER SCHOOL TODAY. CAN YOU COME?
CHOIR PRACTICE?
THERE'S GOING TO BE A WELCOMING EVENT FOR NEW STUDENTS IN A COUPLE DAYS.
WE'RE GOING TO SING AND DO A SHORT PRESENTATION.
WE'D LIKE YOU TO JOIN US IN THE SOPRANO SECTION, YUTAKA.

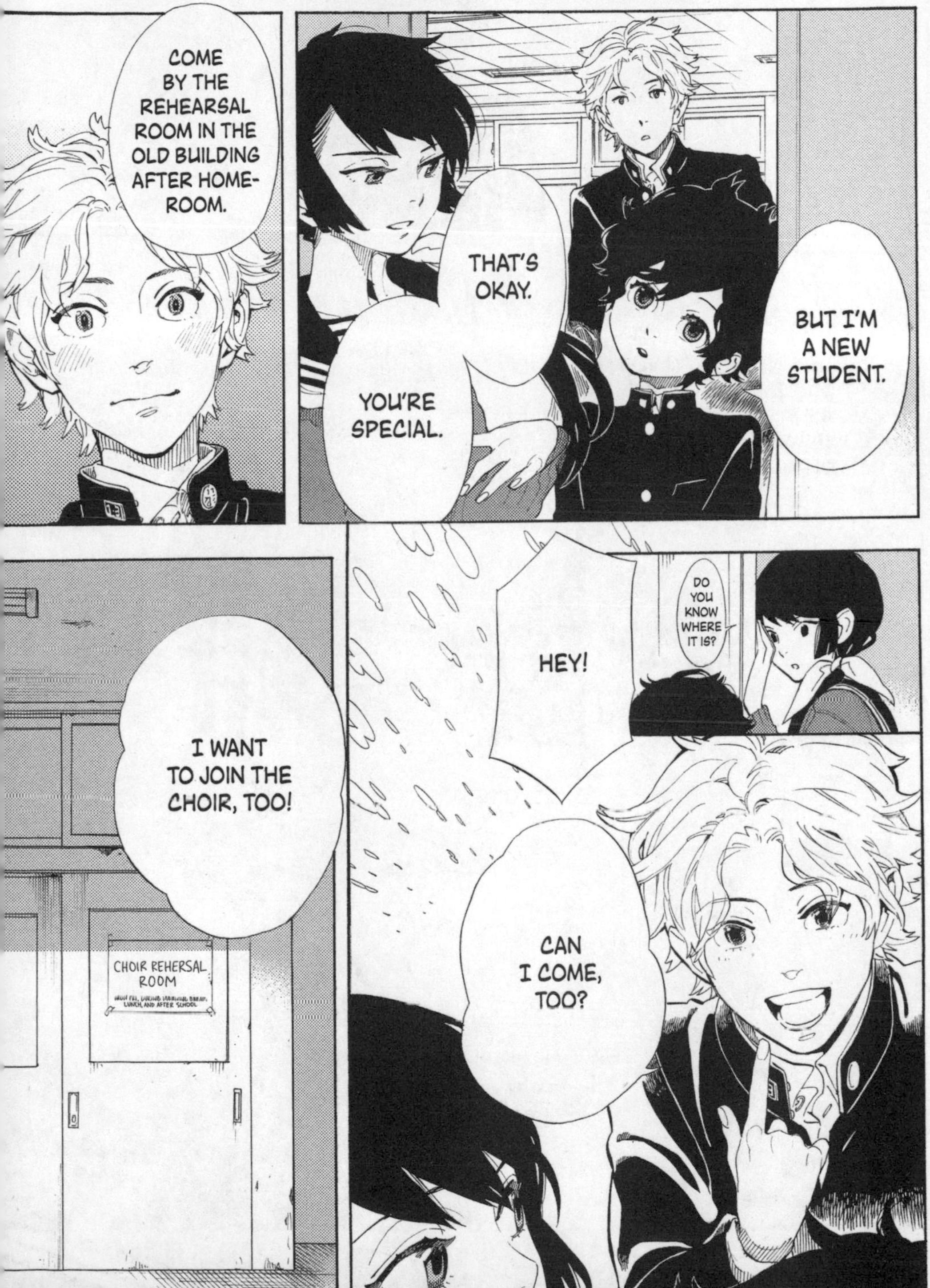
BUT I'M A NEW STUDENT.
THAT'S OKAY.
YOU'RE SPECIAL.
COME BY THE REHEARSAL ROOM IN THE OLD BUILDING AFTER HOME-ROOM.
DO YOU KNOW WHERE IT IS?
HEY!
CAN I COME, TOO?
I WANT TO JOIN THE CHOIR, TOO!
CHOIR REHERSAL ROOM
LUNCH, AND AFTER SCHOOL

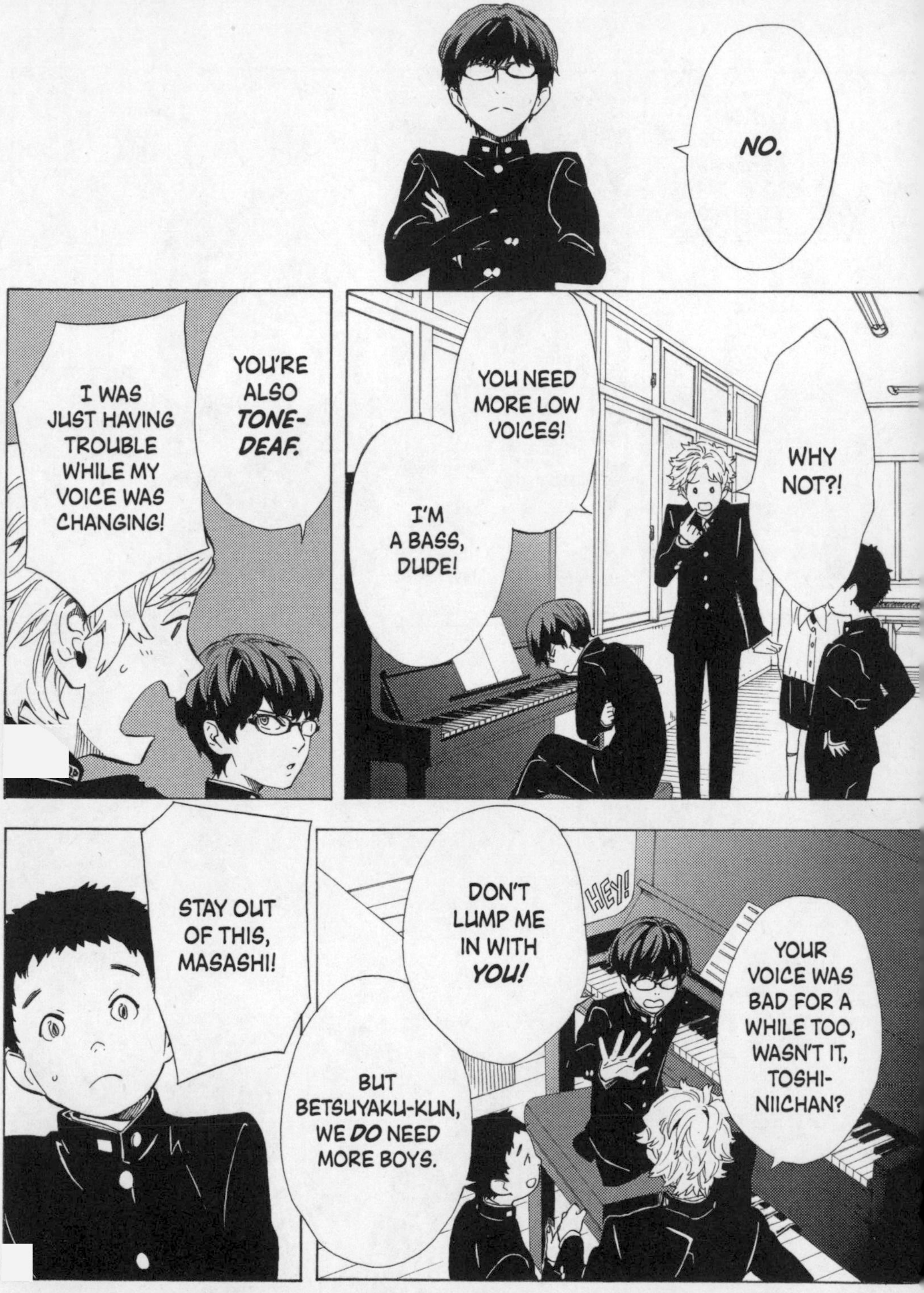
NO.
WHY NOT?!
YOU NEED MORE LOW VOICES!
I'M A BASS, DUDE!
YOU'RE ALSO TONE-DEAF.
I WAS JUST HAVING TROUBLE WHILE MY VOICE WAS CHANGING!
YOUR VOICE WAS BAD FOR A WHILE TOO, WASN'T IT, TOSHI-NIICHAN?
HEY!
DON'T LUMP ME IN WITH YOU!
BUT BETSUYAKU-KUN, WE DO NEED MORE BOYS.
STAY OUT OF THIS, MASASHI!

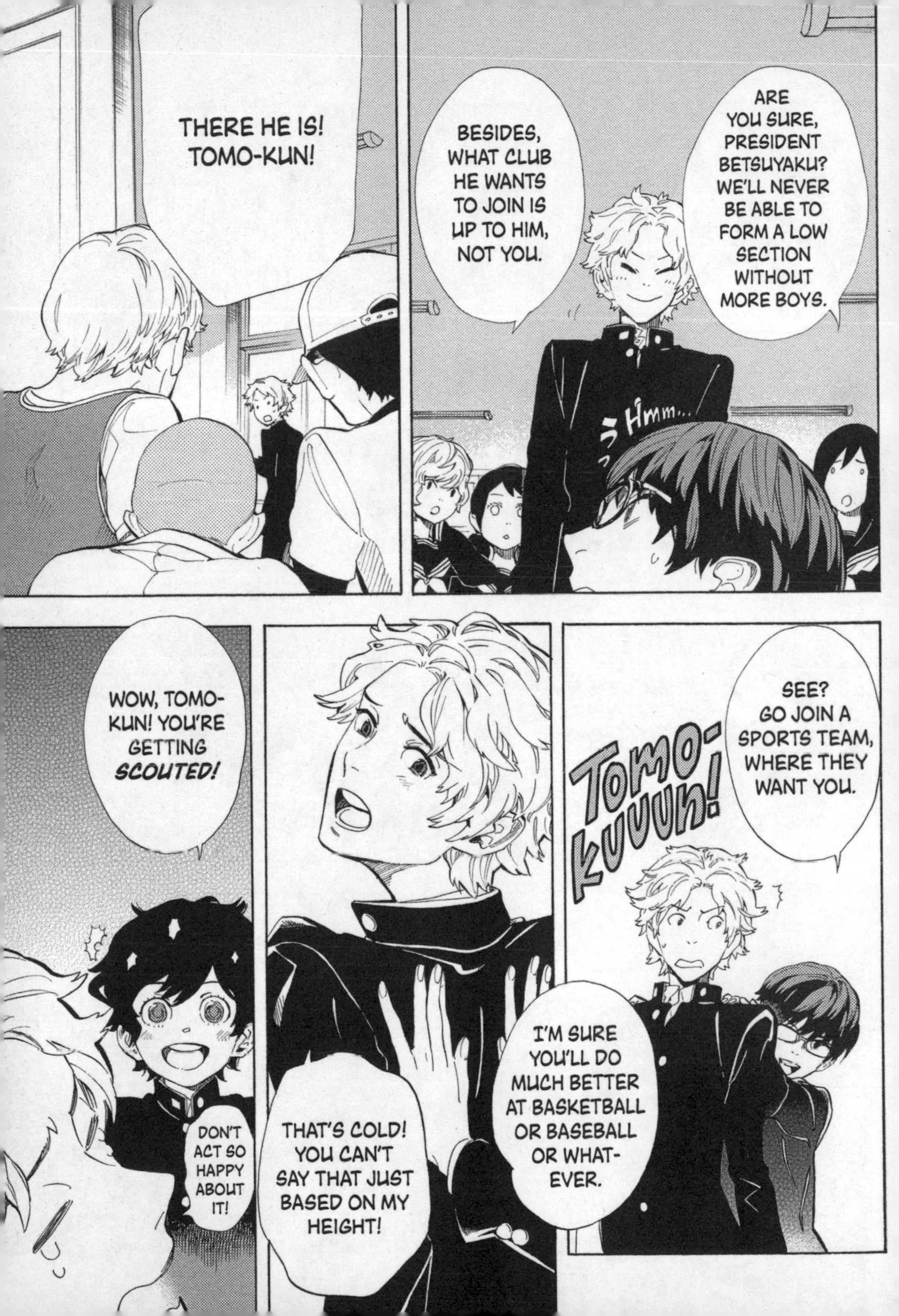
ARE YOU SURE, PRESIDENT BETSUYAKU? WE'LL NEVER BE ABLE TO FORM A LOW SECTION WITHOUT MORE BOYS.
BESIDES, WHAT CLUB HE WANTS TO JOIN IS UP TO HIM, NOT YOU.
Hmm...
THERE HE IS! TOMO-KUN!
SEE? GO JOIN A SPORTS TEAM, WHERE THEY WANT YOU.
Tomo-kuuun!
I'M SURE YOU'LL DO MUCH BETTER AT BASKETBALL OR BASEBALL OR WHATEVER.
THAT'S COLD! YOU CAN'T SAY THAT JUST BASED ON MY HEIGHT!
WOW, TOMO-KUN! YOU'RE GETTING *SCOUTED!*
DON'T ACT SO HAPPY ABOUT IT!

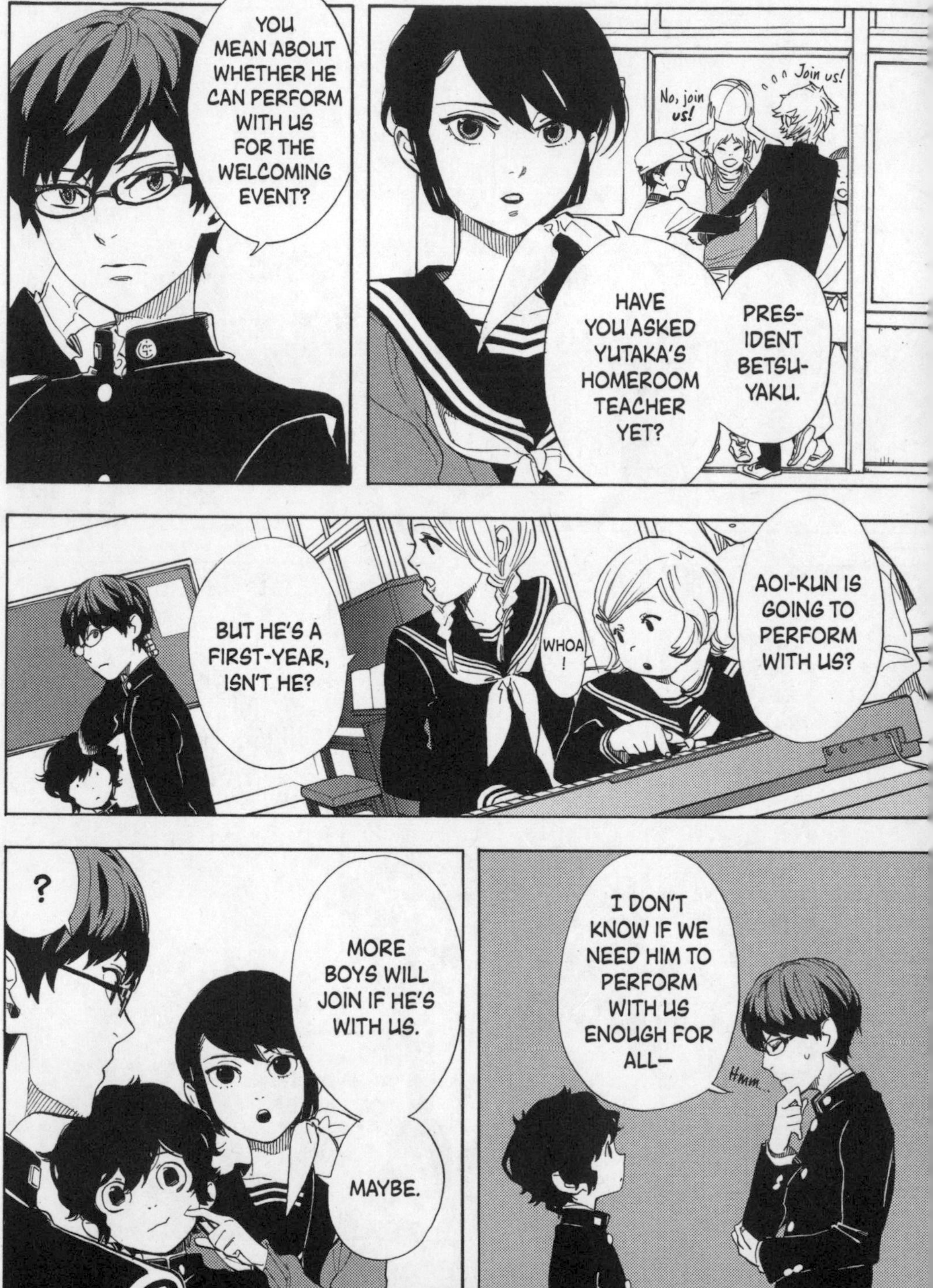
Join us!
No, join us!
PRES-IDENT BETSU-YAKU.
HAVE YOU ASKED YUTAKA'S HOMEROOM TEACHER YET?
YOU MEAN ABOUT WHETHER HE CAN PERFORM WITH US FOR THE WELCOMING EVENT?
AOI-KUN IS GOING TO PERFORM WITH US?
WHOA!
BUT HE'S A FIRST-YEAR, ISN'T HE?
I DON'T KNOW IF WE NEED HIM TO PERFORM WITH US ENOUGH FOR ALL—
Hmm...
MORE BOYS WILL JOIN IF HE'S WITH US.
MAYBE.
?

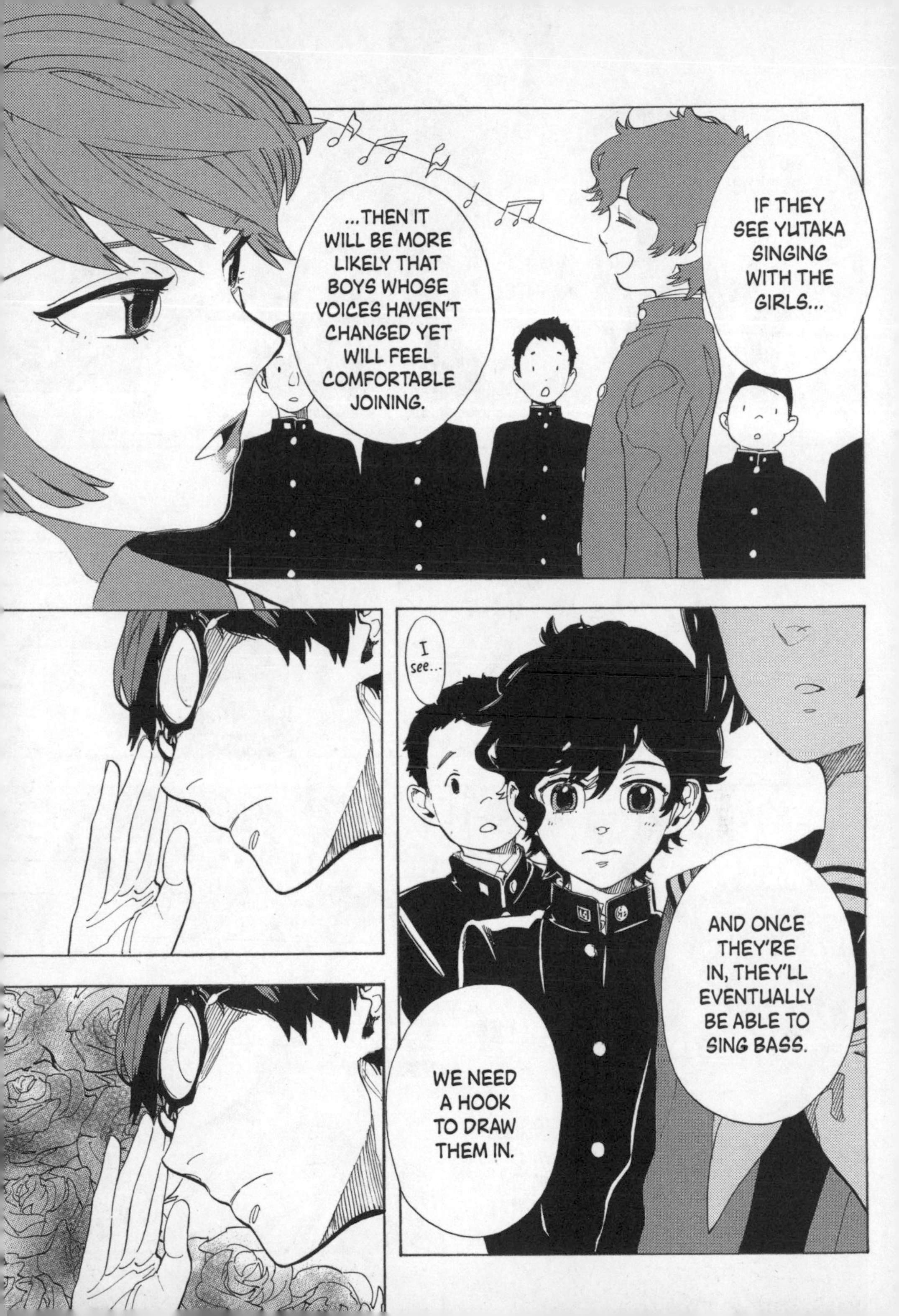
IF THEY SEE YUTAKA SINGING WITH THE GIRLS...
...THEN IT WILL BE MORE LIKELY THAT BOYS WHOSE VOICES HAVEN'T CHANGED YET WILL FEEL COMFORTABLE JOINING.
I see...
AND ONCE THEY'RE IN, THEY'LL EVENTUALLY BE ABLE TO SING BASS.
WE NEED A HOOK TO DRAW THEM IN.

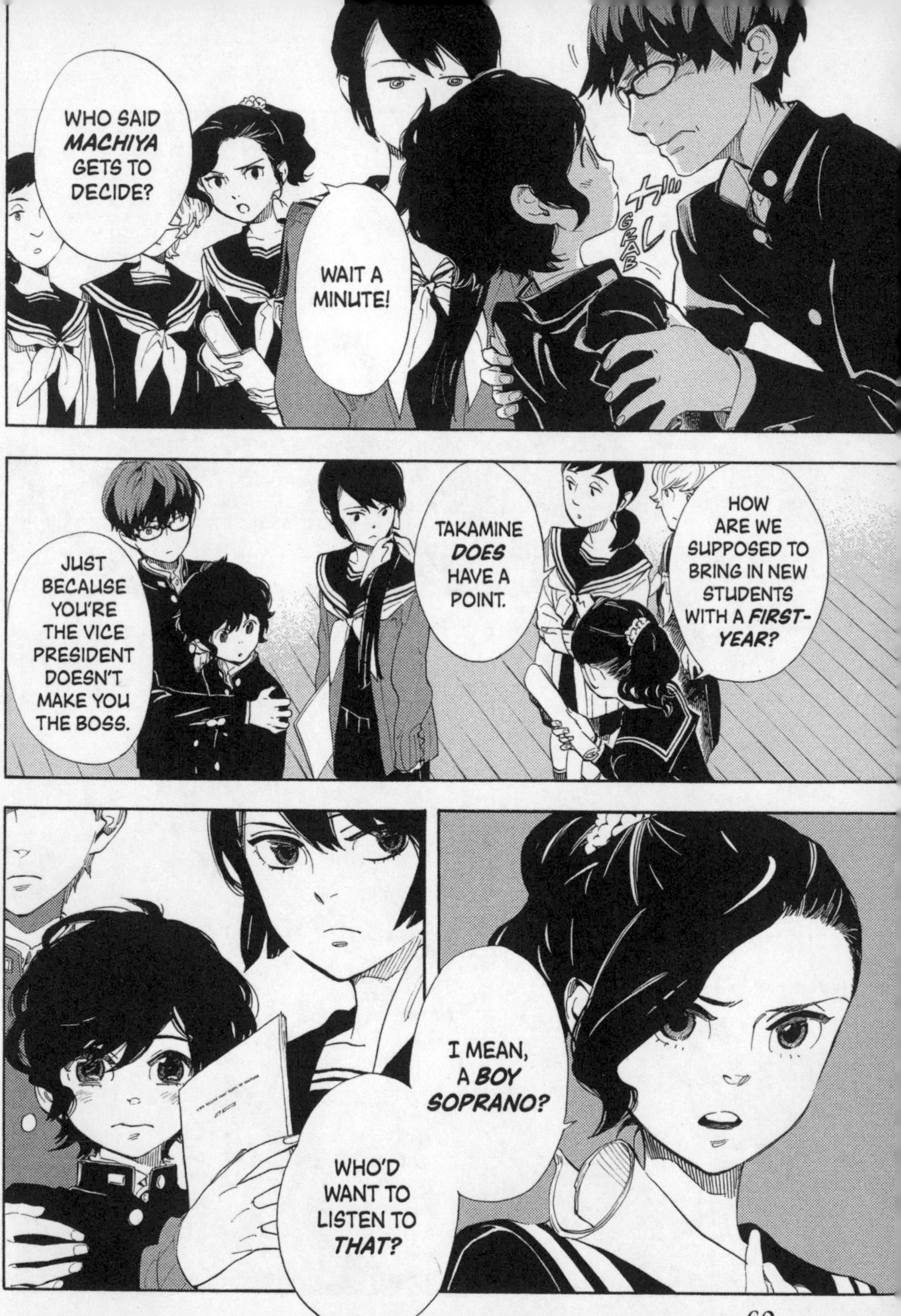
GRAB
WAIT A MINUTE!
WHO SAID MACHIYA GETS TO DECIDE?
HOW ARE WE SUPPOSED TO BRING IN NEW STUDENTS WITH A FIRST-YEAR?
TAKAMINE DOES HAVE A POINT.
JUST BECAUSE YOU'RE THE VICE PRESIDENT DOESN'T MAKE YOU THE BOSS.
I MEAN, A BOY SOPRANO?
WHO'D WANT TO LISTEN TO THAT?

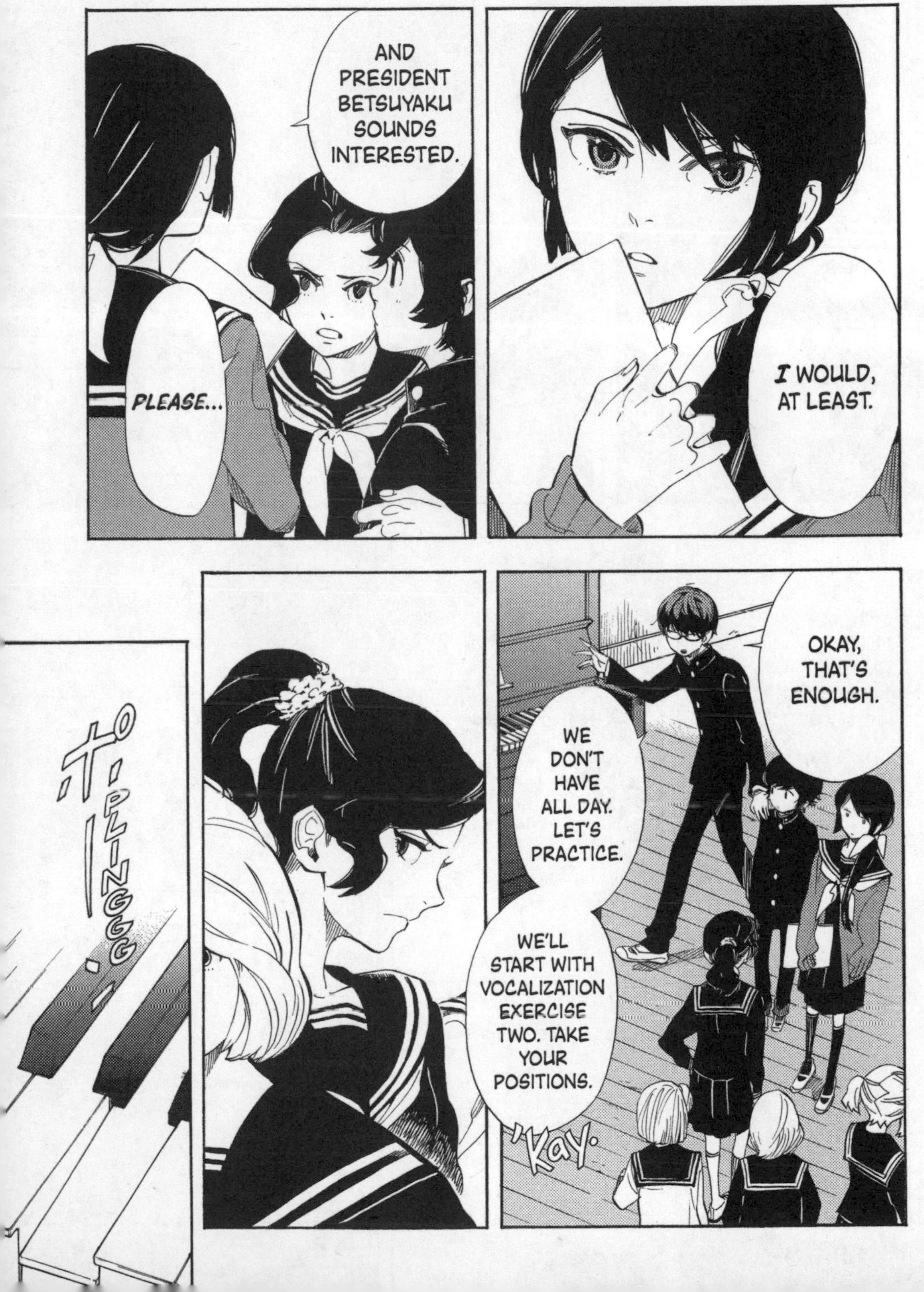
I WOULD, AT LEAST.
AND PRESIDENT BETSUYAKU SOUNDS INTERESTED.
PLEASE...
OKAY, THAT'S ENOUGH.
WE DON'T HAVE ALL DAY. LET'S PRACTICE.
WE'LL START WITH VOCALIZATION EXERCISE TWO. TAKE YOUR POSITIONS.
'Kay.
PLINGGG.

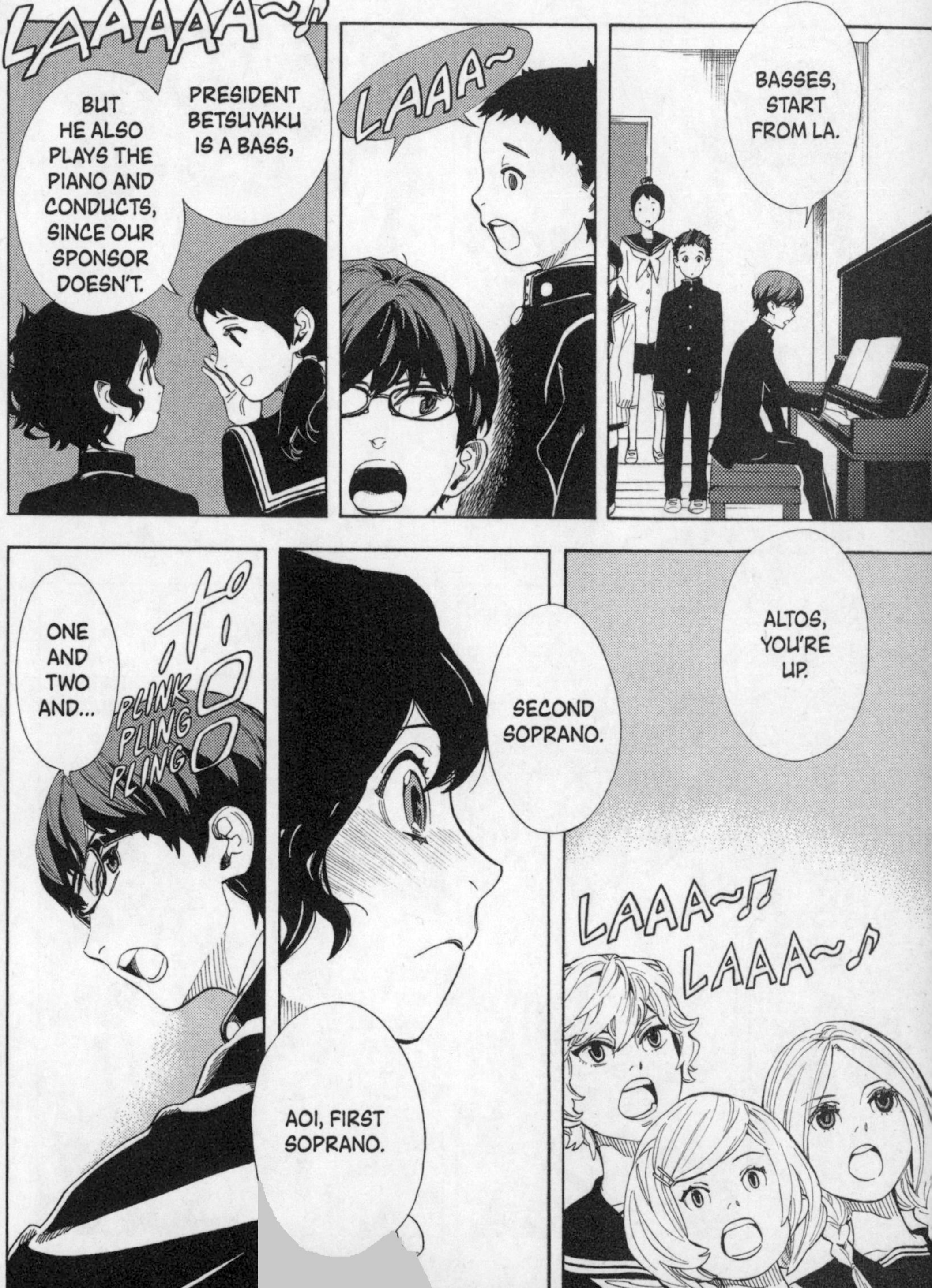
BASSES, START FROM LA.
LAAA~
LAAAAA~♪
PRESIDENT BETSUYAKU IS A BASS,
BUT HE ALSO PLAYS THE PIANO AND CONDUCTS, SINCE OUR SPONSOR DOESN'T.
ALTOS, YOU'RE UP.
LAAA~♪
LAAA~♪
SECOND SOPRANO.
AOI, FIRST SOPRANO.
ONE AND TWO AND...
PLINK PLING PLING

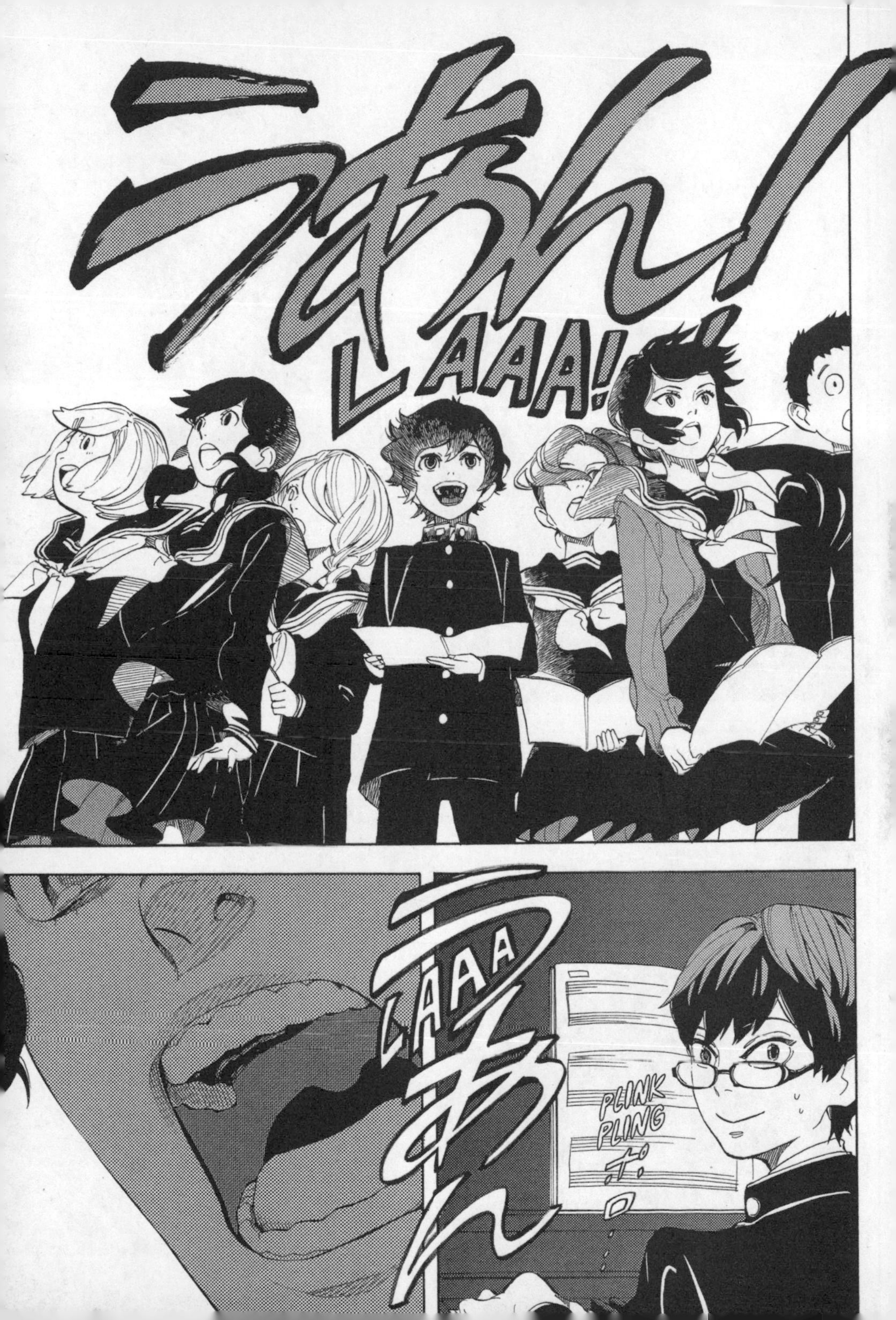

うわん!
LAAA!
う
LAAA
あ
ん
PLINK
PLING

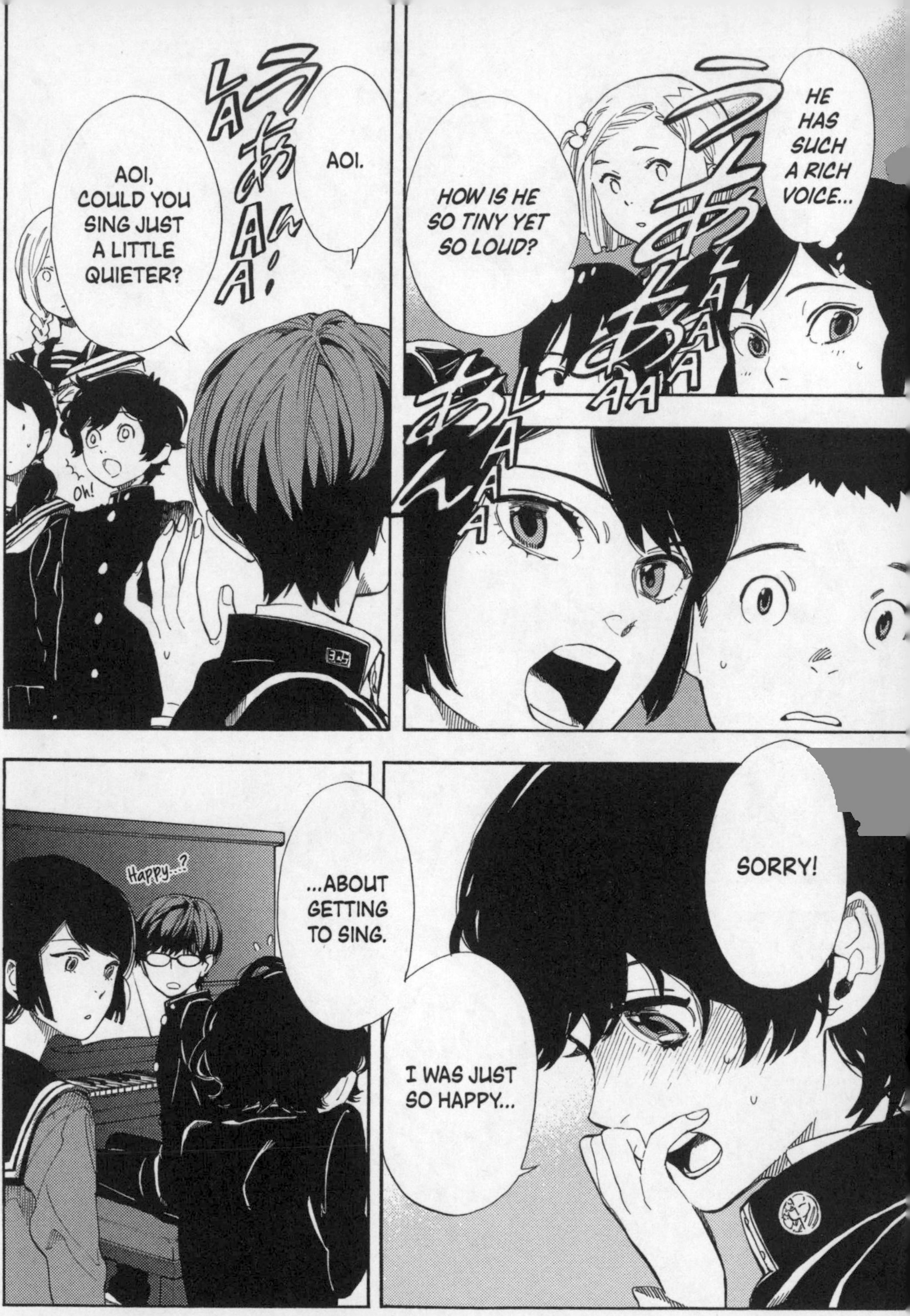
HE HAS SUCH A RICH VOICE...
HOW IS HE SO TINY YET SO LOUD?
LAAAAA
LAAA
LAAAA
AOI.
AOI, COULD YOU SING JUST A LITTLE QUIETER?
LAAA!
Oh!
SORRY!
I WAS JUST SO HAPPY...
...ABOUT GETTING TO SING.
Happy...?

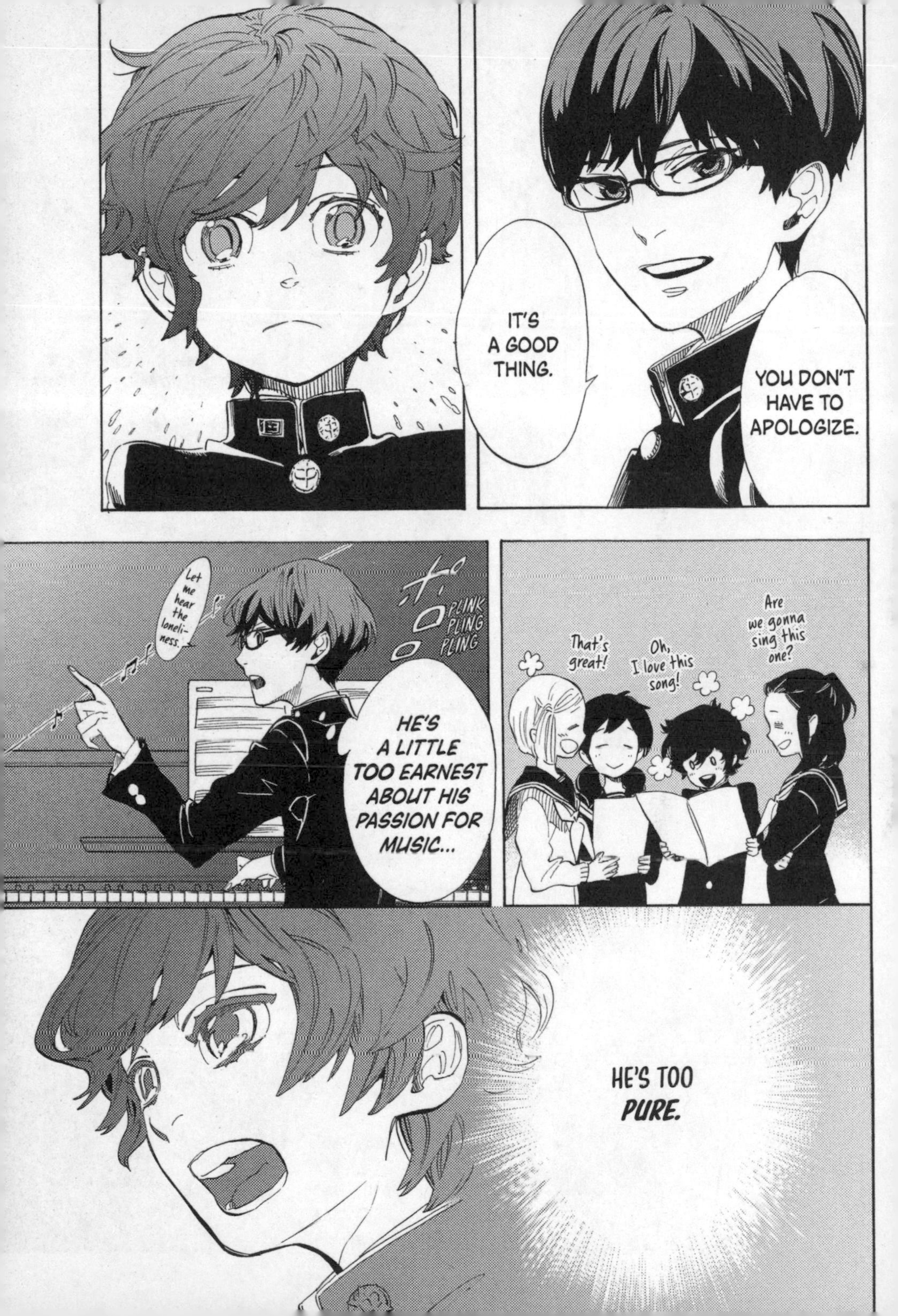
YOU DON'T HAVE TO APOLOGIZE.
IT'S A GOOD THING.
Are we gonna sing this one?
Oh, I love this song!
That's great!
HE'S A LITTLE TOO EARNEST ABOUT HIS PASSION FOR MUSIC...
PLINK PLING PLING
Let me hear the loneli-ness.
HE'S TOO PURE.

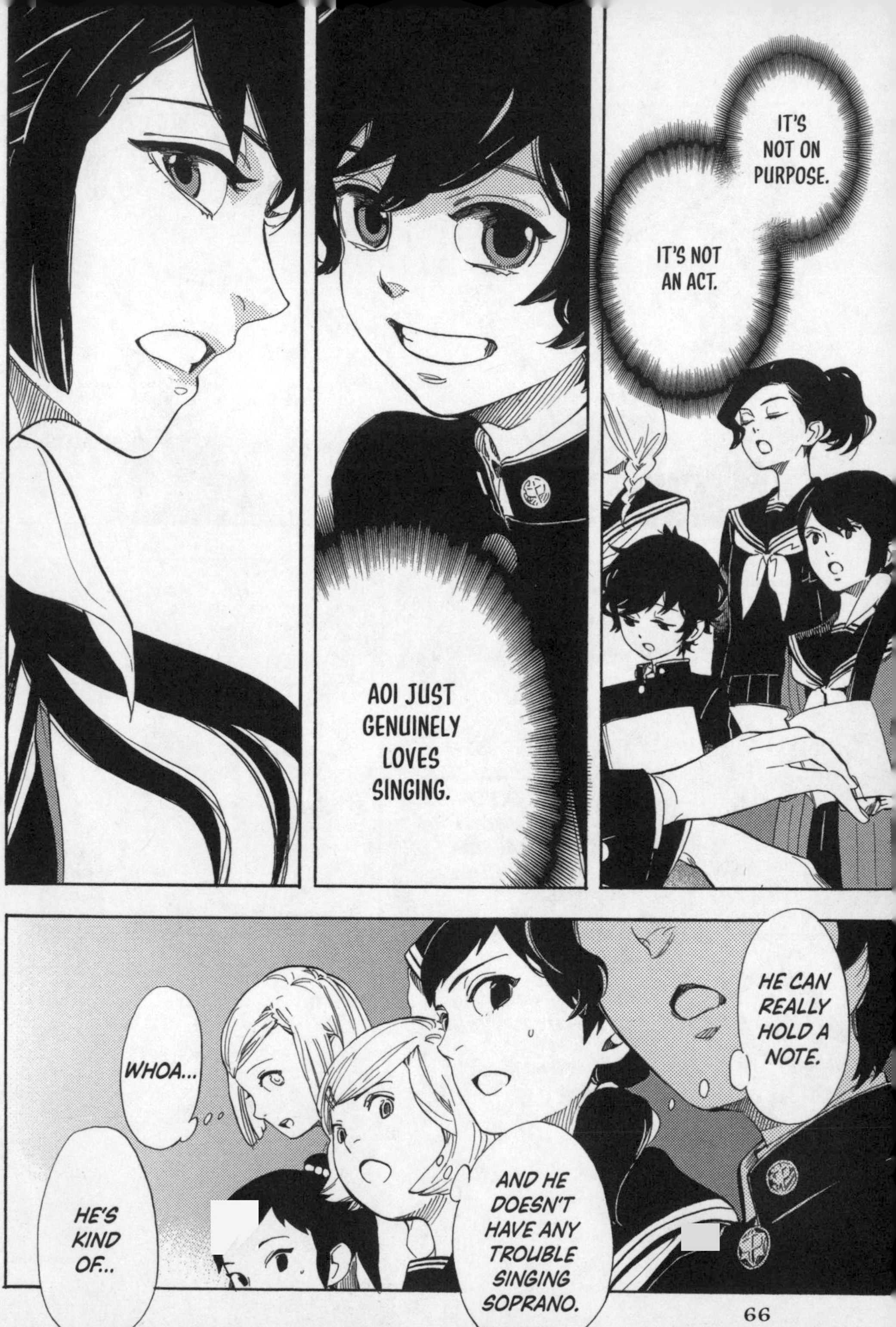
IT'S NOT ON PURPOSE.
IT'S NOT AN ACT.
AOI JUST GENUINELY LOVES SINGING.
HE CAN REALLY HOLD A NOTE.
AND HE DOESN'T HAVE ANY TROUBLE SINGING SOPRANO.
WHOA...
HE'S KIND OF...

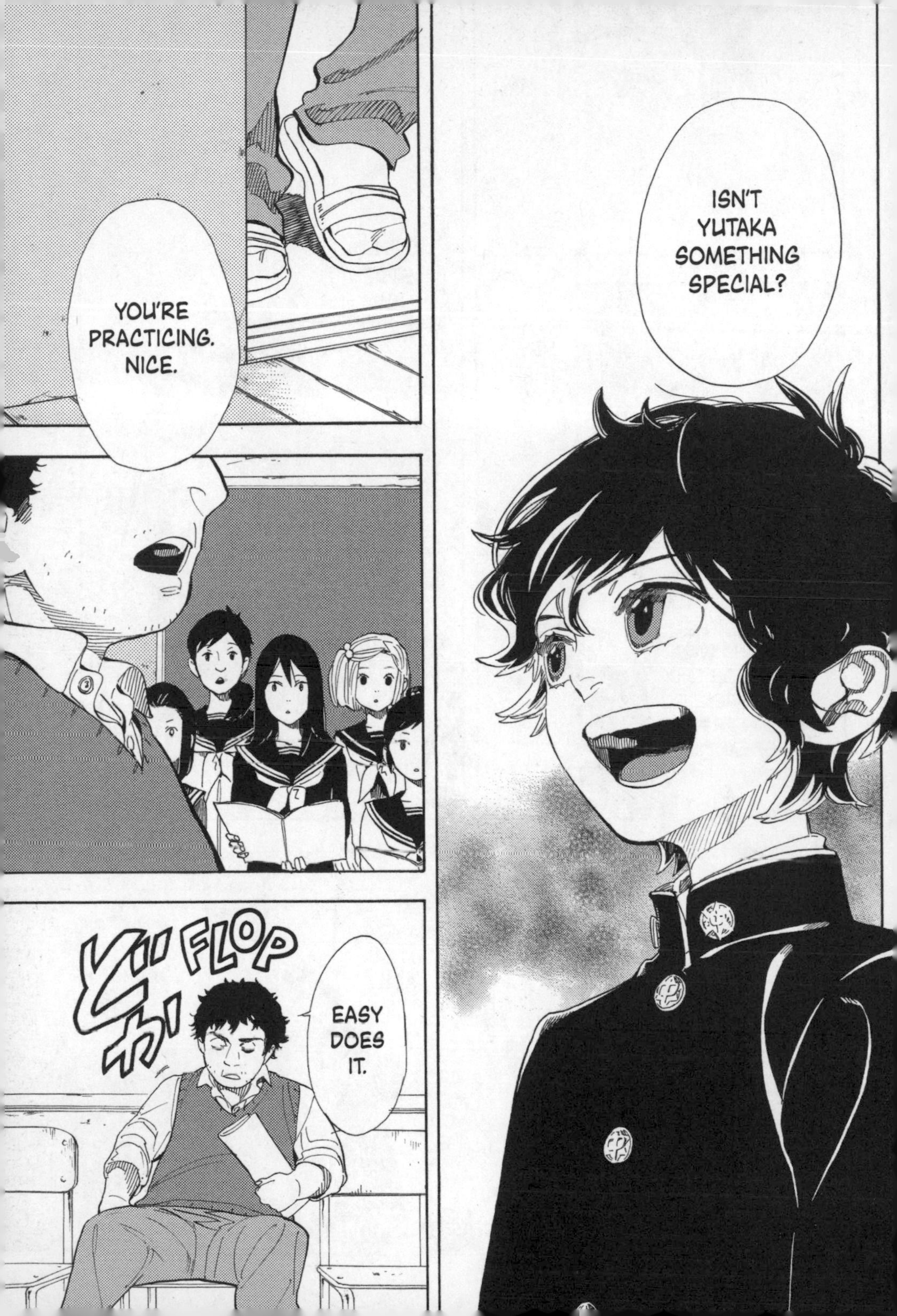
ISN'T YUTAKA SOMETHING SPECIAL?
YOU'RE PRACTICING. NICE.
FLOP
EASY DOES IT.

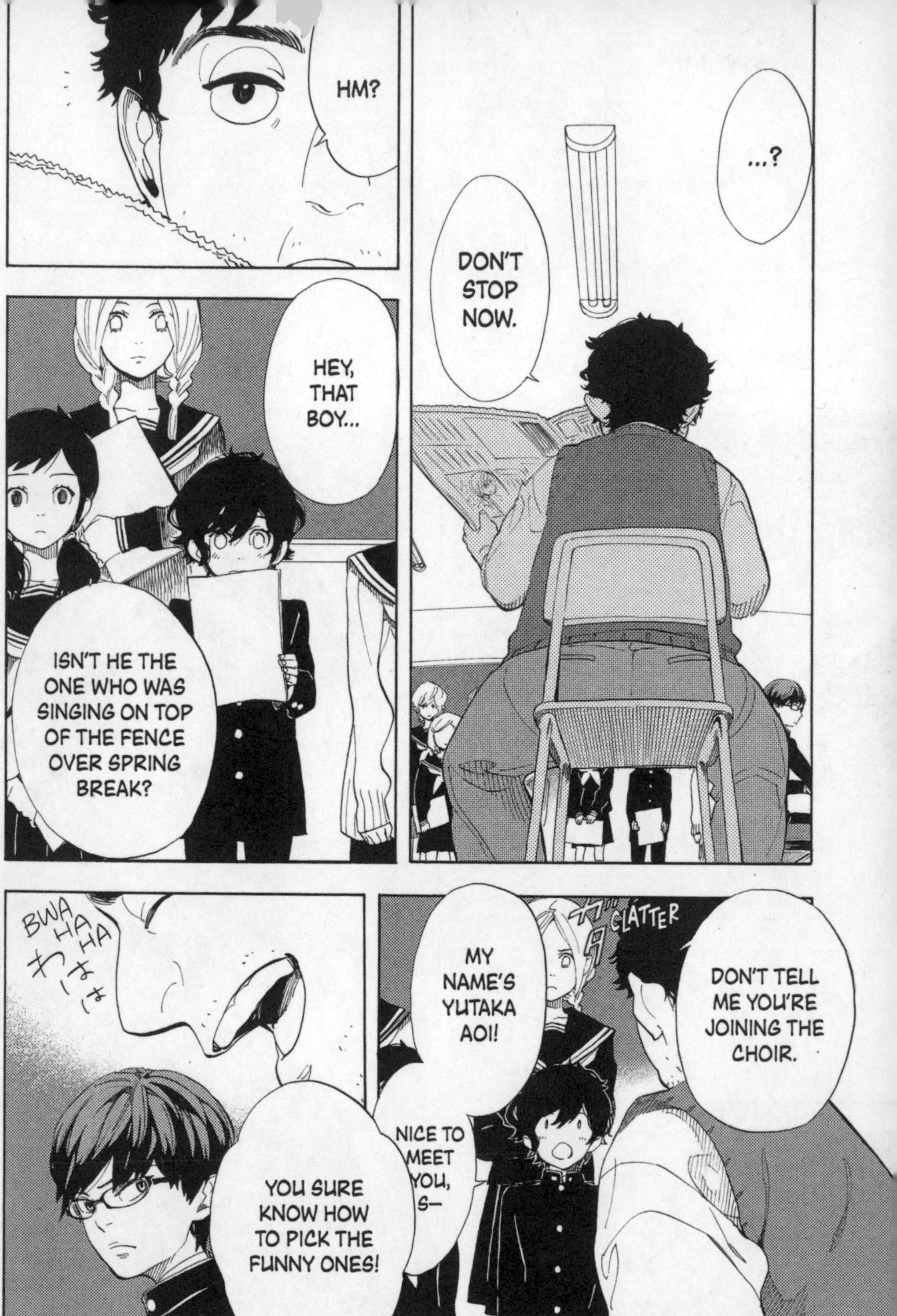
...?
DON'T STOP NOW.
HM?
HEY, THAT BOY...
ISN'T HE THE ONE WHO WAS SINGING ON TOP OF THE FENCE OVER SPRING BREAK?
DON'T TELL ME YOU'RE JOINING THE CHOIR.
CLATTER
MY NAME'S YUTAKA AOI!
NICE TO MEET YOU, S—
BWA HA HA
わはは
YOU SURE KNOW HOW TO PICK THE FUNNY ONES!

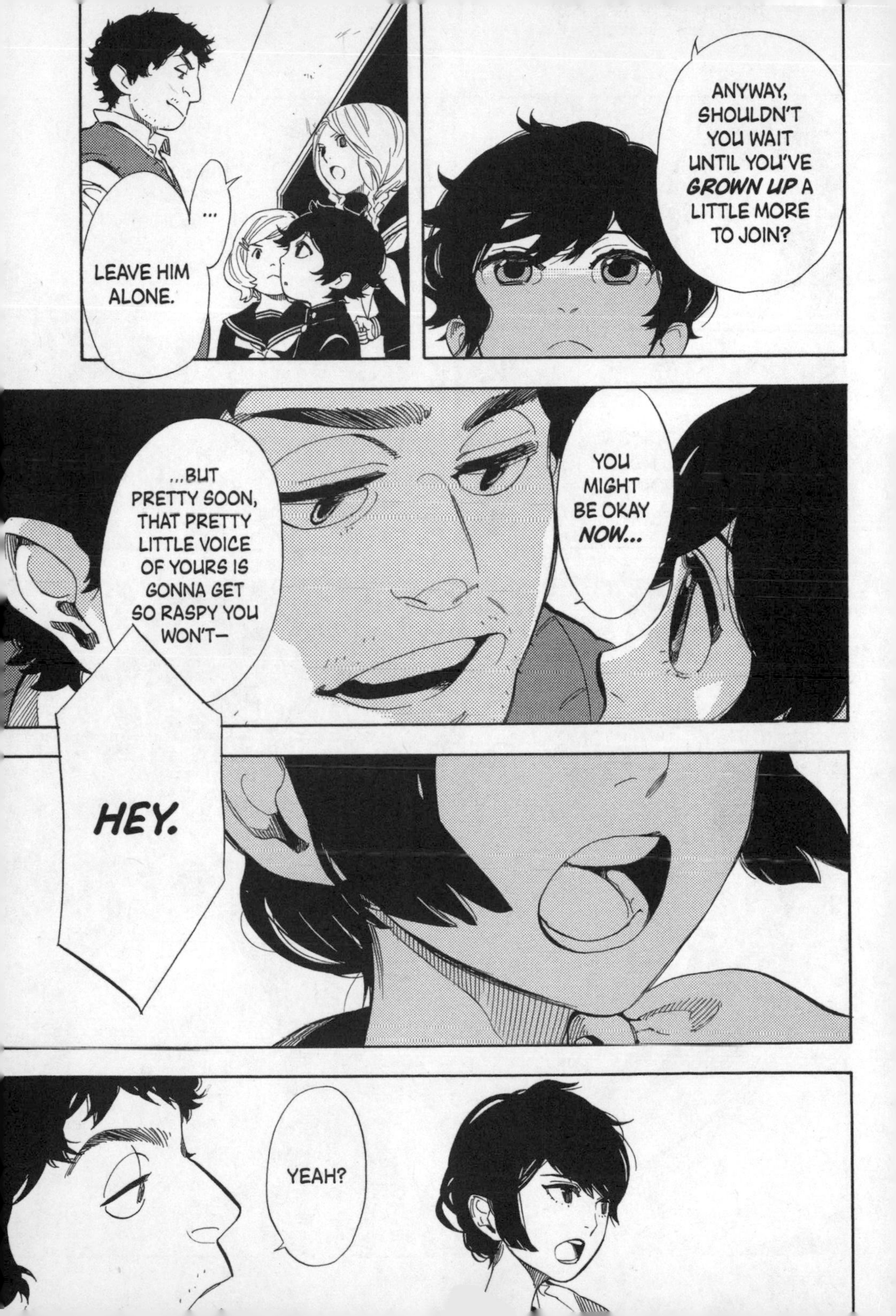
ANYWAY, SHOULDN'T YOU WAIT UNTIL YOU'VE *GROWN UP* A LITTLE MORE TO JOIN?
...
LEAVE HIM ALONE.
YOU MIGHT BE OKAY *NOW...*
...BUT PRETTY SOON, THAT PRETTY LITTLE VOICE OF YOURS IS GONNA GET SO RASPY YOU WON'T—
HEY.
YEAH?

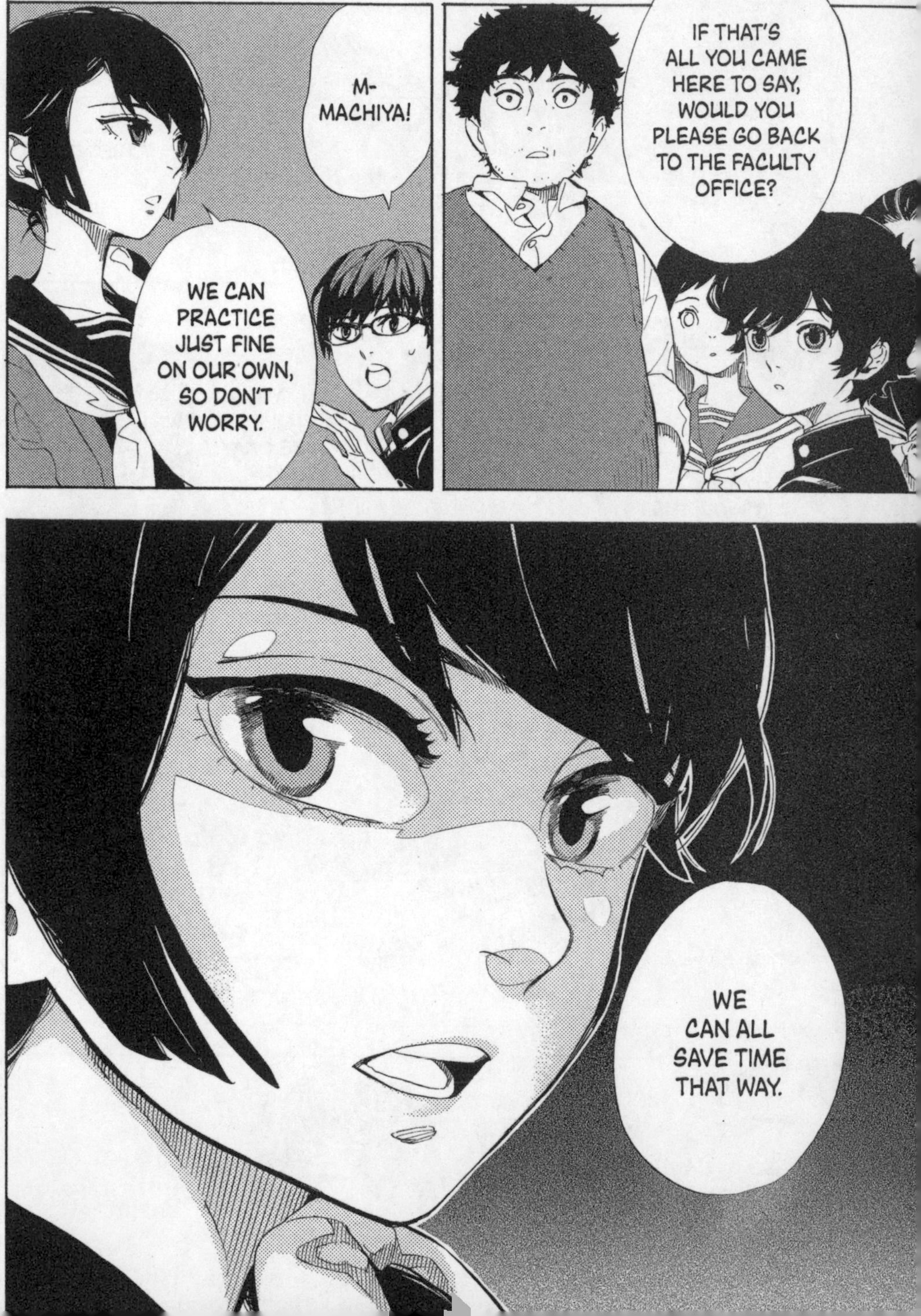
IF THAT'S ALL YOU CAME HERE TO SAY, WOULD YOU PLEASE GO BACK TO THE FACULTY OFFICE?
M-MACHIYA!
WE CAN PRACTICE JUST FINE ON OUR OWN, SO DON'T WORRY.
WE CAN ALL SAVE TIME THAT WAY.

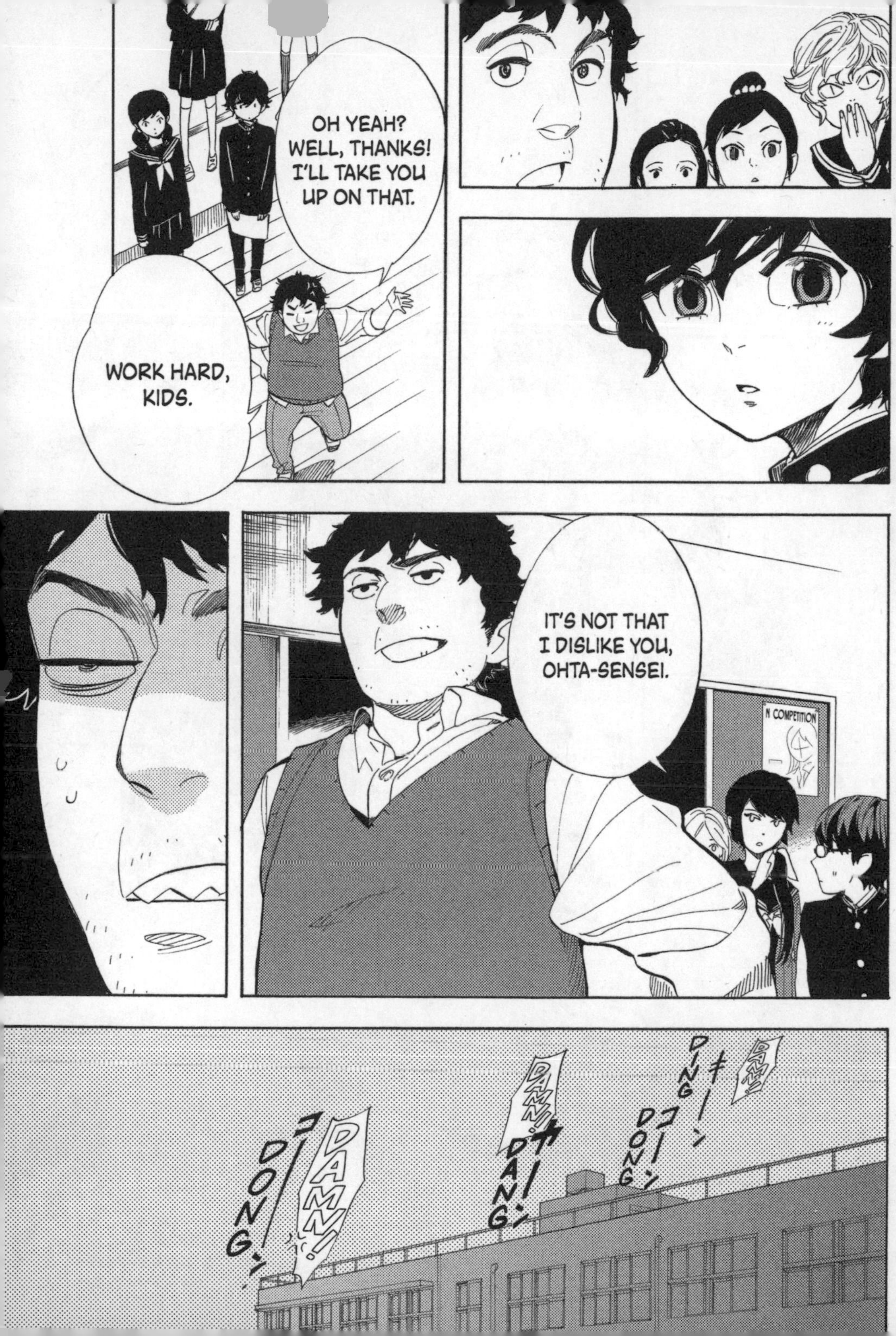
OH YEAH? WELL, THANKS! I'LL TAKE YOU UP ON THAT.
WORK HARD, KIDS.
IT'S NOT THAT I DISLIKE YOU, OHTA-SENSEI.
N COMPETITION
DAMN!
DING DONG
DAMN!
DANG
DAMMN!
DOONG

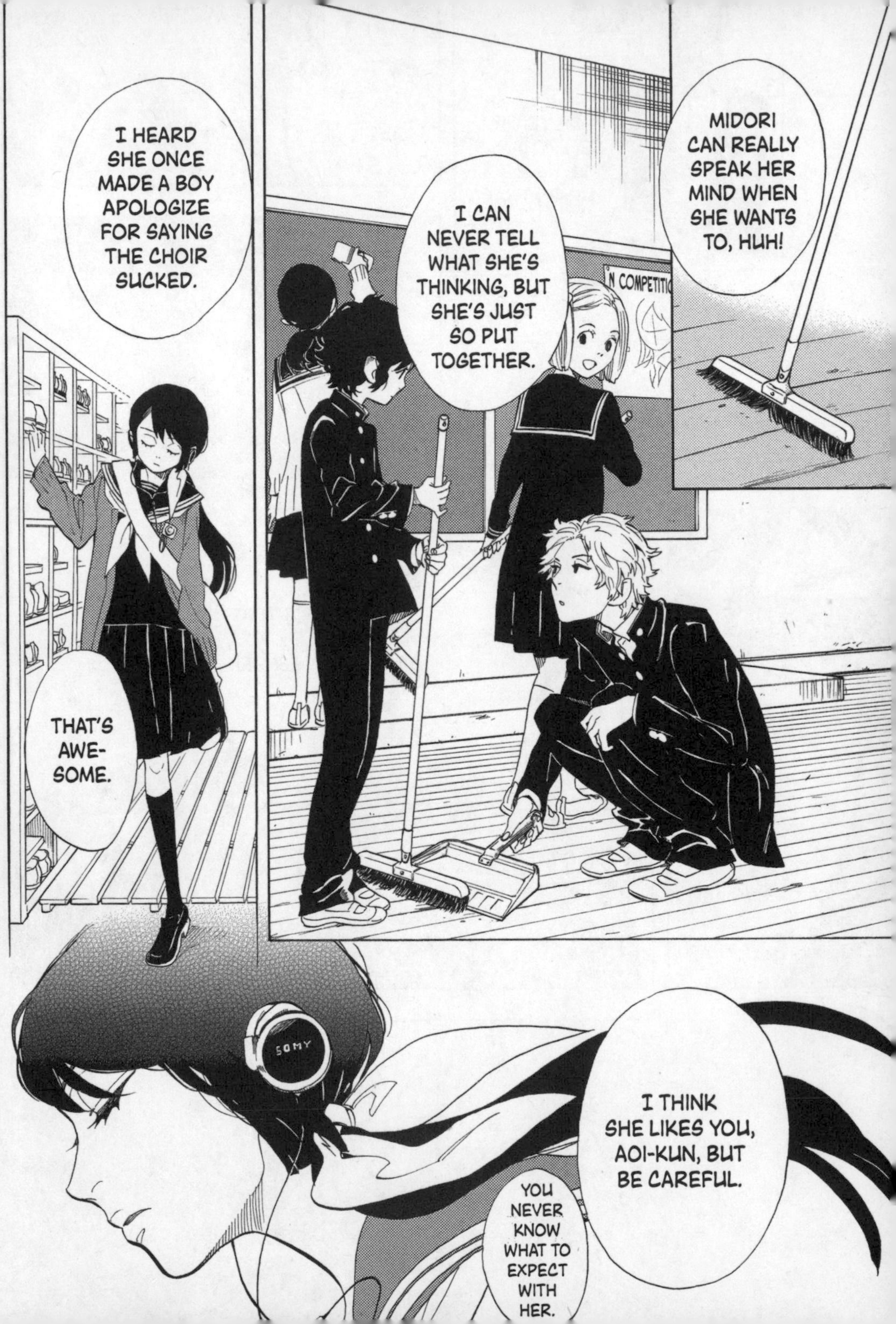
MIDORI CAN REALLY SPEAK HER MIND WHEN SHE WANTS TO, HUH!
I CAN NEVER TELL WHAT SHE'S THINKING, BUT SHE'S JUST SO PUT TOGETHER.
N COMPETITIO
I HEARD SHE ONCE MADE A BOY APOLOGIZE FOR SAYING THE CHOIR SUCKED.
THAT'S AWE-SOME.
I THINK SHE LIKES YOU, AOI-KUN, BUT BE CAREFUL.
YOU NEVER KNOW WHAT TO EXPECT WITH HER.

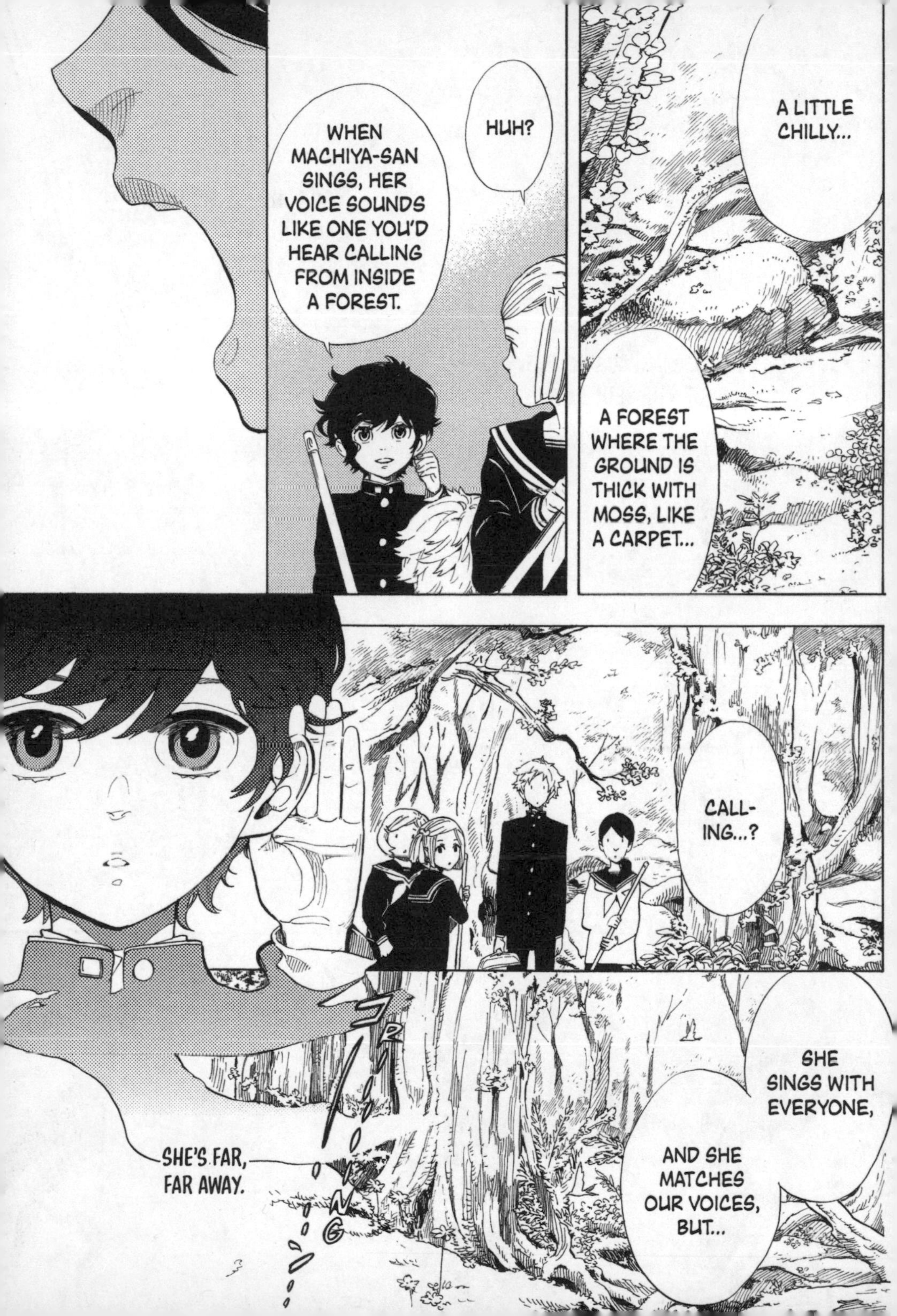
A LITTLE CHILLY...
A FOREST WHERE THE GROUND IS THICK WITH MOSS, LIKE A CARPET...
HUH?
WHEN MACHIYA-SAN SINGS, HER VOICE SOUNDS LIKE ONE YOU'D HEAR CALLING FROM INSIDE A FOREST.
CALL-ING...?
SHE SINGS WITH EVERYONE,
AND SHE MATCHES OUR VOICES, BUT...
SHE'S FAR, FAR AWAY.

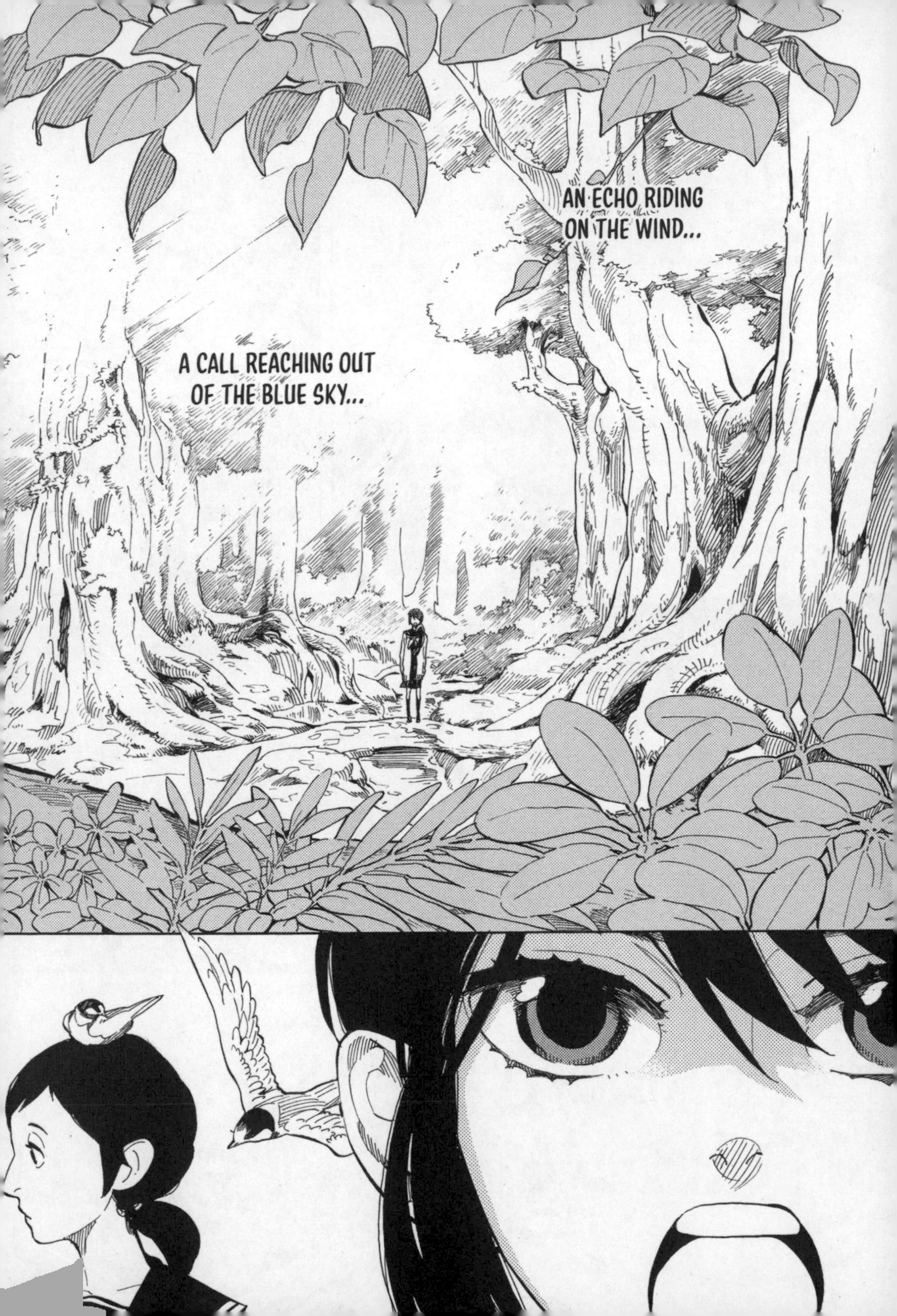
AN ECHO RIDING ON THE WIND...
A CALL REACHING OUT OF THE BLUE SKY...

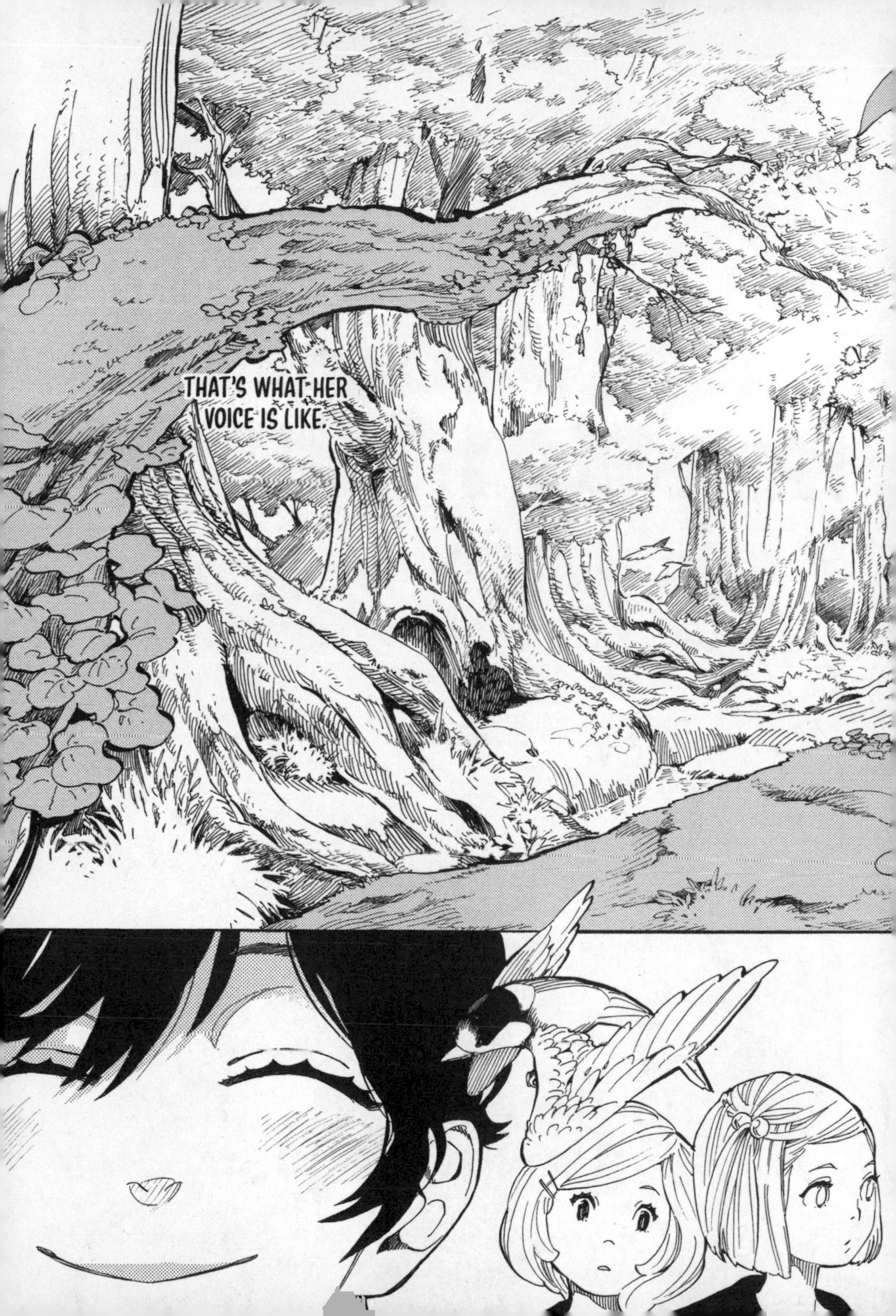
THAT'S WHAT HER VOICE IS LIKE.

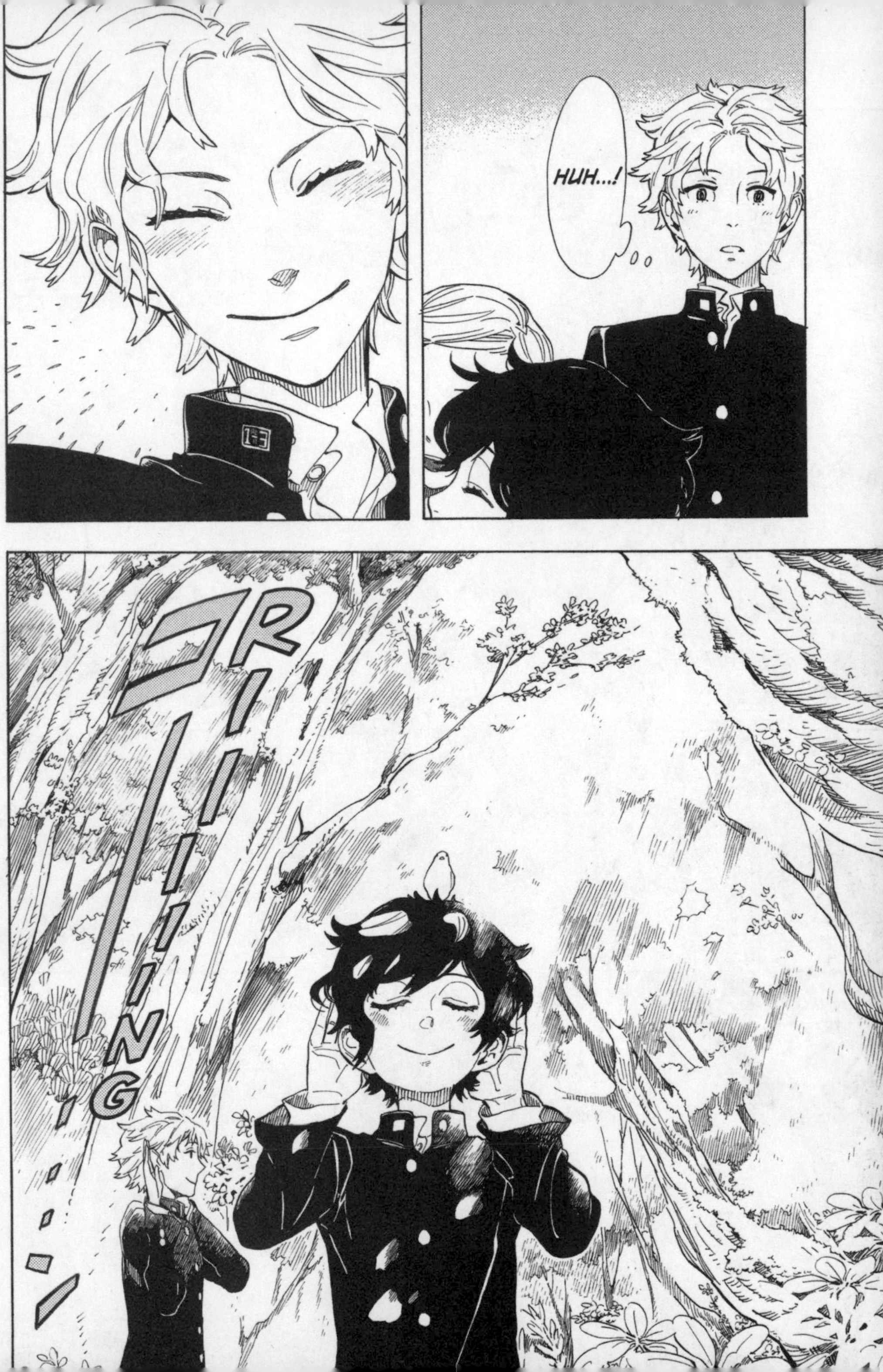
HUH...!
RIIIIING

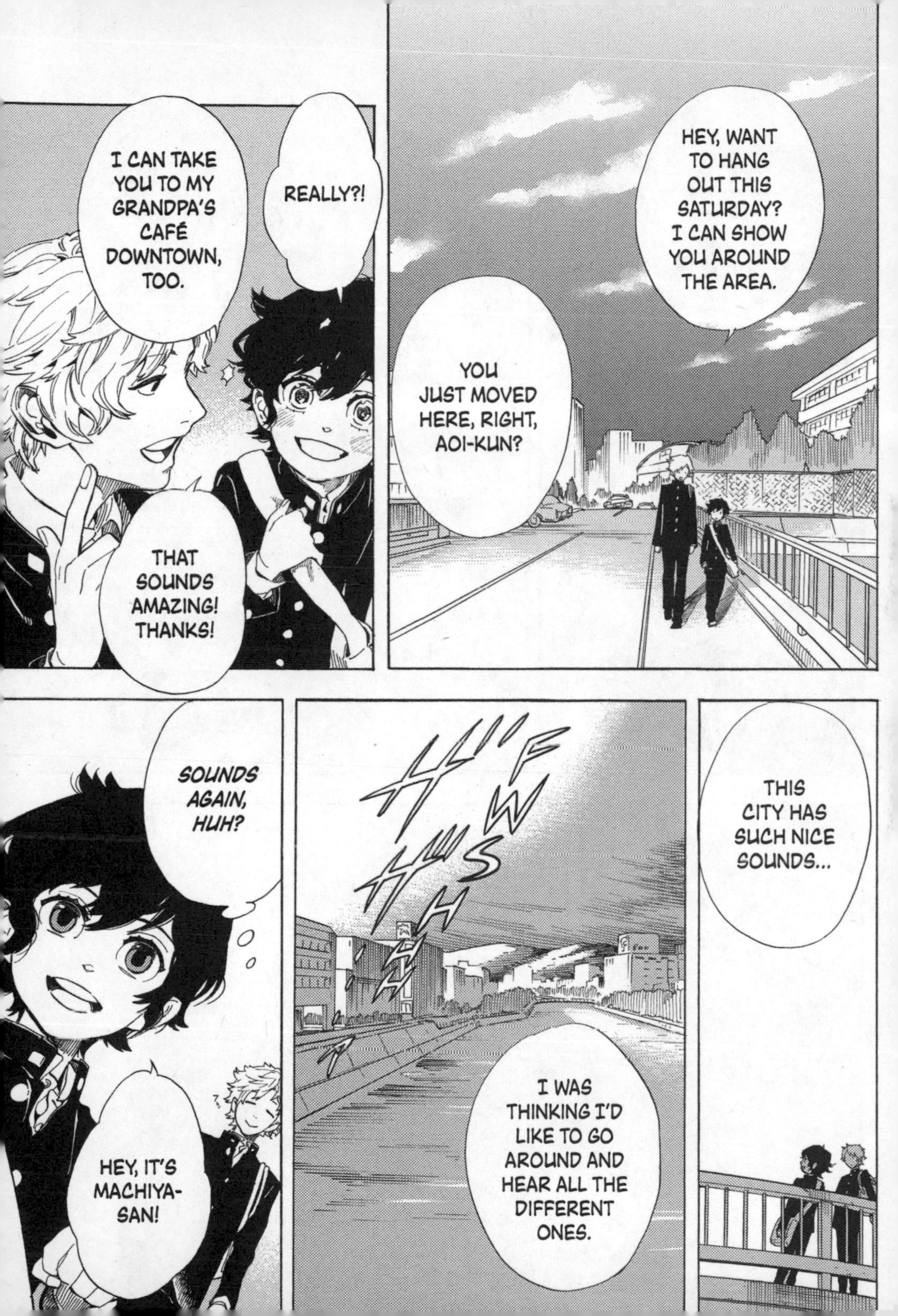
HEY, WANT TO HANG OUT THIS SATURDAY? I CAN SHOW YOU AROUND THE AREA.
YOU JUST MOVED HERE, RIGHT, AOI-KUN?
REALLY?!
I CAN TAKE YOU TO MY GRANDPA'S CAFÉ DOWNTOWN, TOO.
THAT SOUNDS AMAZING! THANKS!
THIS CITY HAS SUCH NICE SOUNDS...
I WAS THINKING I'D LIKE TO GO AROUND AND HEAR ALL THE DIFFERENT ONES.
SOUNDS AGAIN, HUH?
HEY, IT'S MACHIYA-SAN!

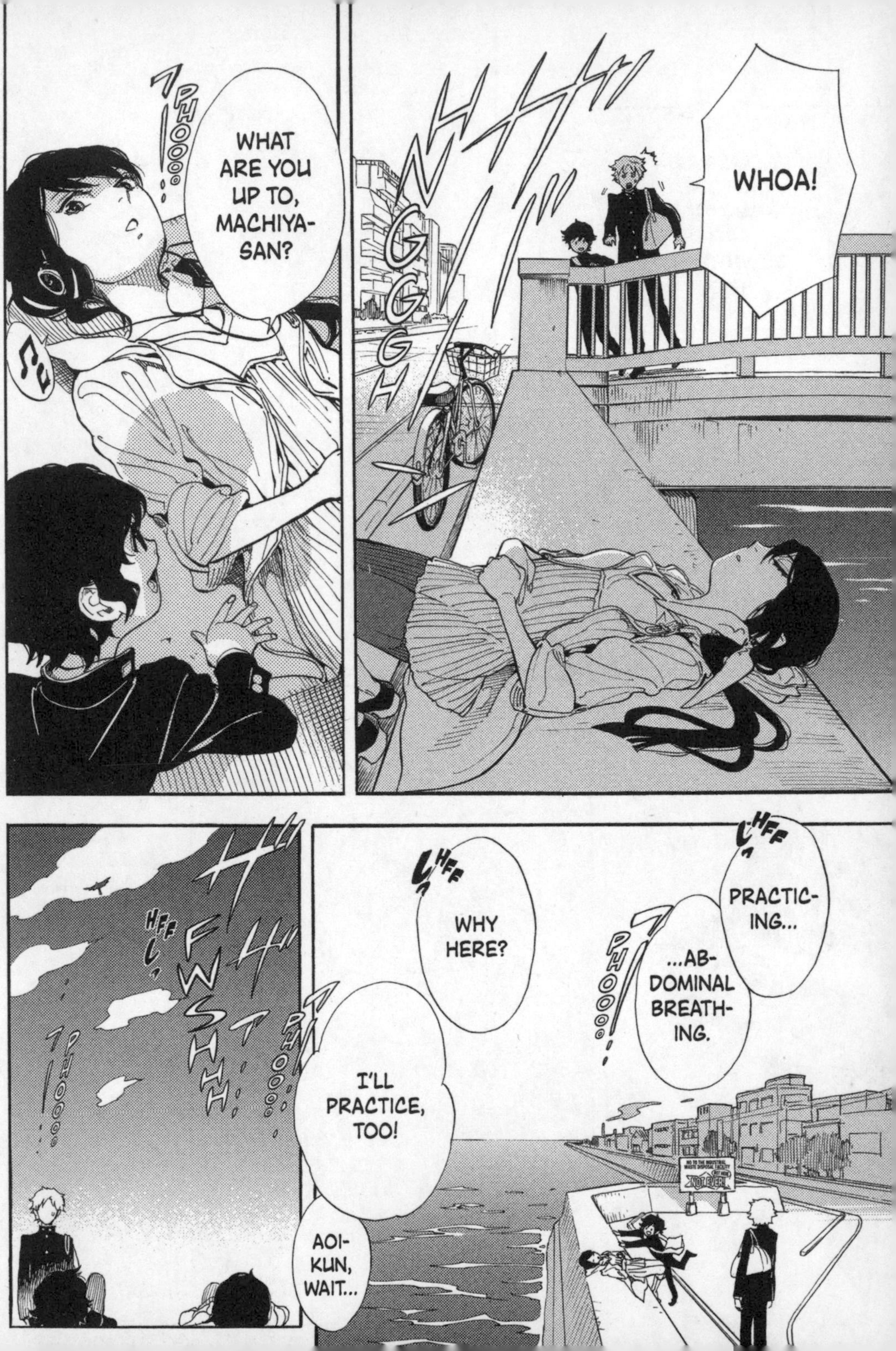
WHOA!
PHOOOOO...!
WHAT ARE YOU UP TO, MACHIYA-SAN?
HFF
PRACTIC-ING...
PHOOOOO...!
...AB-DOMINAL BREATH-ING.
HFF
WHY HERE?
I'LL PRACTICE, TOO!
AOI-KUN, WAIT...
HFF
FWSHHH
PHOOOOO...

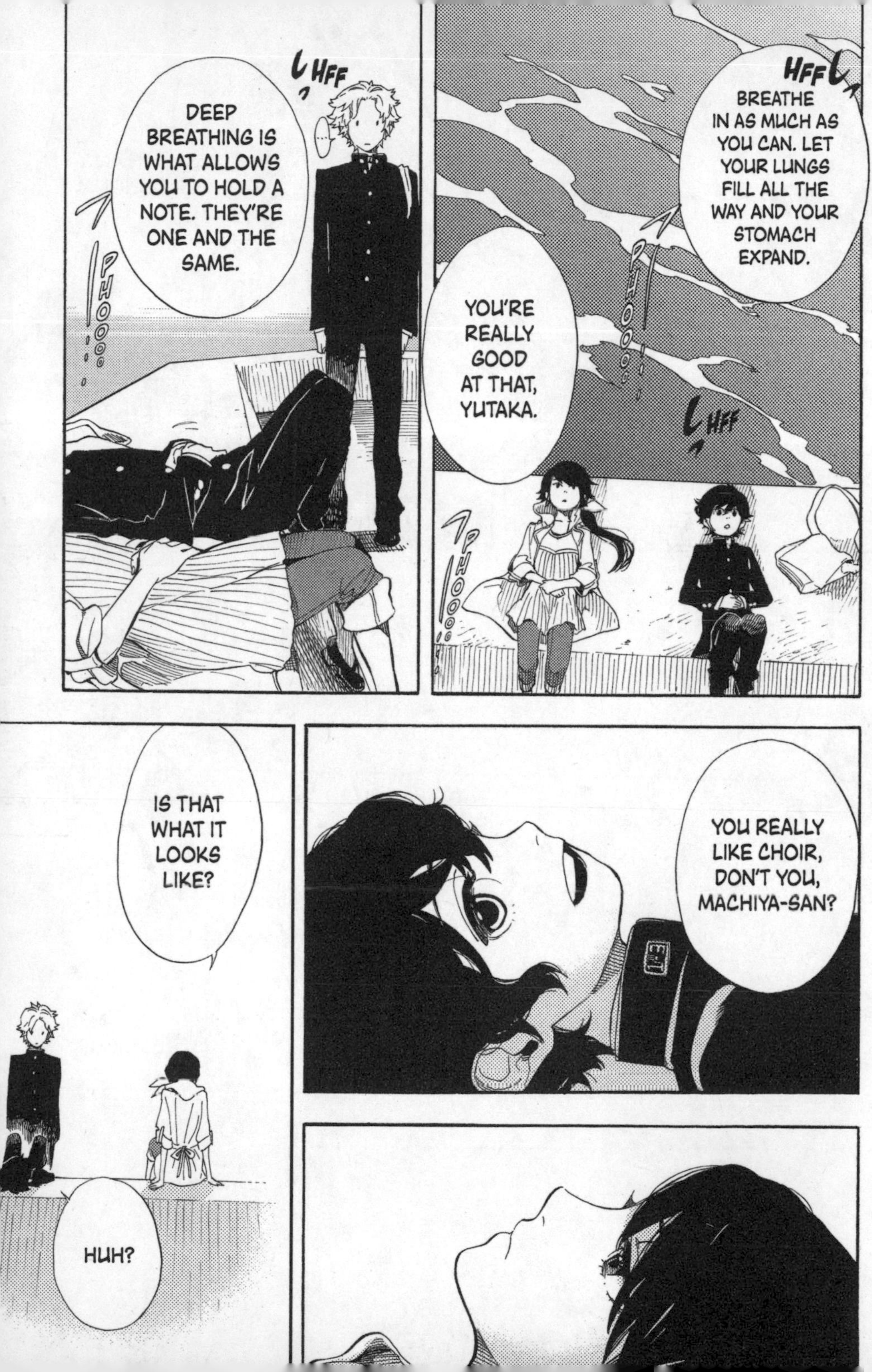
HFF
BREATHE IN AS MUCH AS YOU CAN. LET YOUR LUNGS FILL ALL THE WAY AND YOUR STOMACH EXPAND.
PHOOO...
YOU'RE REALLY GOOD AT THAT, YUTAKA.
HFF
PHOOO...
HFF
DEEP BREATHING IS WHAT ALLOWS YOU TO HOLD A NOTE. THEY'RE ONE AND THE SAME.
...
PHOOO...
YOU REALLY LIKE CHOIR, DON'T YOU, MACHIYA-SAN?
IS THAT WHAT IT LOOKS LIKE?
HUH?

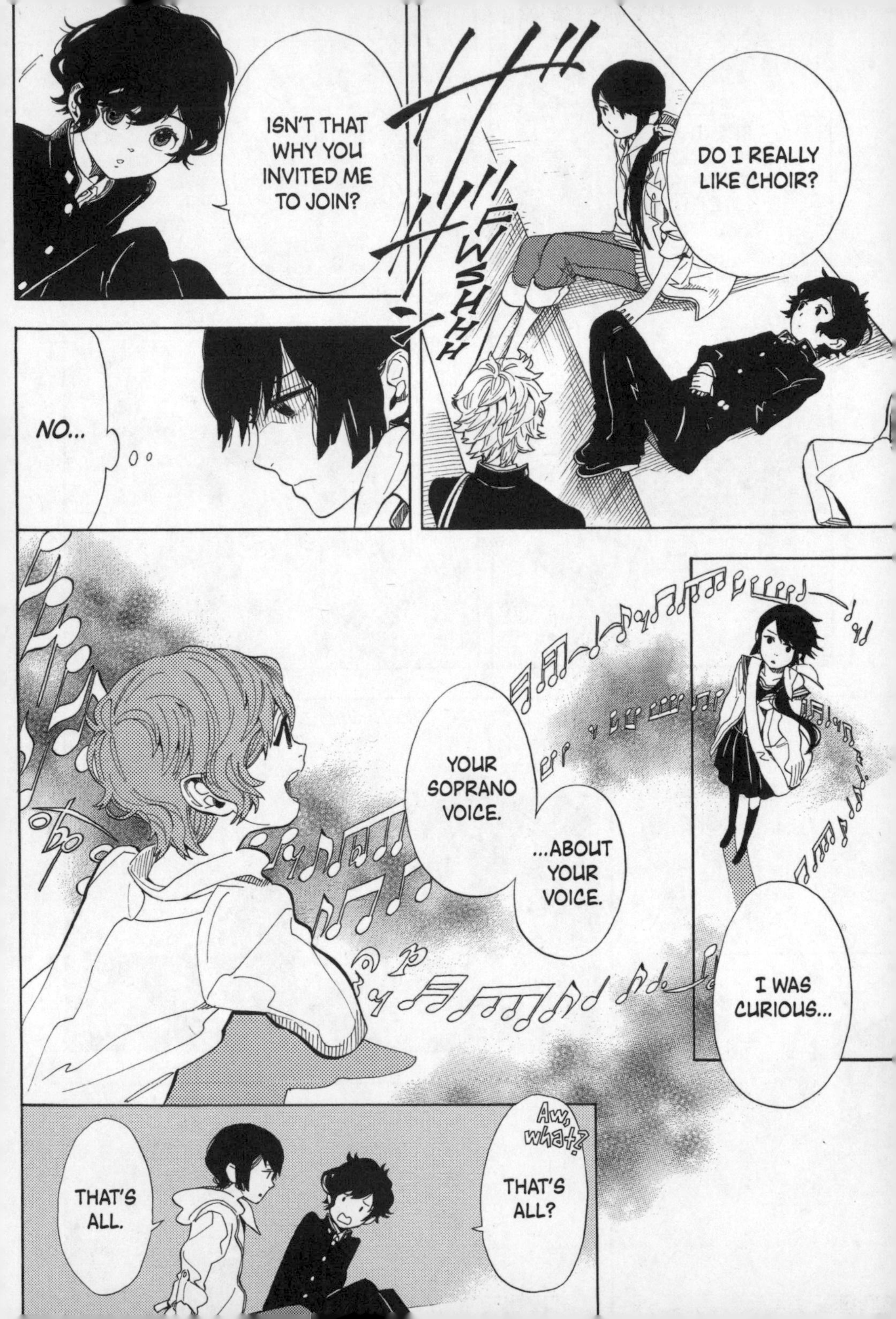
DO I REALLY LIKE CHOIR?
FWSHHH
ISN'T THAT WHY YOU INVITED ME TO JOIN?
NO...
I WAS CURIOUS...
...ABOUT YOUR VOICE.
YOUR SOPRANO VOICE.
Aw, what?
THAT'S ALL?
THAT'S ALL.

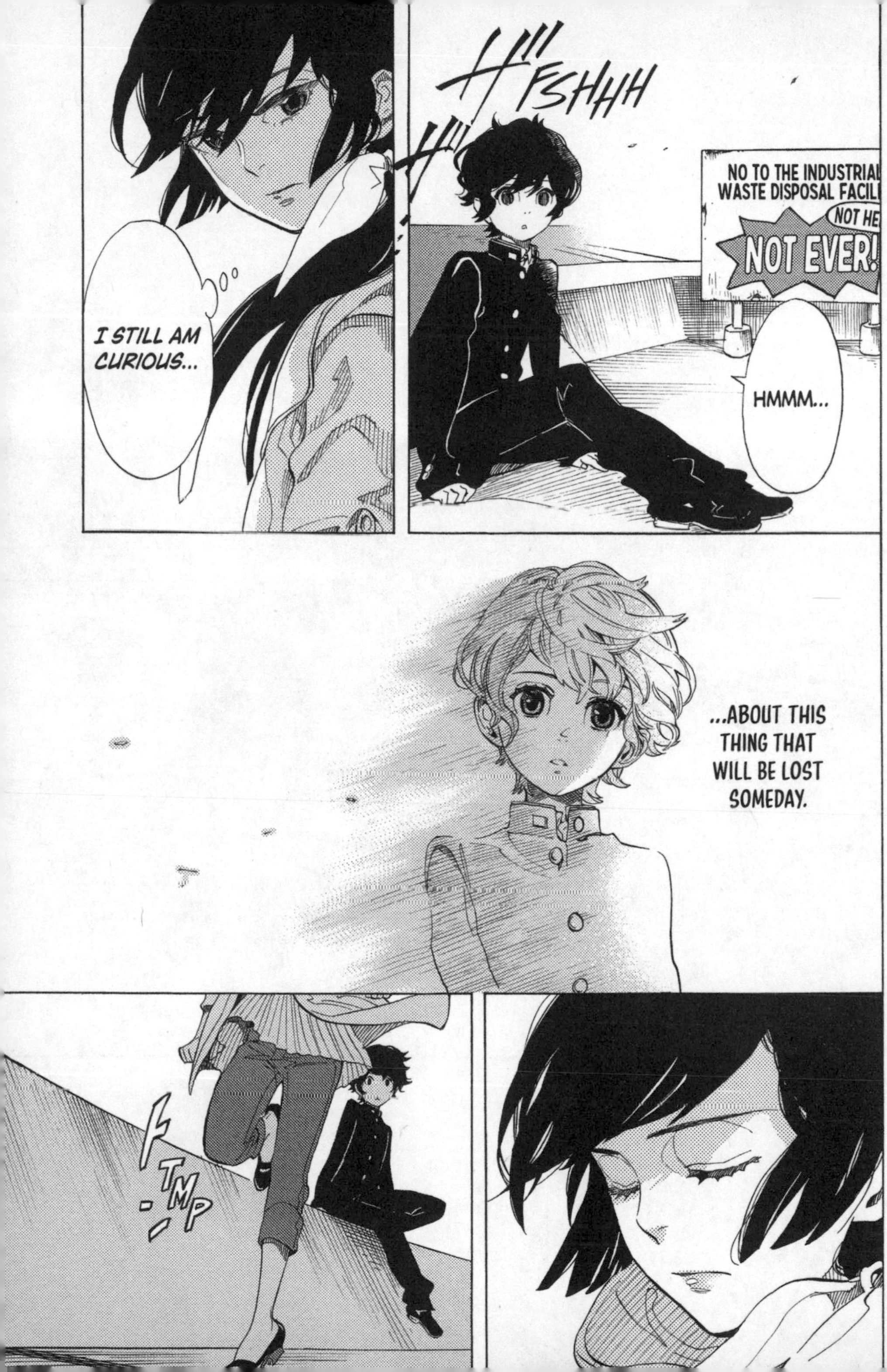

NO TO THE INDUSTRIAL
WASTE DISPOSAL FACIL
NOT HE
NOT EVER!
H'' FSHHH
HMMM...
I STILL AM CURIOUS...
...ABOUT THIS THING THAT WILL BE LOST SOMEDAY.
TMP

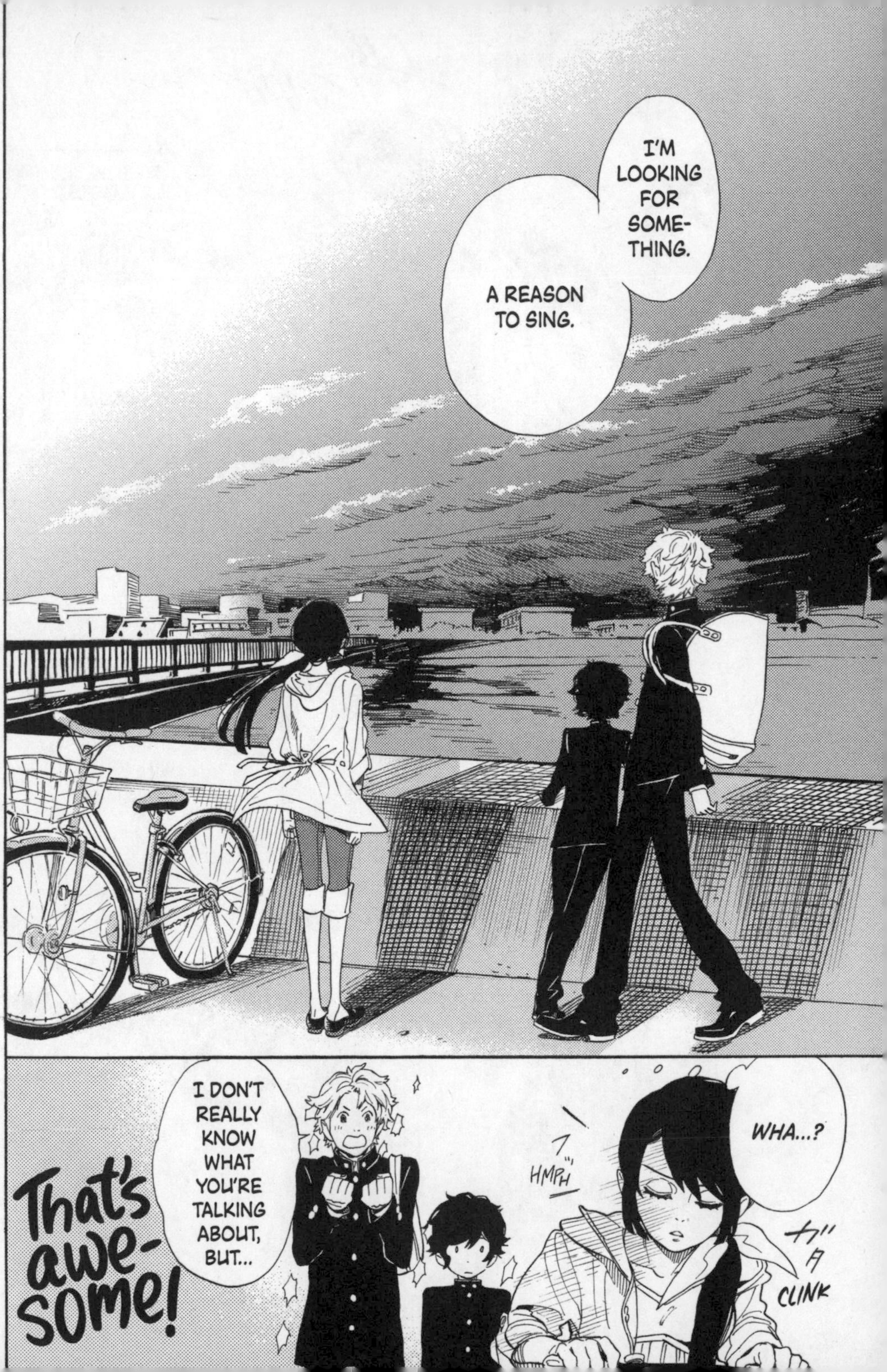
I'M LOOKING FOR SOME-THING.
A REASON TO SING.
WHA...?
CLINK
HMPH
I DON'T REALLY KNOW WHAT YOU'RE TALKING ABOUT, BUT...
That's awe-some!

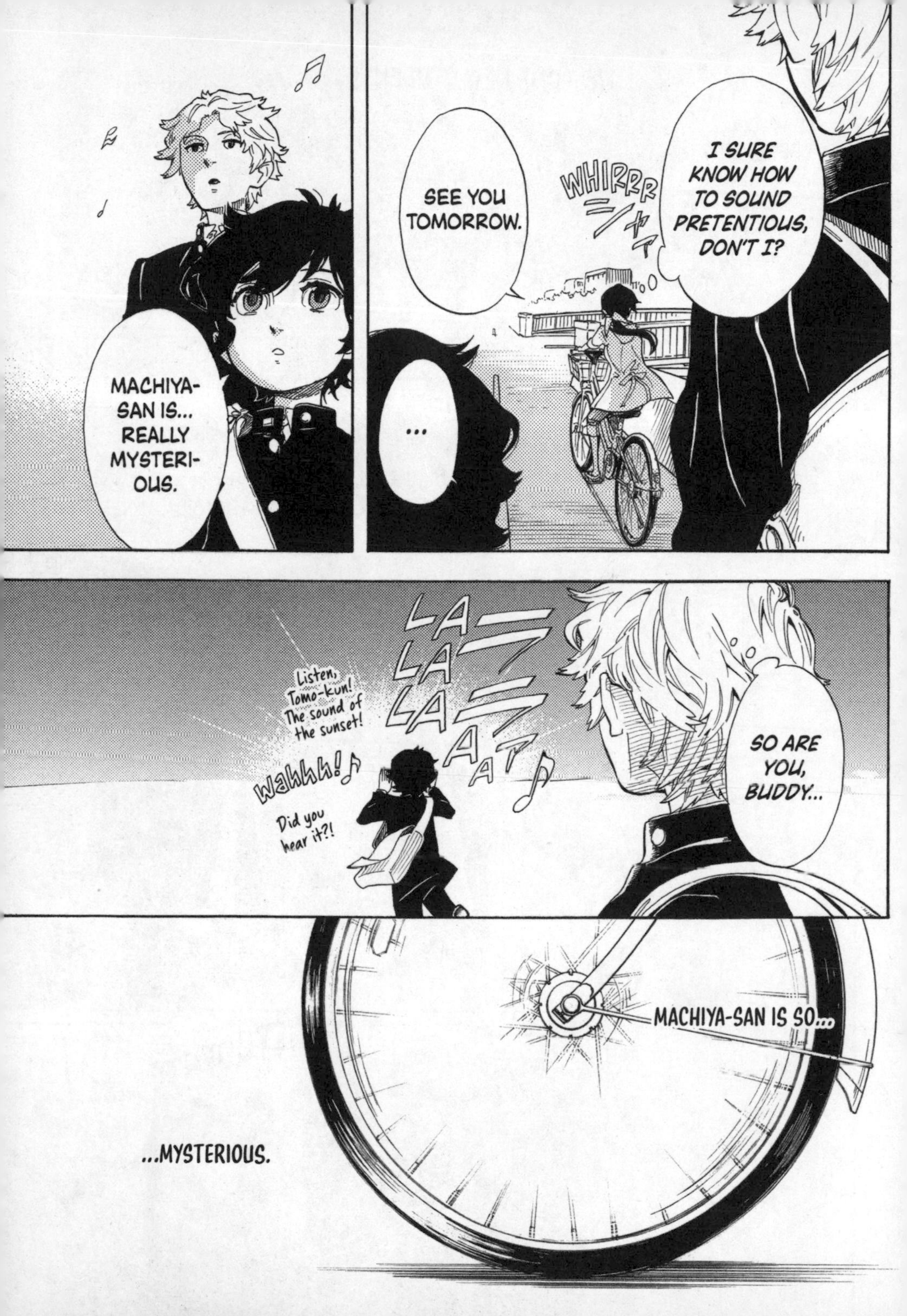
I SURE KNOW HOW TO SOUND PRETENTIOUS, DON'T I?
WHIRRR
SEE YOU TOMORROW.
...
MACHIYA-SAN IS... REALLY MYSTERI-OUS.
SO ARE YOU, BUDDY...
LA LA LA A A
Listen, Tomo-kun! The sound of the sunset!
wahhh!
Did you hear it?!
MACHIYA-SAN IS SO...
...MYSTERIOUS.

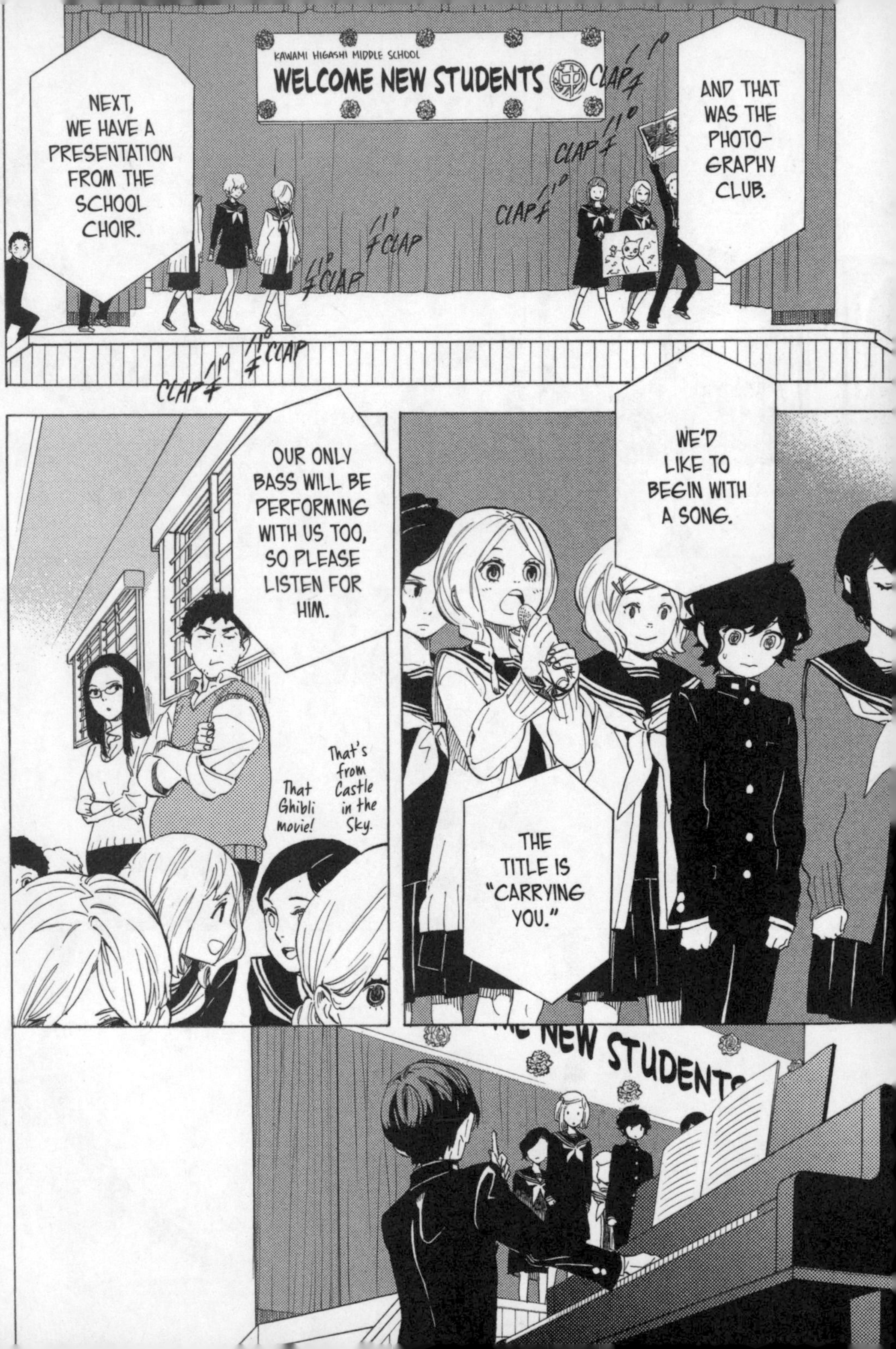
KAWAMI HIGASHI MIDDLE SCHOOL
WELCOME NEW STUDENTS
AND THAT WAS THE PHOTO-GRAPHY CLUB.
CLAP
CLAP
CLAP
CLAP
CLAP
CLAP
CLAP
NEXT, WE HAVE A PRESENTATION FROM THE SCHOOL CHOIR.
WE'D LIKE TO BEGIN WITH A SONG.
THE TITLE IS "CARRYING YOU."
OUR ONLY BASS WILL BE PERFORMING WITH US TOO, SO PLEASE LISTEN FOR HIM.
That's from Castle in the Sky.
That Ghibli movie!
NEW STUDENTS

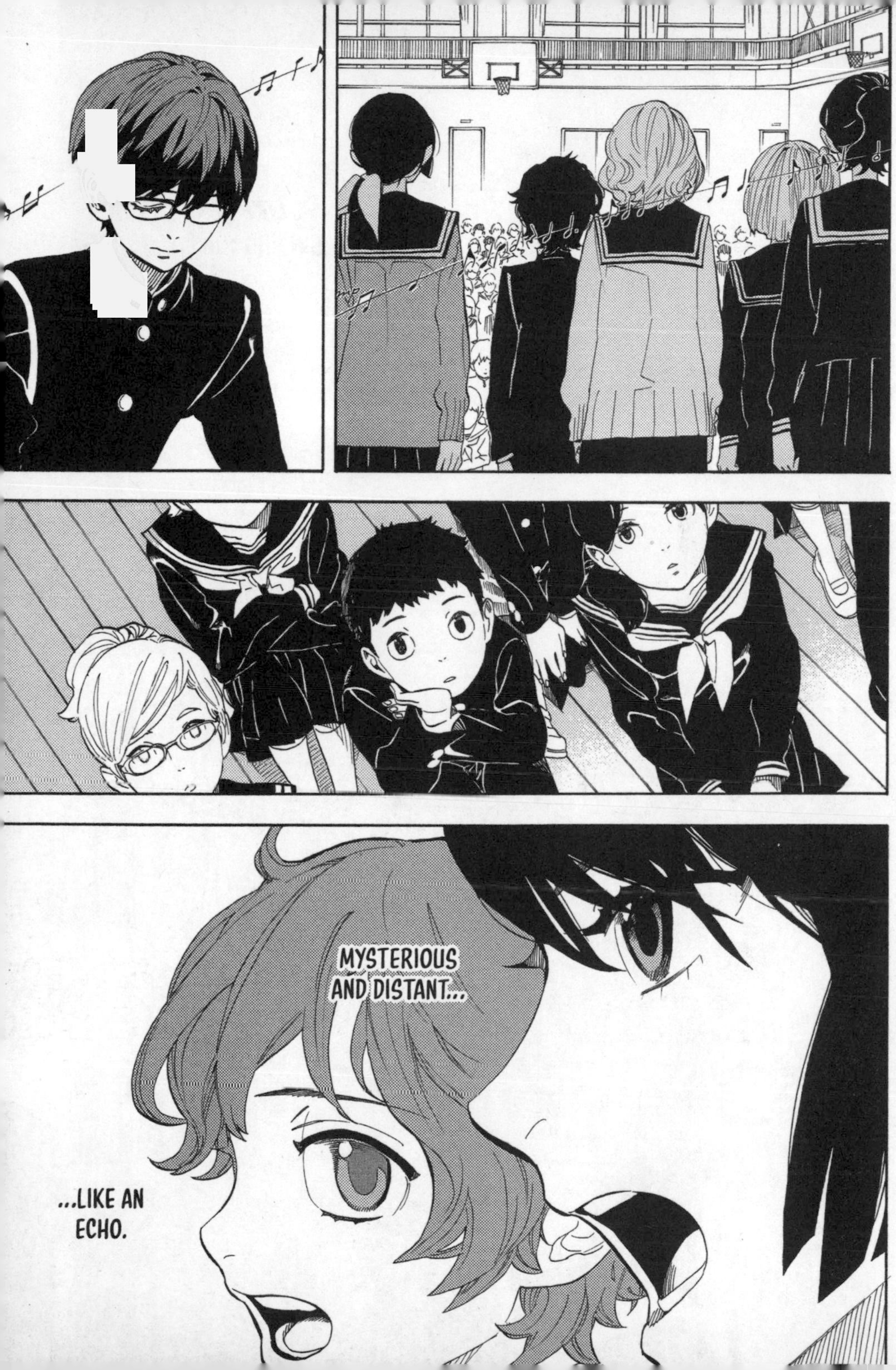
MYSTERIOUS AND DISTANT...
...LIKE AN ECHO.

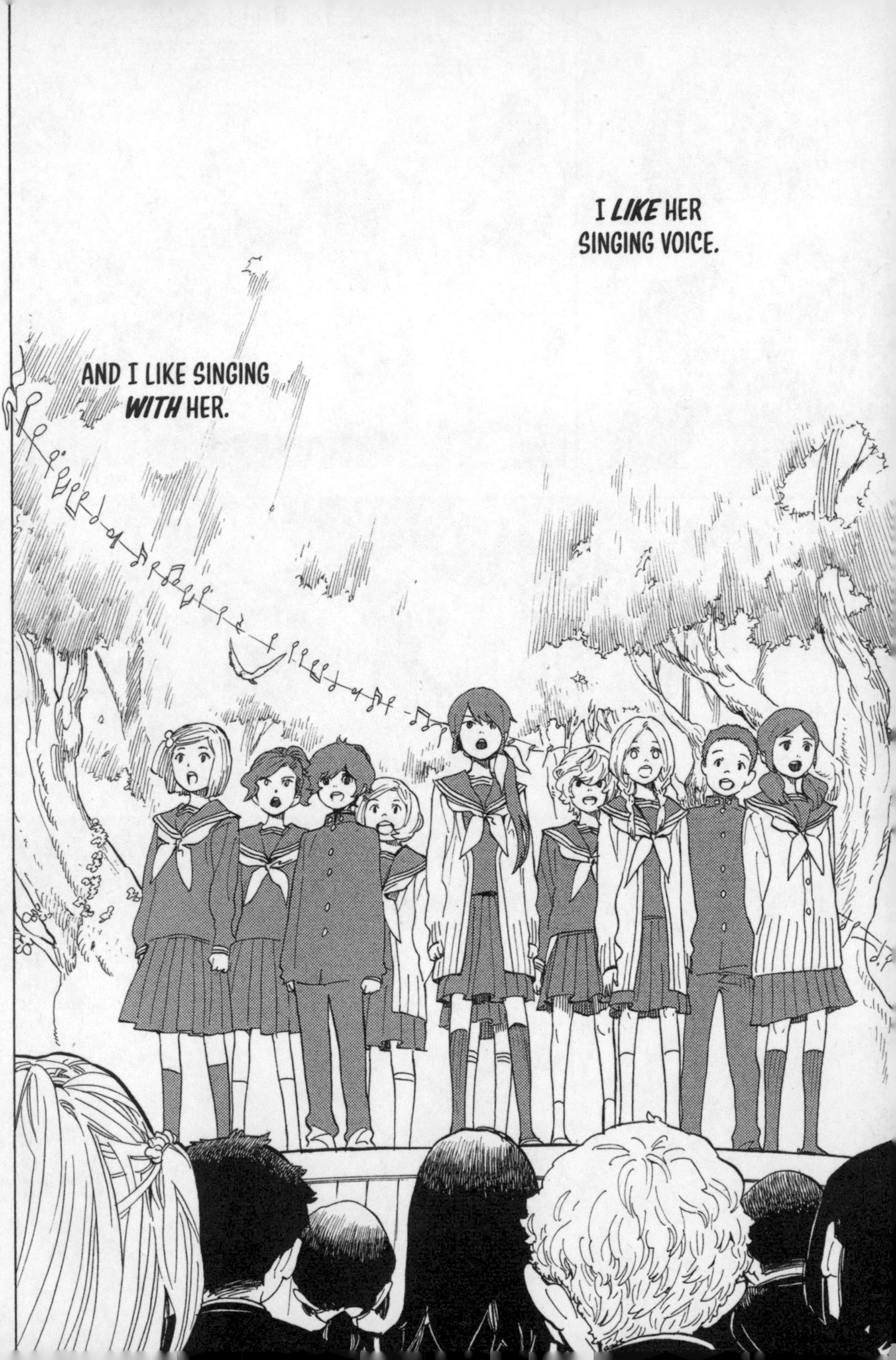
I *LIKE* HER SINGING VOICE.
AND I LIKE SINGING *WITH* HER.

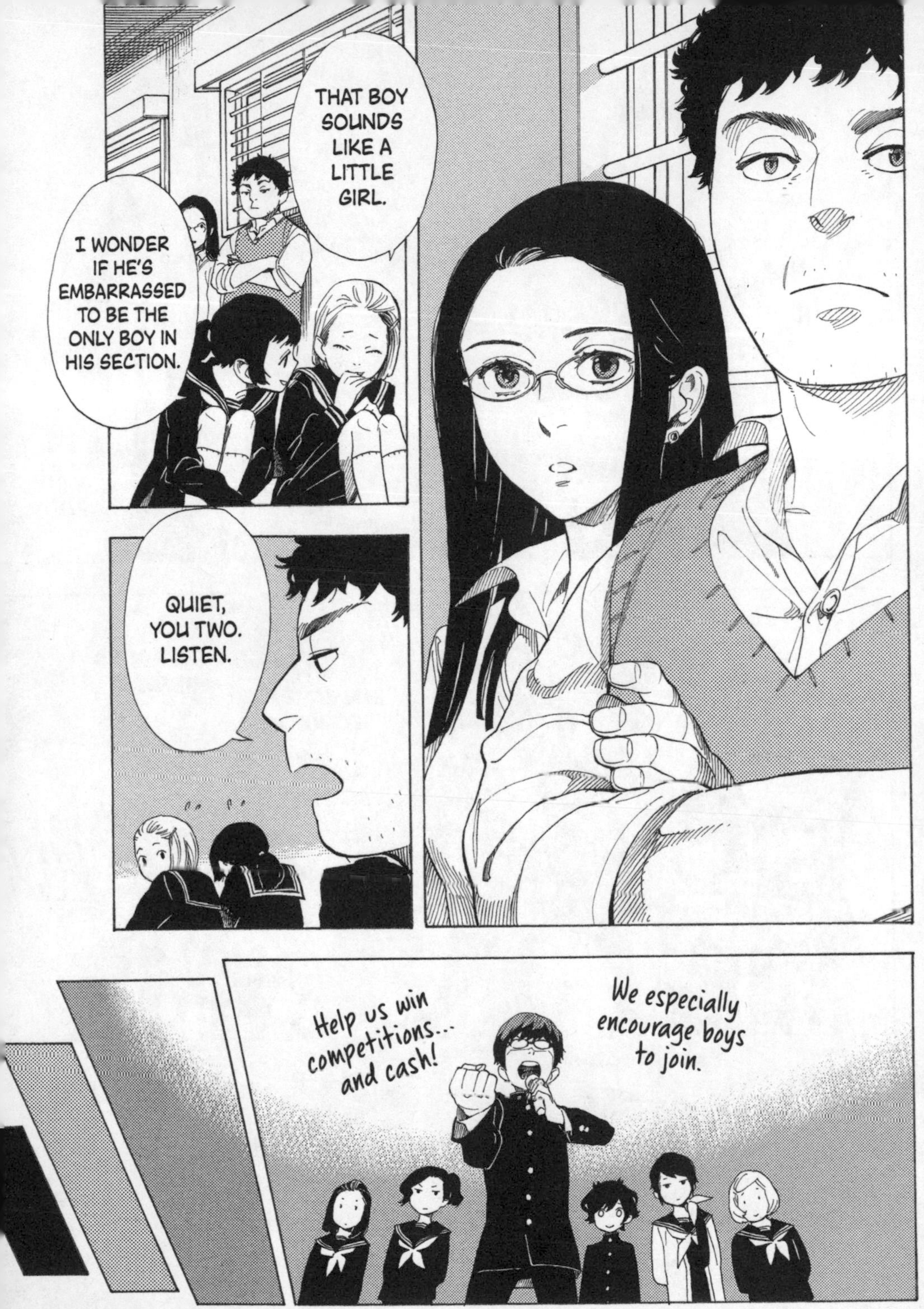
THAT BOY SOUNDS LIKE A LITTLE GIRL.
I WONDER IF HE'S EMBARRASSED TO BE THE ONLY BOY IN HIS SECTION.
QUIET, YOU TWO. LISTEN.
We especially encourage boys to join.
Help us win competitions... and cash!

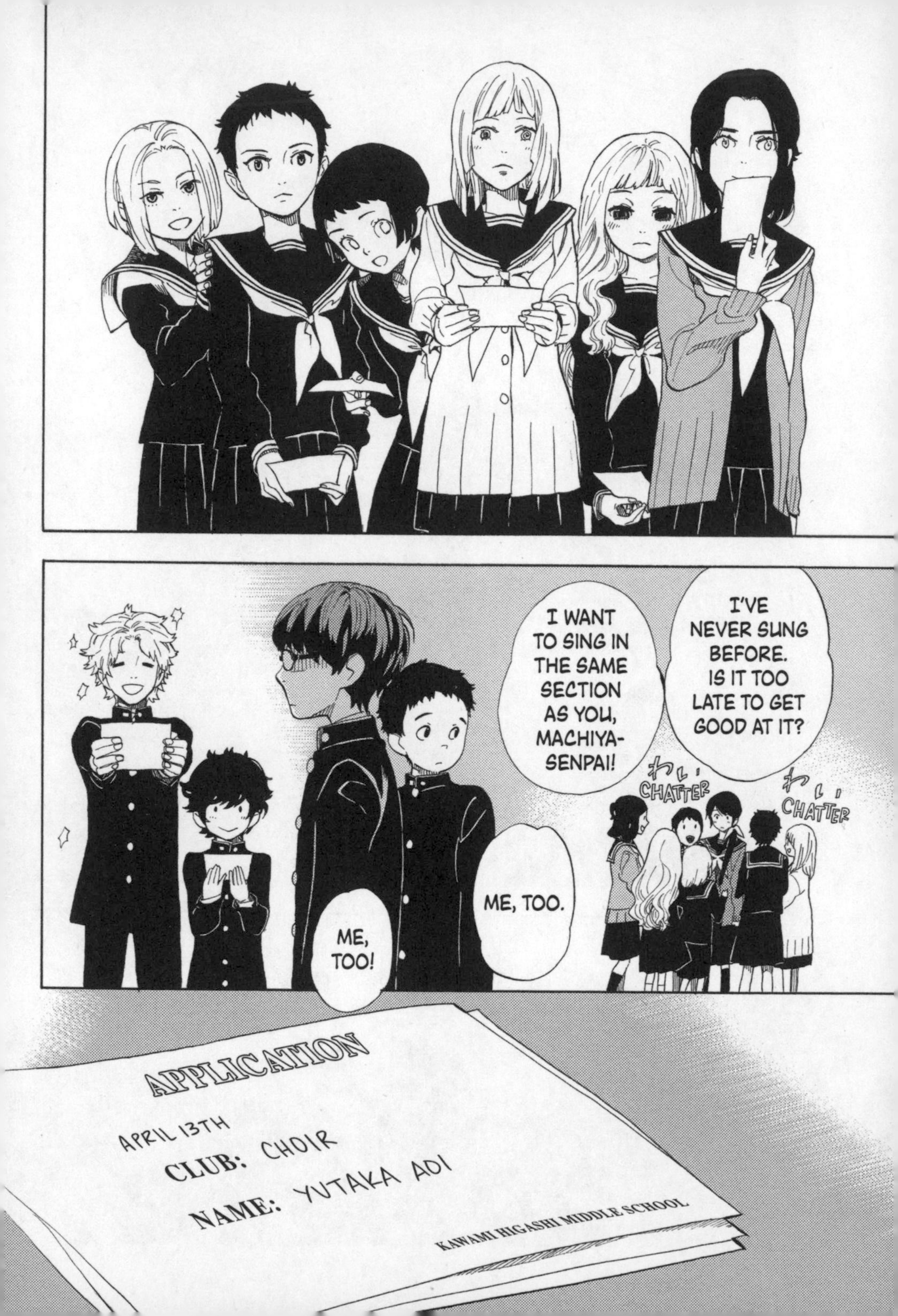
I'VE NEVER SUNG BEFORE. IS IT TOO LATE TO GET GOOD AT IT?
CHATTER
I WANT TO SING IN THE SAME SECTION AS YOU, MACHIYA-SENPAI!
CHATTER
ME, TOO.
ME, TOO!
APPLICATION
APRIL 13TH
CLUB: CHOIR
NAME: YUTAKA AOI
KAWAMI HIGASHI MIDDLE SCHOOL

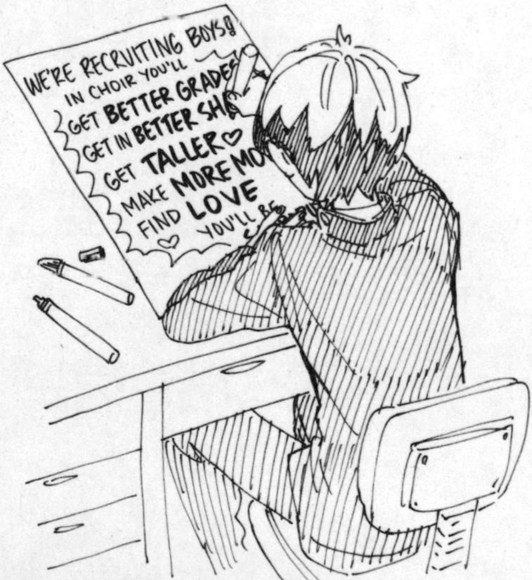
WE'RE RECRUITING BOYS!
IN CHOIR YOU'LL
GET BETTER GRADES
GET IN BETTER SH
GET TALLER
MAKE MORE MO
FIND LOVE
YOU'LL BE

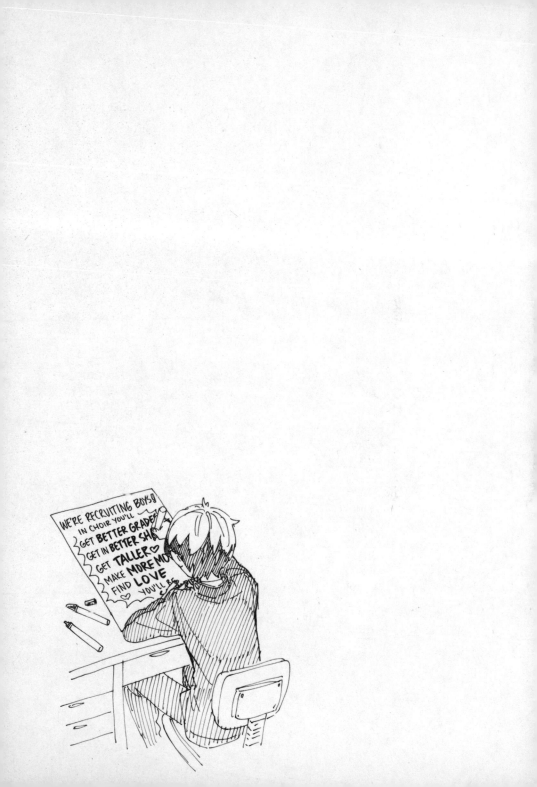

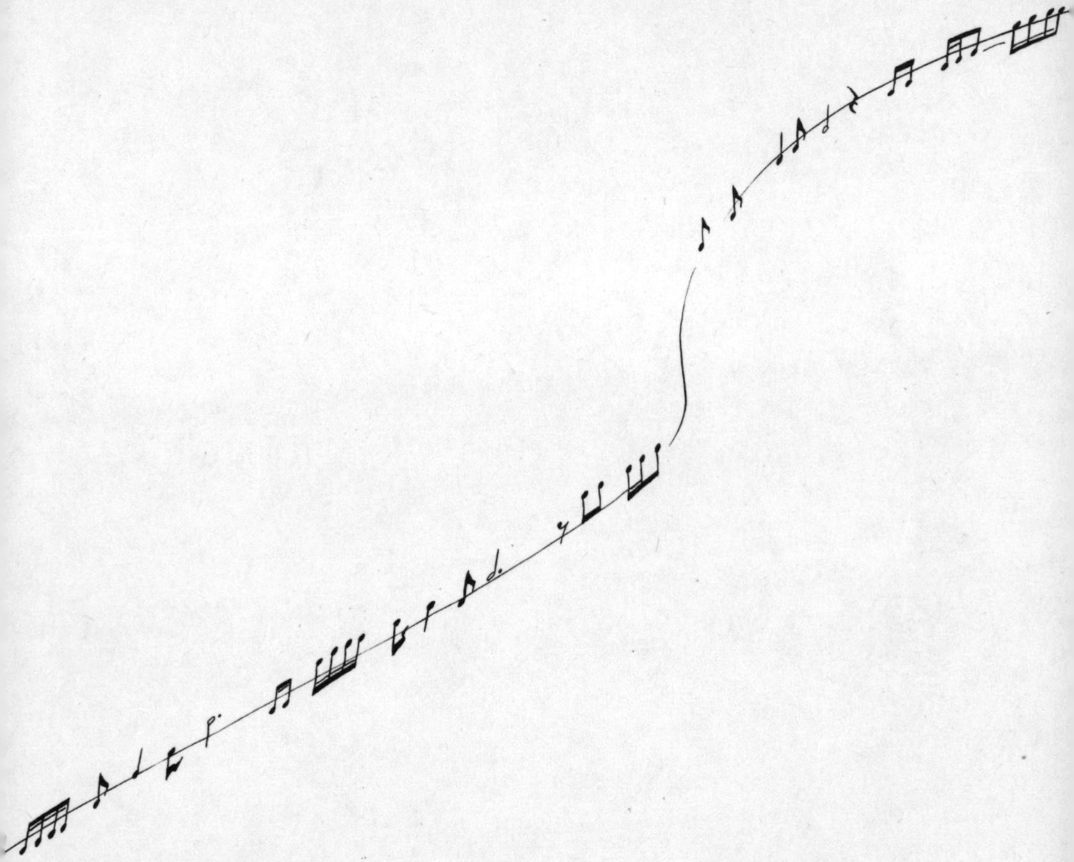

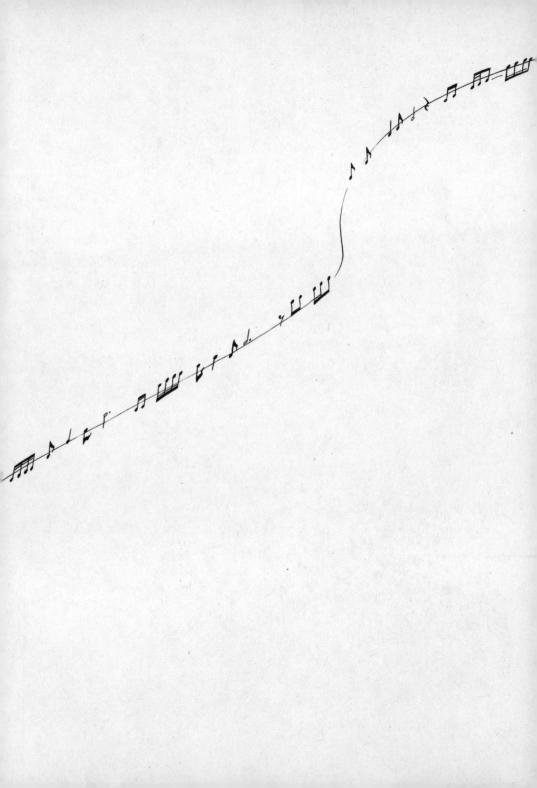

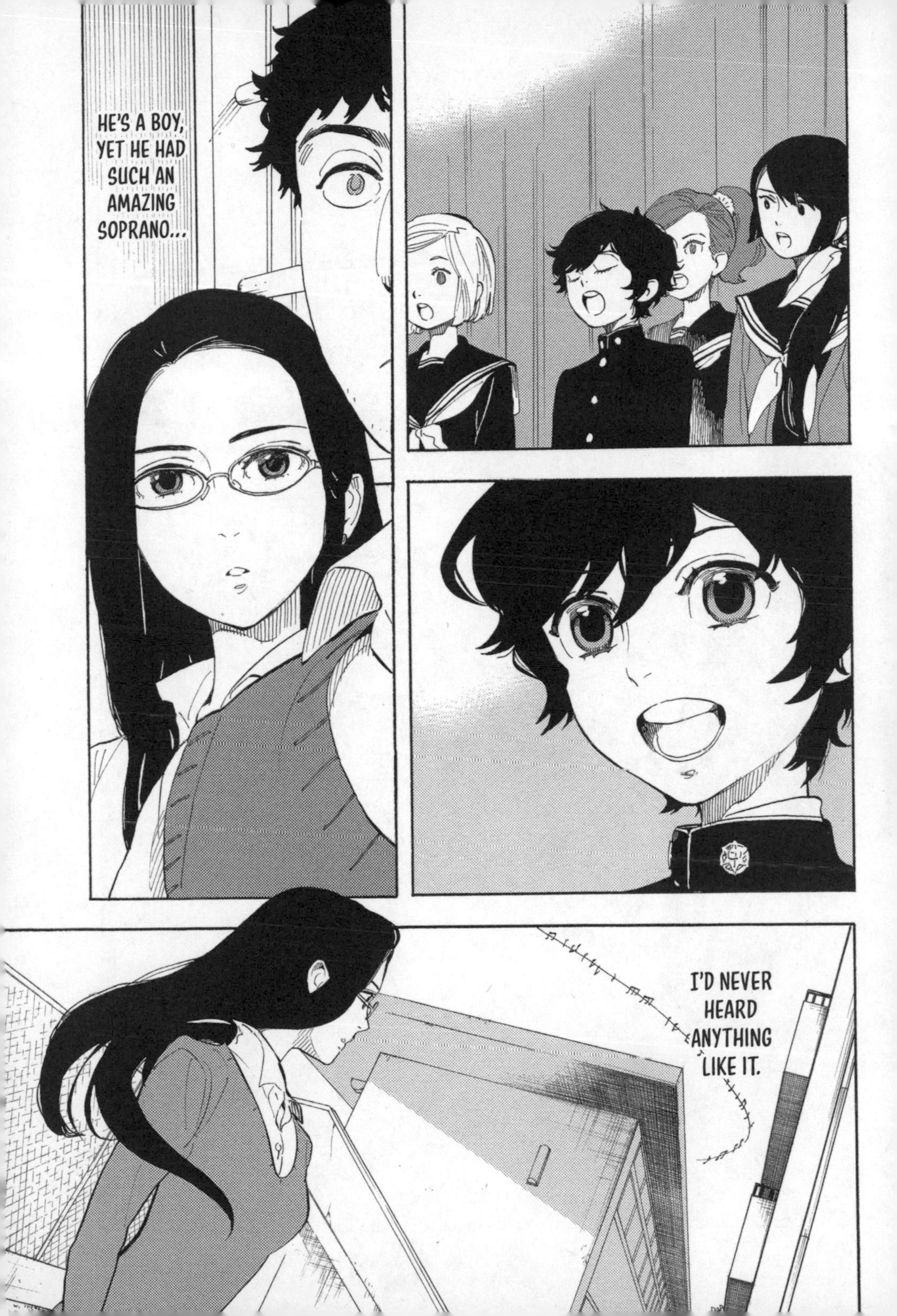
HE'S A BOY, YET HE HAD SUCH AN AMAZING SOPRANO...
I'D NEVER HEARD ANYTHING LIKE IT.

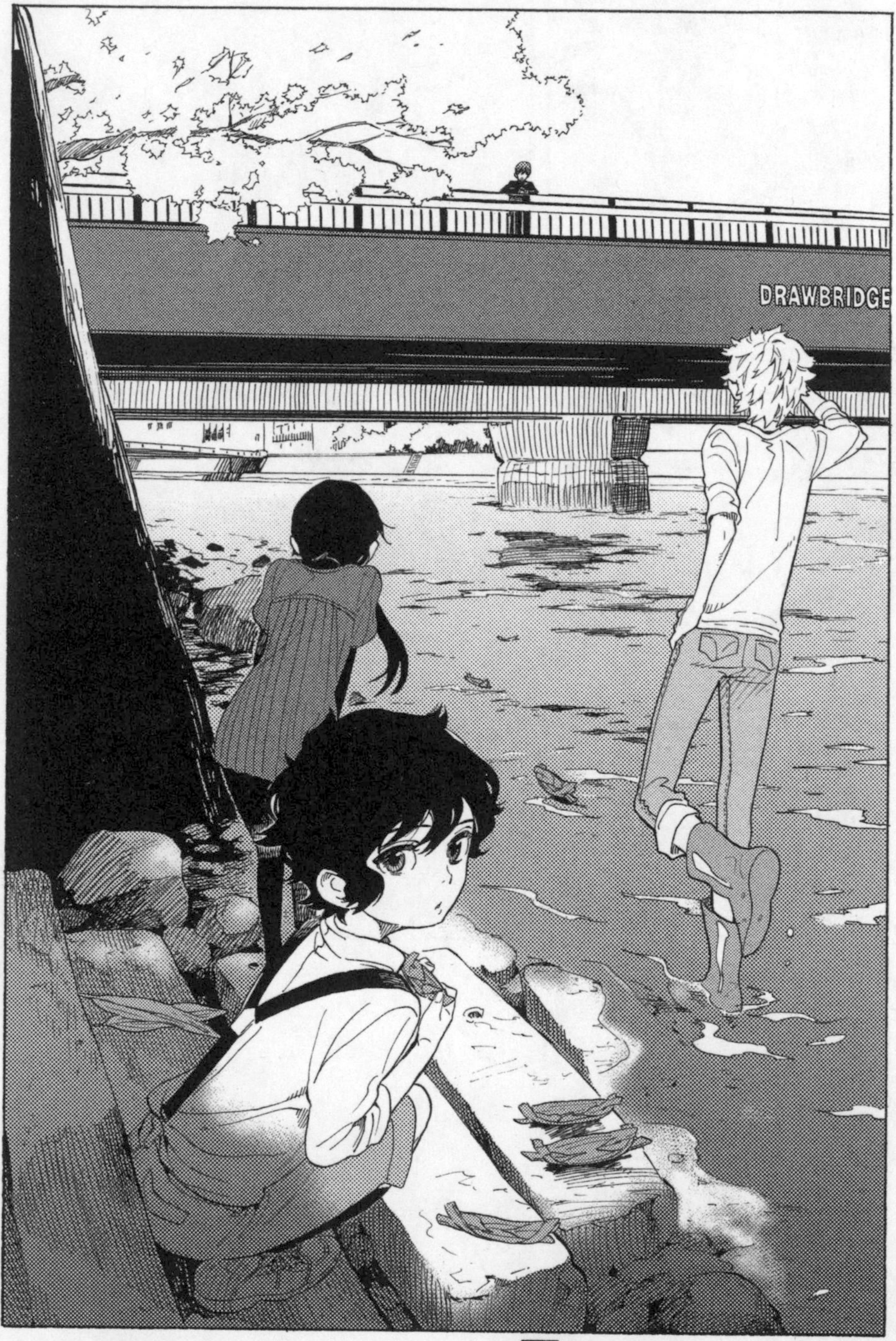
DRAWBRIDGE

note 𝄢: 03 Café Muse

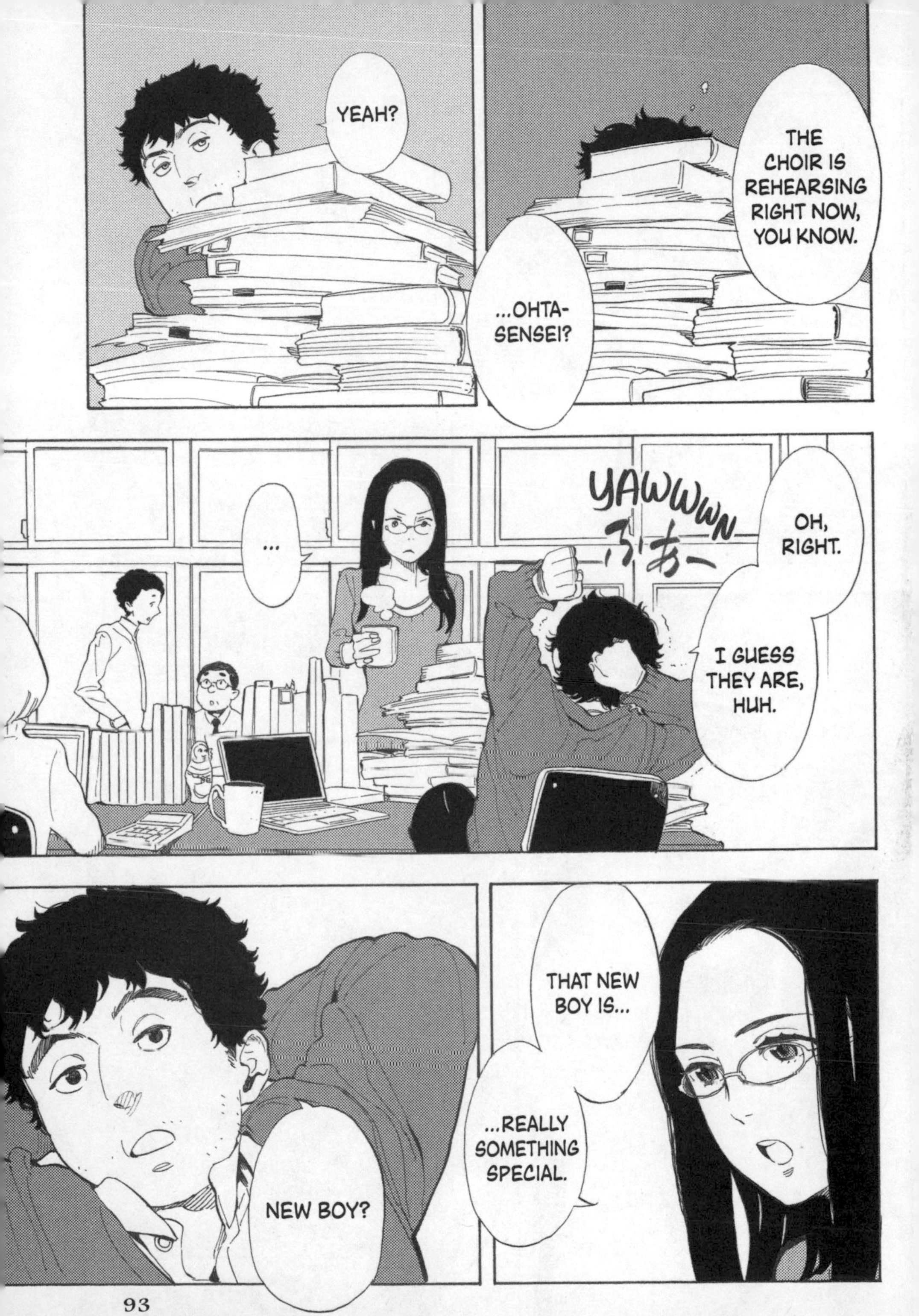
THE CHOIR IS REHEARSING RIGHT NOW, YOU KNOW.
...OHTA-SENSEI?
YEAH?
OH, RIGHT.
YAWWWN
ふあ〜
I GUESS THEY ARE, HUH.
...
THAT NEW BOY IS...
...REALLY SOMETHING SPECIAL.
NEW BOY?

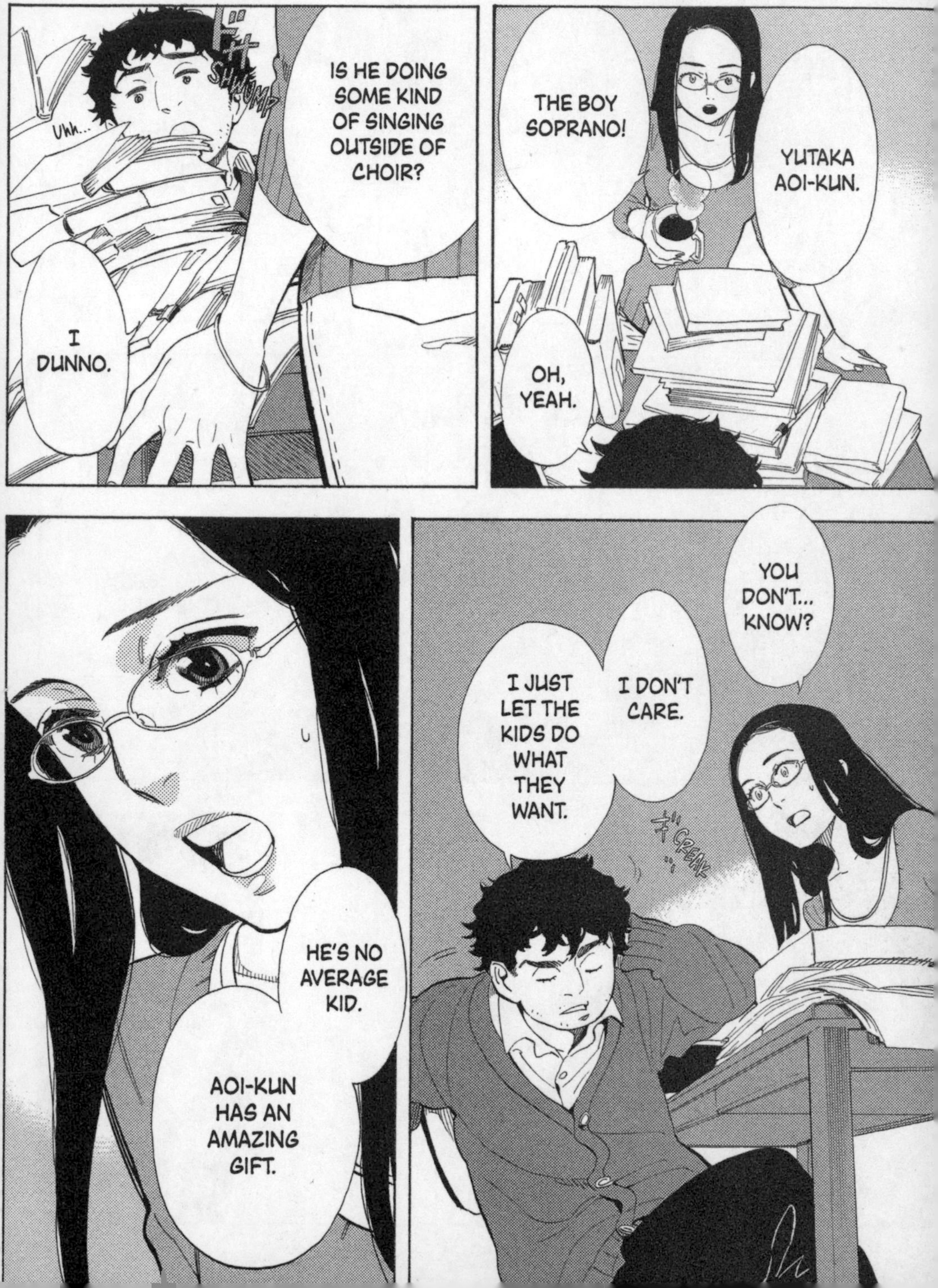
YUTAKA AOI-KUN.
THE BOY SOPRANO!
OH, YEAH.
IS HE DOING SOME KIND OF SINGING OUTSIDE OF CHOIR?
SHWOMP
Uhh...
I DUNNO.
YOU DON'T... KNOW?
I DON'T CARE.
I JUST LET THE KIDS DO WHAT THEY WANT.
CREAK
HE'S NO AVERAGE KID.
AOI-KUN HAS AN AMAZING GIFT.

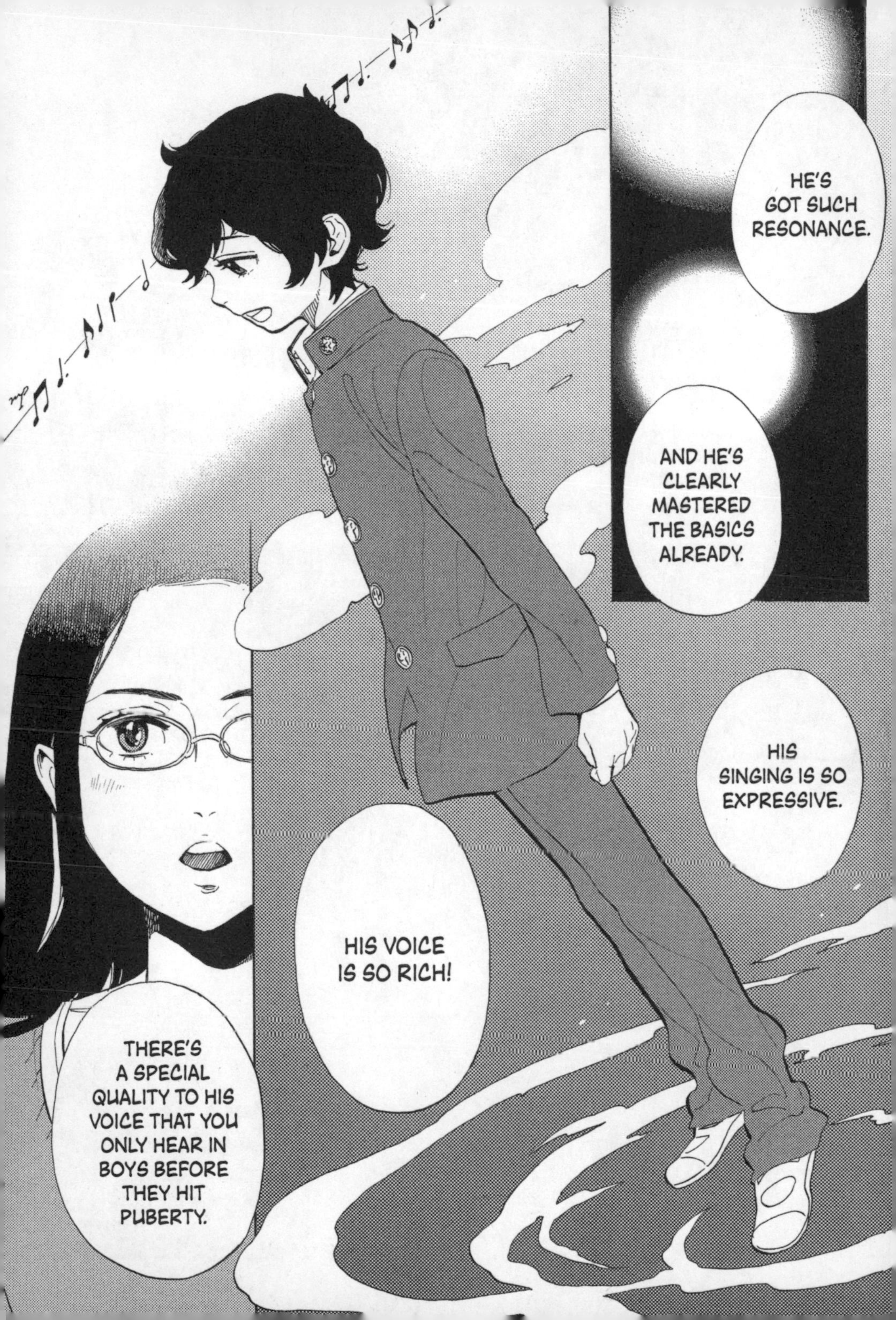
HE'S GOT SUCH RESONANCE.
AND HE'S CLEARLY MASTERED THE BASICS ALREADY.
HIS SINGING IS SO EXPRESSIVE.
HIS VOICE IS SO RICH!
THERE'S A SPECIAL QUALITY TO HIS VOICE THAT YOU ONLY HEAR IN BOYS BEFORE THEY HIT PUBERTY.

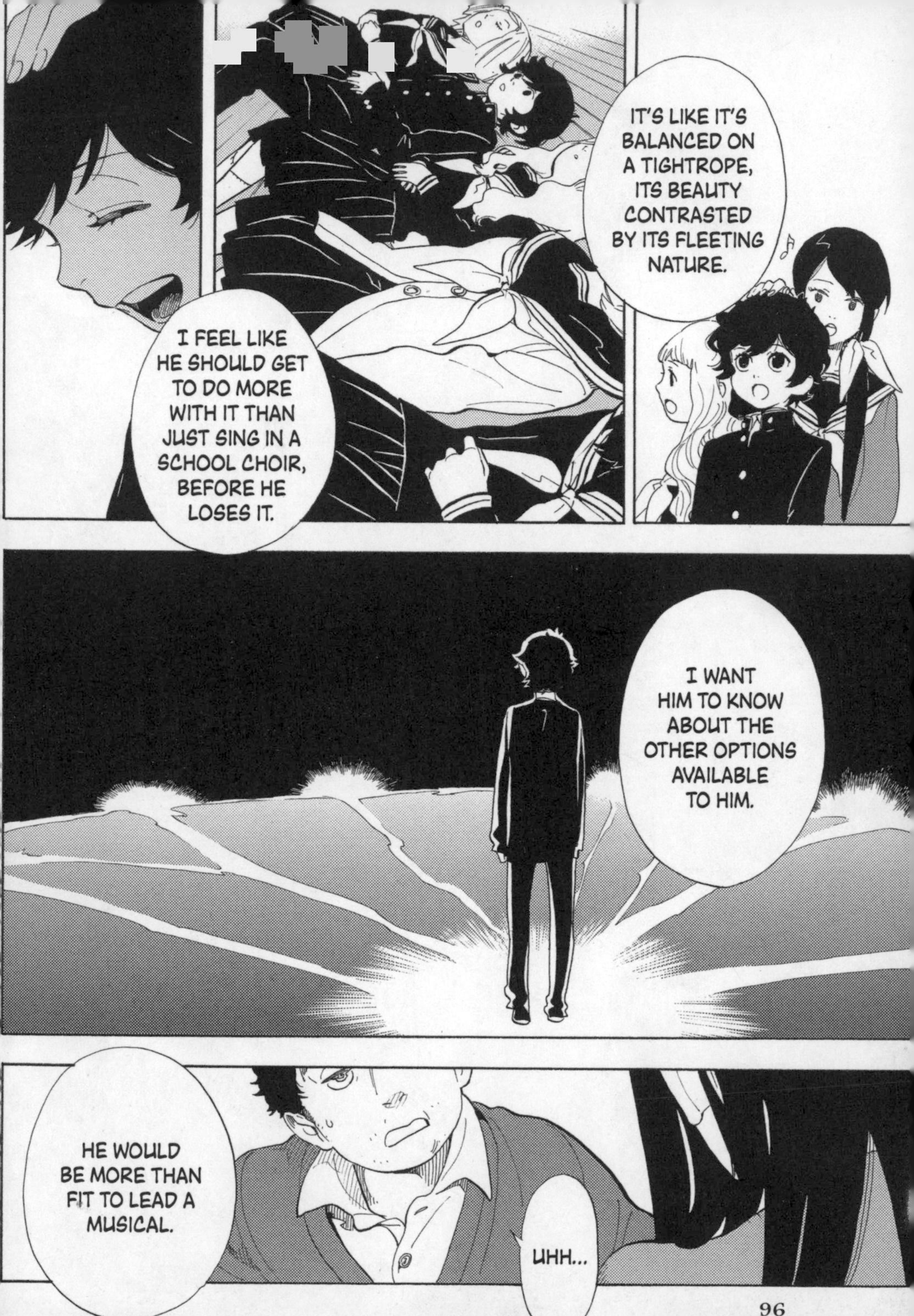
IT'S LIKE IT'S BALANCED ON A TIGHTROPE, ITS BEAUTY CONTRASTED BY ITS FLEETING NATURE.
I FEEL LIKE HE SHOULD GET TO DO MORE WITH IT THAN JUST SING IN A SCHOOL CHOIR, BEFORE HE LOSES IT.
I WANT HIM TO KNOW ABOUT THE OTHER OPTIONS AVAILABLE TO HIM.
HE WOULD BE MORE THAN FIT TO LEAD A MUSICAL.
UHH...

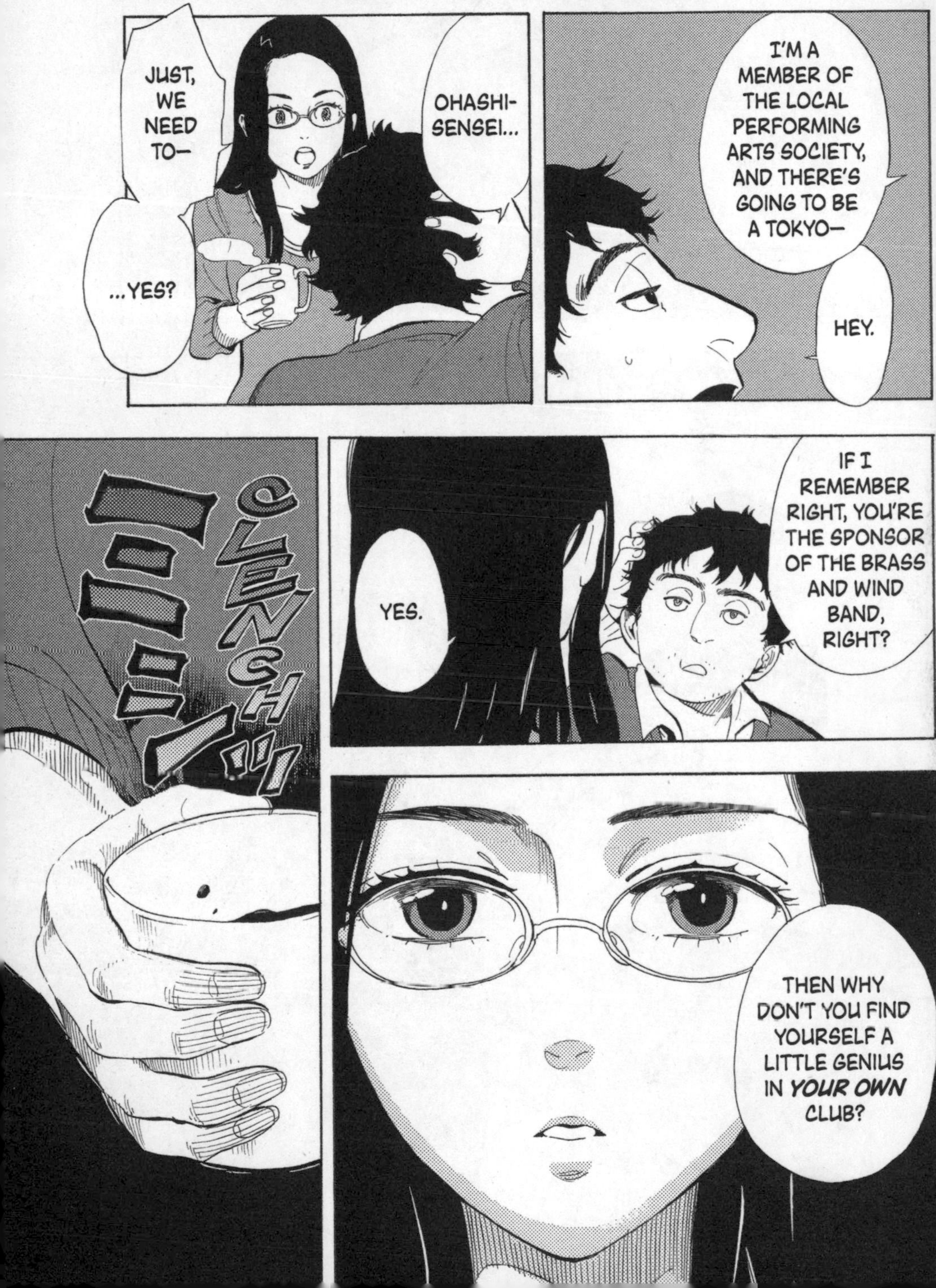
I'M A MEMBER OF THE LOCAL PERFORMING ARTS SOCIETY, AND THERE'S GOING TO BE A TOKYO—
HEY.
OHASHI-SENSEI...
JUST, WE NEED TO—
...YES?
IF I REMEMBER RIGHT, YOU'RE THE SPONSOR OF THE BRASS AND WIND BAND, RIGHT?
YES.
THEN WHY DON'T YOU FIND YOURSELF A LITTLE GENIUS IN ***YOUR OWN*** CLUB?
CLENCH

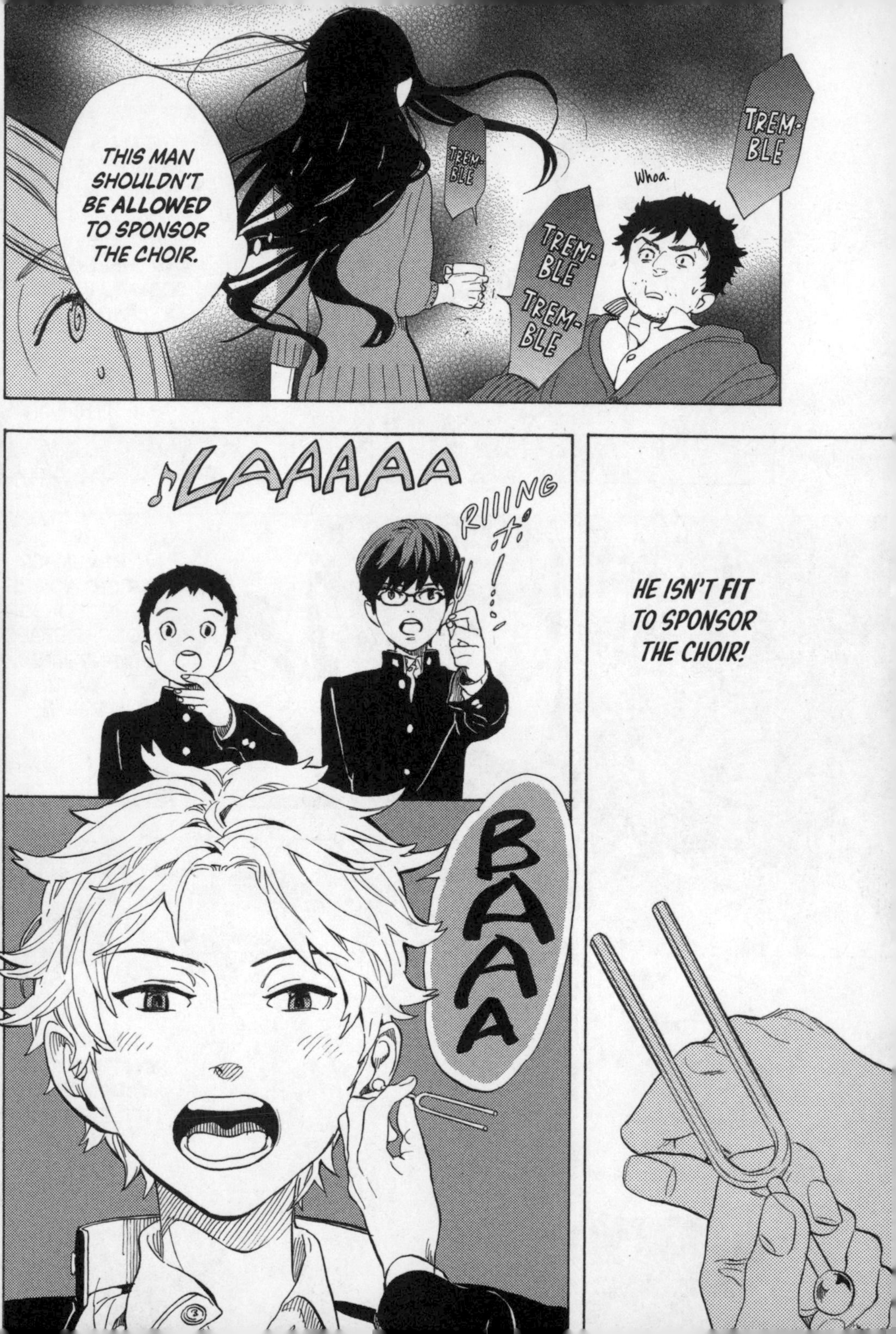
TREM-BLE
Whoa.
TREM-BLE
TREM-BLE
TREM-BLE
TREM-BLE
THIS MAN SHOULDN'T BE ALLOWED TO SPONSOR THE CHOIR.
HE ISN'T FIT TO SPONSOR THE CHOIR!
LAAAAA
RIIING
BAAA

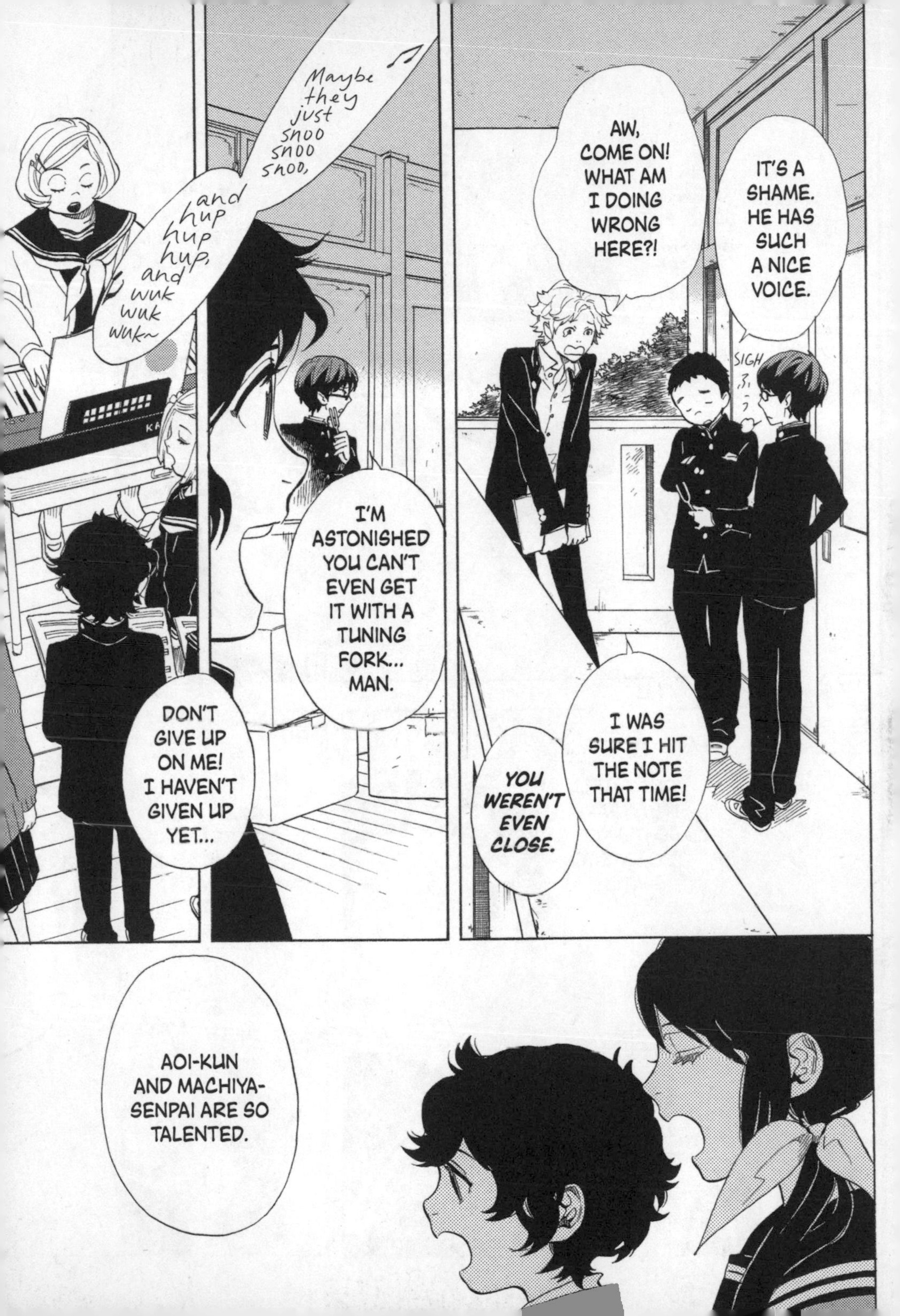
IT'S A SHAME. HE HAS SUCH A NICE VOICE.
SIGH
AW, COME ON! WHAT AM I DOING WRONG HERE?!
I WAS SURE I HIT THE NOTE THAT TIME!
YOU WEREN'T EVEN CLOSE.
I'M ASTONISHED YOU CAN'T EVEN GET IT WITH A TUNING FORK... MAN.
Maybe they just snoo snoo snoo,
and hup hup hup, and wuk wuk wuk~
DON'T GIVE UP ON ME! I HAVEN'T GIVEN UP YET...
AOI-KUN AND MACHIYA-SENPAI ARE SO TALENTED.

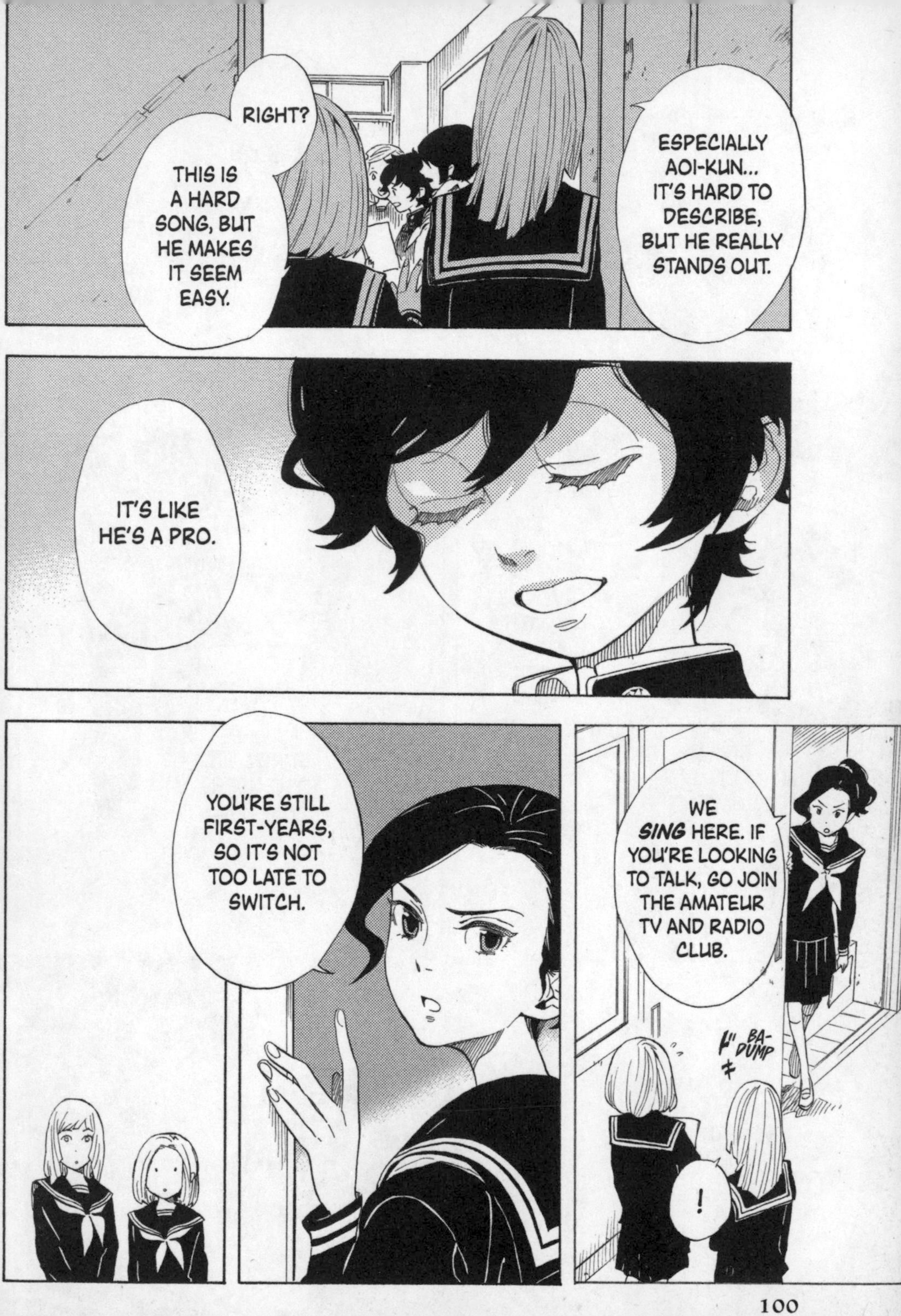
ESPECIALLY AOI-KUN... IT'S HARD TO DESCRIBE, BUT HE REALLY STANDS OUT.
RIGHT?
THIS IS A HARD SONG, BUT HE MAKES IT SEEM EASY.
IT'S LIKE HE'S A PRO.
WE *SING* HERE. IF YOU'RE LOOKING TO TALK, GO JOIN THE AMATEUR TV AND RADIO CLUB.
BA-DUMP
!
YOU'RE STILL FIRST-YEARS, SO IT'S NOT TOO LATE TO SWITCH.

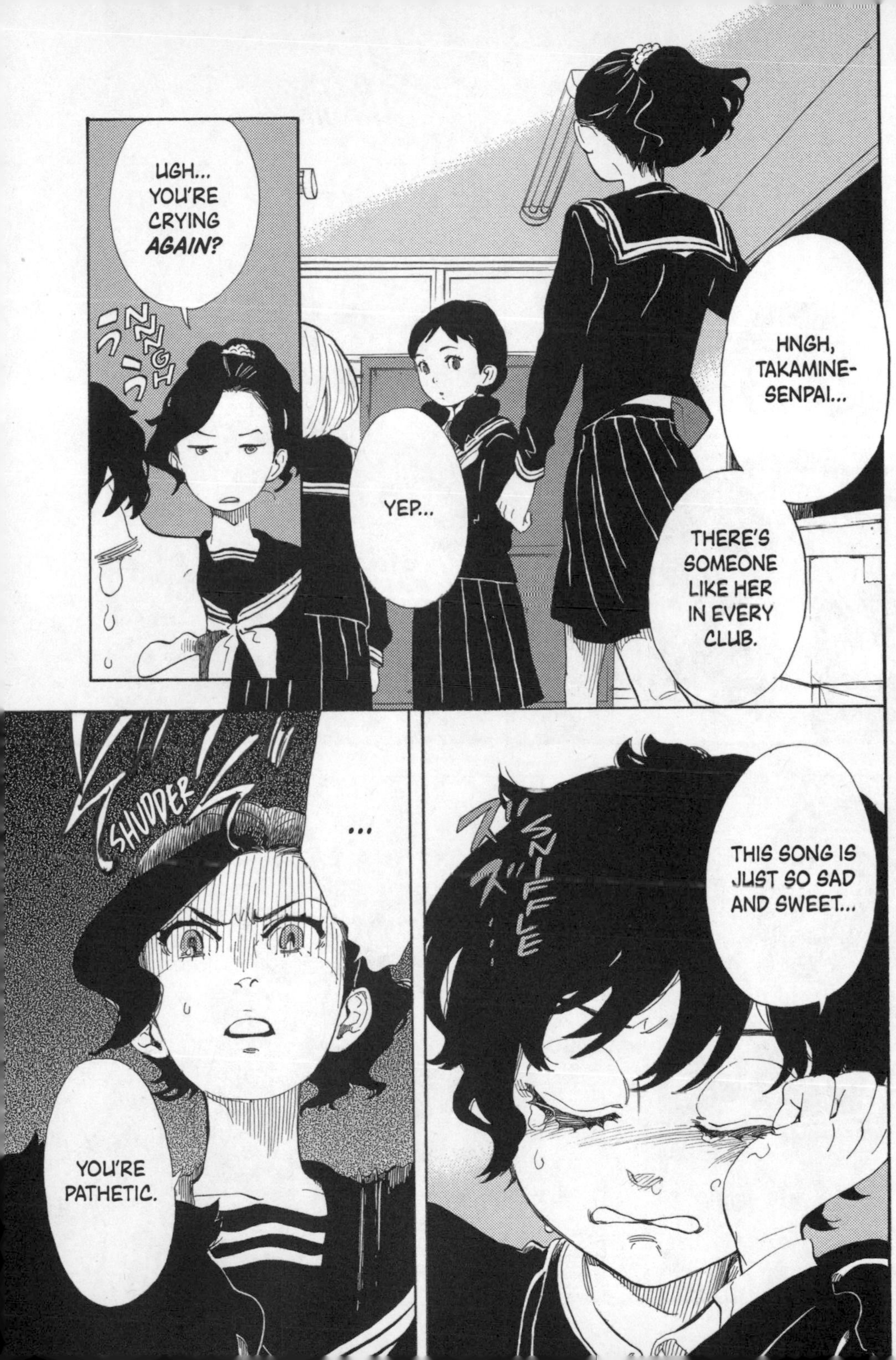
HNGH, TAKAMINE-SENPAI...
THERE'S SOMEONE LIKE HER IN EVERY CLUB.
YEP...
UGH... YOU'RE CRYING AGAIN?
NNGH
SNIFFLE
THIS SONG IS JUST SO SAD AND SWEET...
SHUDDER
...
YOU'RE PATHETIC.

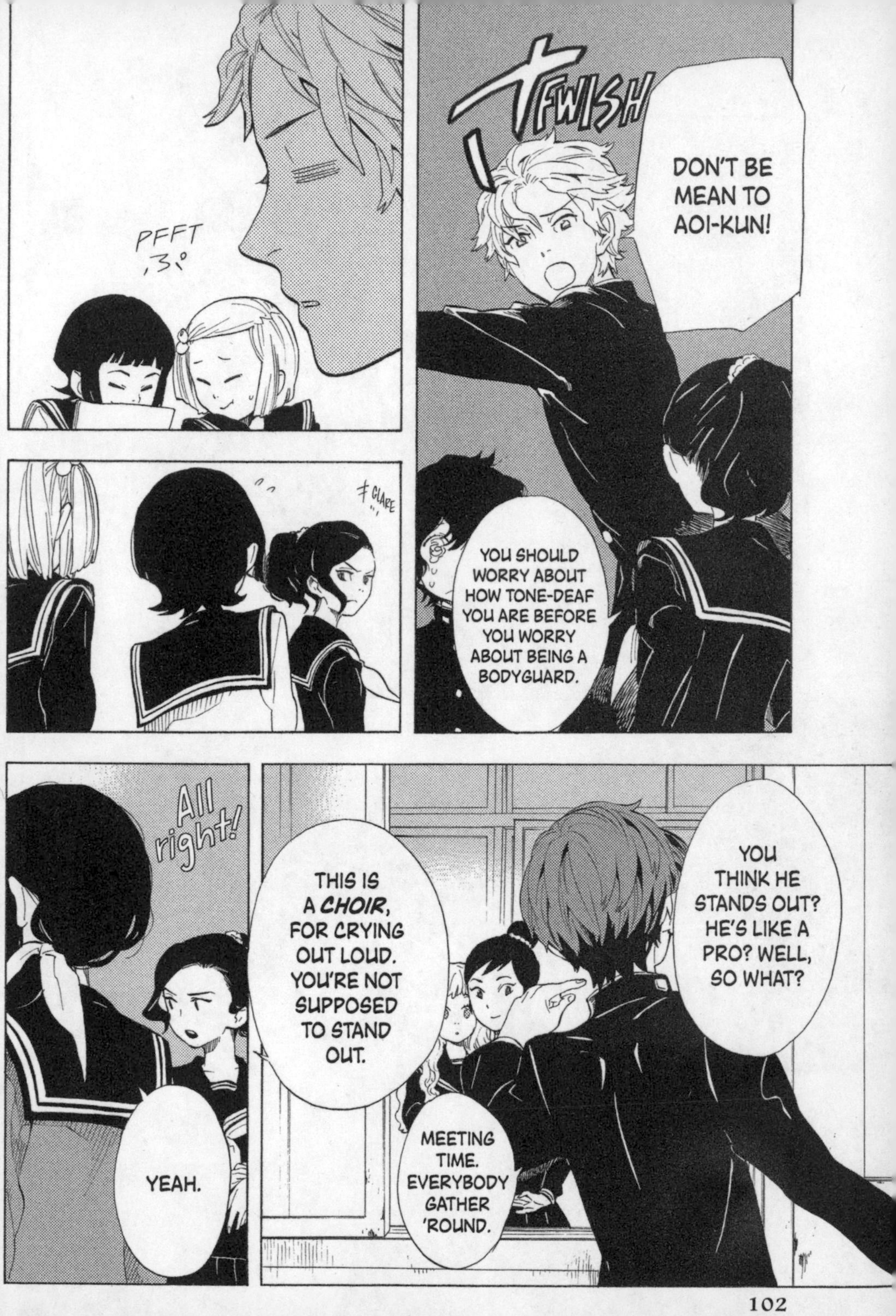
FWISH
DON'T BE MEAN TO AOI-KUN!
PFFT
YOU SHOULD WORRY ABOUT HOW TONE-DEAF YOU ARE BEFORE YOU WORRY ABOUT BEING A BODYGUARD.
GLARE
YOU THINK HE STANDS OUT? HE'S LIKE A PRO? WELL, SO WHAT?
THIS IS A *CHOIR*, FOR CRYING OUT LOUD. YOU'RE NOT SUPPOSED TO STAND OUT.
MEETING TIME. EVERYBODY GATHER 'ROUND.
All right!
YEAH.

YUTAKA IS...TOO GOOD.

OUR MAIN GOAL IS GETTING TO COMPETE IN THE NHK NATIONAL SCHOOL MUSIC COMPETITION THIS OCTOBER. OR, WELL...

THE CASH PRIZE...

HERE'S WHAT OUR SCHEDULE LOOKS LIKE FOR THIS YEAR.

• VOCALIZATI[ON] EXERCISES
• PRACTICE BY SECTIO[N]
• REHEARSA[L]

TWO BILLIO[N] LIGHT YEAR[S]

CHOIR SCHEDUL[E]

4	ENTRANCE CERE[MONY]
5	
6	APPLICATION FOR N COMPETITION
7	VISITING CONCE[RT]
	N COMPETITION REGI[ONAL] SUMMER TRAINING C[AMP]
	[S]CHOOL FESTIVA[L]
	[CH]OIR COMPETITION [N] COMPETITION NATI[ONAL]
	REGION[AL]
	LAST DAY FOR THIRD-YEAR STUDE[NTS]
1	
2	
3	GRADUATION

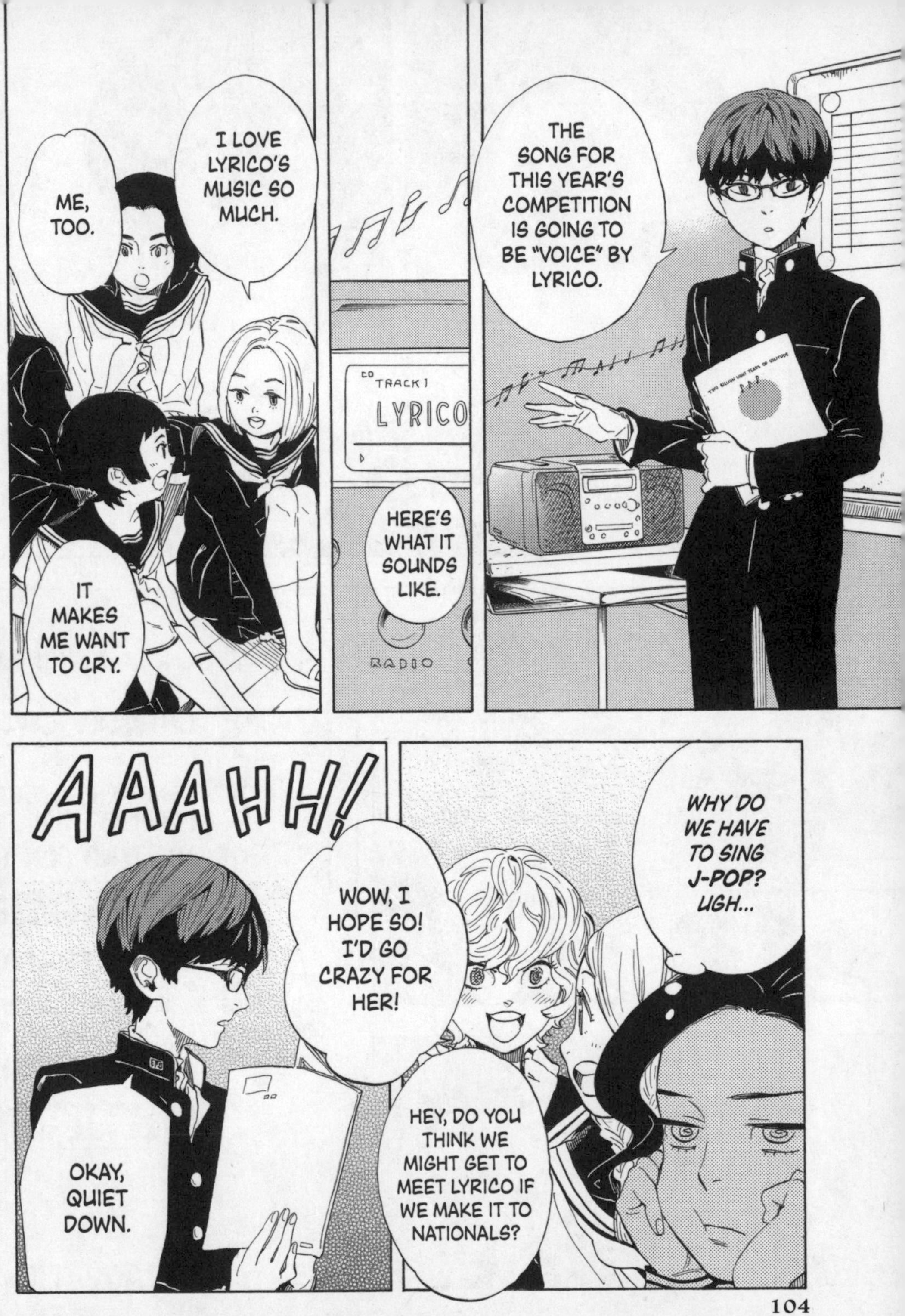
THE SONG FOR THIS YEAR'S COMPETITION IS GOING TO BE "VOICE" BY LYRICO.
CD TRACK 1
LYRICO
HERE'S WHAT IT SOUNDS LIKE.
RADIO
I LOVE LYRICO'S MUSIC SO MUCH.
ME, TOO.
IT MAKES ME WANT TO CRY.
WHY DO WE HAVE TO SING J-POP? UGH...
HEY, DO YOU THINK WE MIGHT GET TO MEET LYRICO IF WE MAKE IT TO NATIONALS?
WOW, I HOPE SO! I'D GO CRAZY FOR HER!
AAAHH!
OKAY, QUIET DOWN.

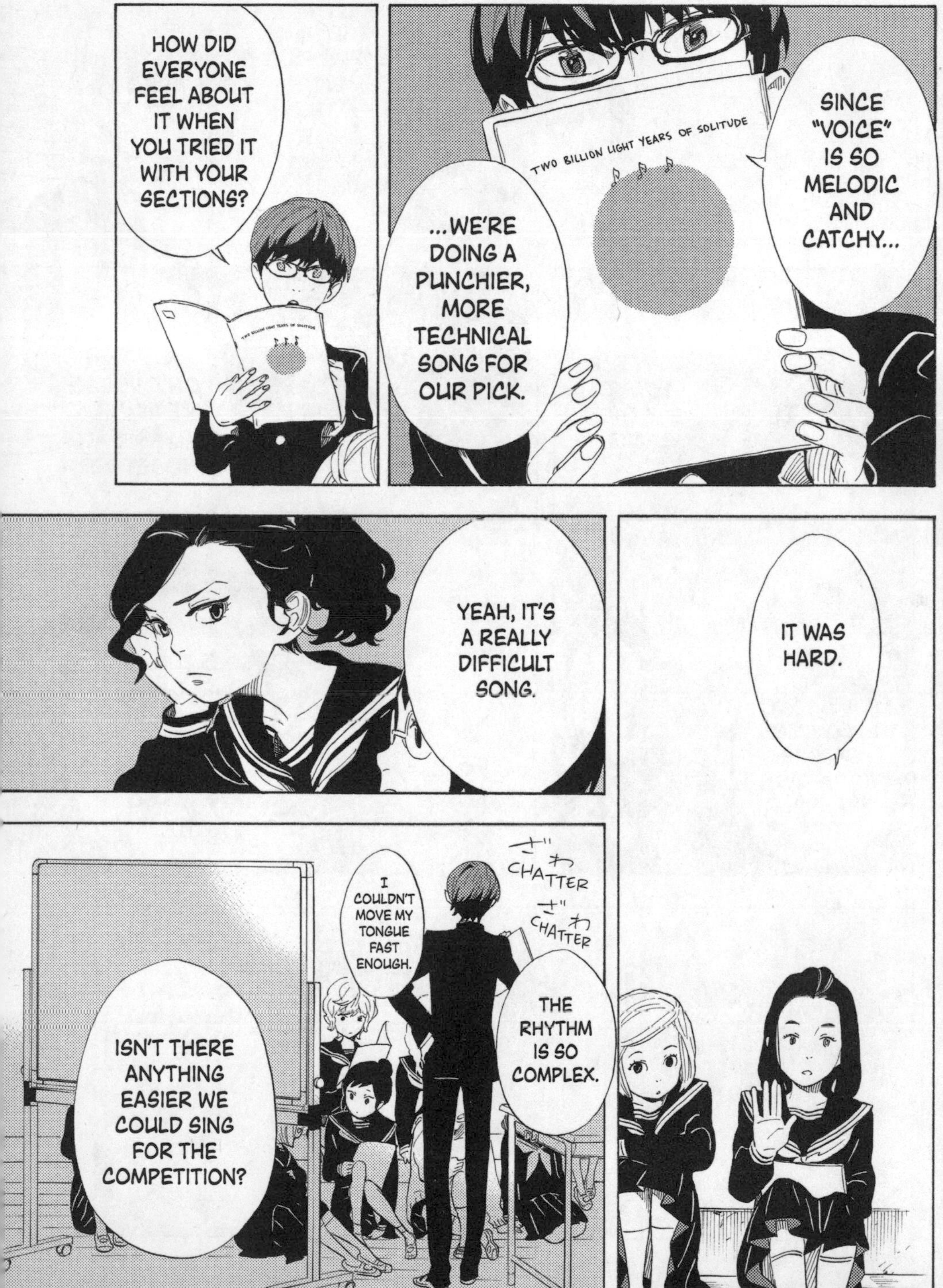
SINCE "VOICE" IS SO MELODIC AND CATCHY...
TWO BILLION LIGHT YEARS OF SOLITUDE
...WE'RE DOING A PUNCHIER, MORE TECHNICAL SONG FOR OUR PICK.
HOW DID EVERYONE FEEL ABOUT IT WHEN YOU TRIED IT WITH YOUR SECTIONS?
IT WAS HARD.
YEAH, IT'S A REALLY DIFFICULT SONG.
ざわ CHATTER
ざわ CHATTER
THE RHYTHM IS SO COMPLEX.
I COULDN'T MOVE MY TONGUE FAST ENOUGH.
ISN'T THERE ANYTHING EASIER WE COULD SING FOR THE COMPETITION?

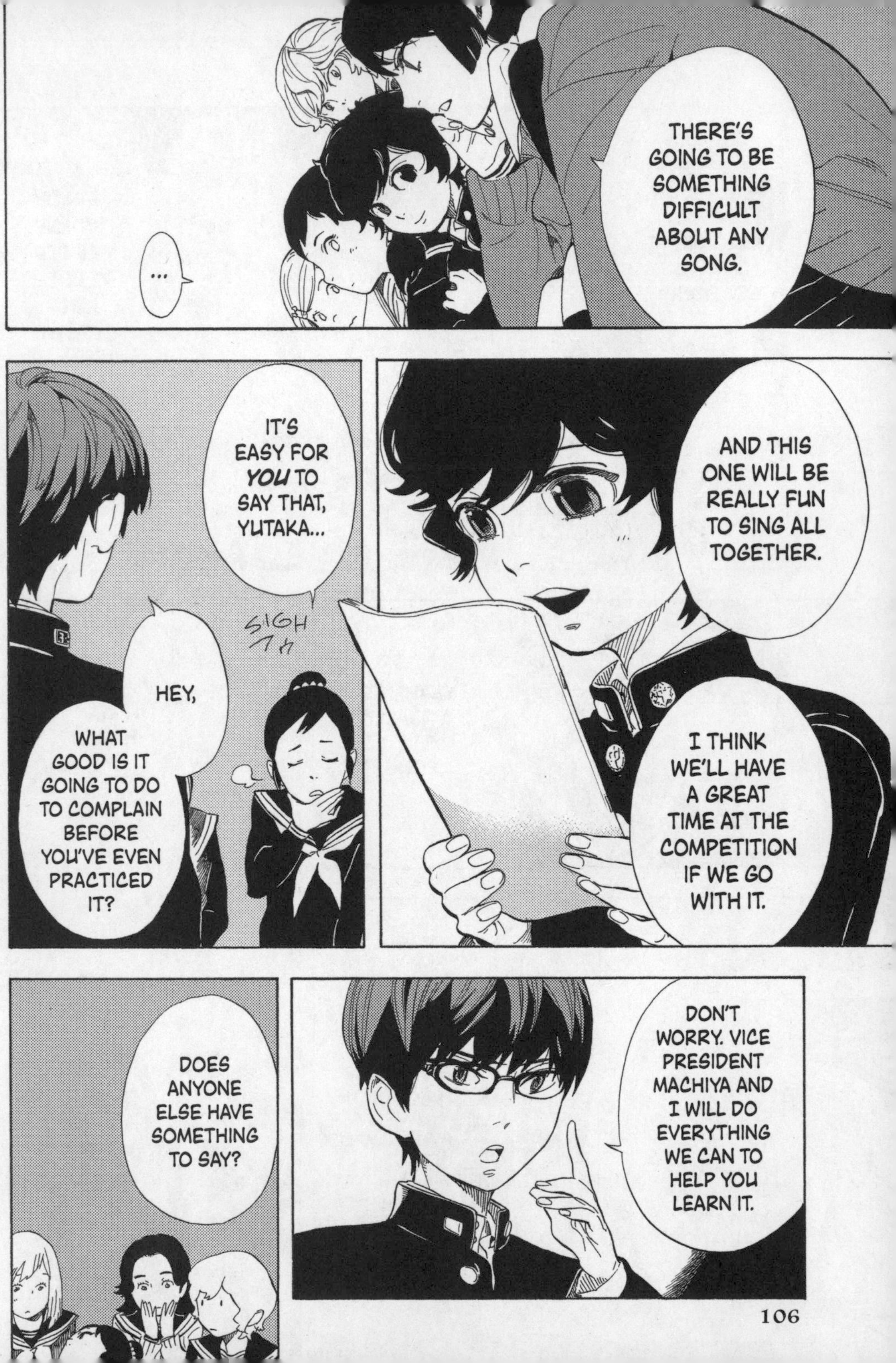
THERE'S GOING TO BE SOMETHING DIFFICULT ABOUT ANY SONG.
...
AND THIS ONE WILL BE REALLY FUN TO SING ALL TOGETHER.
I THINK WE'LL HAVE A GREAT TIME AT THE COMPETITION IF WE GO WITH IT.
IT'S EASY FOR *YOU* TO SAY THAT, YUTAKA...
SIGH
HEY,
WHAT GOOD IS IT GOING TO DO TO COMPLAIN BEFORE YOU'VE EVEN PRACTICED IT?
DON'T WORRY. VICE PRESIDENT MACHIYA AND I WILL DO EVERYTHING WE CAN TO HELP YOU LEARN IT.
DOES ANYONE ELSE HAVE SOMETHING TO SAY?

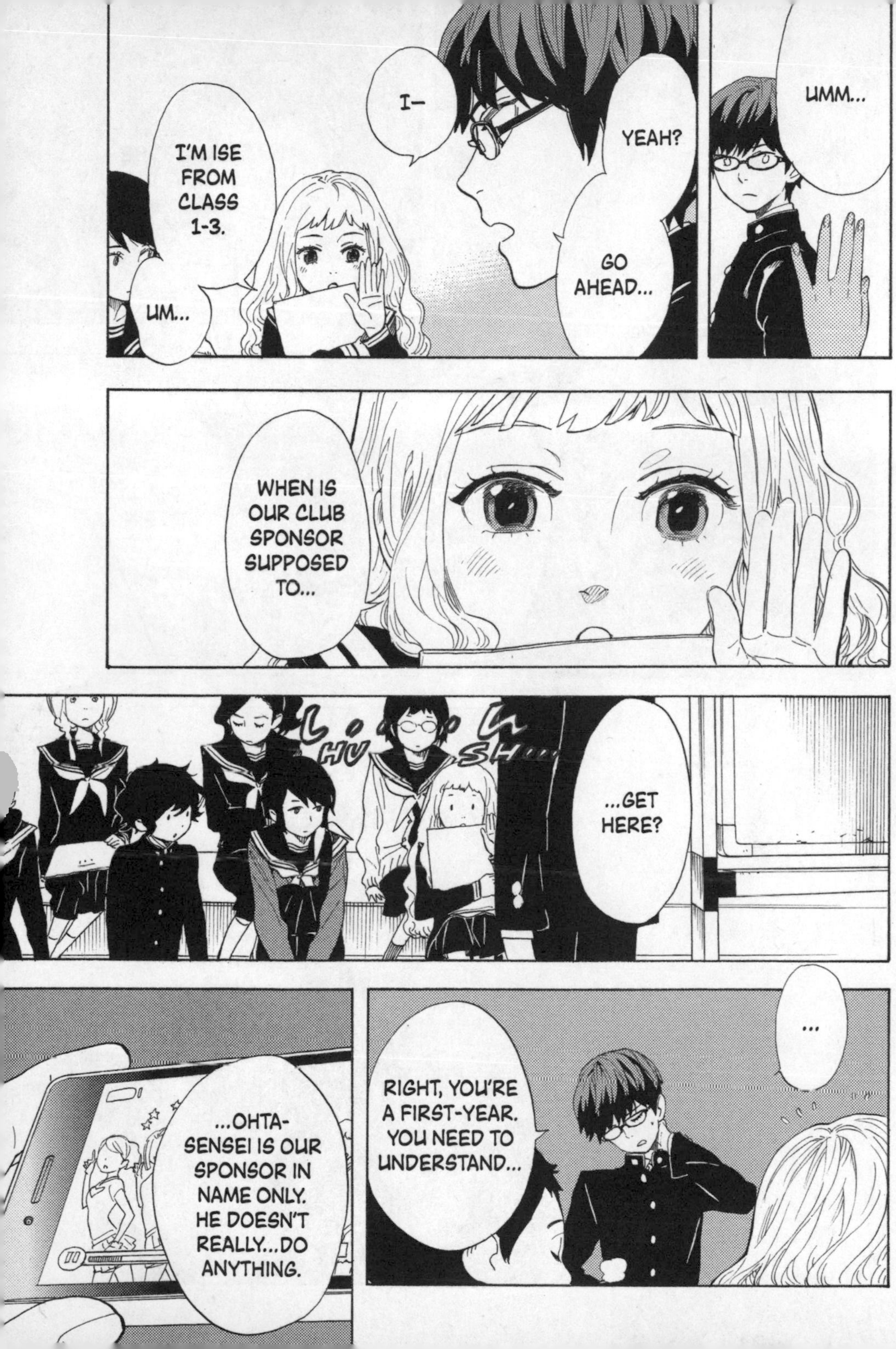
UMM...
YEAH?
GO AHEAD...
I—
I'M ISE FROM CLASS 1-3.
UM...
WHEN IS OUR CLUB SPONSOR SUPPOSED TO...
...GET HERE?
HUSH...
...
RIGHT, YOU'RE A FIRST-YEAR. YOU NEED TO UNDERSTAND...
...OHTA-SENSEI IS OUR SPONSOR IN NAME ONLY. HE DOESN'T REALLY...DO ANYTHING.

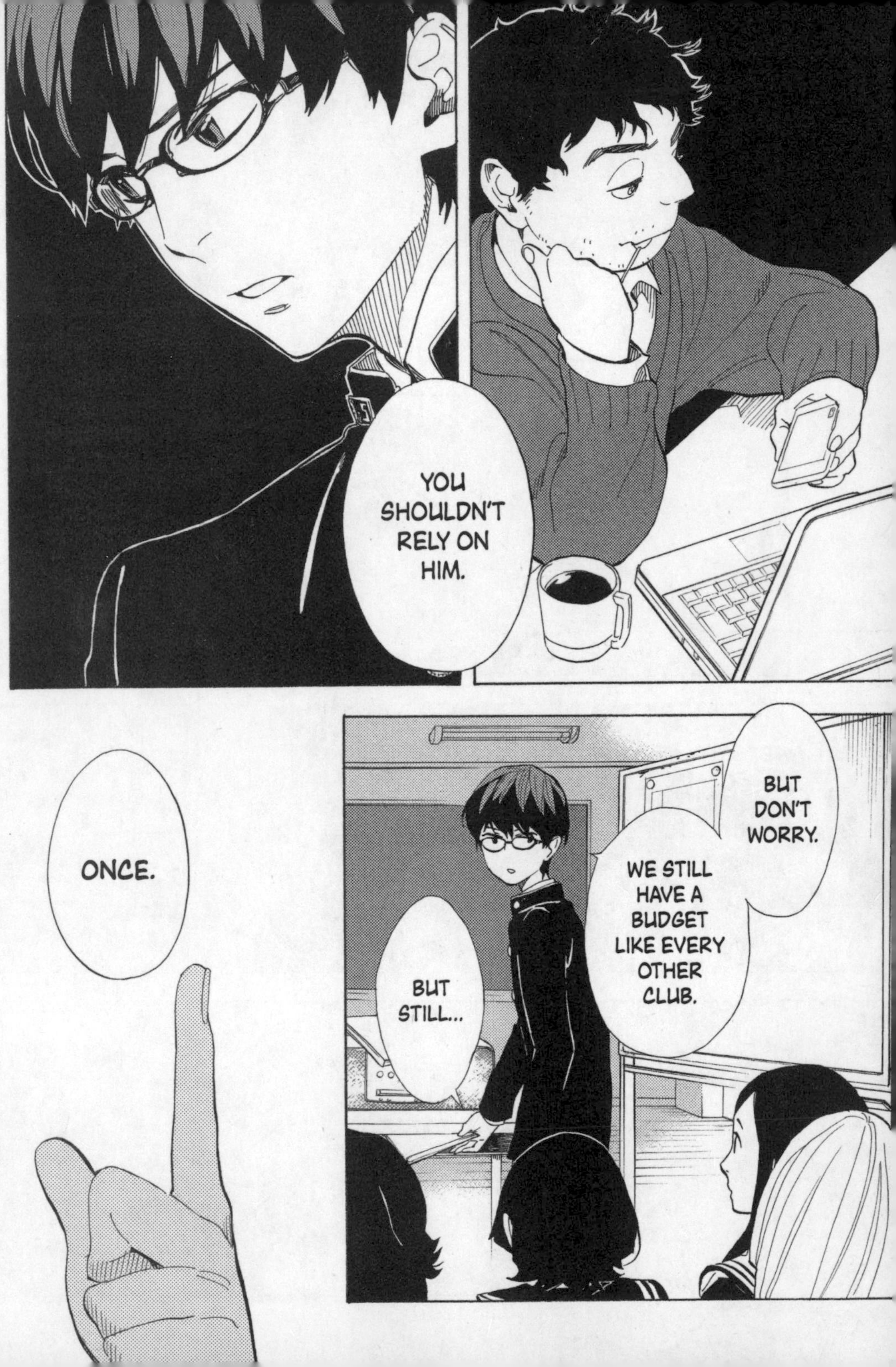
YOU SHOULDN'T RELY ON HIM.
BUT DON'T WORRY.
WE STILL HAVE A BUDGET LIKE EVERY OTHER CLUB.
BUT STILL...
ONCE.

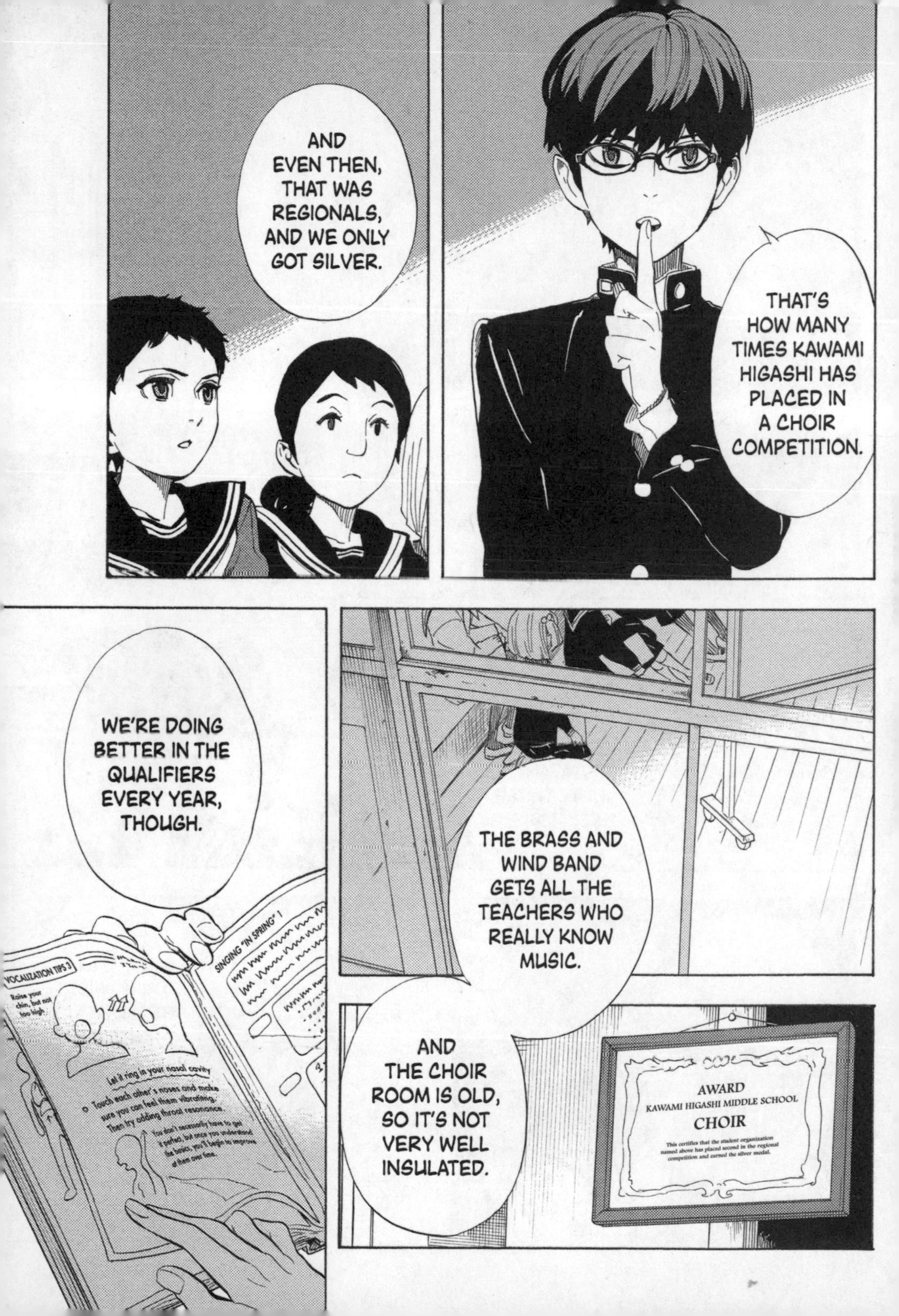
THAT'S HOW MANY TIMES KAWAMI HIGASHI HAS PLACED IN A CHOIR COMPETITION.
AND EVEN THEN, THAT WAS REGIONALS, AND WE ONLY GOT SILVER.
THE BRASS AND WIND BAND GETS ALL THE TEACHERS WHO REALLY KNOW MUSIC.
AND THE CHOIR ROOM IS OLD, SO IT'S NOT VERY WELL INSULATED.
AWARD
KAWAMI HIGASHI MIDDLE SCHOOL
CHOIR
This certifies that the student organization named above has placed second in the regional competition and earned the silver medal.
WE'RE DOING BETTER IN THE QUALIFIERS EVERY YEAR, THOUGH.
VOCALIZATION TIPS 3
Raise your chin, but not too high.
Let it ring in your nasal cavity
Touch each other's noses and make sure you can feel them vibrating. Then try adding throat resonance.
You don't necessarily have to get it perfect, but once you understand the basics, you'll begin to improve at them over time.
SINGING "IN SPRING" 1

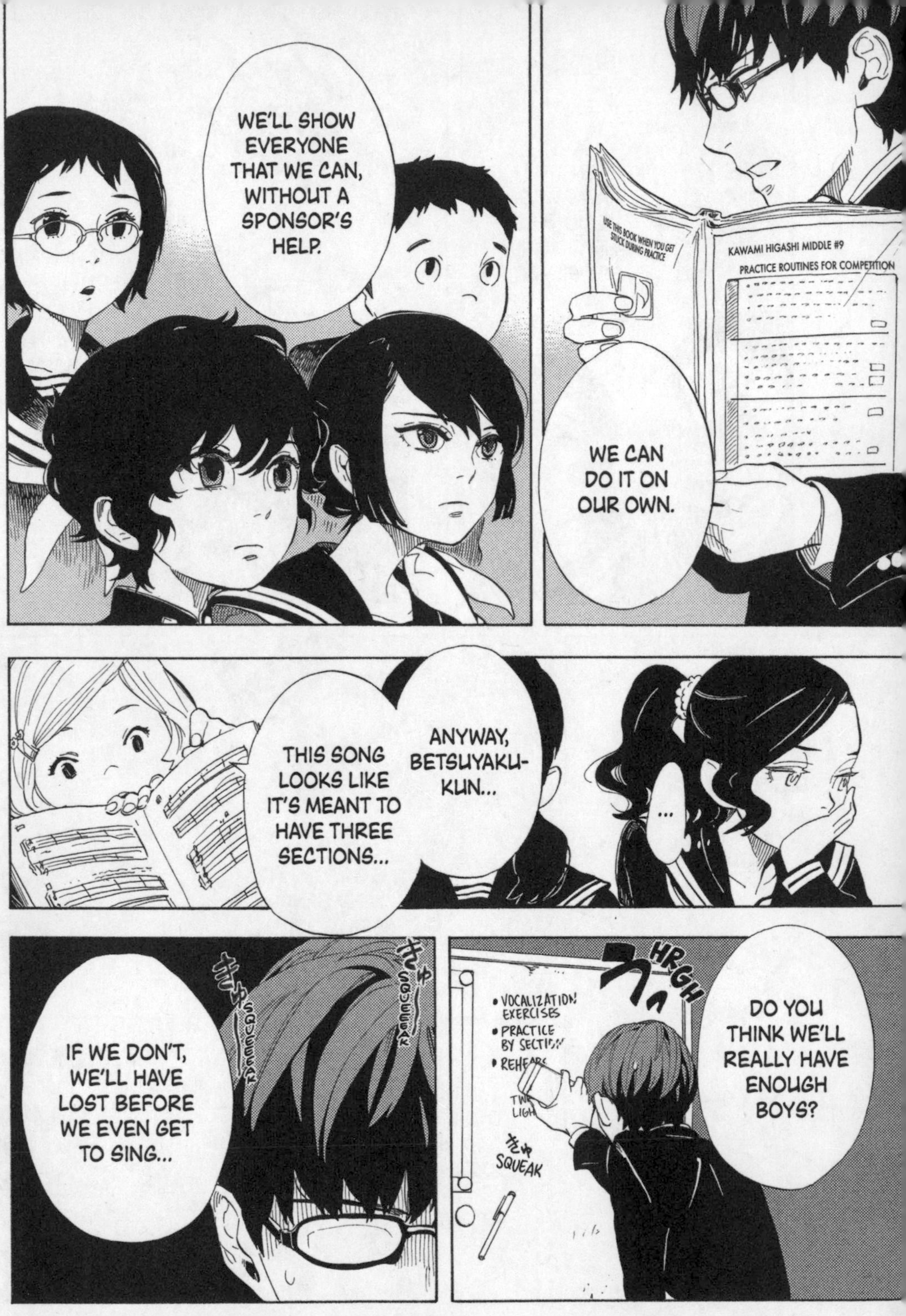
USE THIS BOOK WHEN YOU GET STUCK DURING PRACTICE
KAWAMI HIGASHI MIDDLE #9
PRACTICE ROUTINES FOR COMPETITION
WE CAN DO IT ON OUR OWN.
WE'LL SHOW EVERYONE THAT WE CAN, WITHOUT A SPONSOR'S HELP.
...
ANYWAY, BETSUYAKU-KUN...
THIS SONG LOOKS LIKE IT'S MEANT TO HAVE THREE SECTIONS...
DO YOU THINK WE'LL REALLY HAVE ENOUGH BOYS?
HRGH
• VOCALIZATION EXERCISES
• PRACTICE
SQUEAK
SQUEEAK
SQUEEAK
IF WE DON'T, WE'LL HAVE LOST BEFORE WE EVEN GET TO SING...

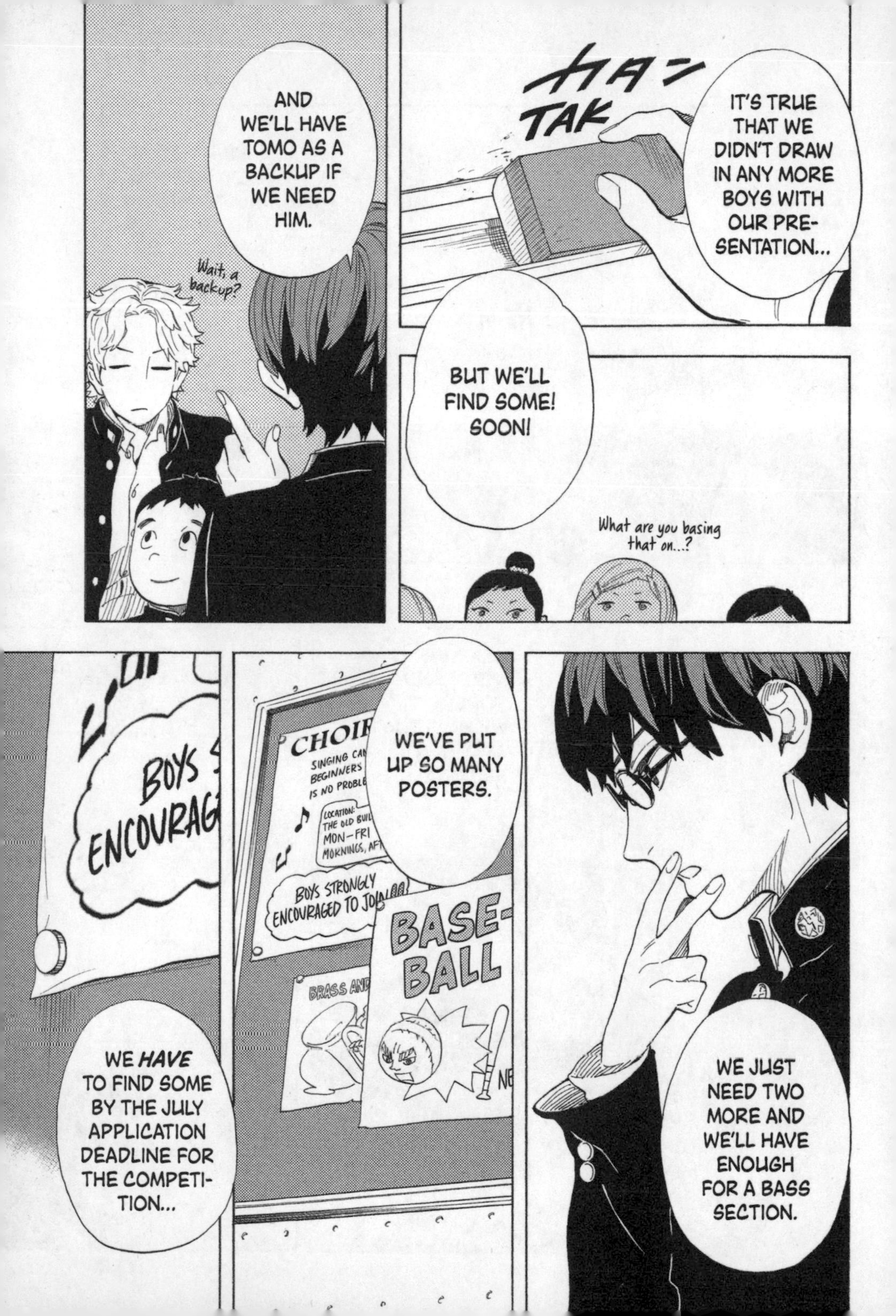

カタン
TAK
IT'S TRUE THAT WE DIDN'T DRAW IN ANY MORE BOYS WITH OUR PRESENTATION...
BUT WE'LL FIND SOME! SOON!
What are you basing that on...?
AND WE'LL HAVE TOMO AS A BACKUP IF WE NEED HIM.
Wait, a backup?
WE JUST NEED TWO MORE AND WE'LL HAVE ENOUGH FOR A BASS SECTION.
WE'VE PUT UP SO MANY POSTERS.
CHOIR
BOYS STRONGLY ENCOURAGED TO JOIN!!
BASE-BALL
WE *HAVE* TO FIND SOME BY THE JULY APPLICATION DEADLINE FOR THE COMPETITION...

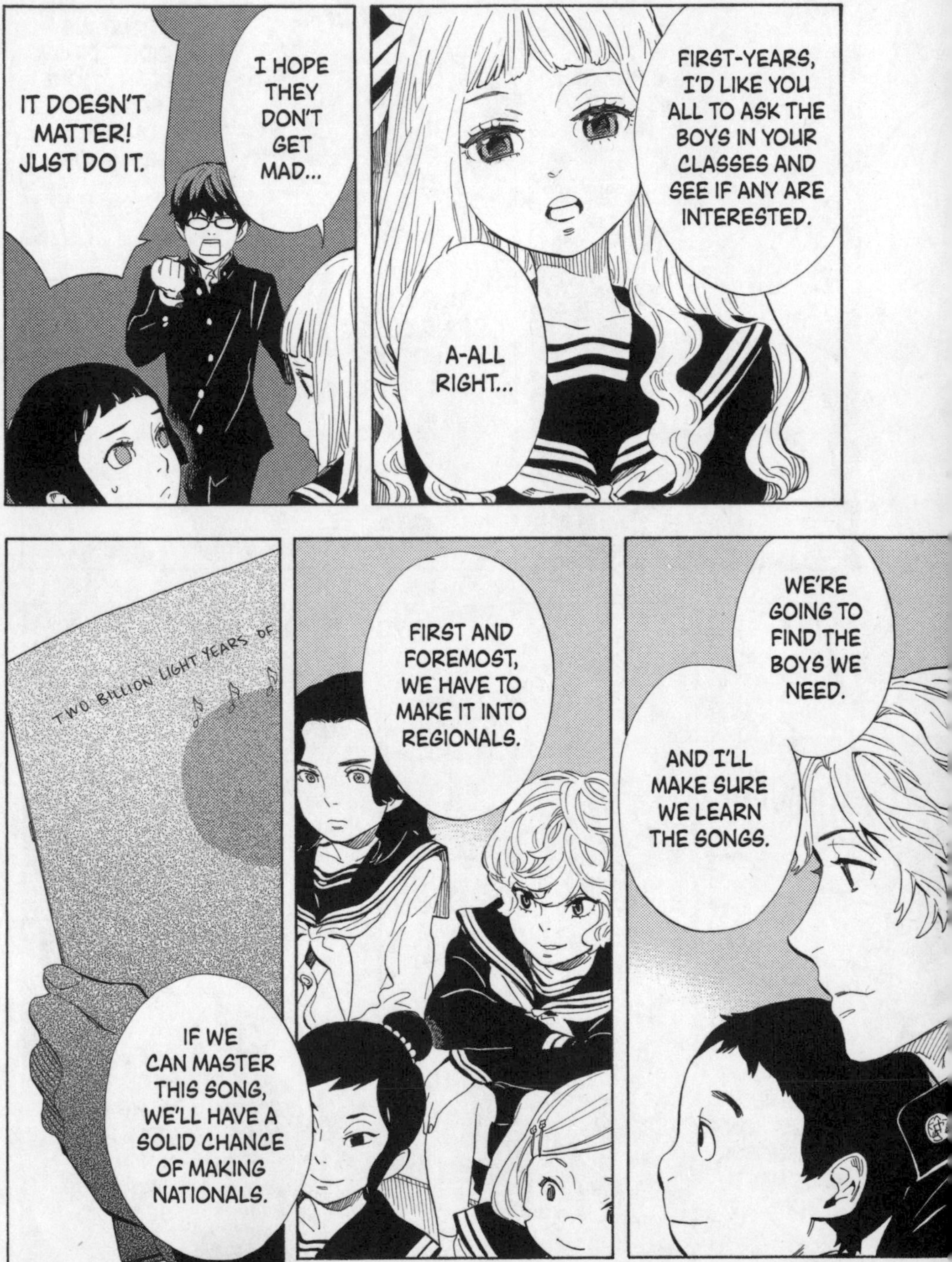
FIRST-YEARS, I'D LIKE YOU ALL TO ASK THE BOYS IN YOUR CLASSES AND SEE IF ANY ARE INTERESTED.
A-ALL RIGHT...
I HOPE THEY DON'T GET MAD...
IT DOESN'T MATTER! JUST DO IT.
WE'RE GOING TO FIND THE BOYS WE NEED.
AND I'LL MAKE SURE WE LEARN THE SONGS.
FIRST AND FOREMOST, WE HAVE TO MAKE IT INTO REGIONALS.
TWO BILLION LIGHT YEARS OF
IF WE CAN MASTER THIS SONG, WE'LL HAVE A SOLID CHANCE OF MAKING NATIONALS.

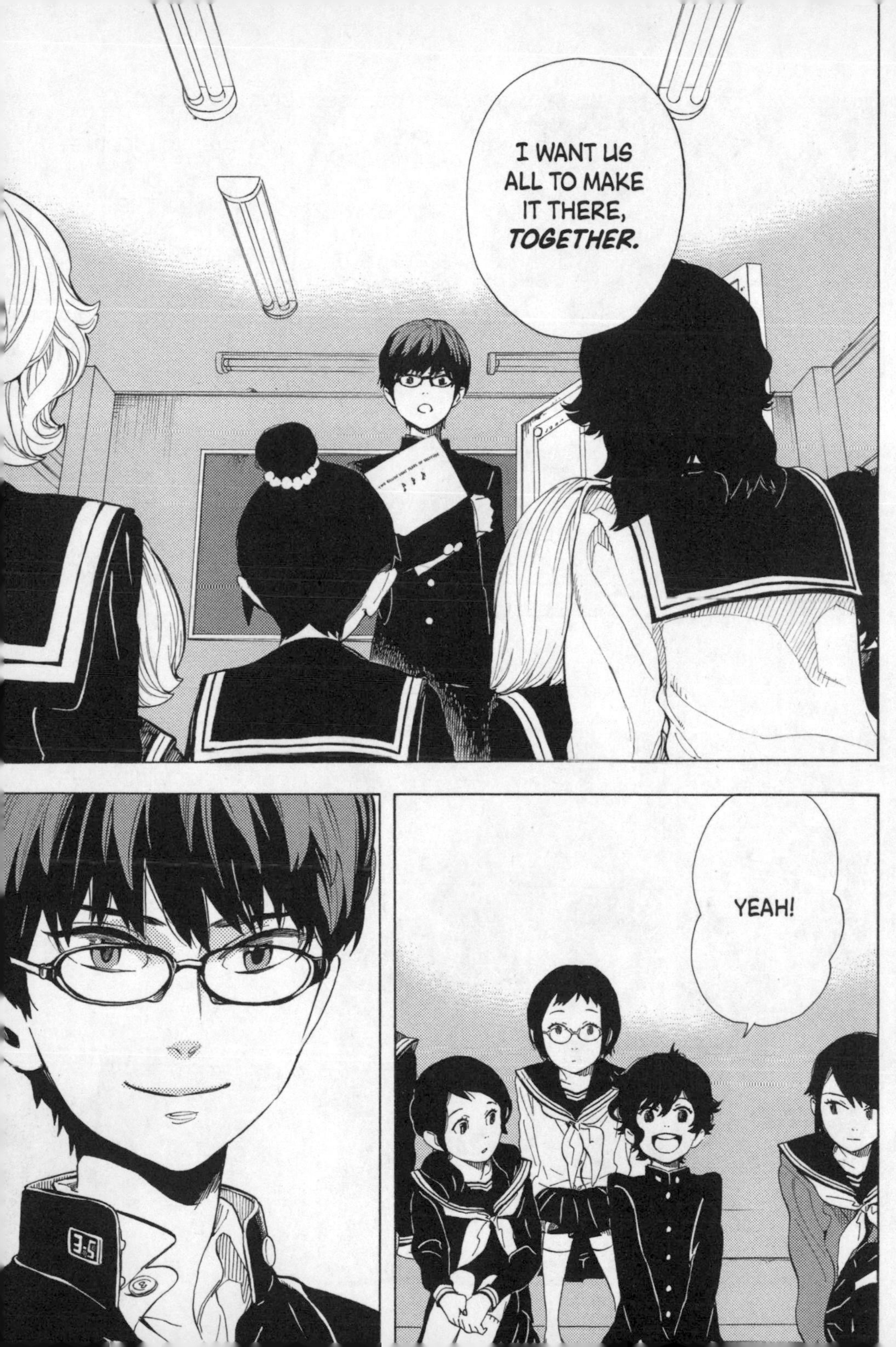
I WANT US ALL TO MAKE IT THERE, TOGETHER.
YEAH!

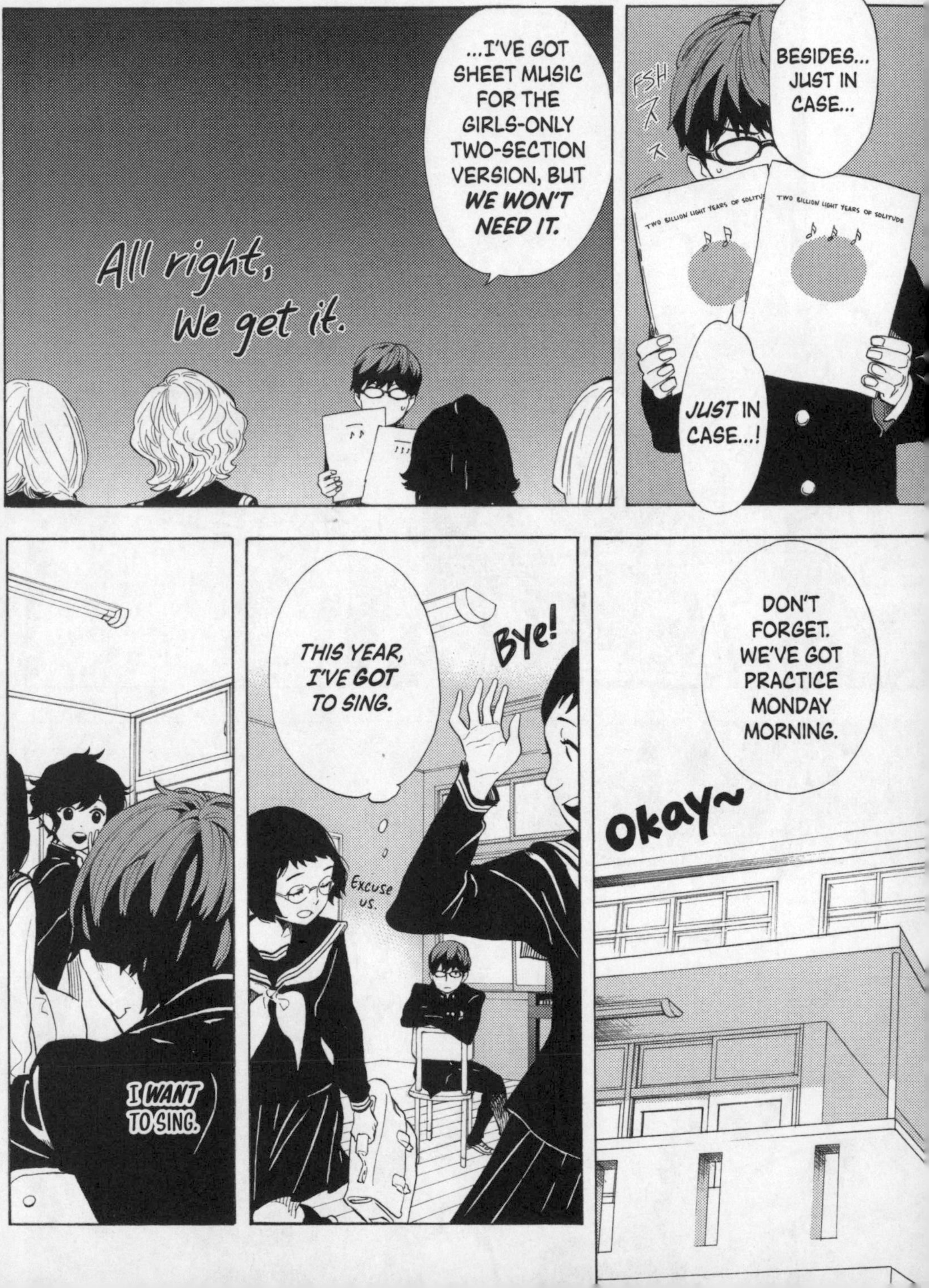
FSH
BESIDES... JUST IN CASE...
TWO BILLION LIGHT YEARS OF SOLITUDE
TWO BILLION LIGHT YEARS OF SOLITU
JUST IN CASE...!
...I'VE GOT SHEET MUSIC FOR THE GIRLS-ONLY TWO-SECTION VERSION, BUT WE WON'T NEED IT.
All right, We get it.
DON'T FORGET. WE'VE GOT PRACTICE MONDAY MORNING.
Okay~
Bye!
THIS YEAR, I'VE GOT TO SING.
Excuse us.
I WANT TO SING.

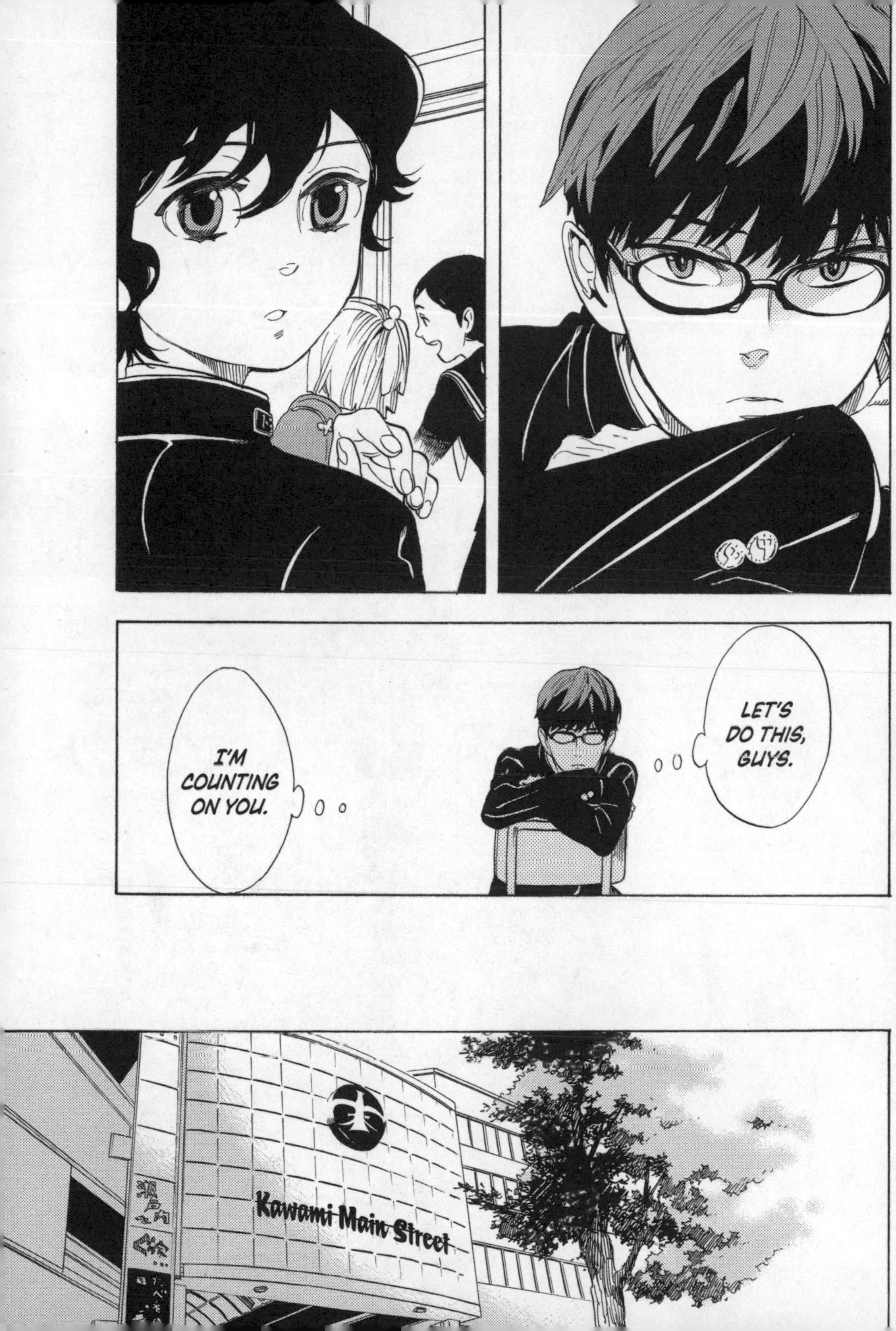
LET'S DO THIS, GUYS.
I'M COUNTING ON YOU.
Kawami Main Street

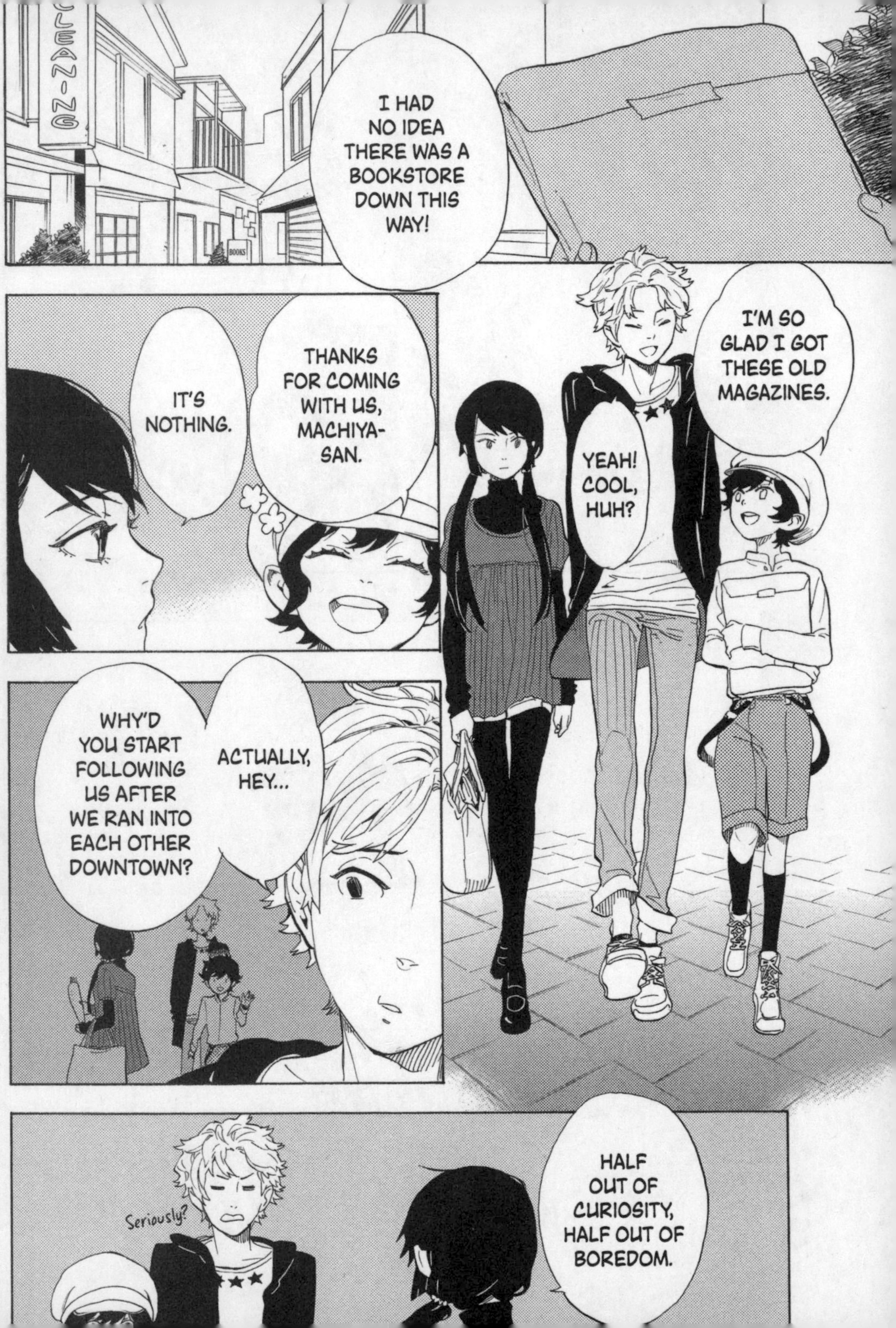
CLEANING
BOOKS
I HAD NO IDEA THERE WAS A BOOKSTORE DOWN THIS WAY!
I'M SO GLAD I GOT THESE OLD MAGAZINES.
YEAH! COOL, HUH?
THANKS FOR COMING WITH US, MACHIYA-SAN.
IT'S NOTHING.
ACTUALLY, HEY...
WHY'D YOU START FOLLOWING US AFTER WE RAN INTO EACH OTHER DOWNTOWN?
HALF OUT OF CURIOSITY, HALF OUT OF BOREDOM.
Seriously?

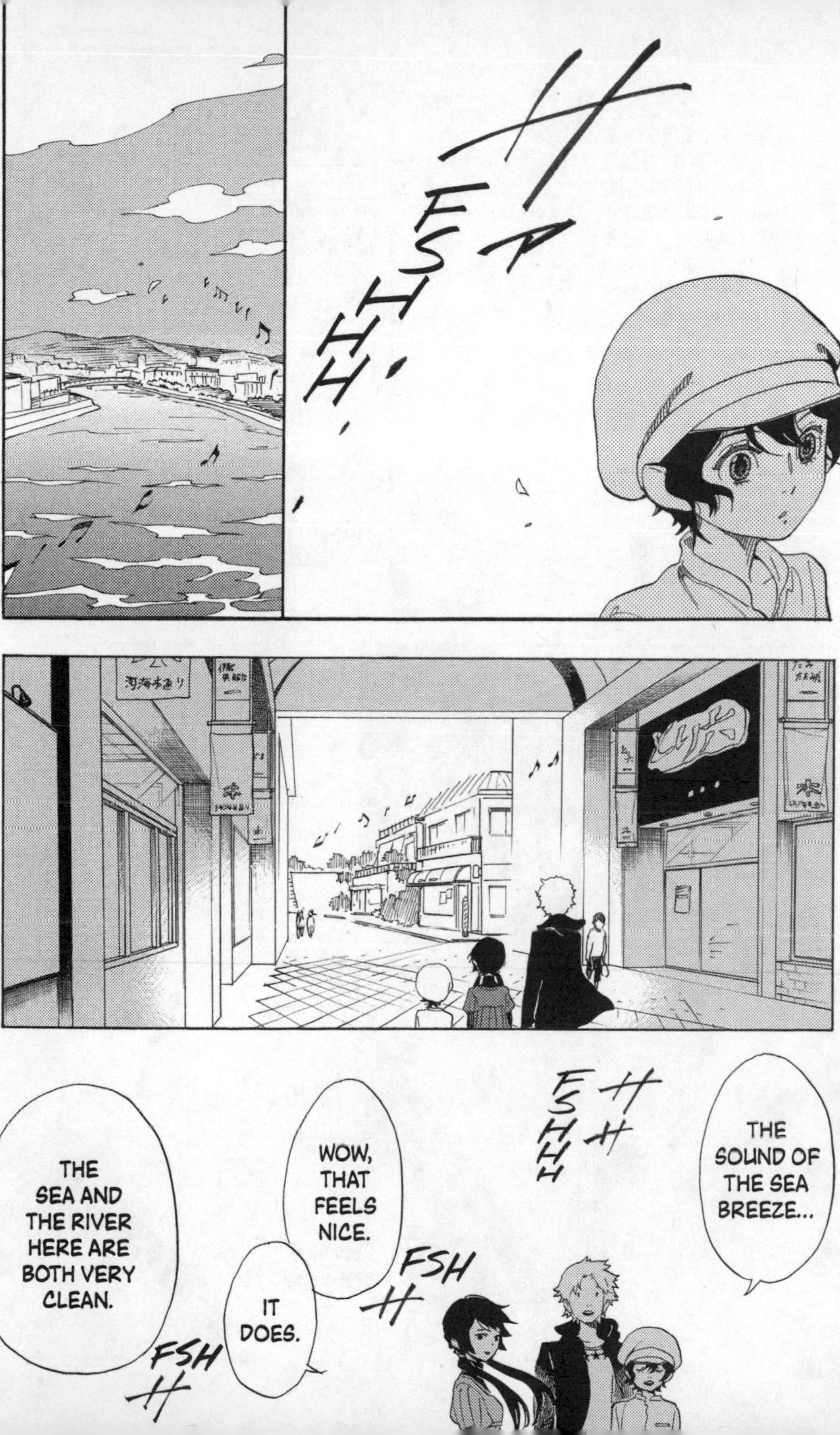
FSHHH
FSHHH
THE SOUND OF THE SEA BREEZE...
WOW, THAT FEELS NICE.
FSH
IT DOES.
THE SEA AND THE RIVER HERE ARE BOTH VERY CLEAN.
FSH

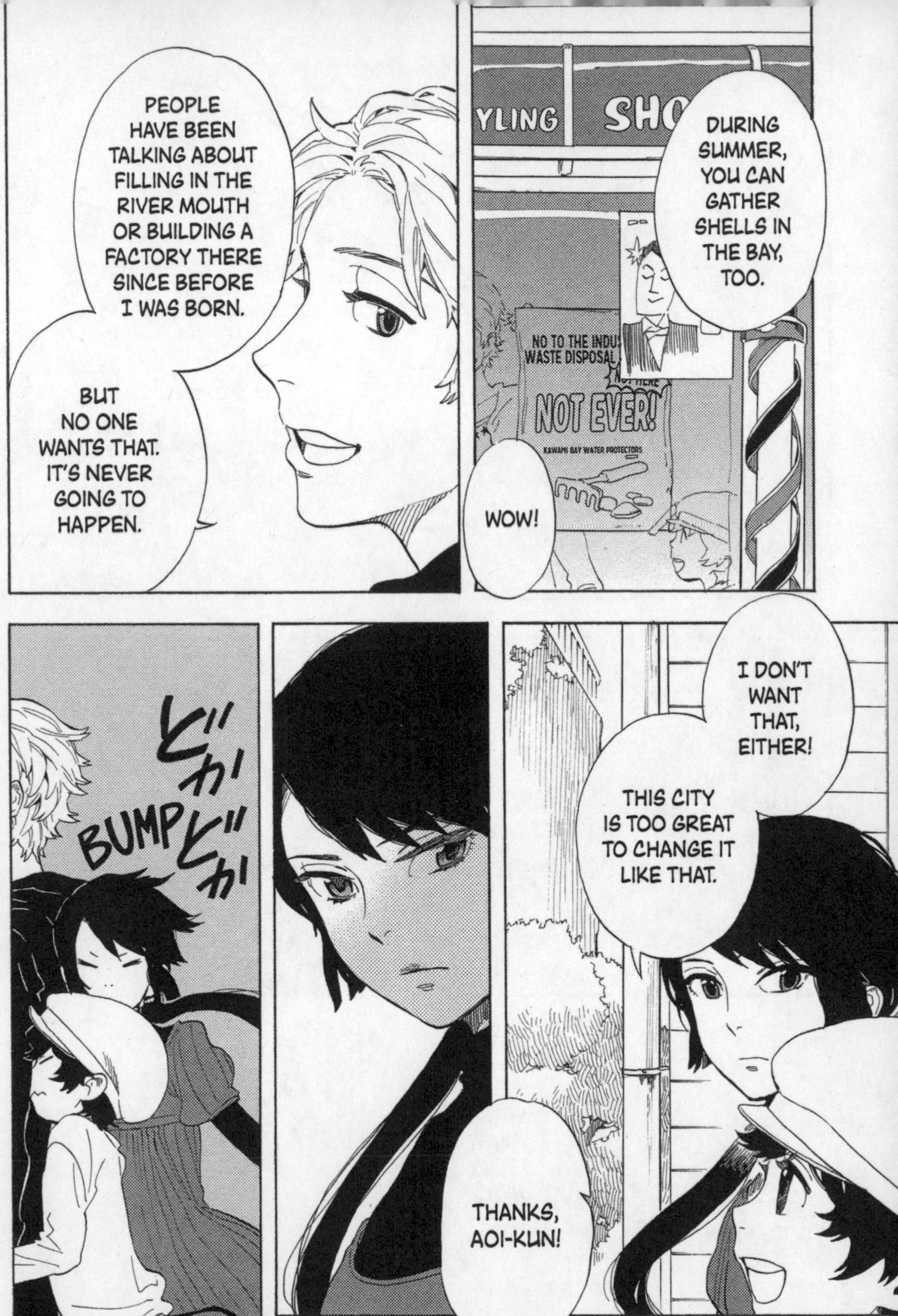
YLING SHO
DURING SUMMER, YOU CAN GATHER SHELLS IN THE BAY, TOO.
NO TO THE INDUS WASTE DISPOSAL
NOT EVER!
KAWAMI BAY WATER PROTECTORS
WOW!
PEOPLE HAVE BEEN TALKING ABOUT FILLING IN THE RIVER MOUTH OR BUILDING A FACTORY THERE SINCE BEFORE I WAS BORN.
BUT NO ONE WANTS THAT. IT'S NEVER GOING TO HAPPEN.
I DON'T WANT THAT, EITHER!
THIS CITY IS TOO GREAT TO CHANGE IT LIKE THAT.
THANKS, AOI-KUN!
どかどか
BUMP

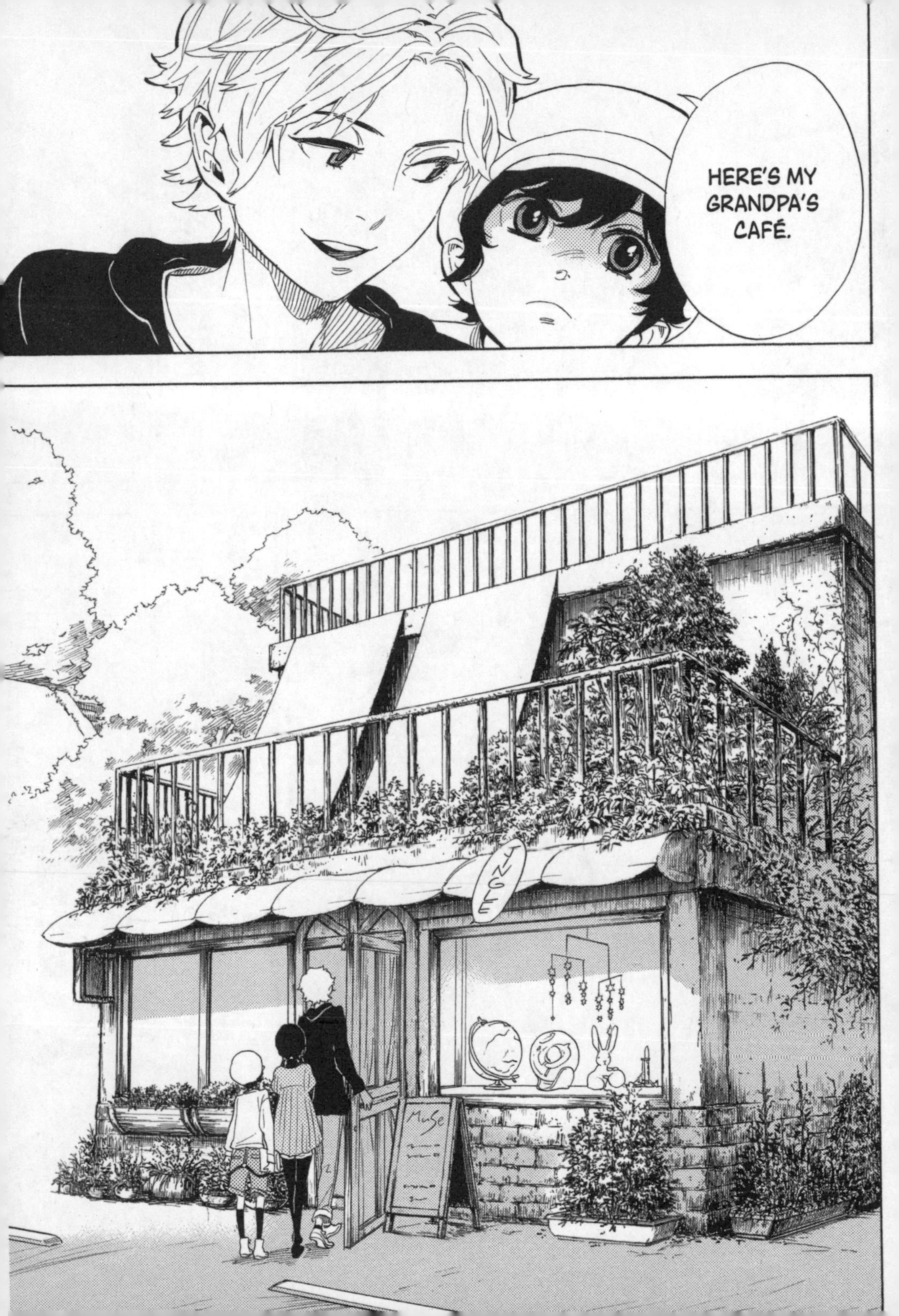
HERE'S MY GRANDPA'S CAFÉ.
JINGLE
MuSe

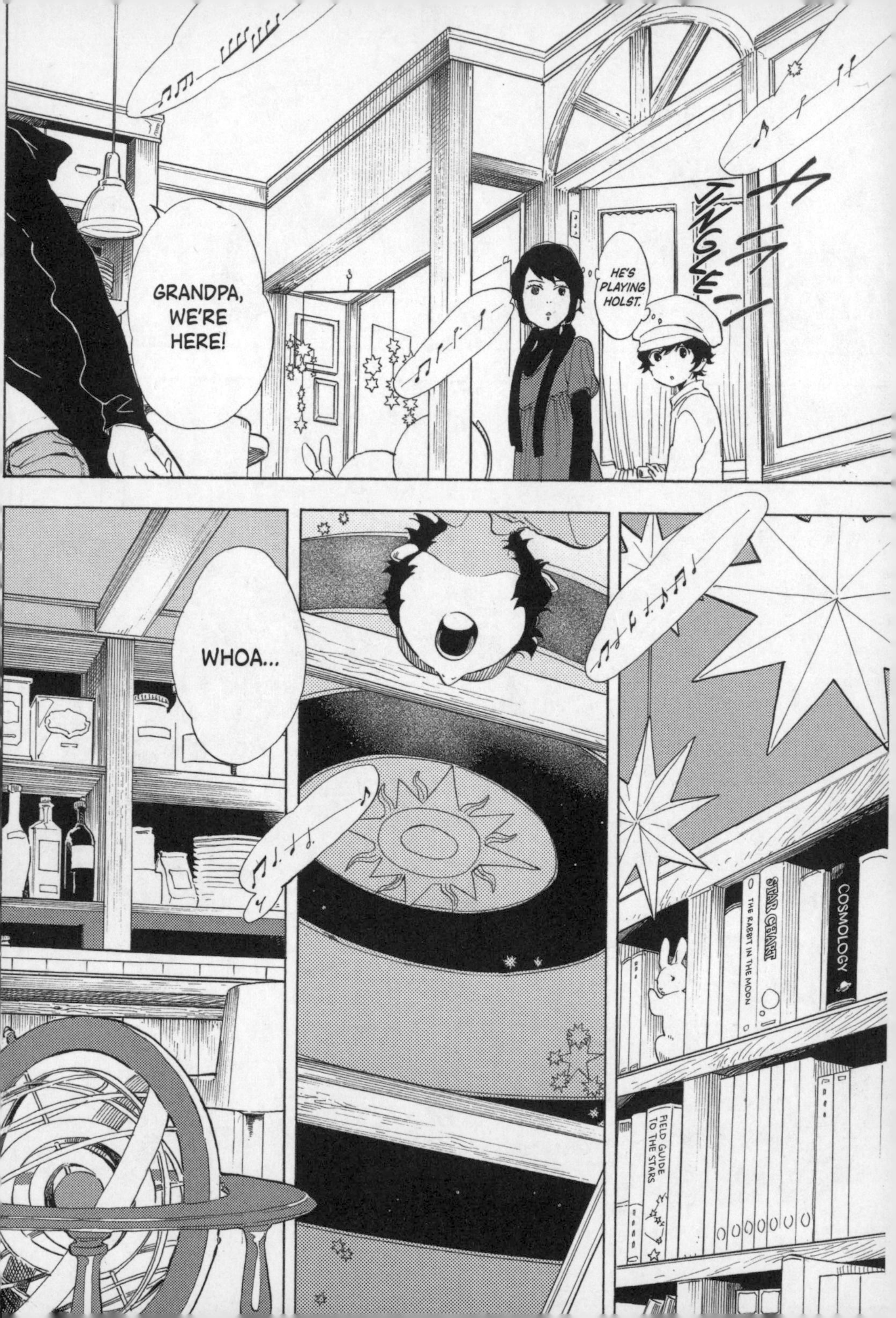
JINGLE
HE'S PLAYING HOLST.
GRANDPA, WE'RE HERE!
COSMOLOGY
STAR CHART
THE RABBIT IN THE MOON
FIELD GUIDE TO THE STARS
WHOA...

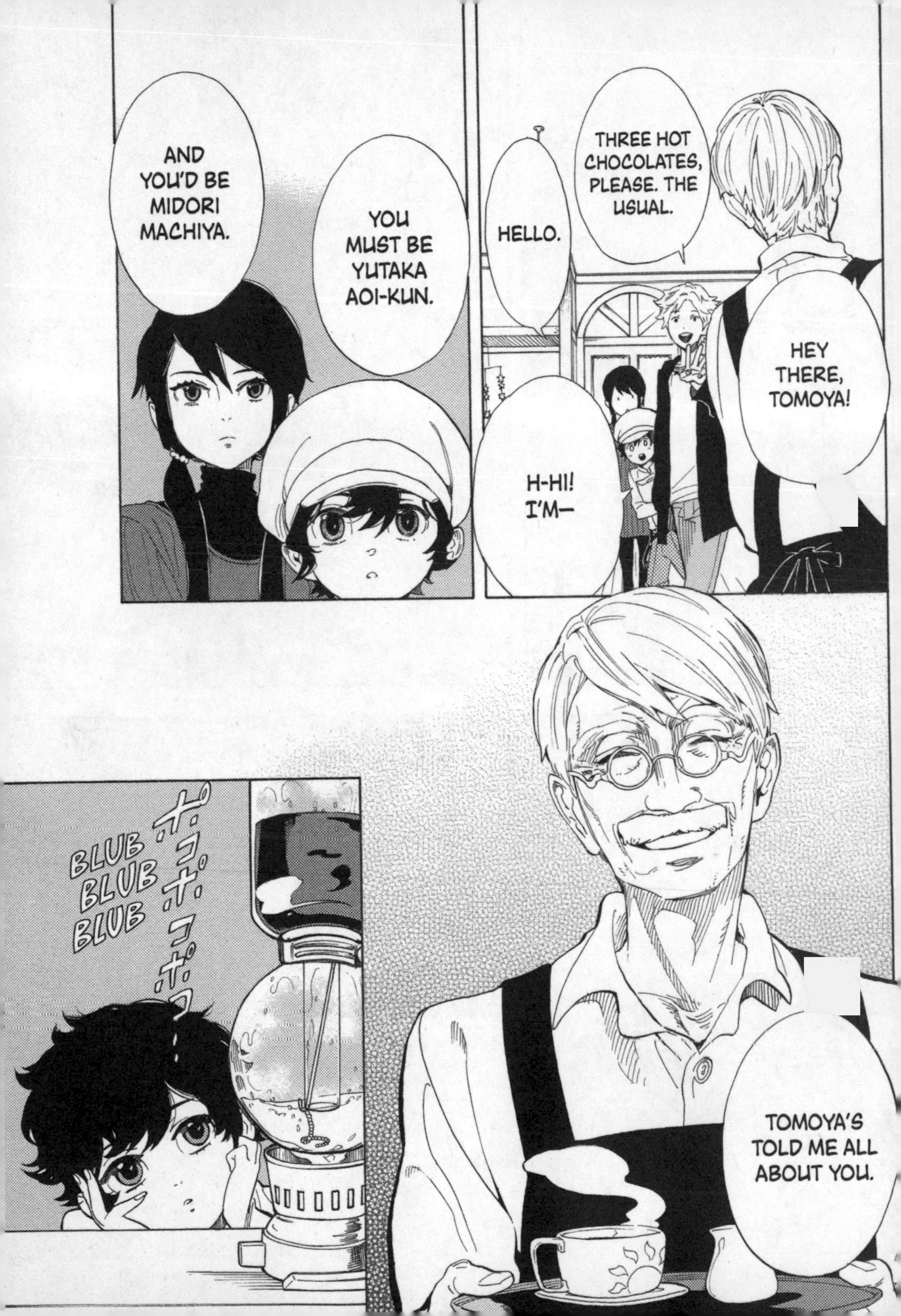
THREE HOT CHOCOLATES, PLEASE. THE USUAL.
HELLO.
HEY THERE, TOMOYA!
H-HI! I'M—
YOU MUST BE YUTAKA AOI-KUN.
AND YOU'D BE MIDORI MACHIYA.
TOMOYA'S TOLD ME ALL ABOUT YOU.
BLUB BLUB BLUB

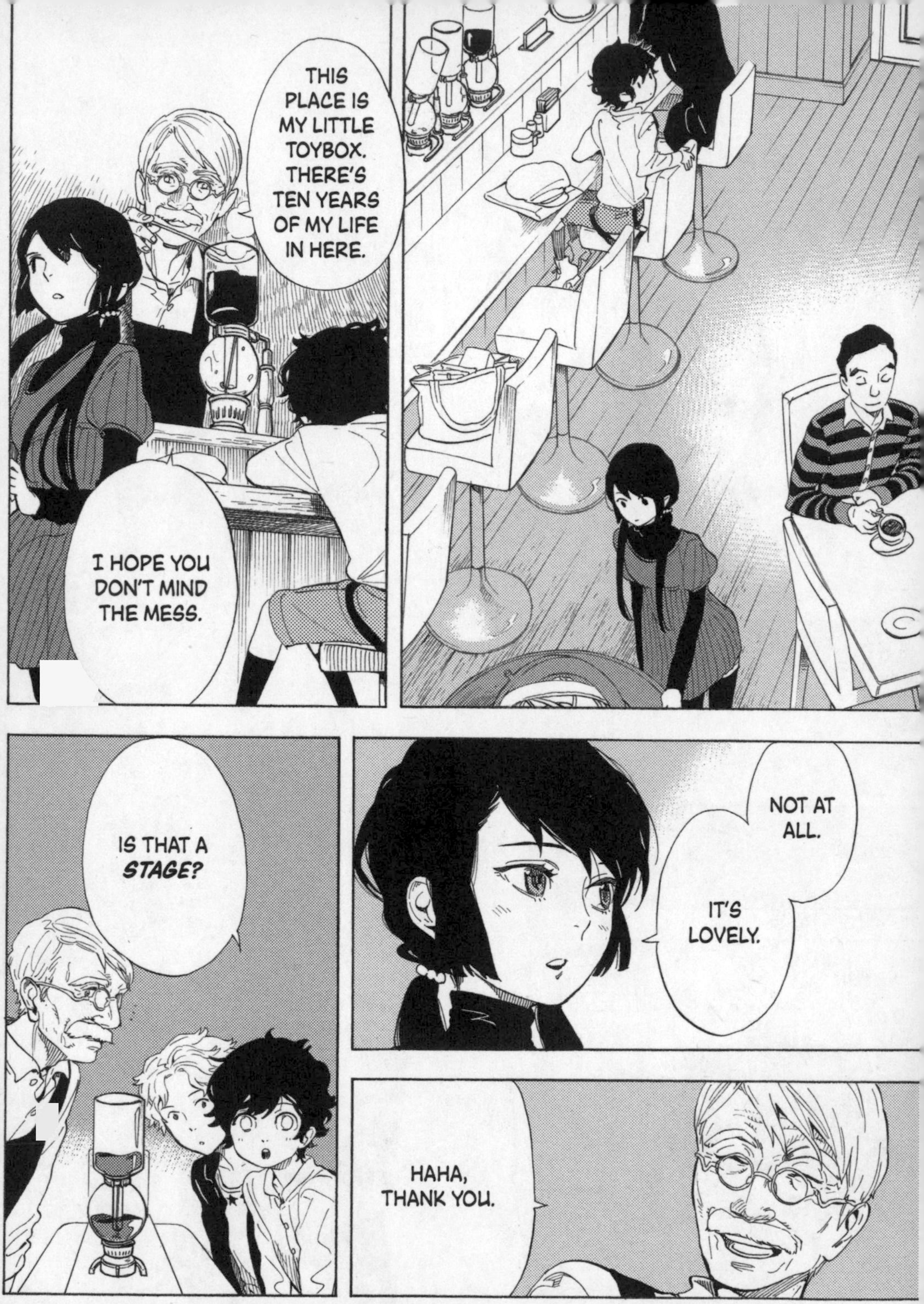
THIS PLACE IS MY LITTLE TOYBOX. THERE'S TEN YEARS OF MY LIFE IN HERE.
I HOPE YOU DON'T MIND THE MESS.
NOT AT ALL.
IT'S LOVELY.
HAHA, THANK YOU.
IS THAT A *STAGE?*

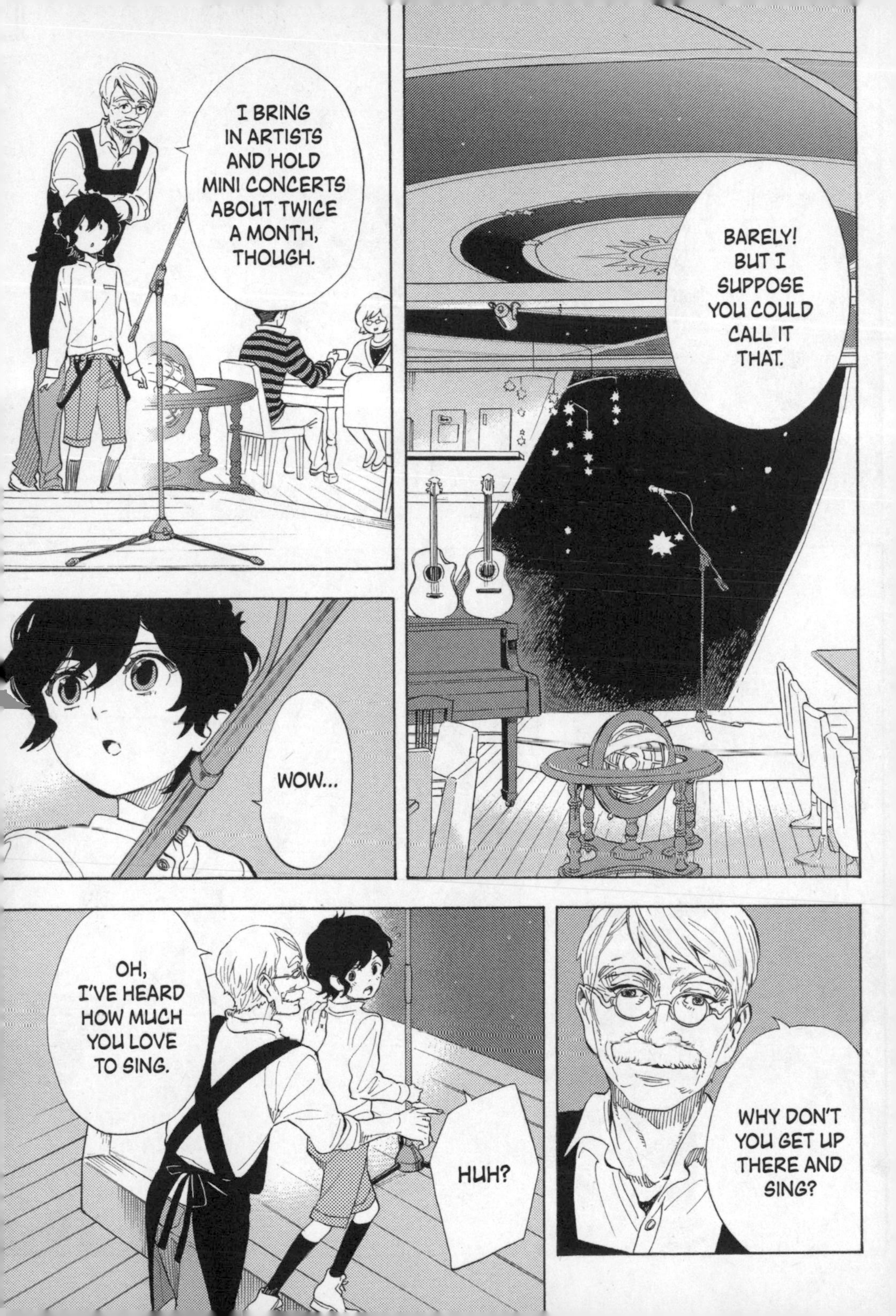
BARELY! BUT I SUPPOSE YOU COULD CALL IT THAT.
I BRING IN ARTISTS AND HOLD MINI CONCERTS ABOUT TWICE A MONTH, THOUGH.
WOW...
WHY DON'T YOU GET UP THERE AND SING?
OH, I'VE HEARD HOW MUCH YOU LOVE TO SING.
HUH?

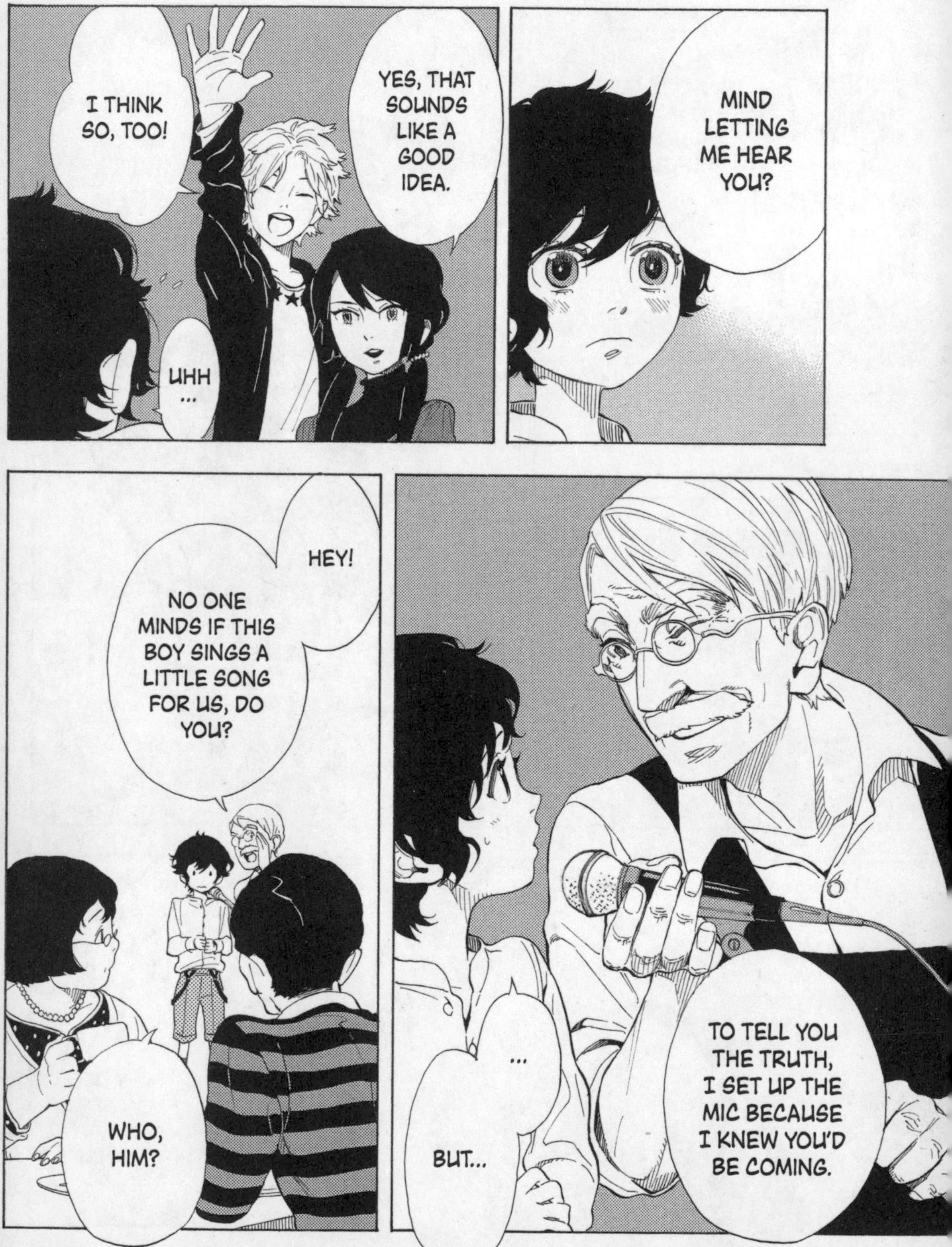
MIND LETTING ME HEAR YOU?
YES, THAT SOUNDS LIKE A GOOD IDEA.
I THINK SO, TOO!
UHH ...
TO TELL YOU THE TRUTH, I SET UP THE MIC BECAUSE I KNEW YOU'D BE COMING.
... BUT...
HEY! NO ONE MINDS IF THIS BOY SINGS A LITTLE SONG FOR US, DO YOU?
WHO, HIM?

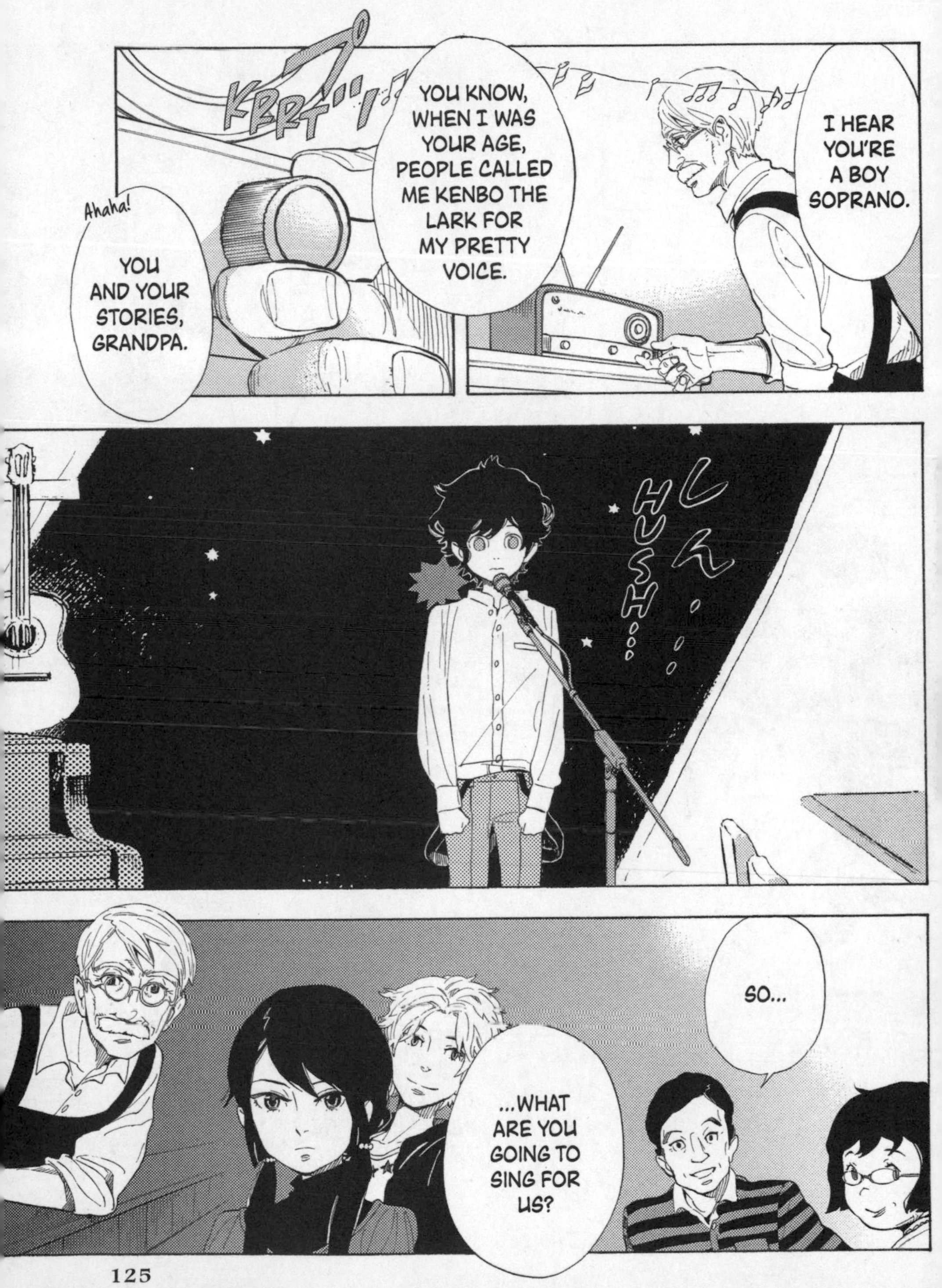
I HEAR YOU'RE A BOY SOPRANO.
YOU KNOW, WHEN I WAS YOUR AGE, PEOPLE CALLED ME KENBO THE LARK FOR MY PRETTY VOICE.
KRRT
Ahaha!
YOU AND YOUR STORIES, GRANDPA.
HUSH...
SO...
...WHAT ARE YOU GOING TO SING FOR US?

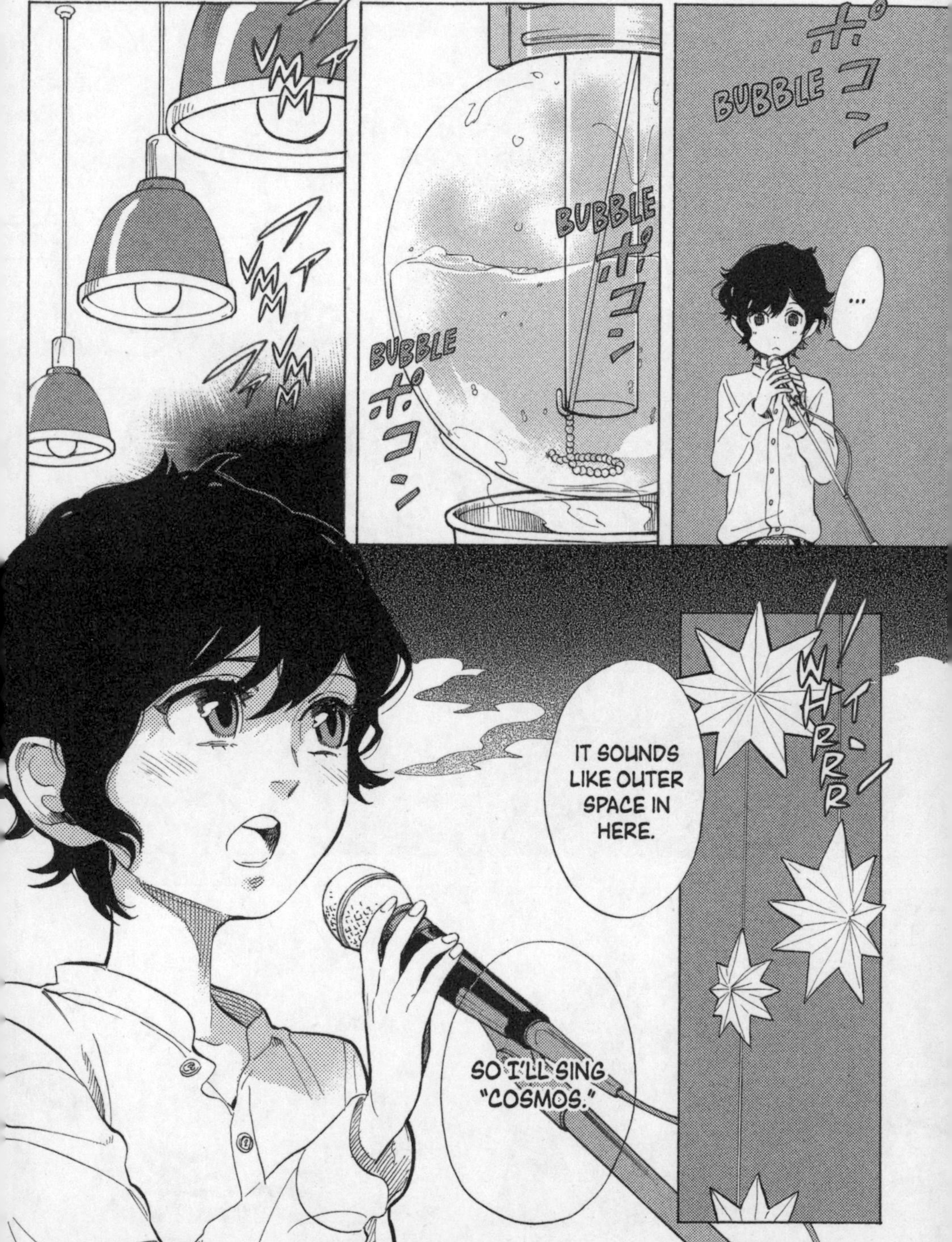
BUBBLE
…
BUBBLE
BUBBLE
VMM
VMM
VMM
WHRRR
!!
IT SOUNDS LIKE OUTER SPACE IN HERE.
SO I'LL SING "COSMOS."

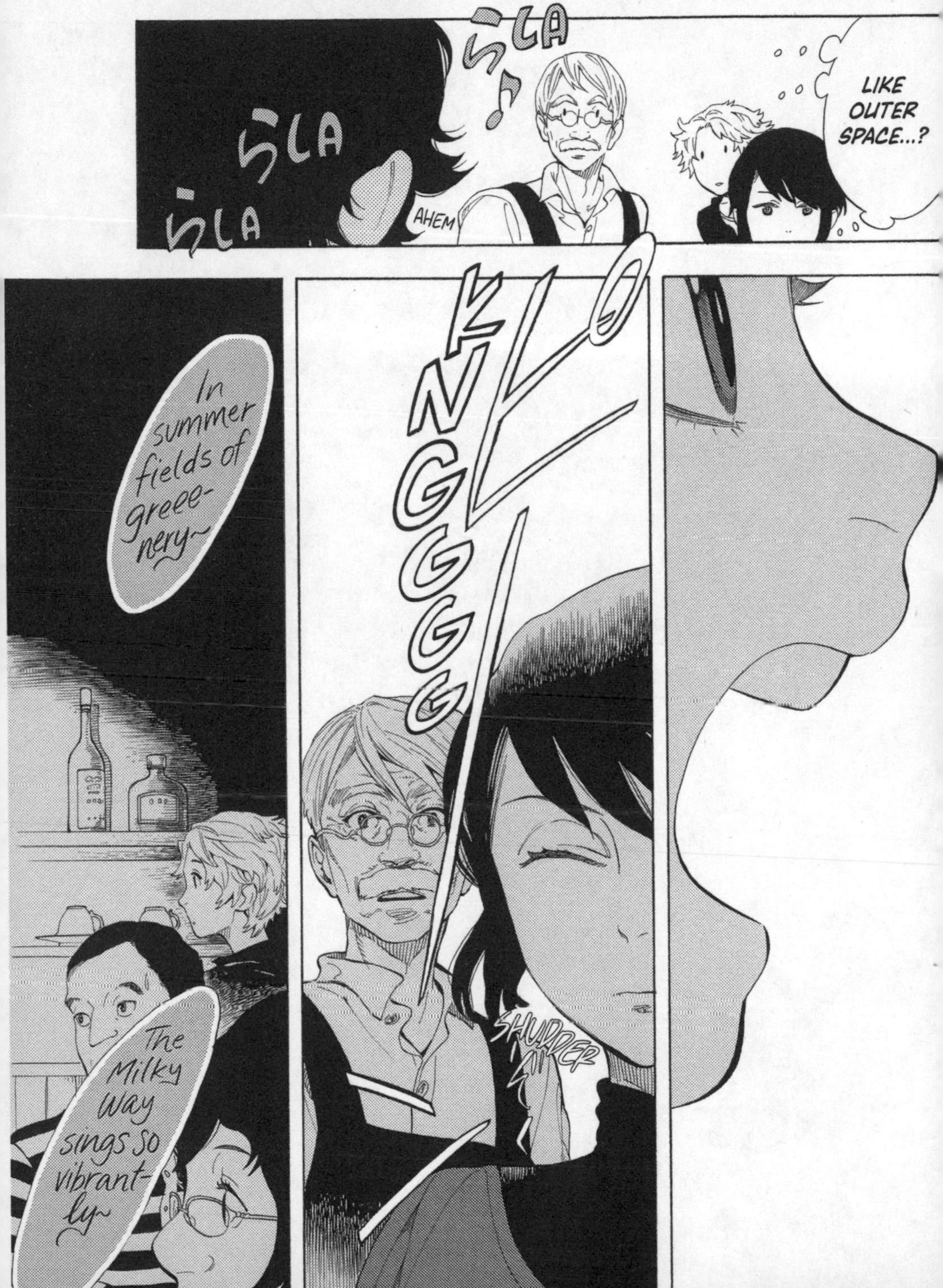
LIKE OUTER SPACE...?
らLA
らLA
AHEM
らLA
KLONGGGG
SHUDDER
In summer fields of greee-nery~
The Milky way sings so vibrant-ly~

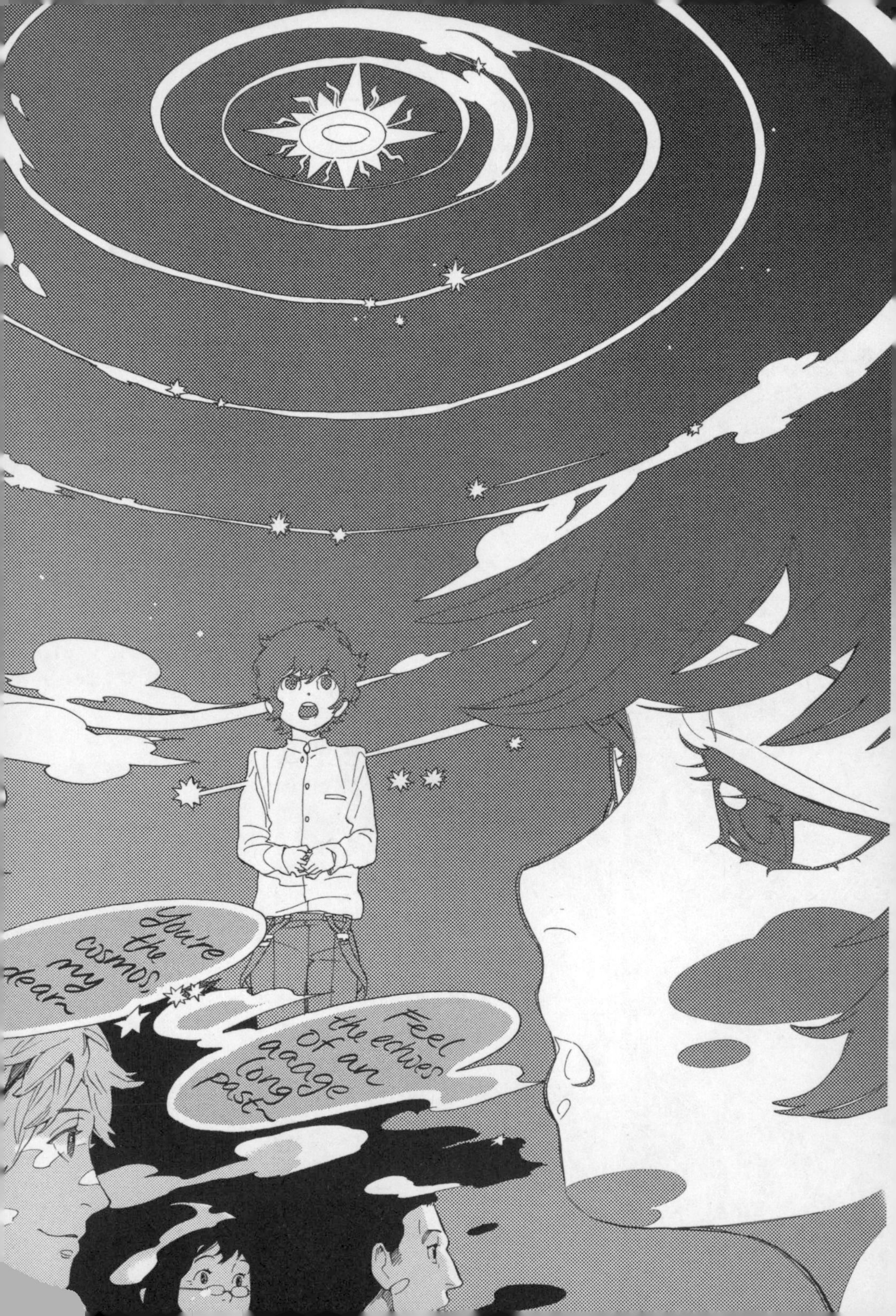
You're the cosmos, my dear~
Feel the echoes of an aaage long past~

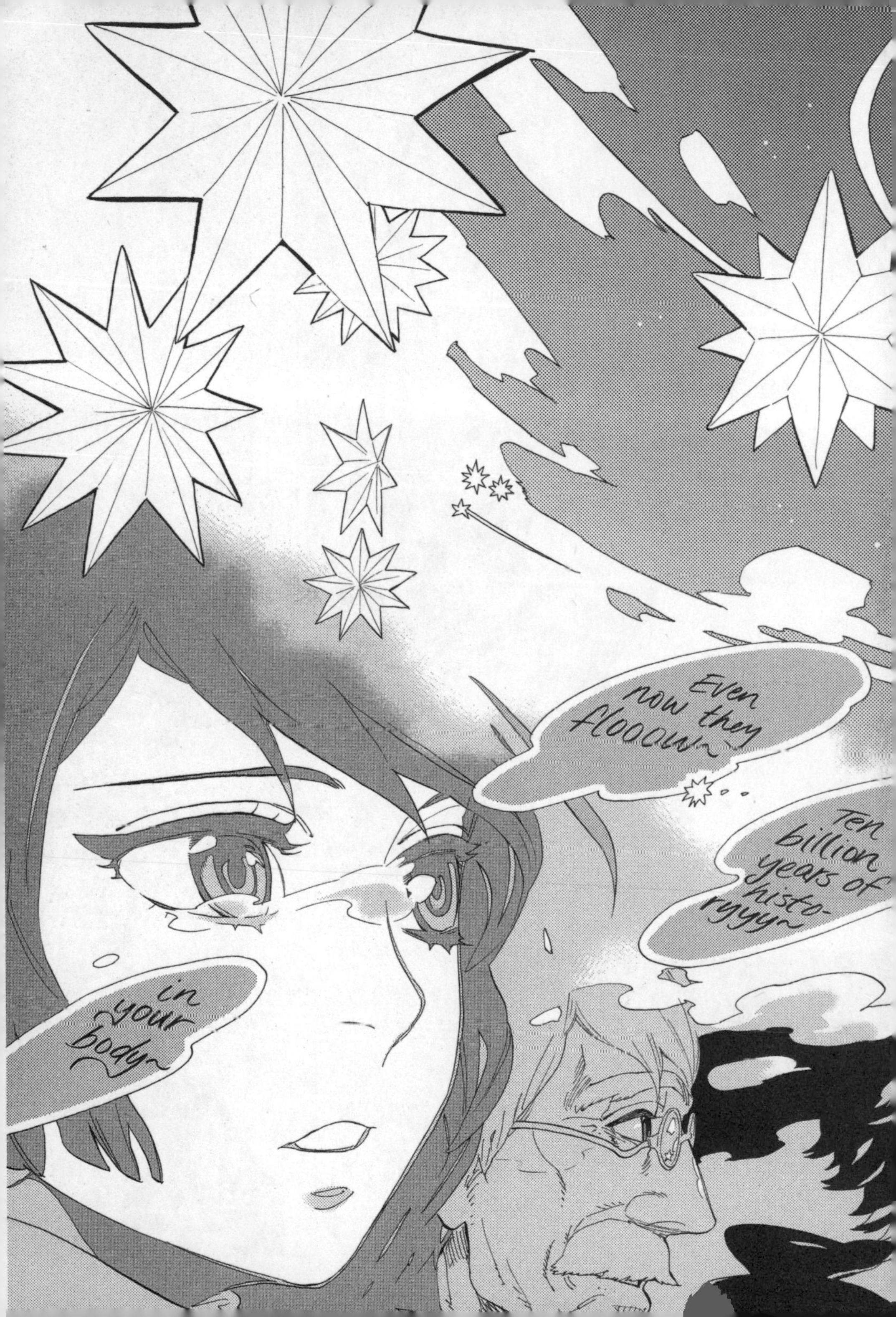
Ten billion years of histo-ryyy~
Even now they flooow~
in your body~

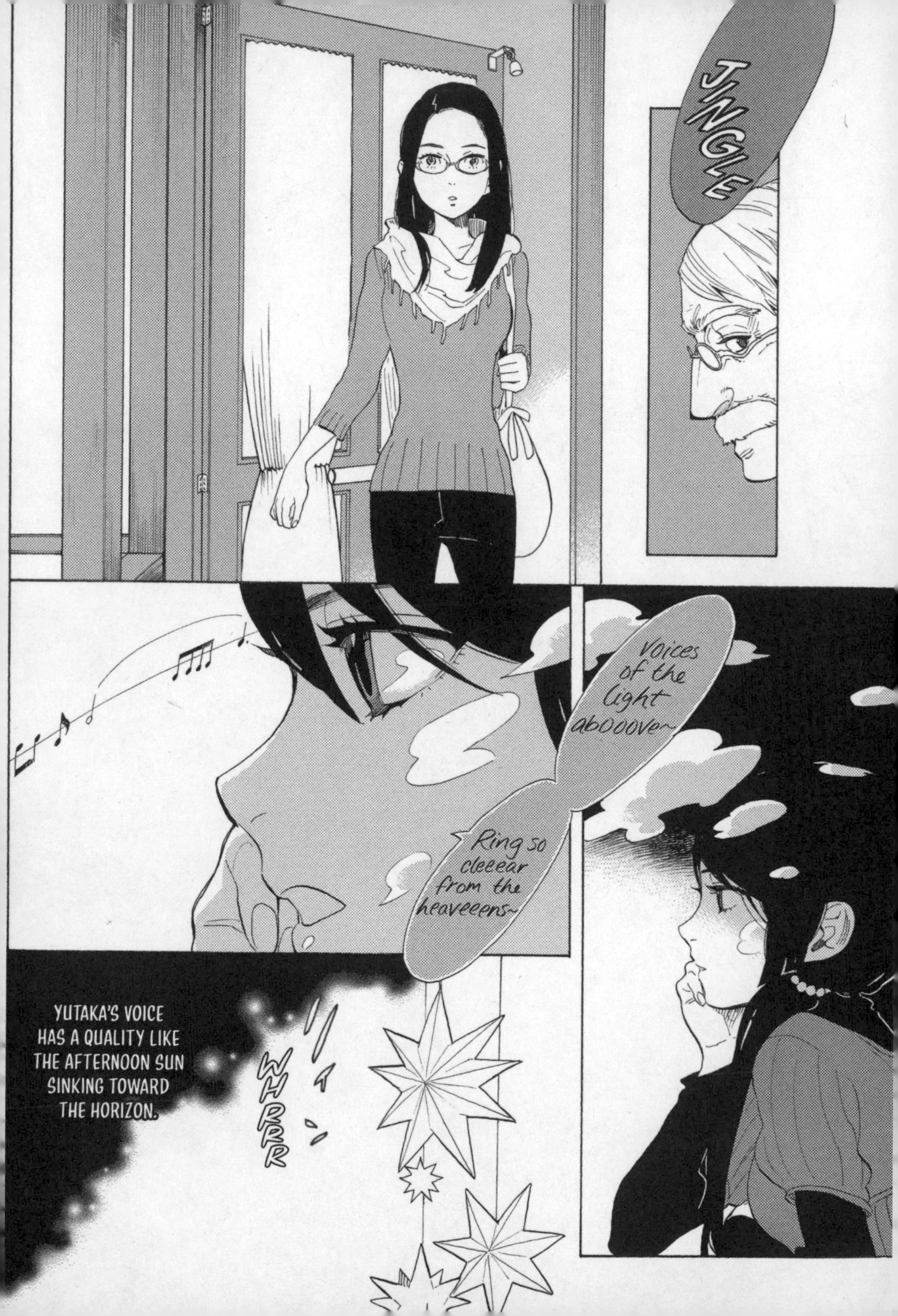
JINGLE
Voices of the light aboooove~
Ring so cleeear from the heaveeens~
WHRRR
YUTAKA'S VOICE HAS A QUALITY LIKE THE AFTERNOON SUN SINKING TOWARD THE HORIZON.

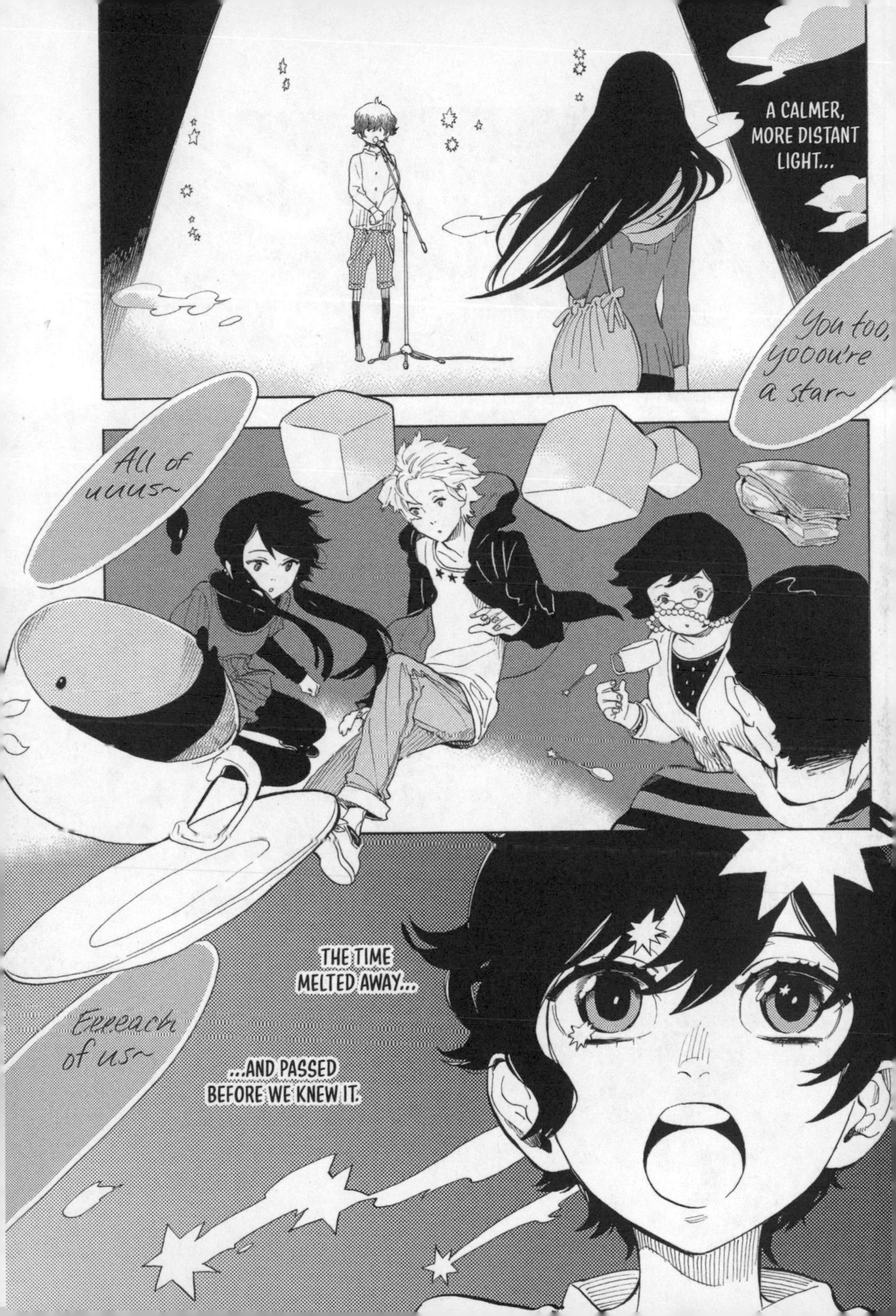
A CALMER, MORE DISTANT LIGHT...
You too, yooou're a star~
All of uuus~
THE TIME MELTED AWAY...
...AND PASSED BEFORE WE KNEW IT.
Eeeeach of us~

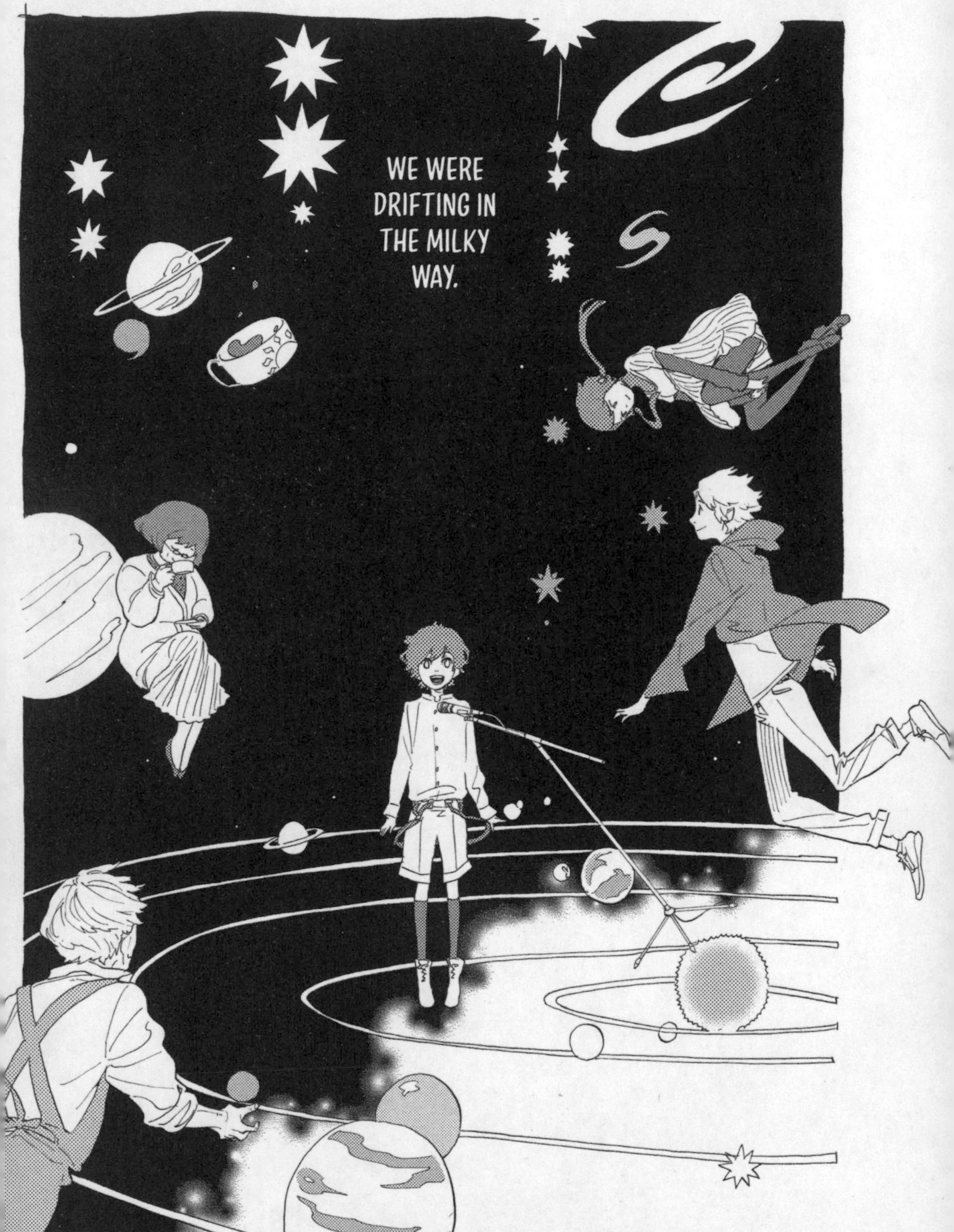
WE WERE DRIFTING IN THE MILKY WAY.

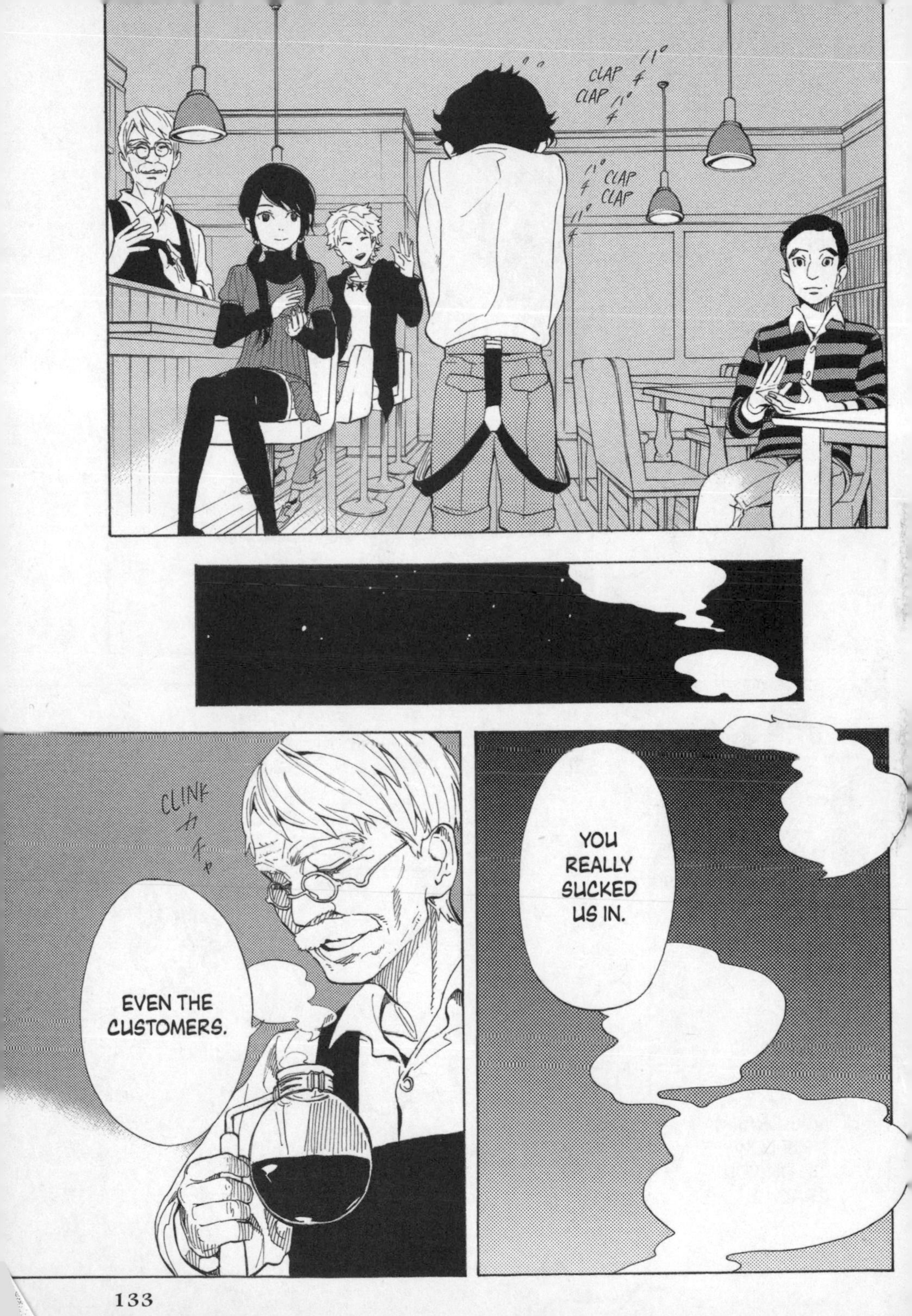
CLAP
CLAP
CLAP
CLAP
YOU REALLY SUCKED US IN.
CLINK
カチャ
EVEN THE CUSTOMERS.

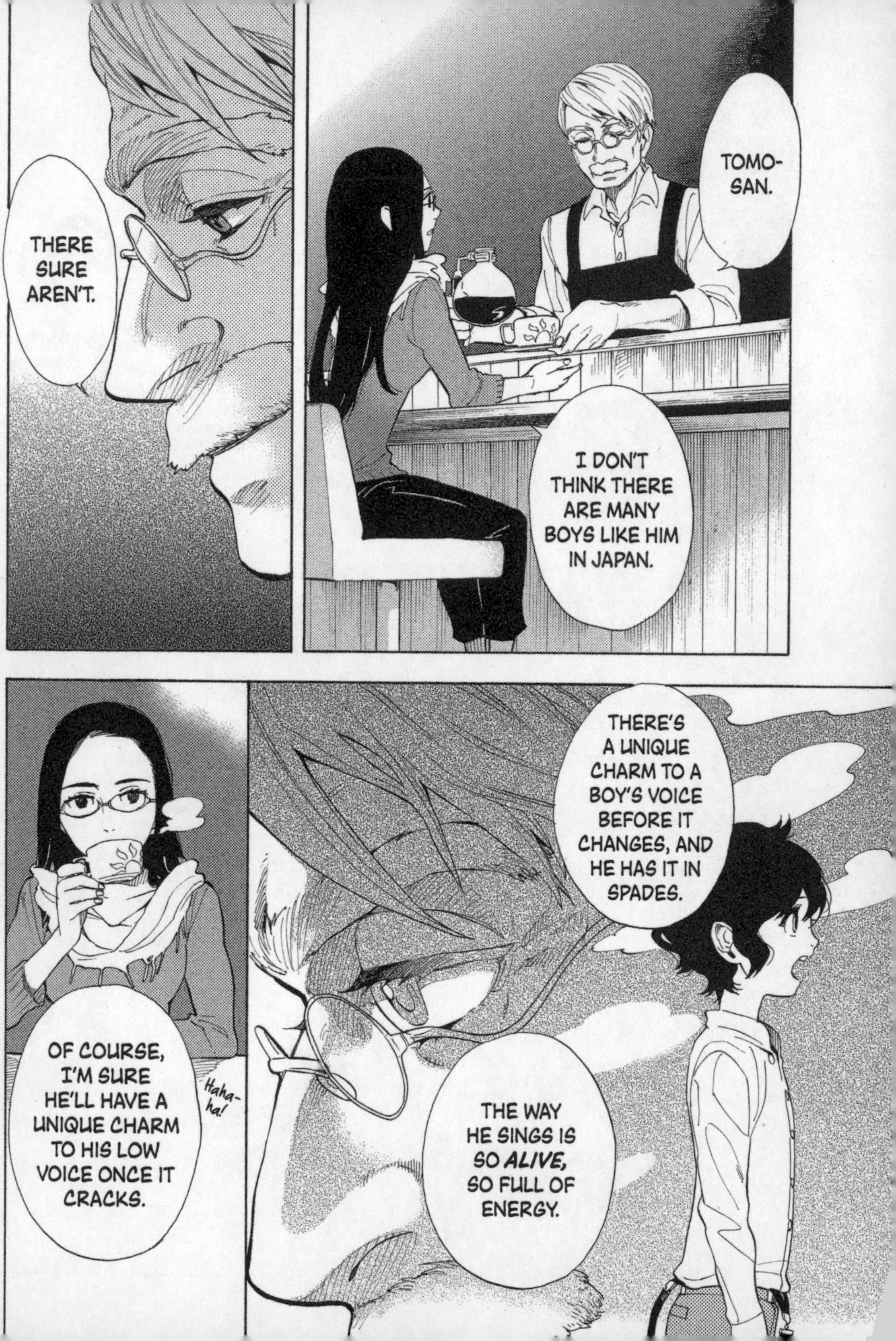
TOMO-SAN.
I DON'T THINK THERE ARE MANY BOYS LIKE HIM IN JAPAN.
THERE SURE AREN'T.
THERE'S A UNIQUE CHARM TO A BOY'S VOICE BEFORE IT CHANGES, AND HE HAS IT IN SPADES.
THE WAY HE SINGS IS SO ALIVE, SO FULL OF ENERGY.
OF COURSE, I'M SURE HE'LL HAVE A UNIQUE CHARM TO HIS LOW VOICE ONCE IT CRACKS.
Haha-ha!

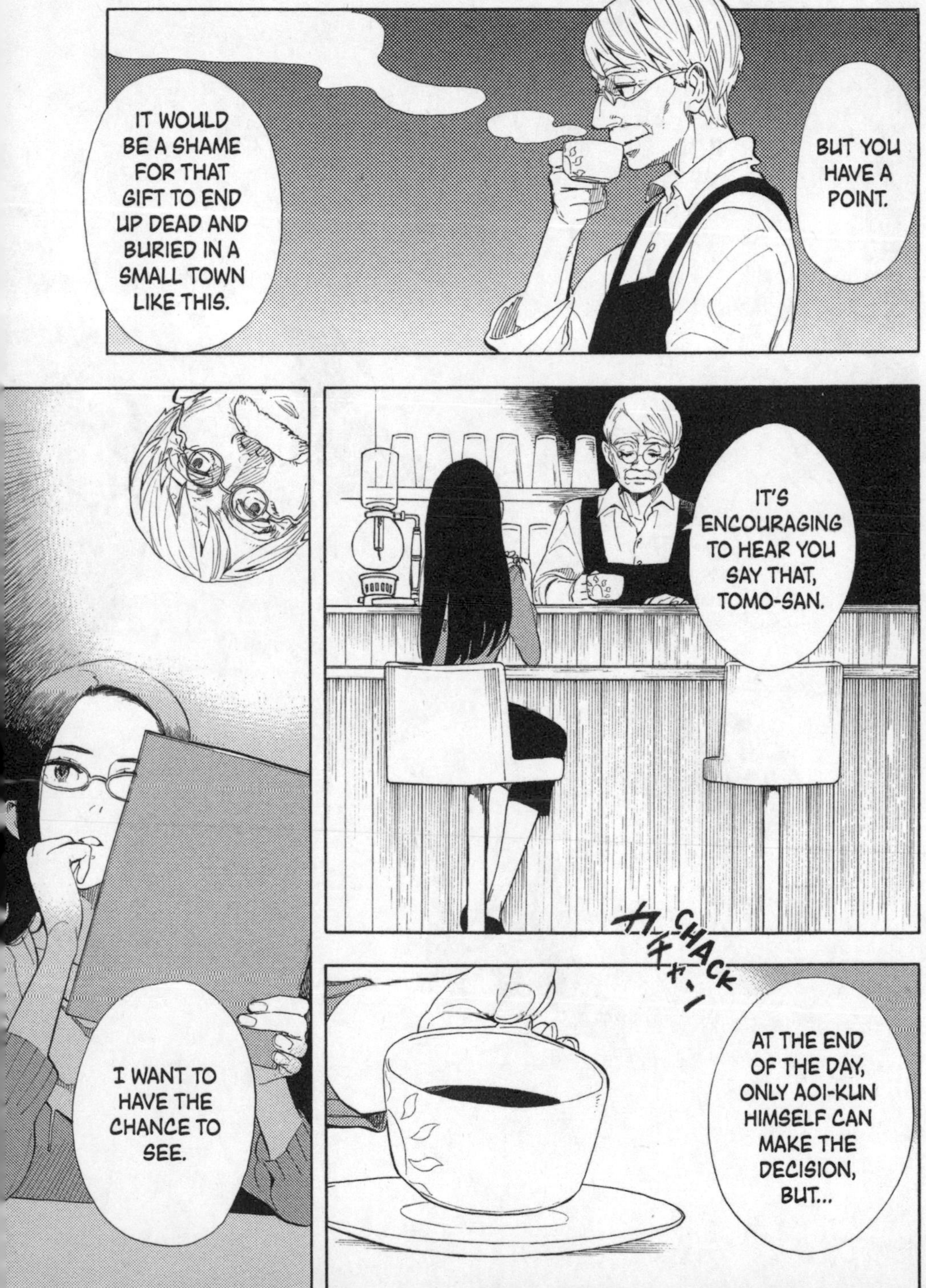
BUT YOU HAVE A POINT.
IT WOULD BE A SHAME FOR THAT GIFT TO END UP DEAD AND BURIED IN A SMALL TOWN LIKE THIS.
IT'S ENCOURAGING TO HEAR YOU SAY THAT, TOMO-SAN.
CHACK
AT THE END OF THE DAY, ONLY AOI-KUN HIMSELF CAN MAKE THE DECISION, BUT...
I WANT TO HAVE THE CHANCE TO SEE.

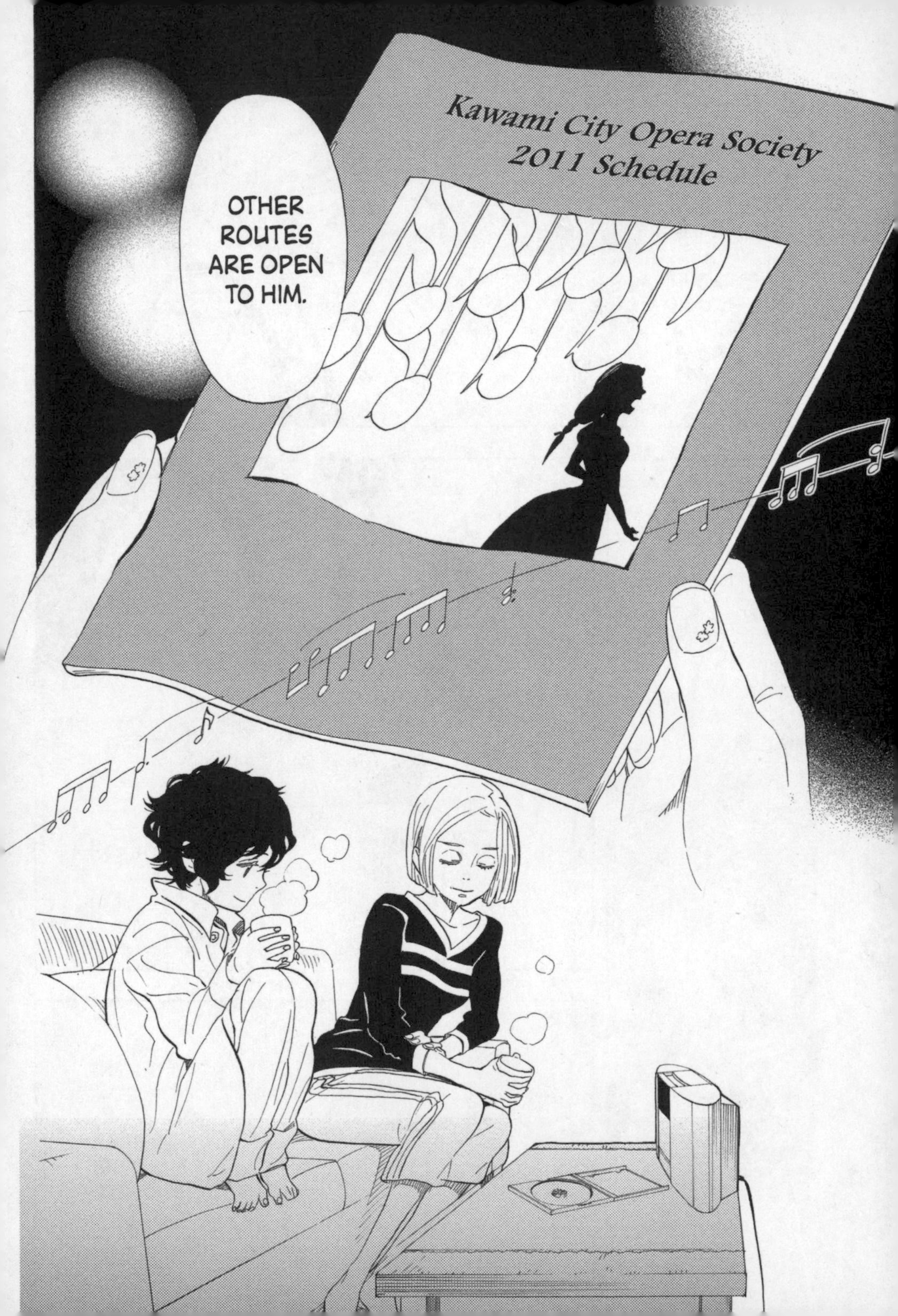
Kawami City Opera Society
2011 Schedule
OTHER ROUTES ARE OPEN TO HIM.

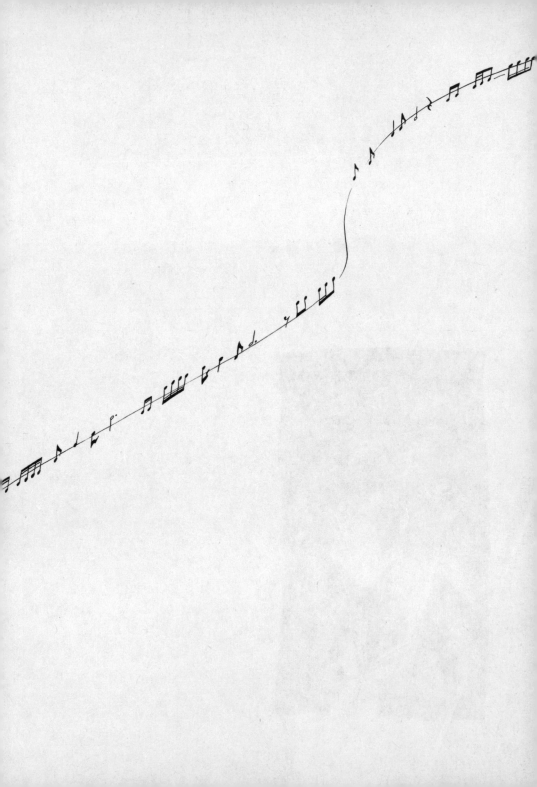

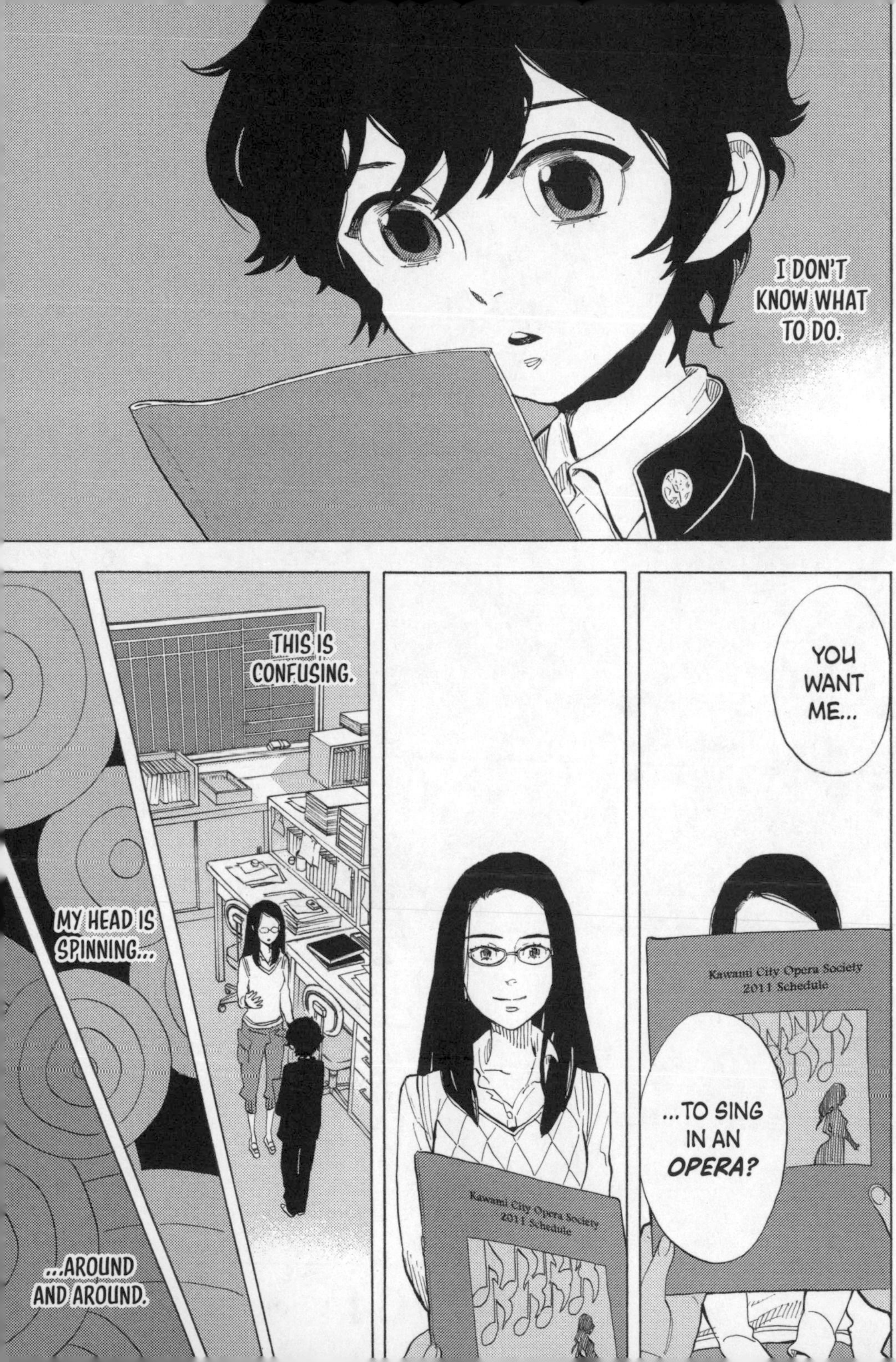
I DON'T KNOW WHAT TO DO.
YOU WANT ME...
Kawami City Opera Society 2011 Schedule
...TO SING IN AN *OPERA?*
Kawami City Opera Society 2011 Schedule
THIS IS CONFUSING.
MY HEAD IS SPINNING...
...AROUND AND AROUND.

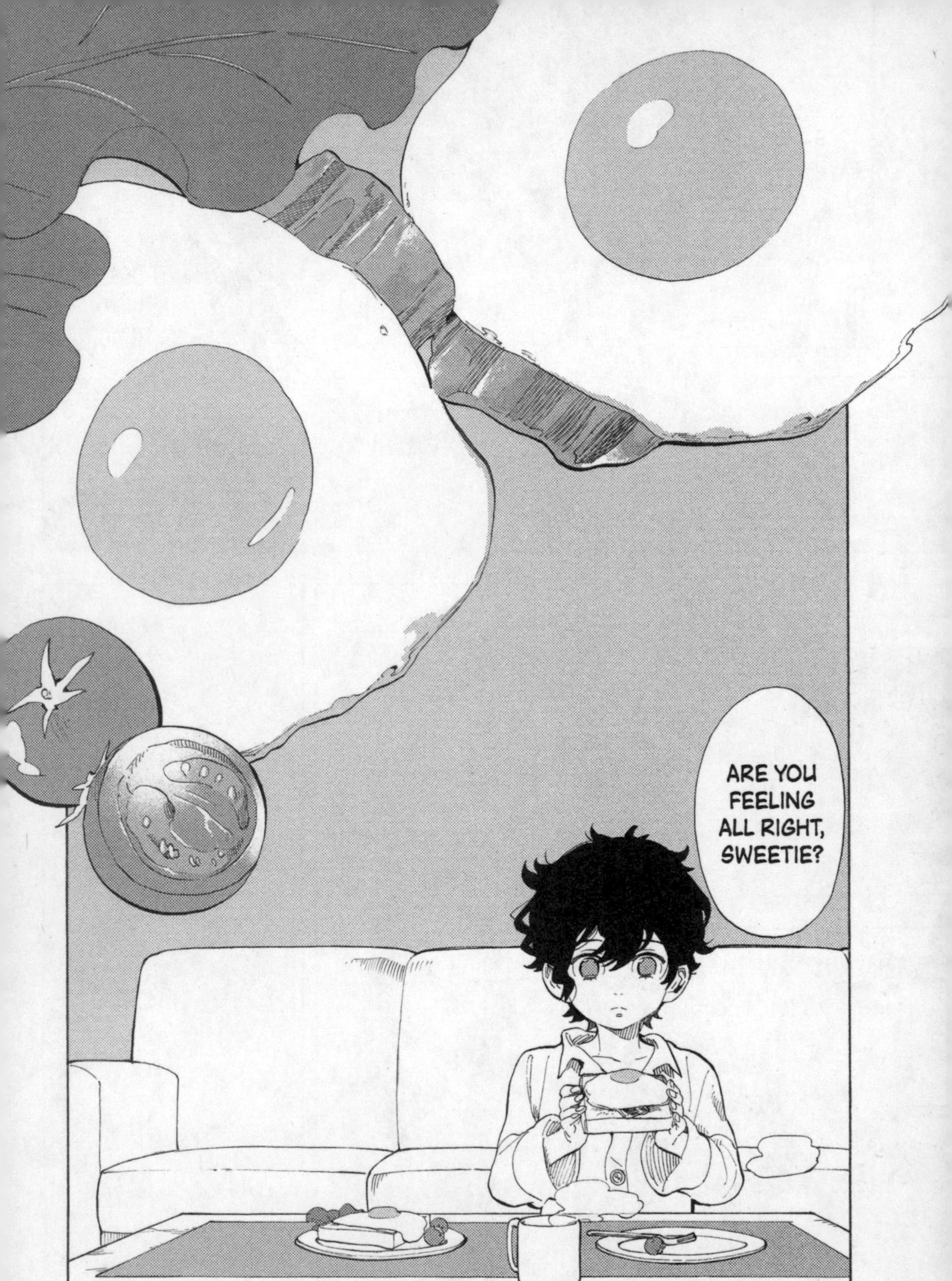
ARE YOU FEELING ALL RIGHT, SWEETIE?

note 𝄢: 04 Choir and Song

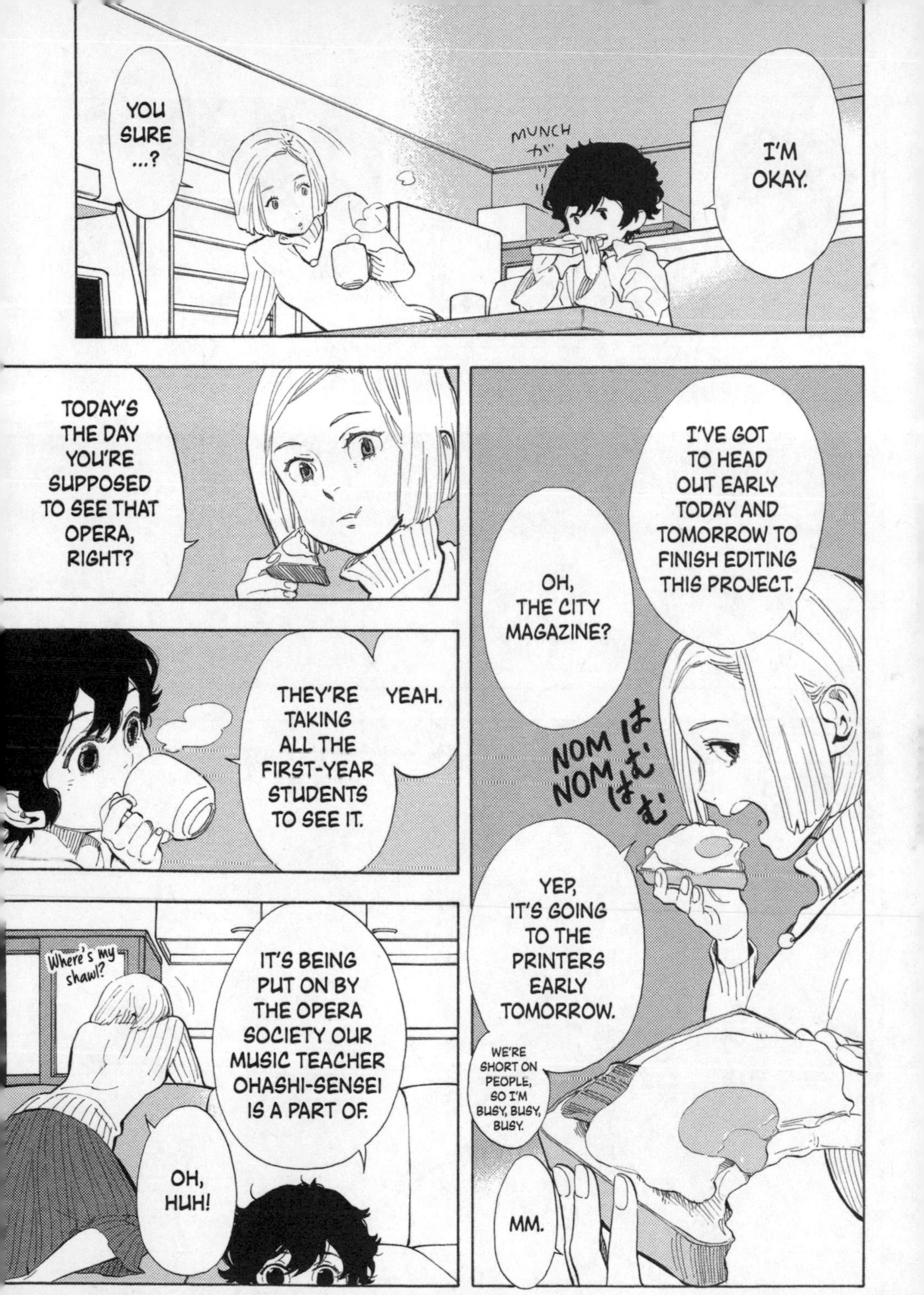
I'M OKAY.
MUNCH
YOU SURE ...?
I'VE GOT TO HEAD OUT EARLY TODAY AND TOMORROW TO FINISH EDITING THIS PROJECT.
OH, THE CITY MAGAZINE?
NOM NOM はむはむ
YEP, IT'S GOING TO THE PRINTERS EARLY TOMORROW.
WE'RE SHORT ON PEOPLE, SO I'M BUSY, BUSY, BUSY.
MM.
TODAY'S THE DAY YOU'RE SUPPOSED TO SEE THAT OPERA, RIGHT?
YEAH.
THEY'RE TAKING ALL THE FIRST-YEAR STUDENTS TO SEE IT.
IT'S BEING PUT ON BY THE OPERA SOCIETY OUR MUSIC TEACHER OHASHI-SENSEI IS A PART OF.
Where's my shawl?
OH, HUH!

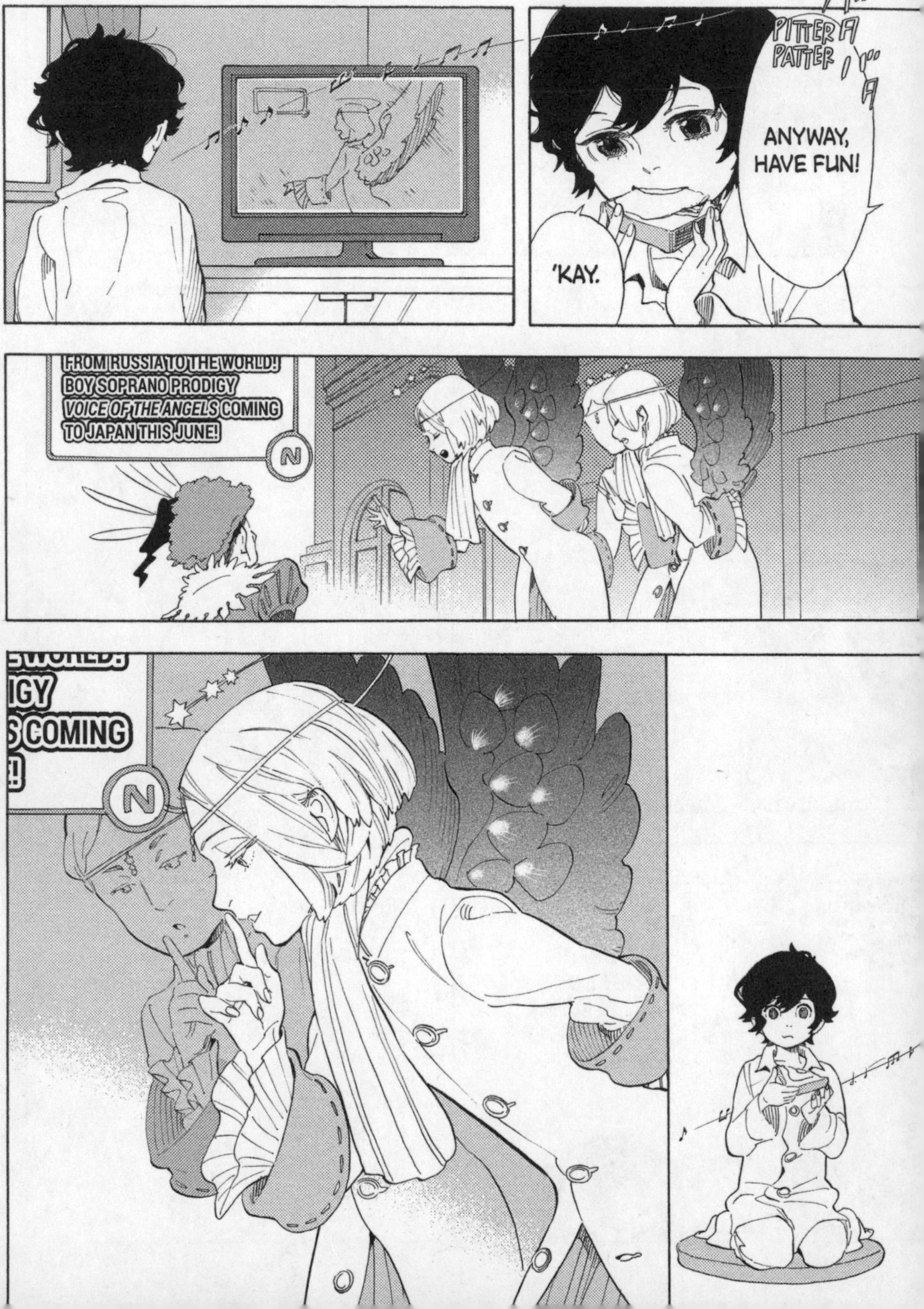
PITTER PATTER
ANYWAY, HAVE FUN!
'KAY.
FROM RUSSIA TO THE WORLD! BOY SOPRANO PRODIGY *VOICE OF THE ANGELS* COMING TO JAPAN THIS JUNE!

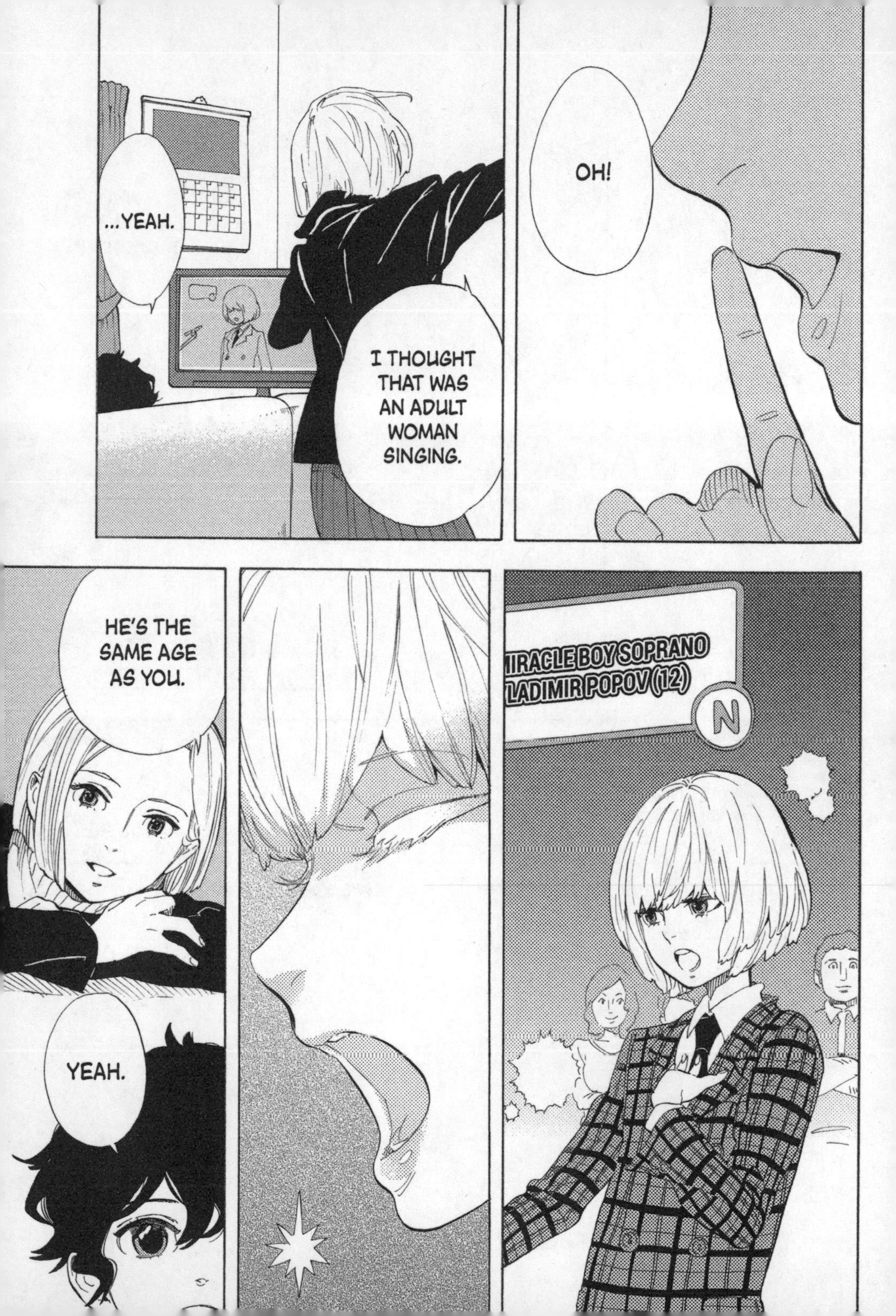
OH!
I THOUGHT THAT WAS AN ADULT WOMAN SINGING.
...YEAH.
MIRACLE BOY SOPRANO
LADIMIR POPOV (12)
N
HE'S THE SAME AGE AS YOU.
YEAH.

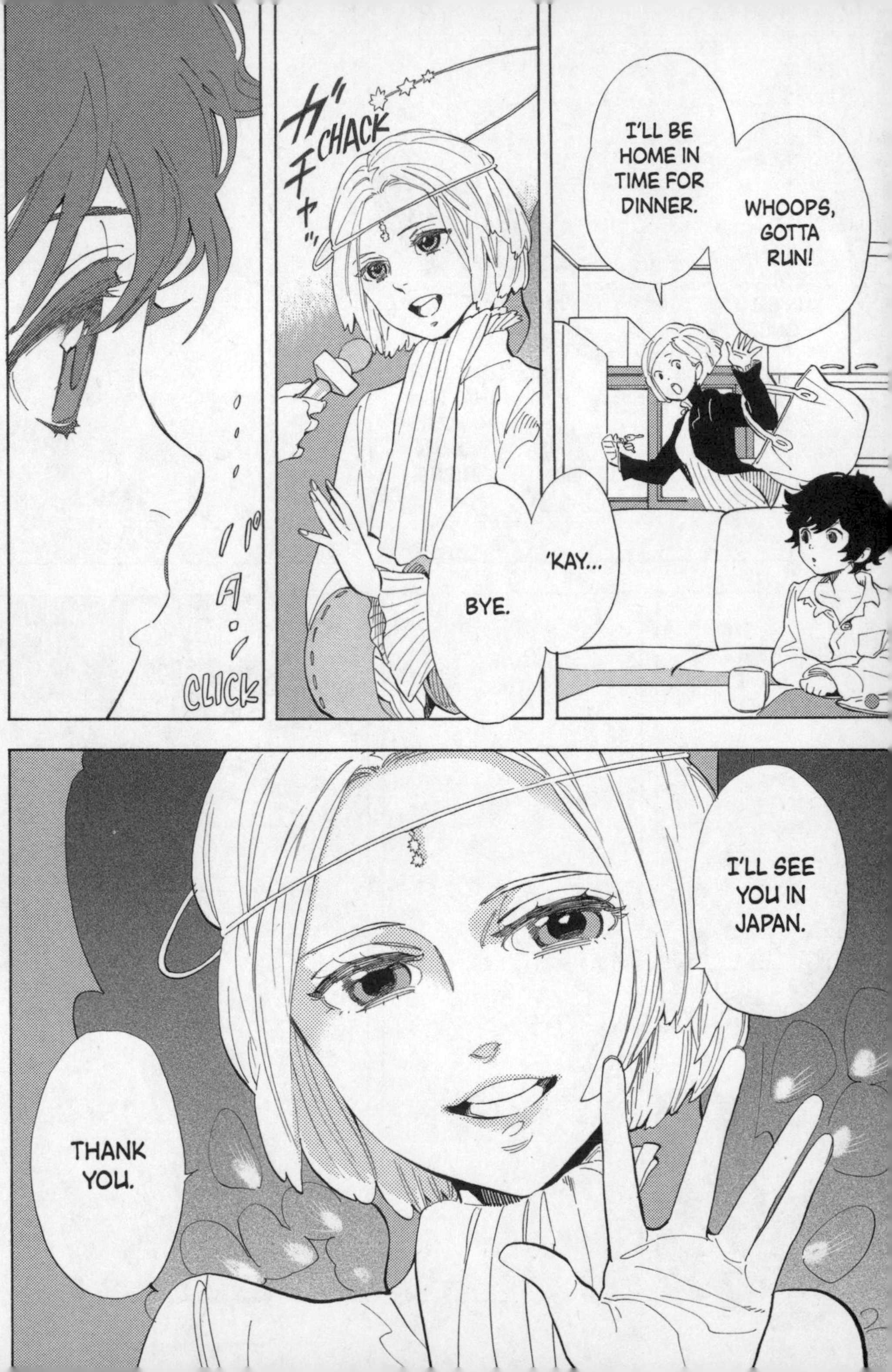
WHOOPS, GOTTA RUN!
I'LL BE HOME IN TIME FOR DINNER.
ガチャッ
CHACK
'KAY...
BYE.
A...
パ
CLICK
I'LL SEE YOU IN JAPAN.
THANK YOU.

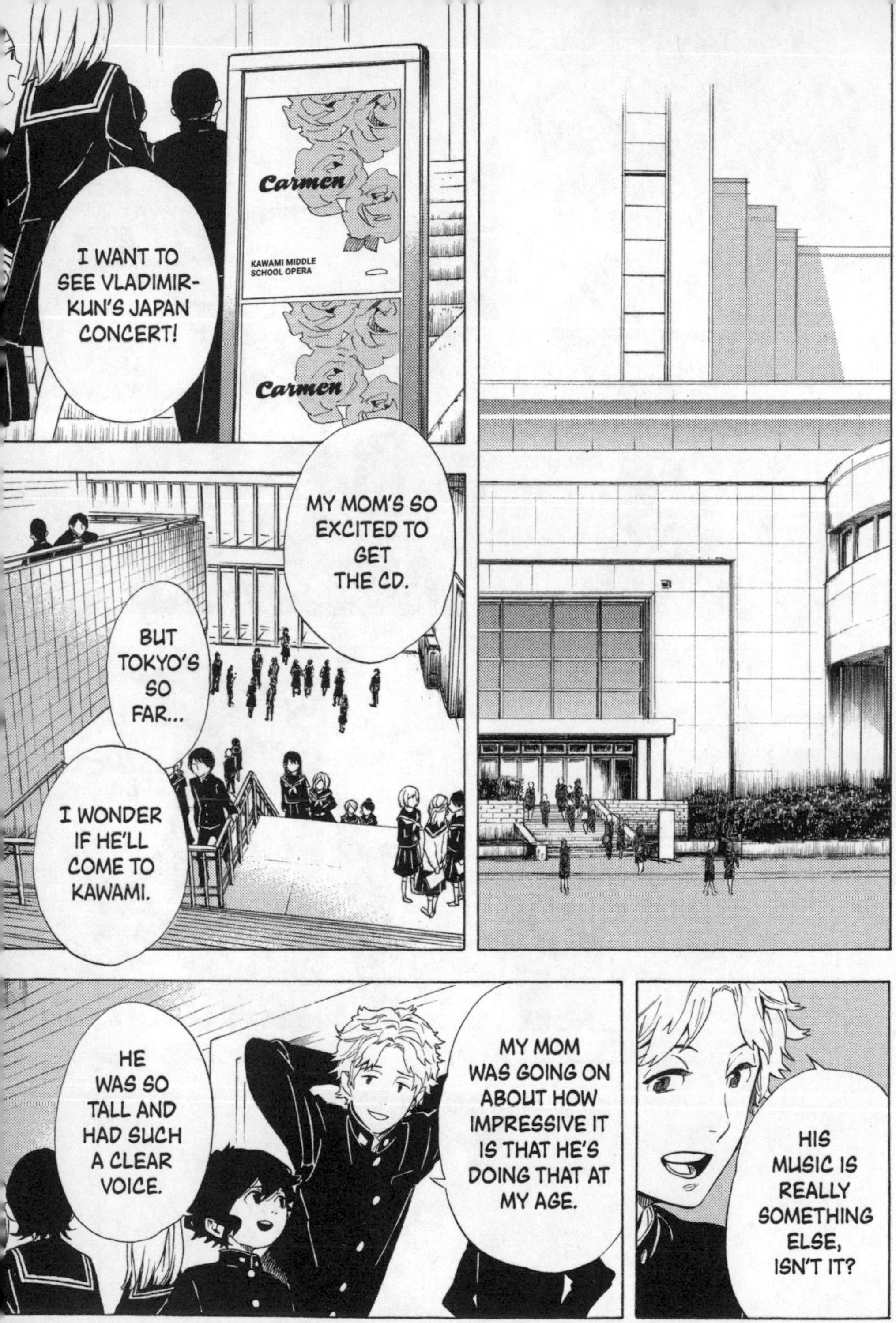
Carmen
KAWAMI MIDDLE SCHOOL OPERA
Carmen
I WANT TO SEE VLADIMIR-KUN'S JAPAN CONCERT!
MY MOM'S SO EXCITED TO GET THE CD.
BUT TOKYO'S SO FAR...
I WONDER IF HE'LL COME TO KAWAMI.
HIS MUSIC IS REALLY SOMETHING ELSE, ISN'T IT?
MY MOM WAS GOING ON ABOUT HOW IMPRESSIVE IT IS THAT HE'S DOING THAT AT MY AGE.
HE WAS SO TALL AND HAD SUCH A CLEAR VOICE.

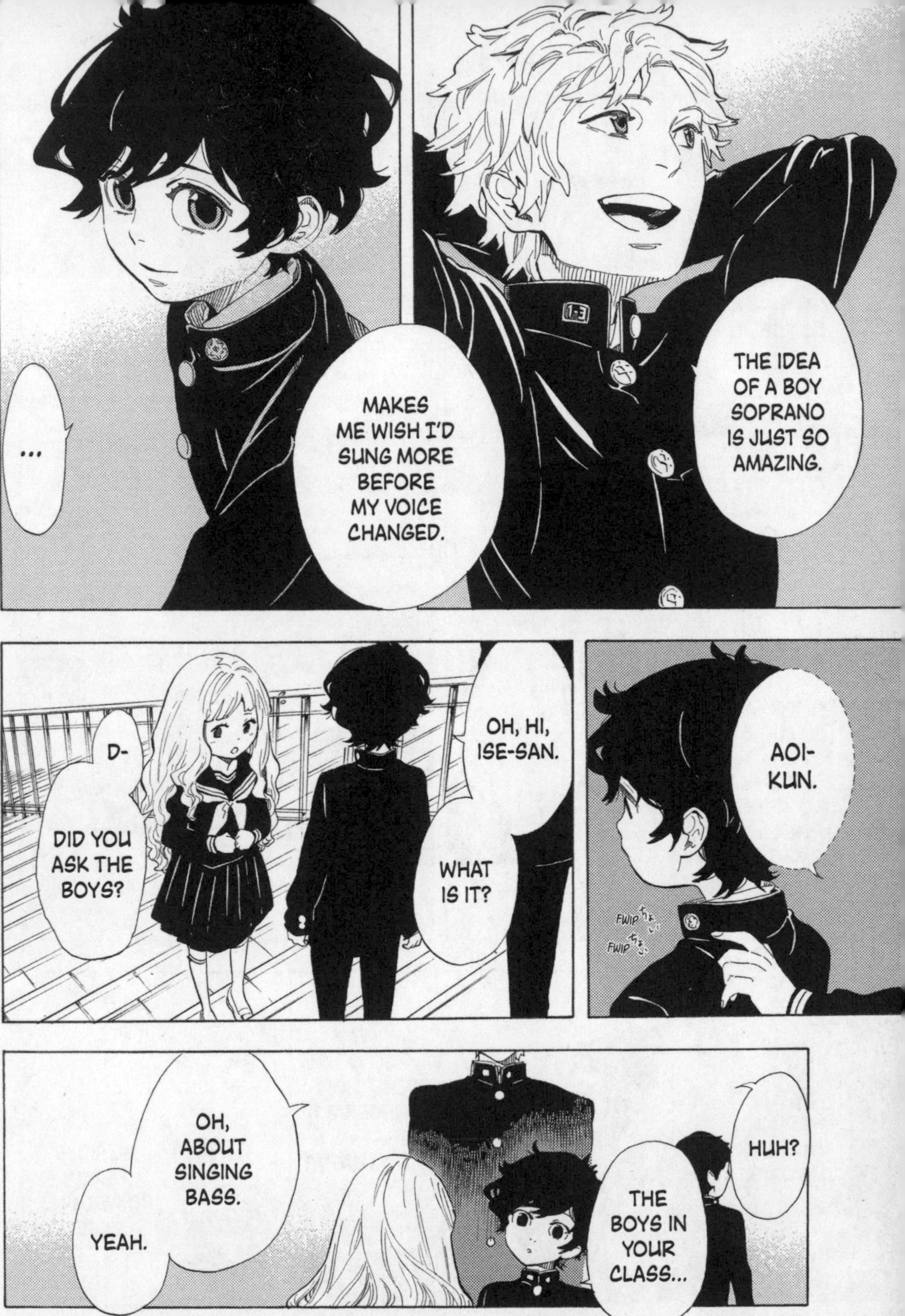
THE IDEA OF A BOY SOPRANO IS JUST SO AMAZING.
MAKES ME WISH I'D SUNG MORE BEFORE MY VOICE CHANGED.
...
AOI-KUN.
FWIP
FWIP
OH, HI, ISE-SAN.
WHAT IS IT?
D-
DID YOU ASK THE BOYS?
HUH?
THE BOYS IN YOUR CLASS...
OH, ABOUT SINGING BASS.
YEAH.

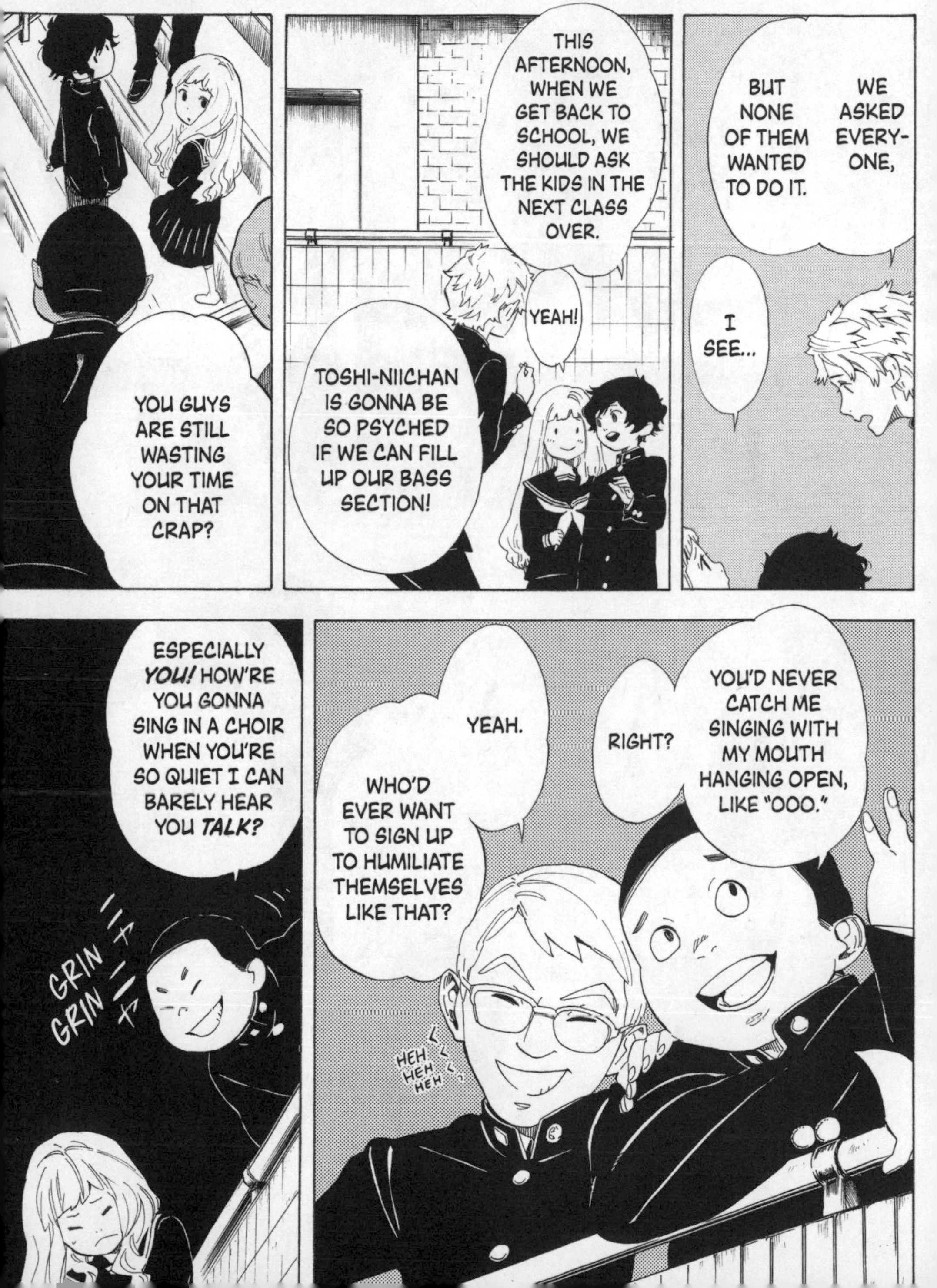
WE ASKED EVERYONE,
BUT NONE OF THEM WANTED TO DO IT.
I SEE...
THIS AFTERNOON, WHEN WE GET BACK TO SCHOOL, WE SHOULD ASK THE KIDS IN THE NEXT CLASS OVER.
YEAH!
TOSHI-NIICHAN IS GONNA BE SO PSYCHED IF WE CAN FILL UP OUR BASS SECTION!
YOU GUYS ARE STILL WASTING YOUR TIME ON THAT CRAP?
YOU'D NEVER CATCH ME SINGING WITH MY MOUTH HANGING OPEN, LIKE "OOO."
RIGHT?
YEAH.
WHO'D EVER WANT TO SIGN UP TO HUMILIATE THEMSELVES LIKE THAT?
HEH HEH HEH
ESPECIALLY *YOU!* HOW'RE YOU GONNA SING IN A CHOIR WHEN YOU'RE SO QUIET I CAN BARELY HEAR YOU *TALK?*
GRIN GRIN

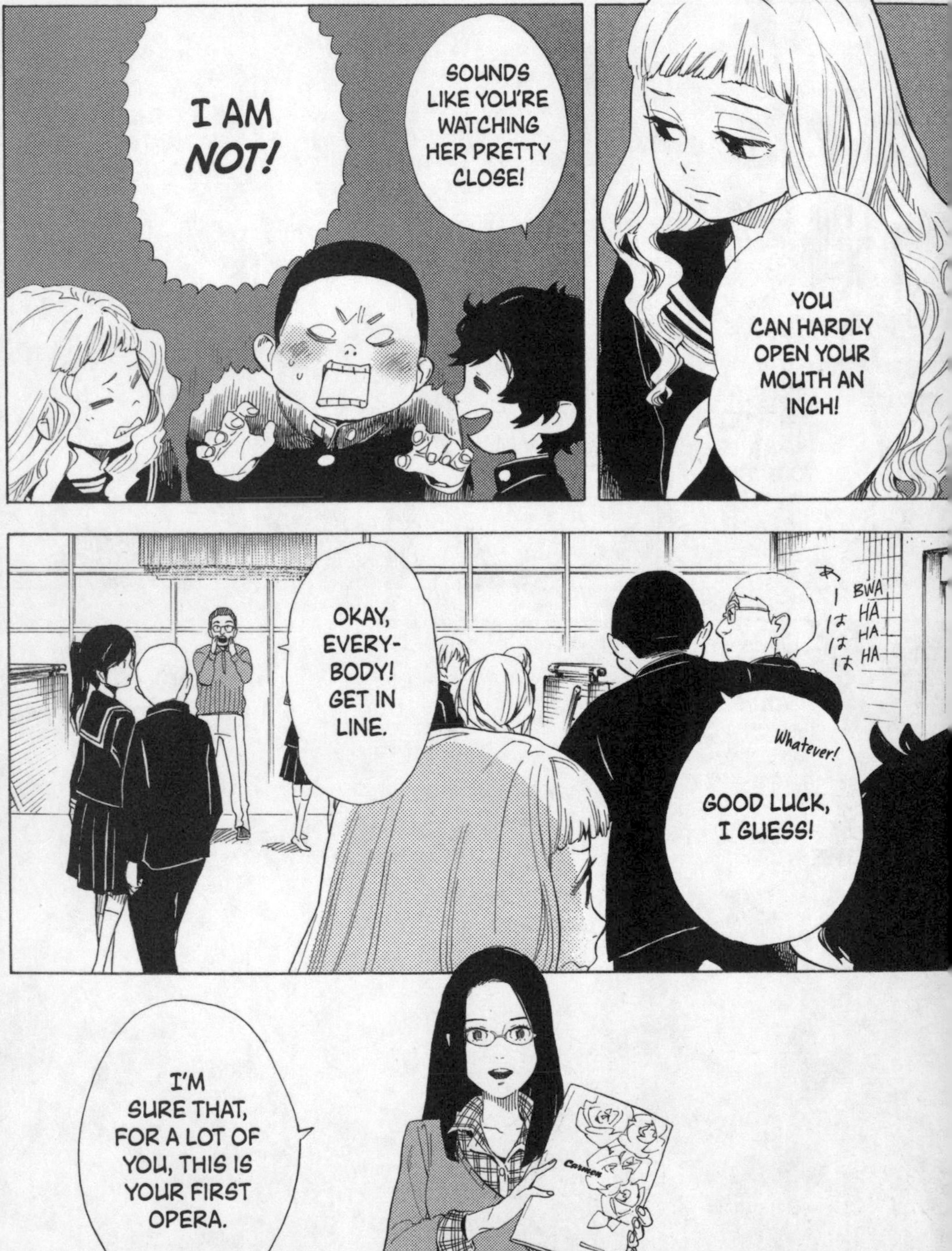
YOU CAN HARDLY OPEN YOUR MOUTH AN INCH!
SOUNDS LIKE YOU'RE WATCHING HER PRETTY CLOSE!
I AM *NOT!*
あーははは
BWA HA HA HA
Whatever!
GOOD LUCK, I GUESS!
OKAY, EVERYBODY! GET IN LINE.
Carmen
I'M SURE THAT, FOR A LOT OF YOU, THIS IS YOUR FIRST OPERA.

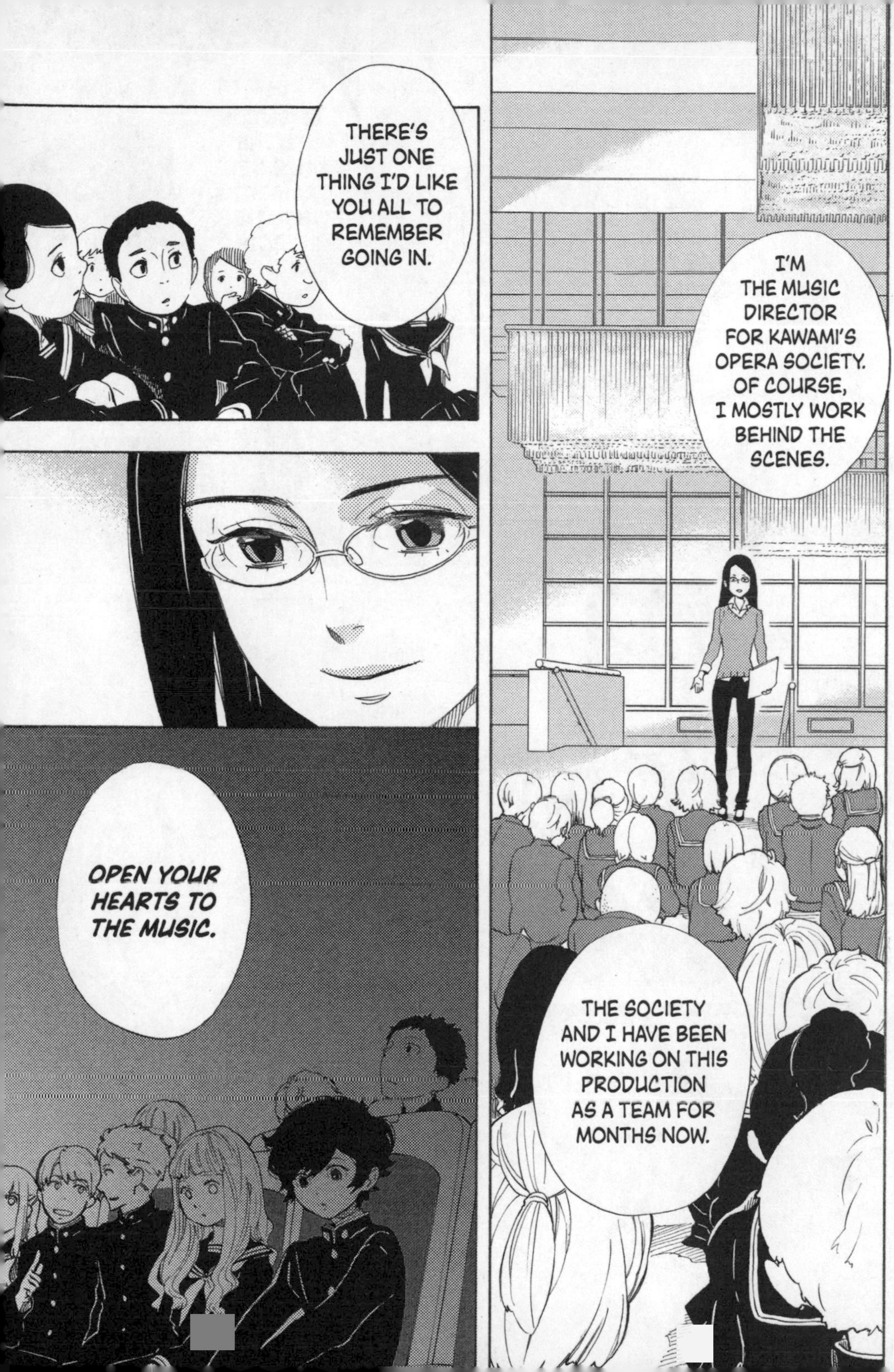
I'M THE MUSIC DIRECTOR FOR KAWAMI'S OPERA SOCIETY. OF COURSE, I MOSTLY WORK BEHIND THE SCENES.
THE SOCIETY AND I HAVE BEEN WORKING ON THIS PRODUCTION AS A TEAM FOR MONTHS NOW.
THERE'S JUST ONE THING I'D LIKE YOU ALL TO REMEMBER GOING IN.
OPEN YOUR HEARTS TO THE MUSIC.

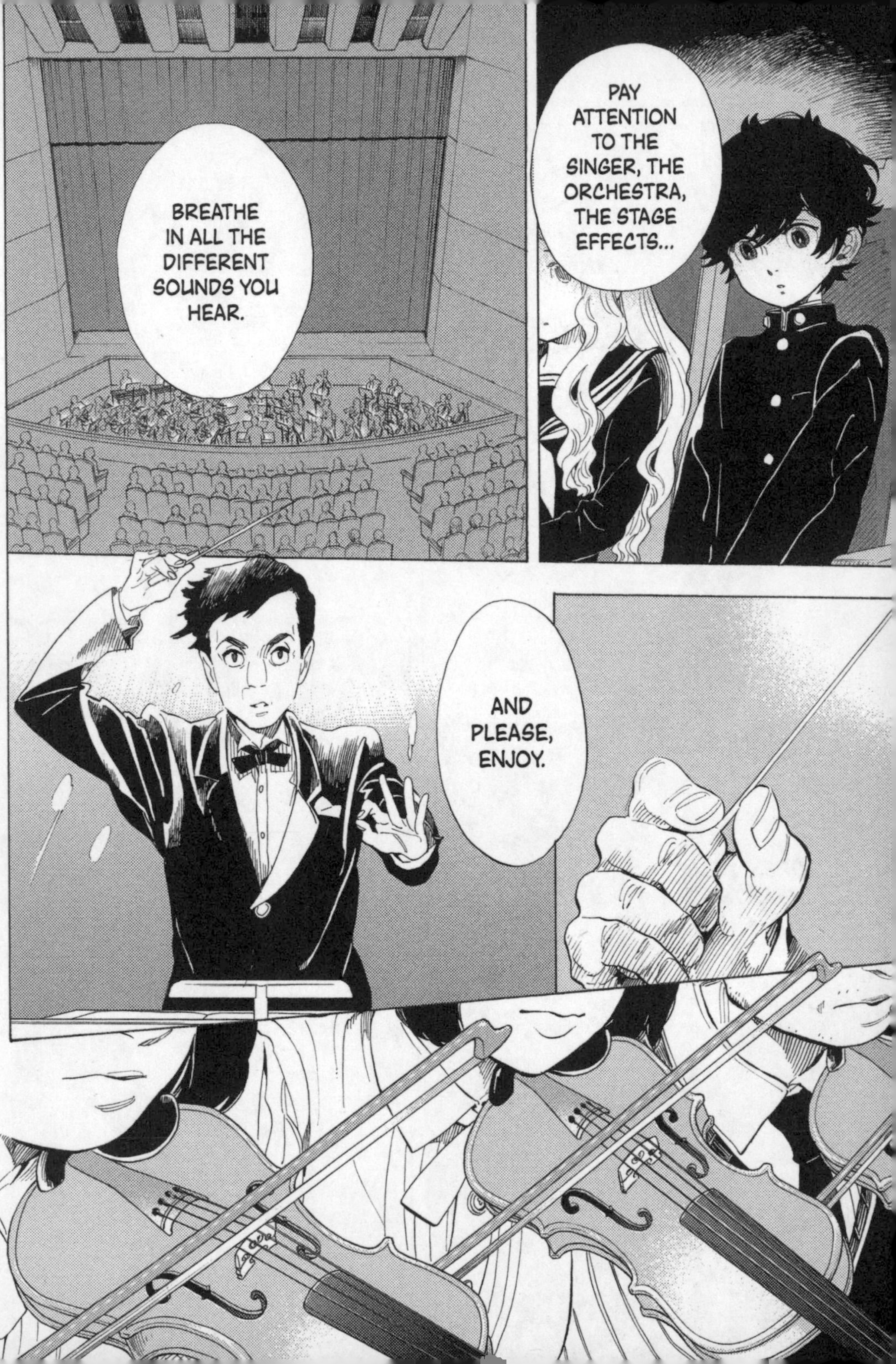
PAY ATTENTION TO THE SINGER, THE ORCHESTRA, THE STAGE EFFECTS...
BREATHE IN ALL THE DIFFERENT SOUNDS YOU HEAR.
AND PLEASE, ENJOY.

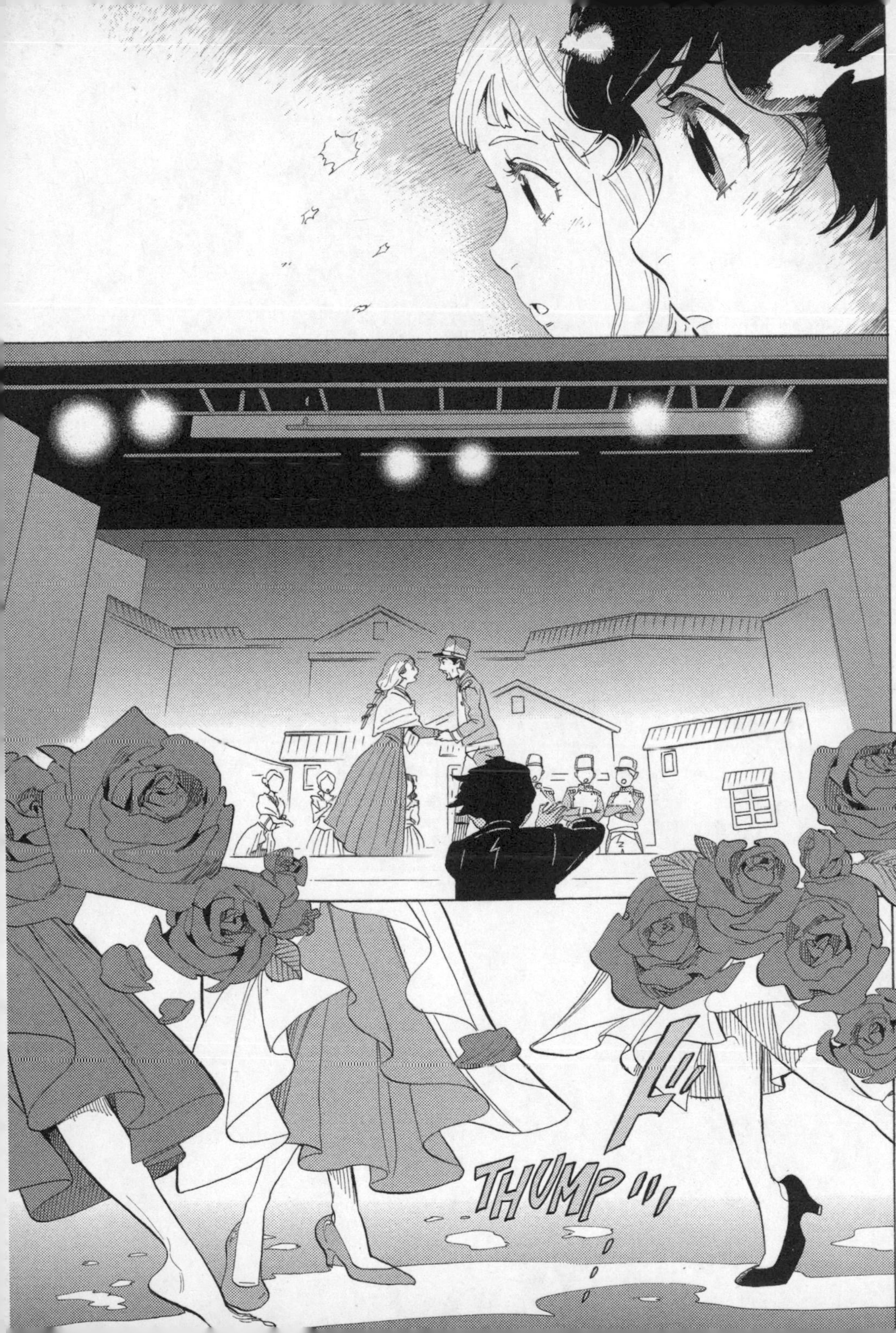
THUMP

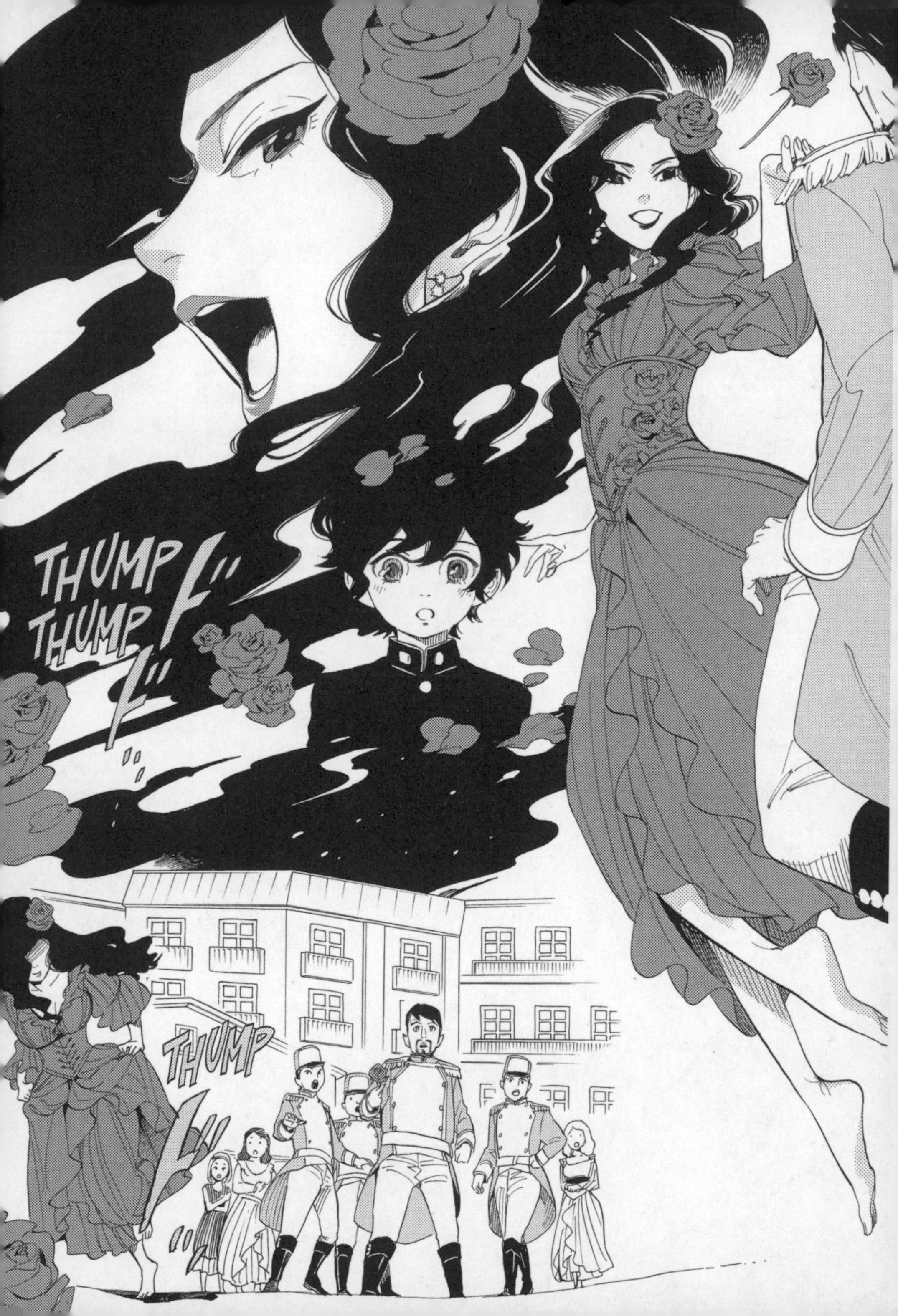
THUMP THUMP
THUMP

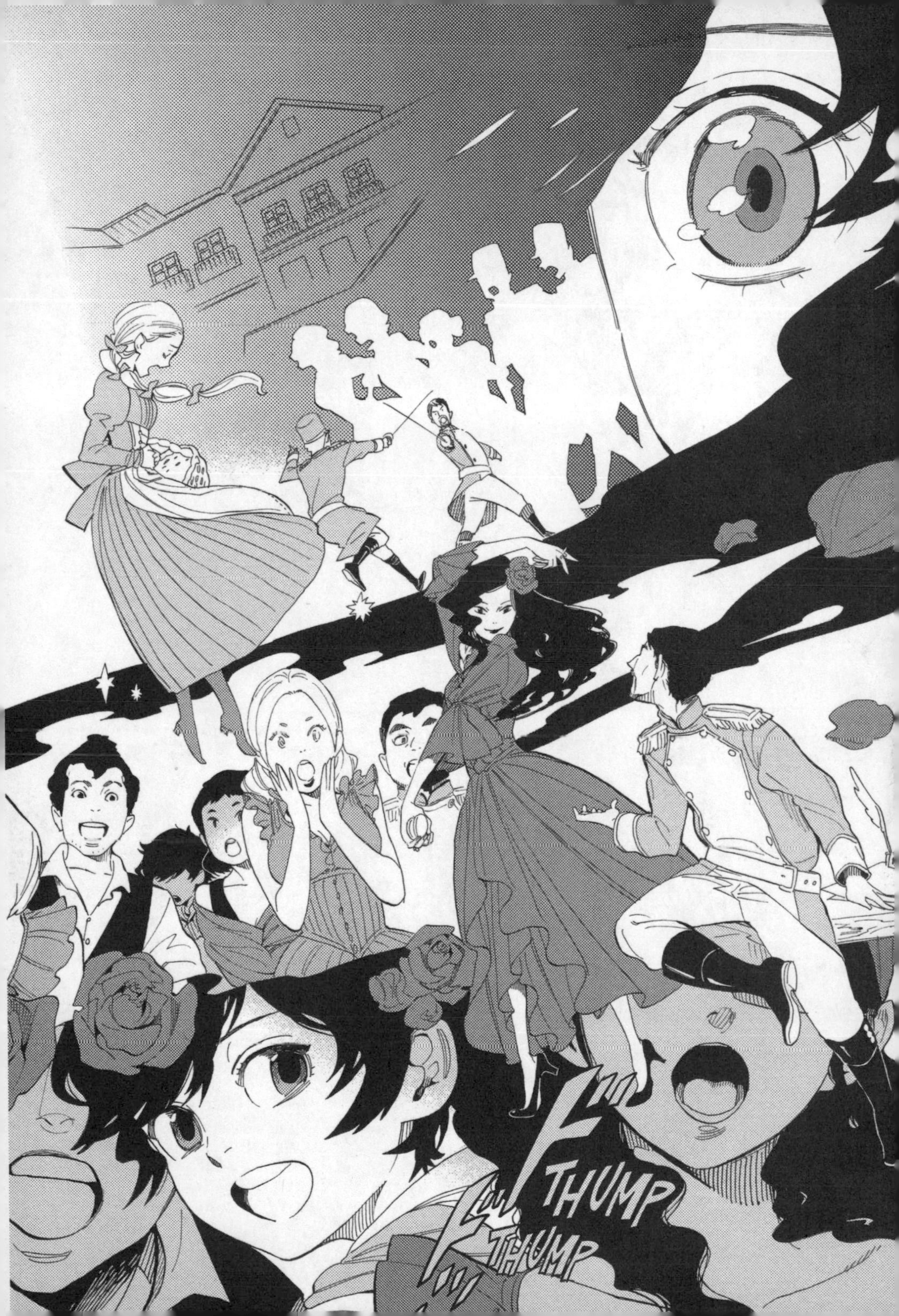
THUMP
THUMP

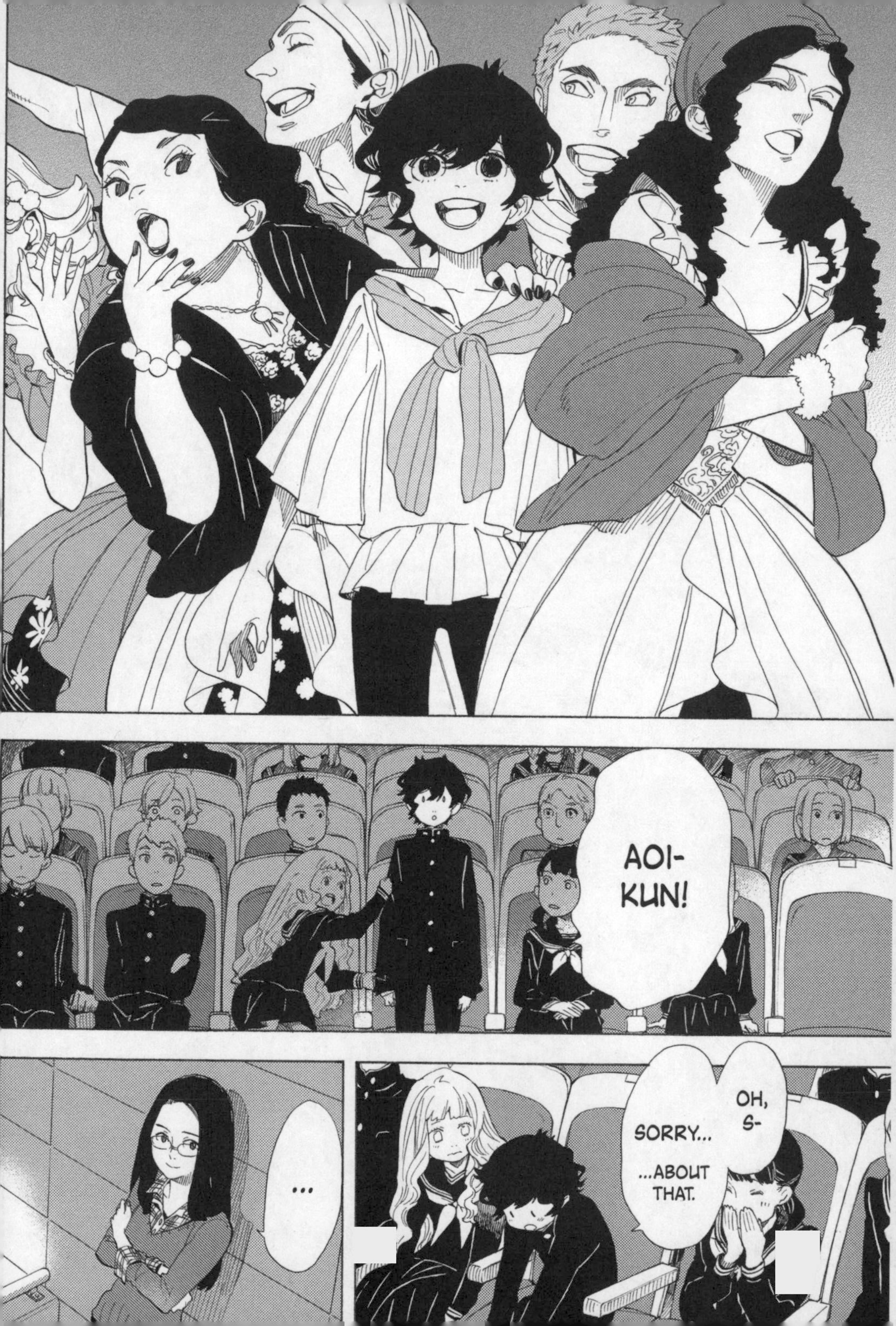
AOI-KUN!
OH, S-
SORRY...
...ABOUT THAT.
...

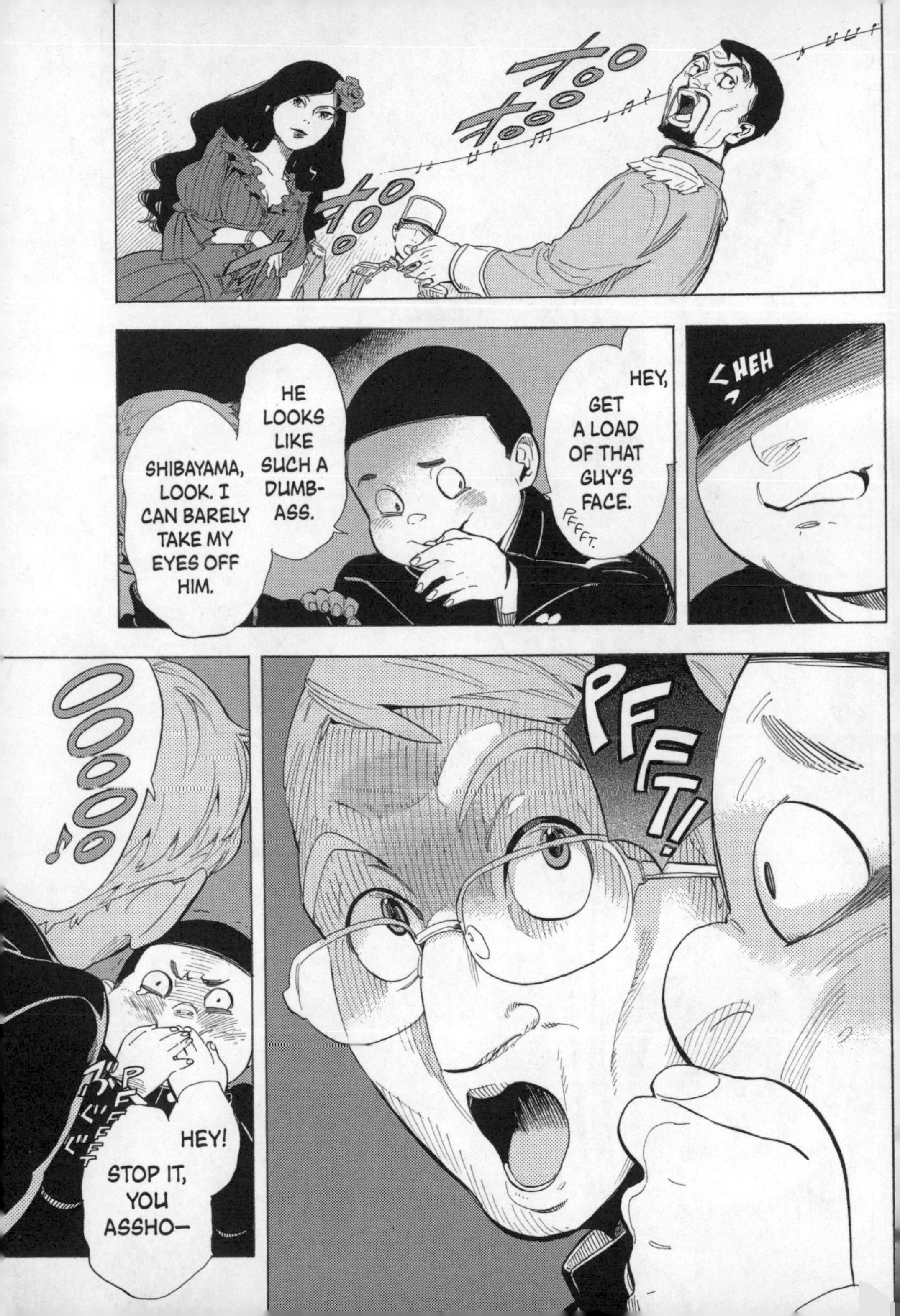
HEH
HEY, GET A LOAD OF THAT GUY'S FACE.
PFFFT.
HE LOOKS LIKE SUCH A DUMB-ASS.
SHIBAYAMA, LOOK. I CAN BARELY TAKE MY EYES OFF HIM.
PFFT!
OOOOO♪
PFFFFT
HEY!
STOP IT, YOU ASSHO—

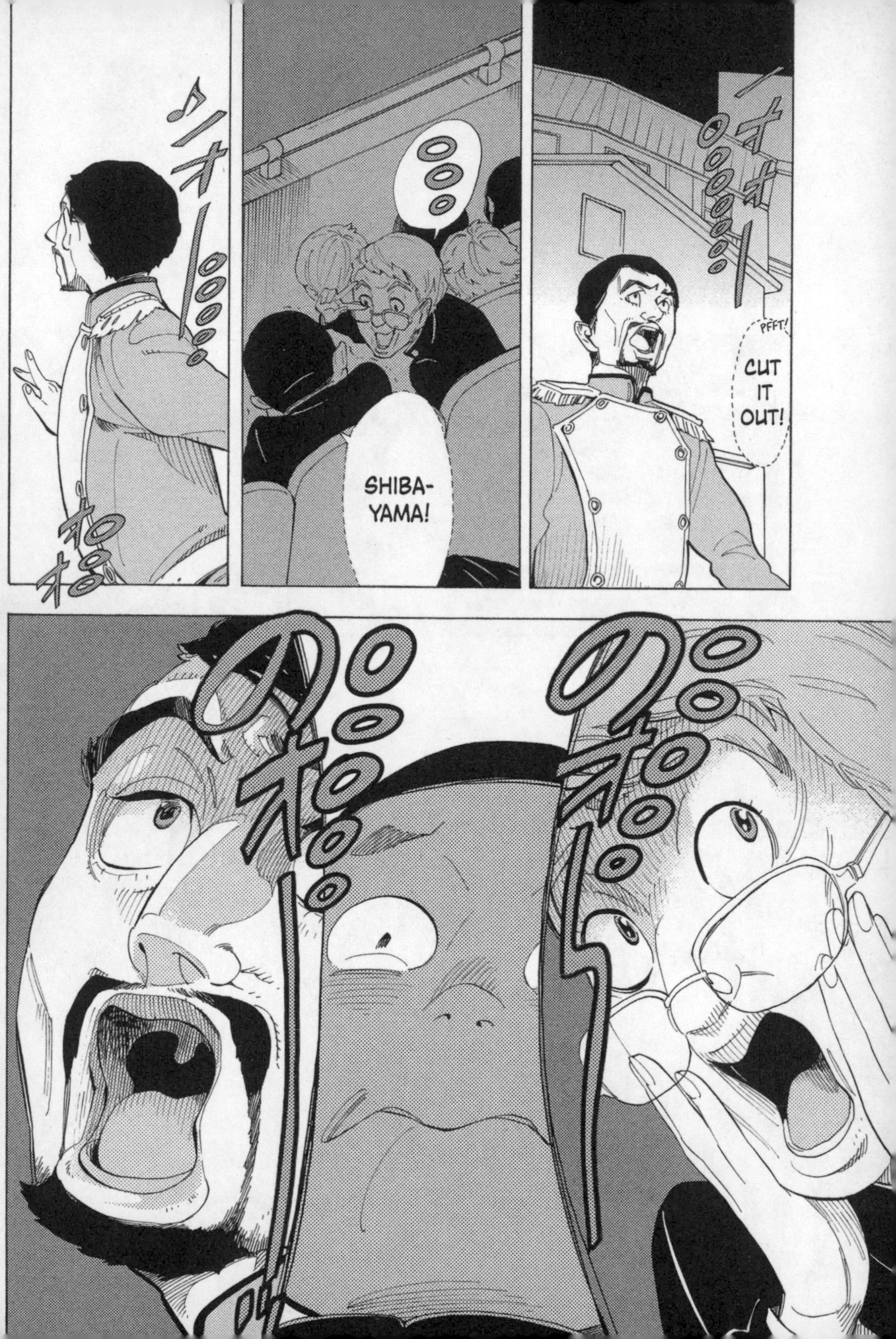
PFFT!
CUT IT OUT!
SHIBA-YAMA!

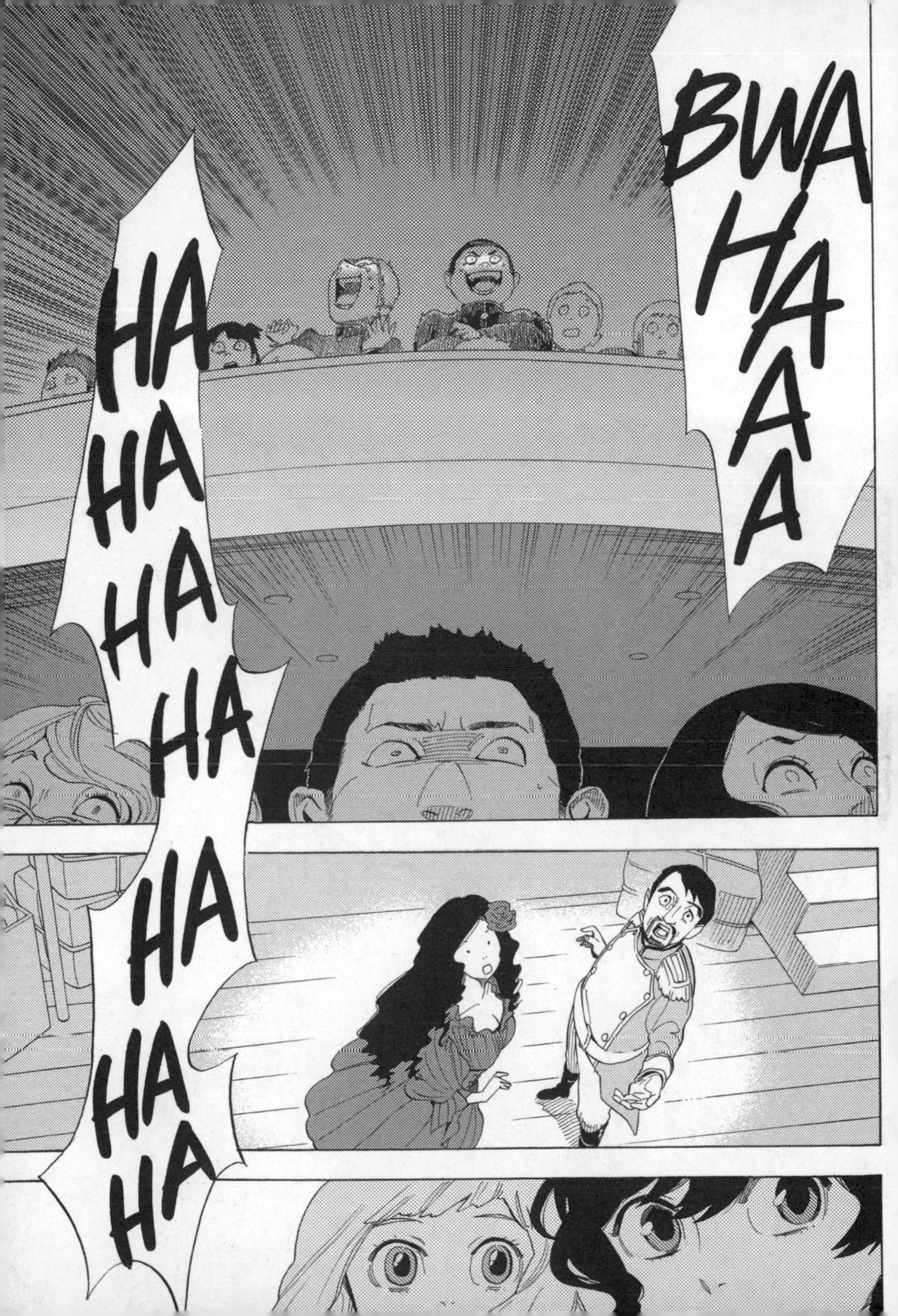
BWA HA HA A A A
HA HA HA HA HA HA HA HA HA

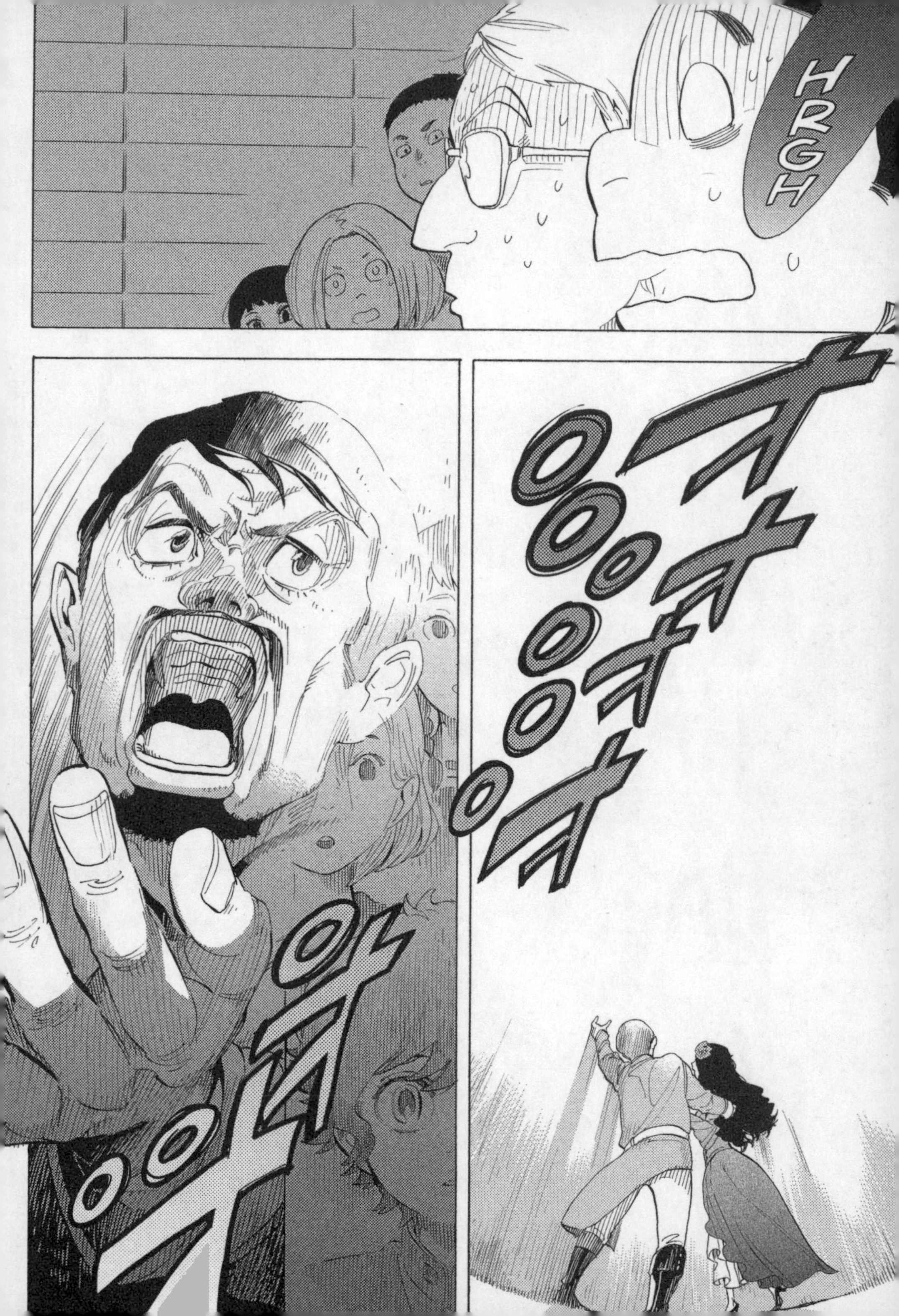
HRGH

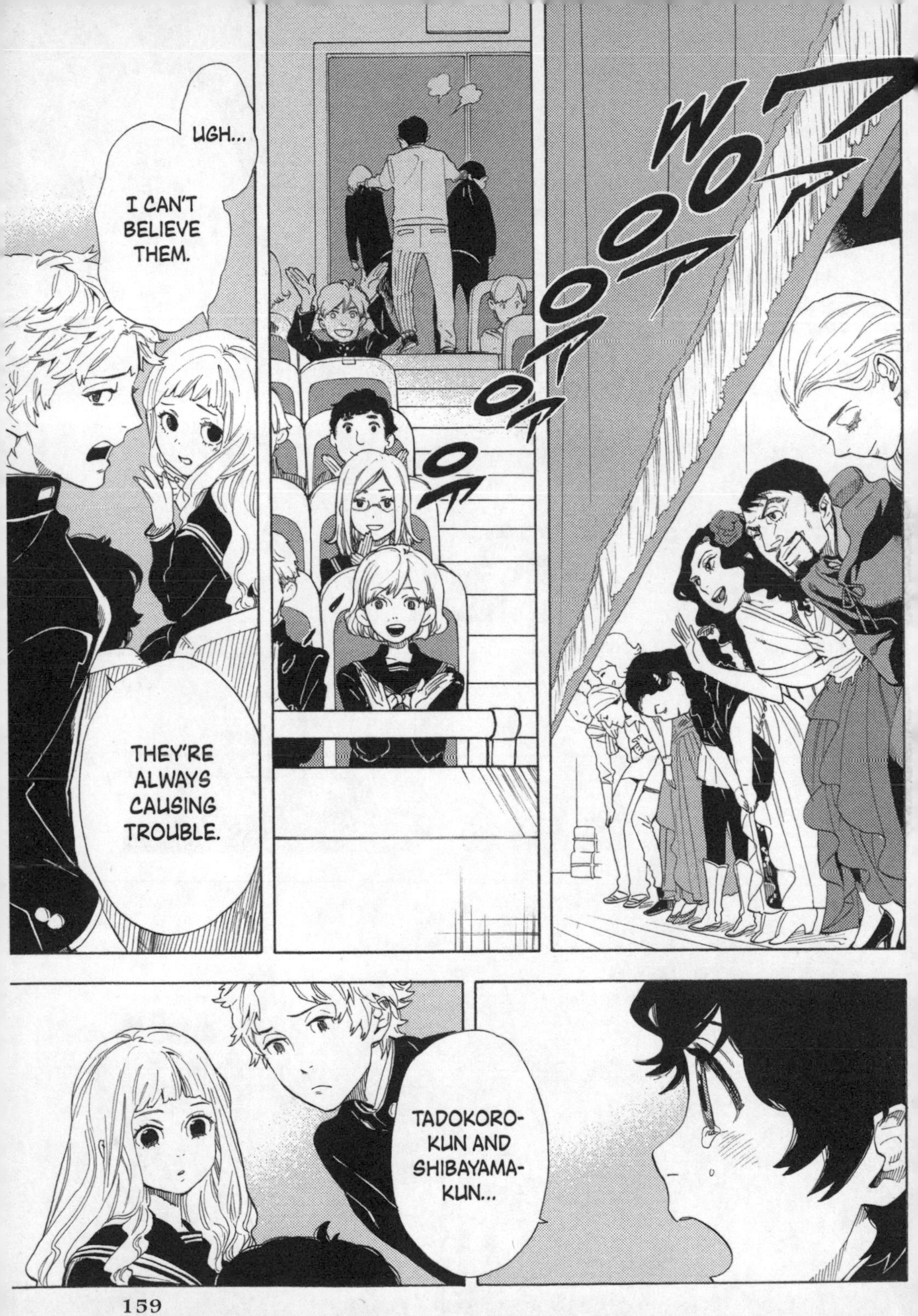
WOOOOOOO
UGH...
I CAN'T BELIEVE THEM.
THEY'RE ALWAYS CAUSING TROUBLE.
TADOKORO-KUN AND SHIBAYAMA-KUN...

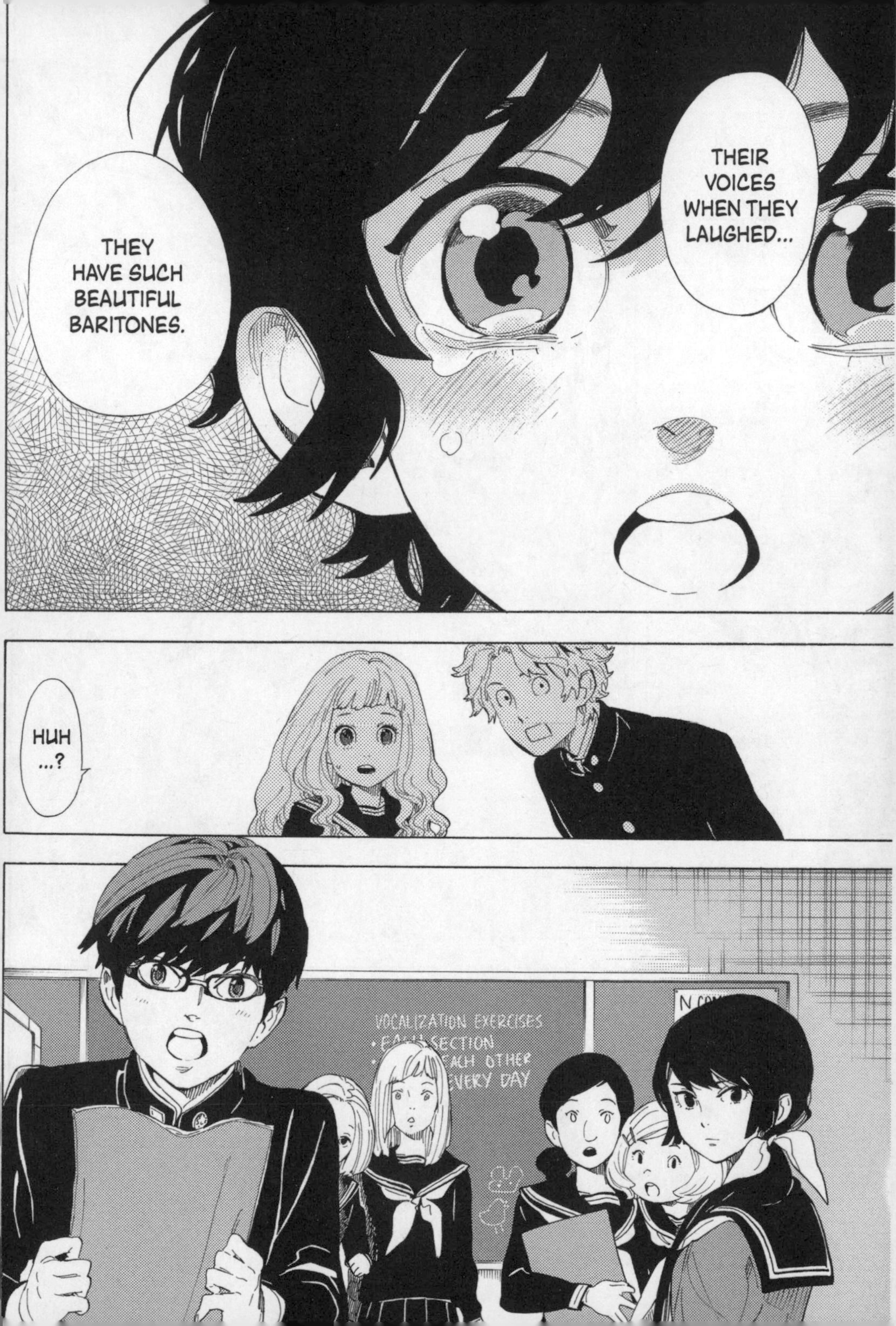
THEIR VOICES WHEN THEY LAUGHED...
THEY HAVE SUCH BEAUTIFUL BARITONES.
HUH ...?
VOCALIZATION EXERCISES
SECTION
EACH OTHER
EVERY DAY

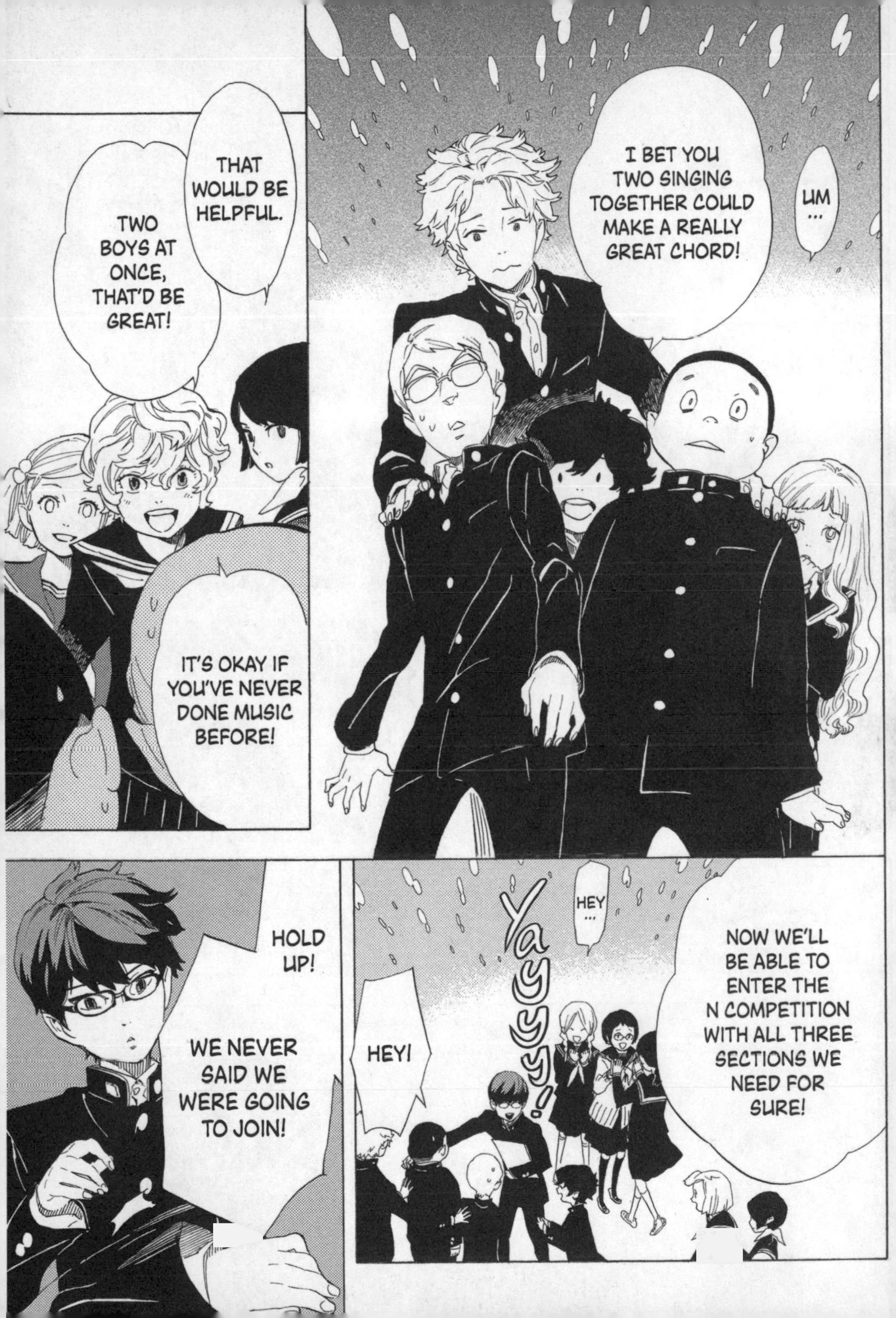
I BET YOU TWO SINGING TOGETHER COULD MAKE A REALLY GREAT CHORD!
UM ...
THAT WOULD BE HELPFUL.
TWO BOYS AT ONCE, THAT'D BE GREAT!
IT'S OKAY IF YOU'VE NEVER DONE MUSIC BEFORE!
NOW WE'LL BE ABLE TO ENTER THE N COMPETITION WITH ALL THREE SECTIONS WE NEED FOR SURE!
Yayyy!
HEY ...
HEY!
HOLD UP!
WE NEVER SAID WE WERE GOING TO JOIN!

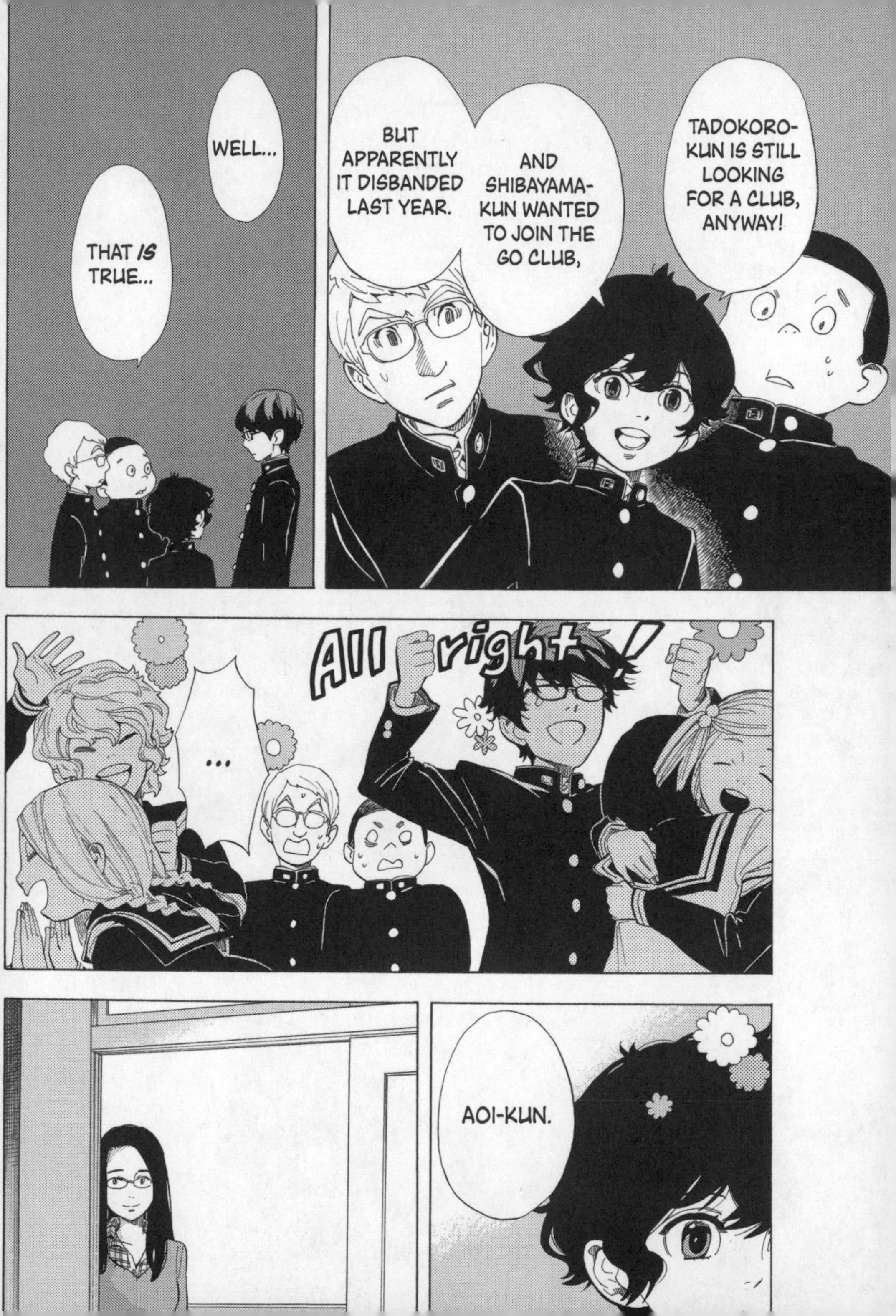
TADOKORO-KUN IS STILL LOOKING FOR A CLUB, ANYWAY!
AND SHIBAYAMA-KUN WANTED TO JOIN THE GO CLUB,
BUT APPARENTLY IT DISBANDED LAST YEAR.
WELL...
THAT *IS* TRUE...
All right!
...
AOI-KUN.

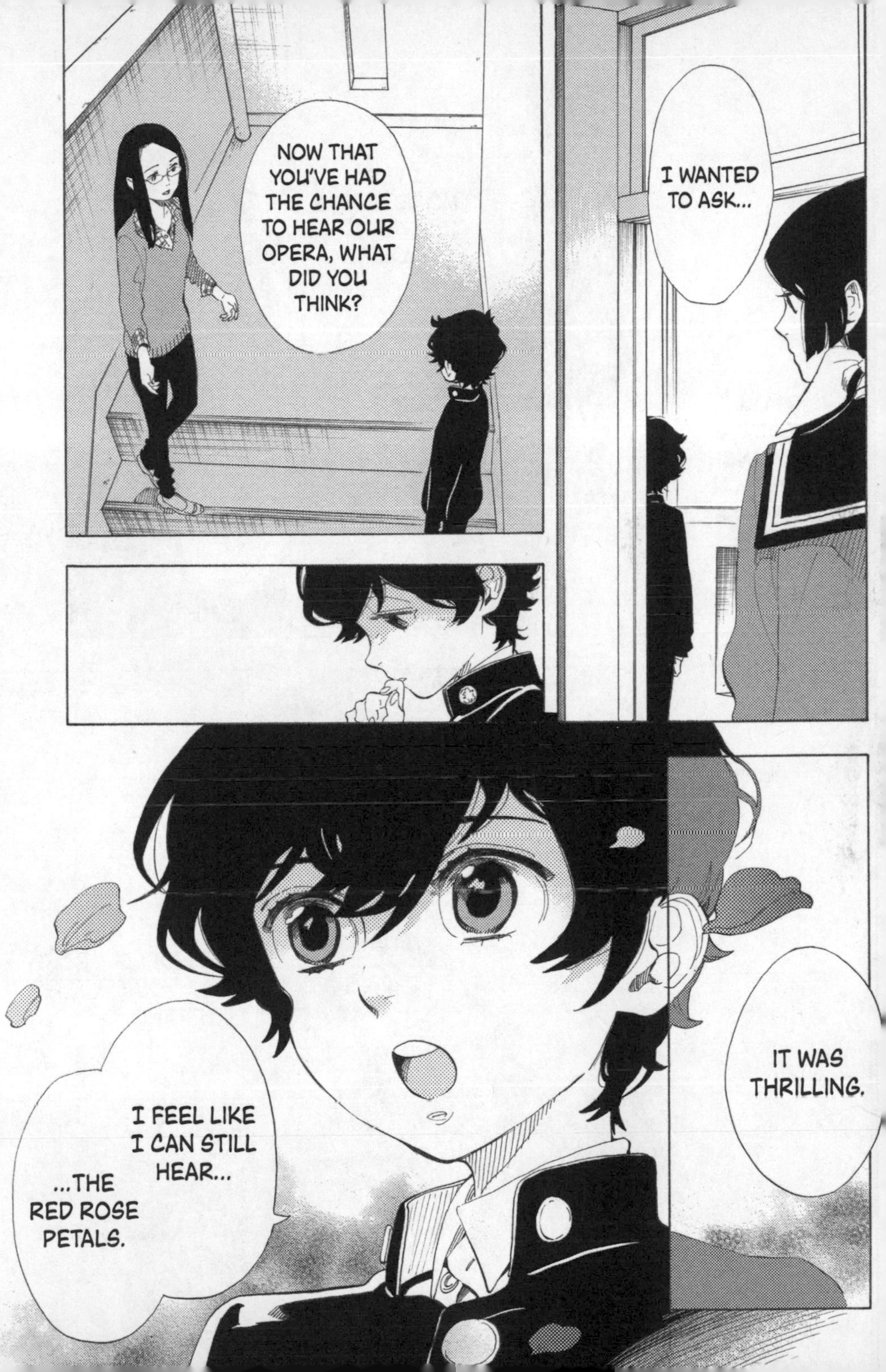
I WANTED TO ASK...
NOW THAT YOU'VE HAD THE CHANCE TO HEAR OUR OPERA, WHAT DID YOU THINK?
IT WAS THRILLING.
I FEEL LIKE I CAN STILL HEAR...
...THE RED ROSE PETALS.

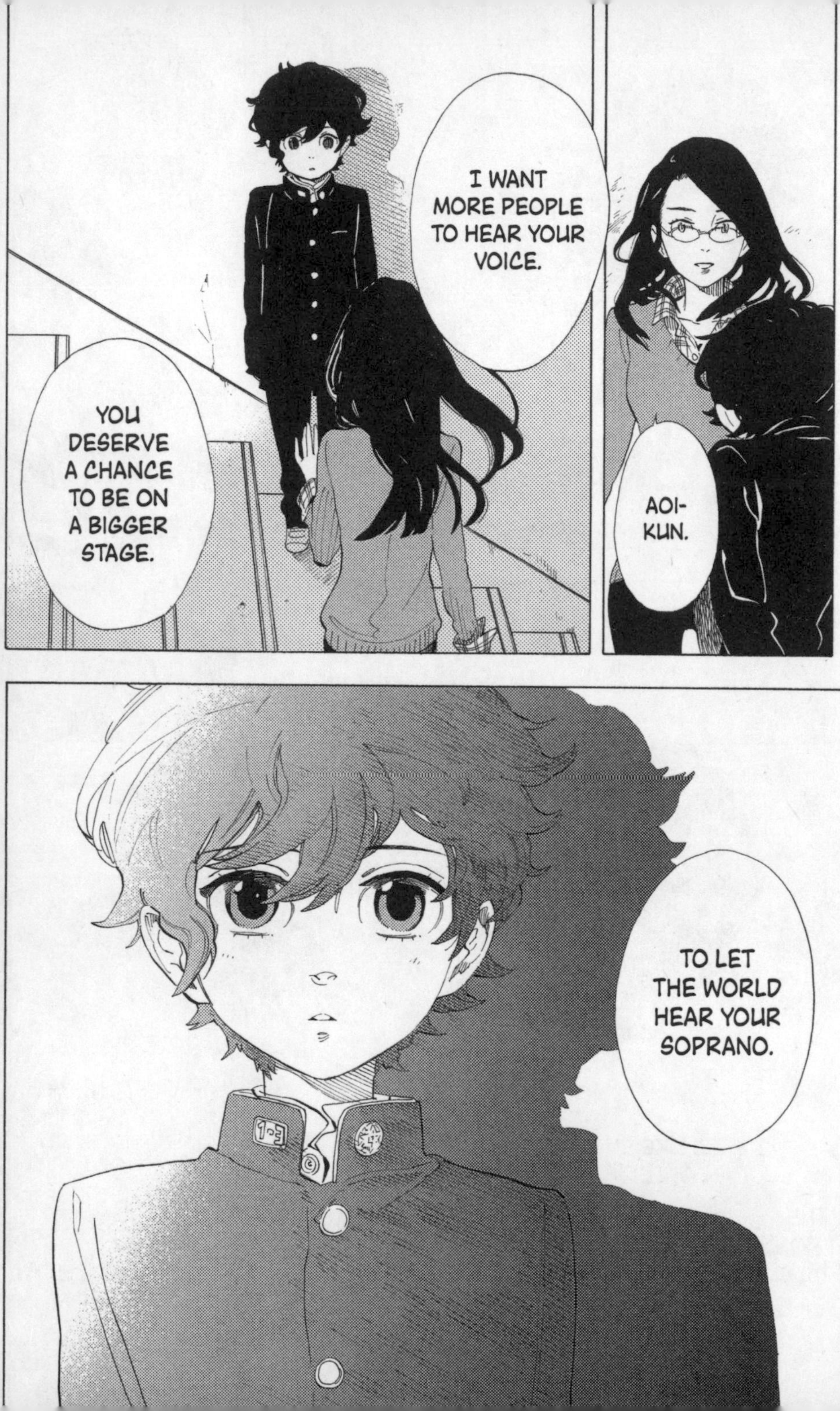
AOI-KUN.
I WANT MORE PEOPLE TO HEAR YOUR VOICE.
YOU DESERVE A CHANCE TO BE ON A BIGGER STAGE.
TO LET THE WORLD HEAR YOUR SOPRANO.

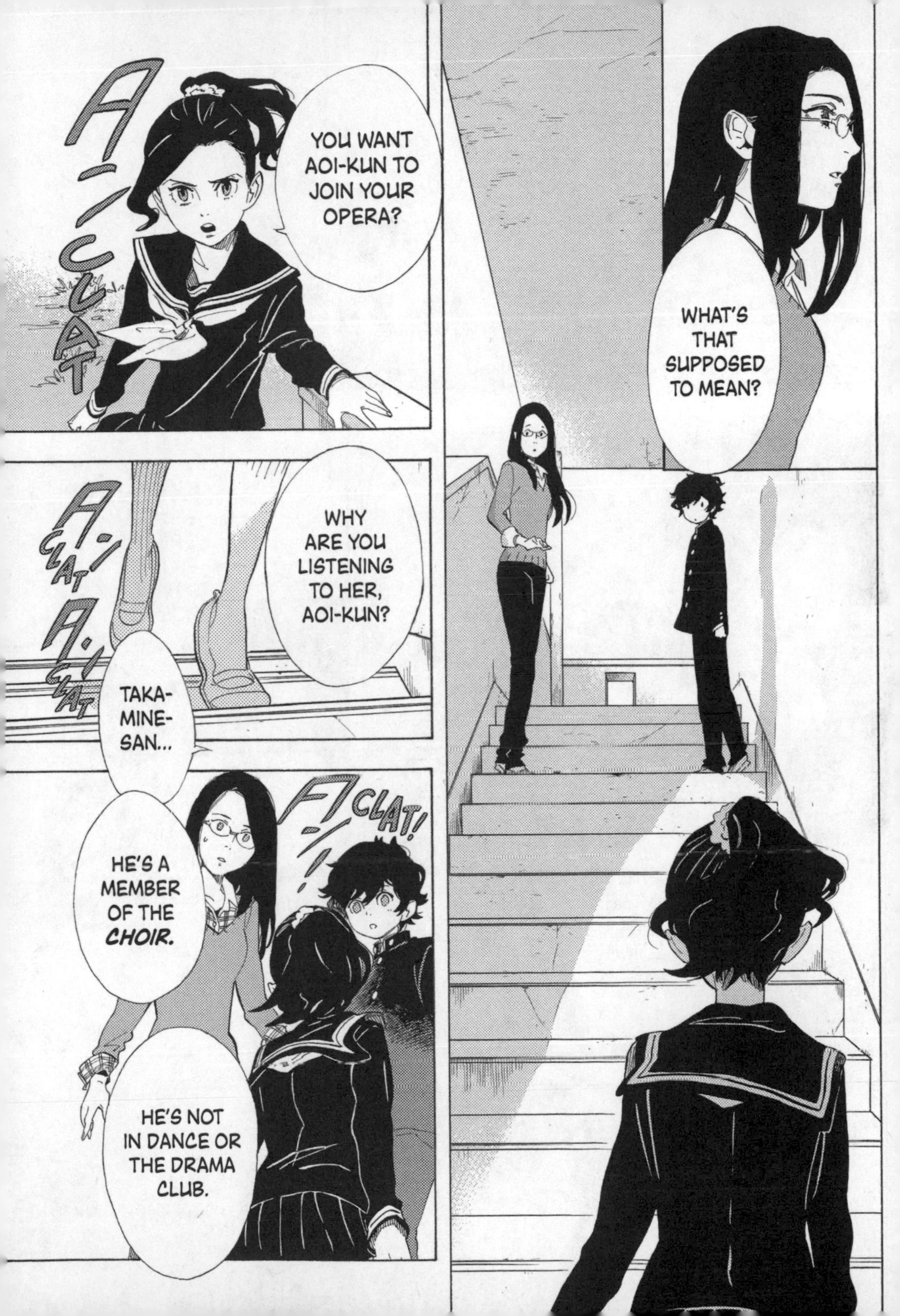
WHAT'S THAT SUPPOSED TO MEAN?
A--CLAT
YOU WANT AOI-KUN TO JOIN YOUR OPERA?
A-! CLAT
A-! CLAT
WHY ARE YOU LISTENING TO HER, AOI-KUN?
TAKA-MINE-SAN...
A! CLAT!
HE'S A MEMBER OF THE *CHOIR.*
HE'S NOT IN DANCE OR THE DRAMA CLUB.

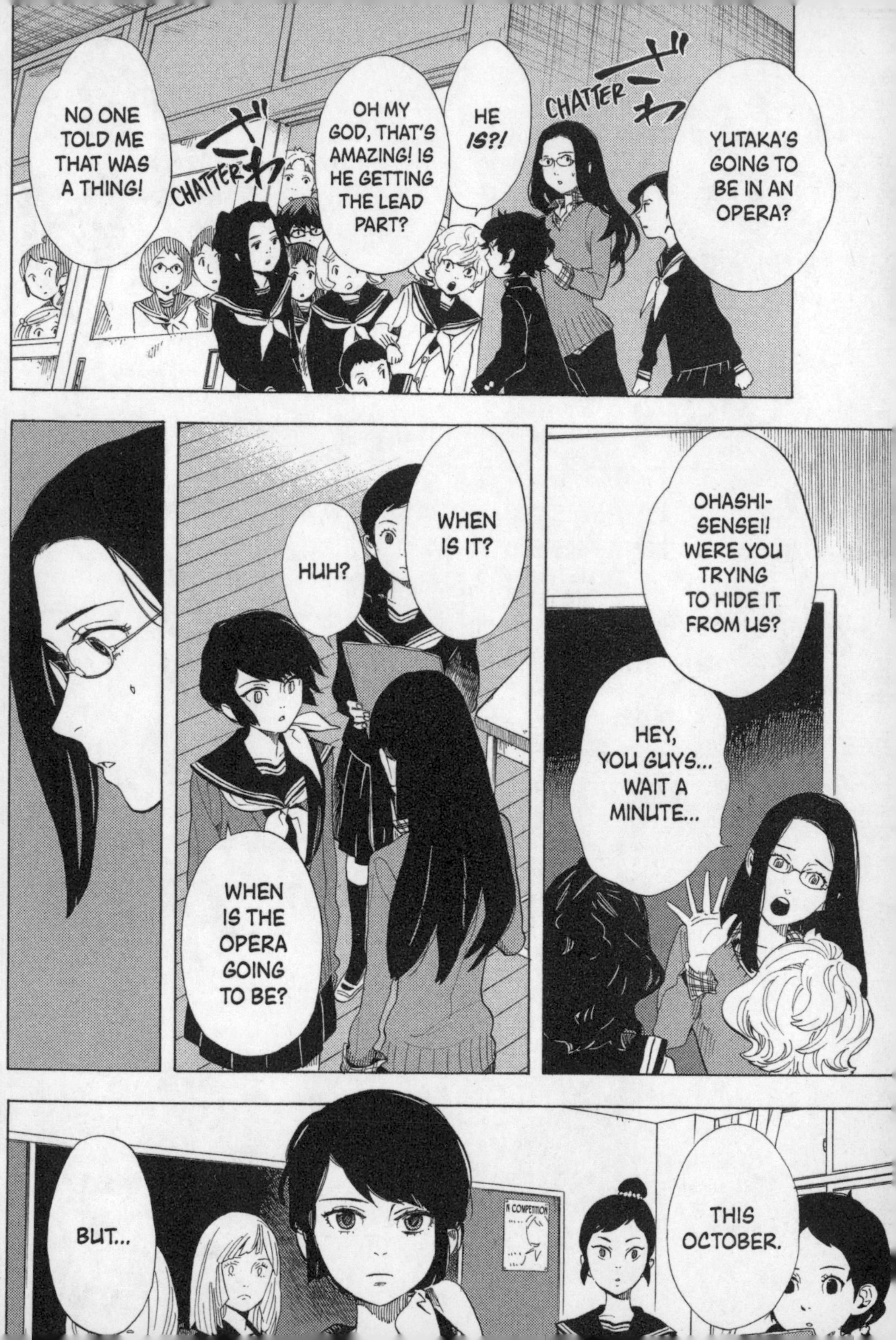
YUTAKA'S GOING TO BE IN AN OPERA?
ざわ CHATTER
HE IS?!
OH MY GOD, THAT'S AMAZING! IS HE GETTING THE LEAD PART?
ざわ CHATTER
NO ONE TOLD ME THAT WAS A THING!
OHASHI-SENSEI! WERE YOU TRYING TO HIDE IT FROM US?
HEY, YOU GUYS... WAIT A MINUTE...
WHEN IS IT?
HUH?
WHEN IS THE OPERA GOING TO BE?
THIS OCTOBER.
N COMPETITION
BUT...

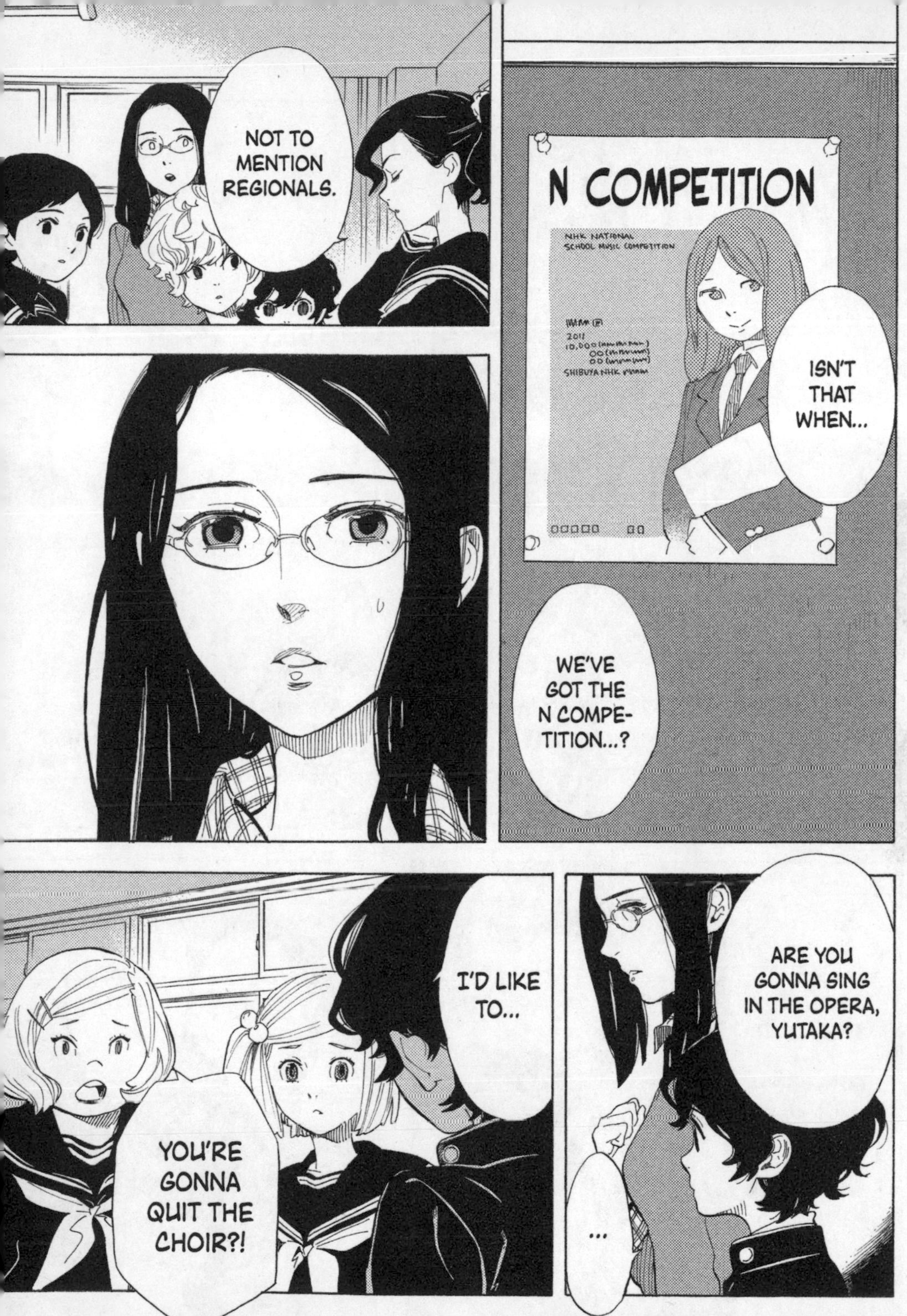

N COMPETITION
NHK NATIONAL SCHOOL MUSIC COMPETITION
2011
SHIBUYA NHK
ISN'T THAT WHEN...
WE'VE GOT THE N COMPETITION...?
NOT TO MENTION REGIONALS.
ARE YOU GONNA SING IN THE OPERA, YUTAKA?
...
I'D LIKE TO...
YOU'RE GONNA QUIT THE CHOIR?!

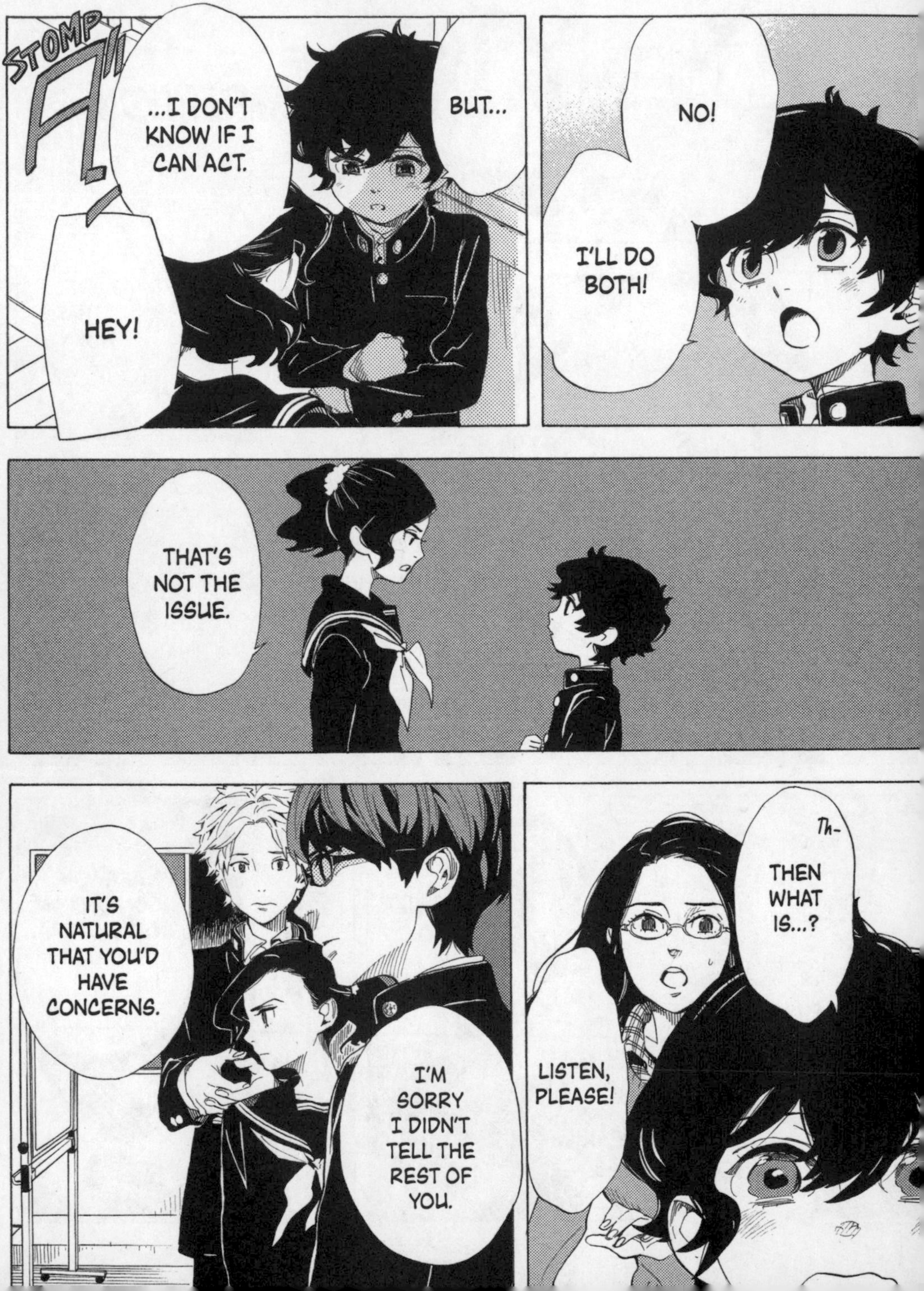
NO!
I'LL DO BOTH!
BUT...
...I DON'T KNOW IF I CAN ACT.
STOMP
HEY!
THAT'S NOT THE ISSUE.
Th- THEN WHAT IS...?
LISTEN, PLEASE!
I'M SORRY I DIDN'T TELL THE REST OF YOU.
IT'S NATURAL THAT YOU'D HAVE CONCERNS.

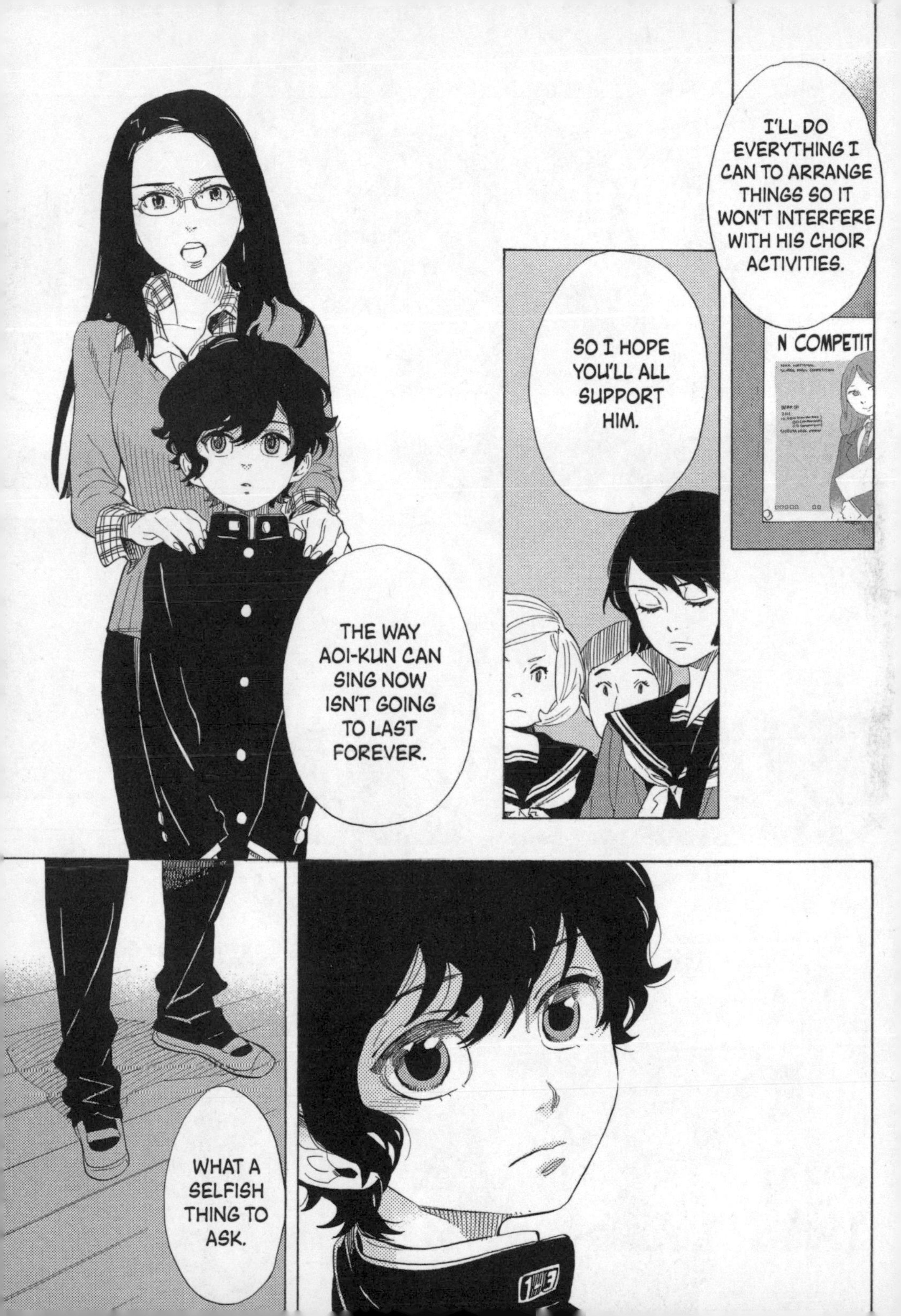
I'LL DO EVERYTHING I CAN TO ARRANGE THINGS SO IT WON'T INTERFERE WITH HIS CHOIR ACTIVITIES.
N COMPETIT
SO I HOPE YOU'LL ALL SUPPORT HIM.
THE WAY AOI-KUN CAN SING NOW ISN'T GOING TO LAST FOREVER.
WHAT A SELFISH THING TO ASK.

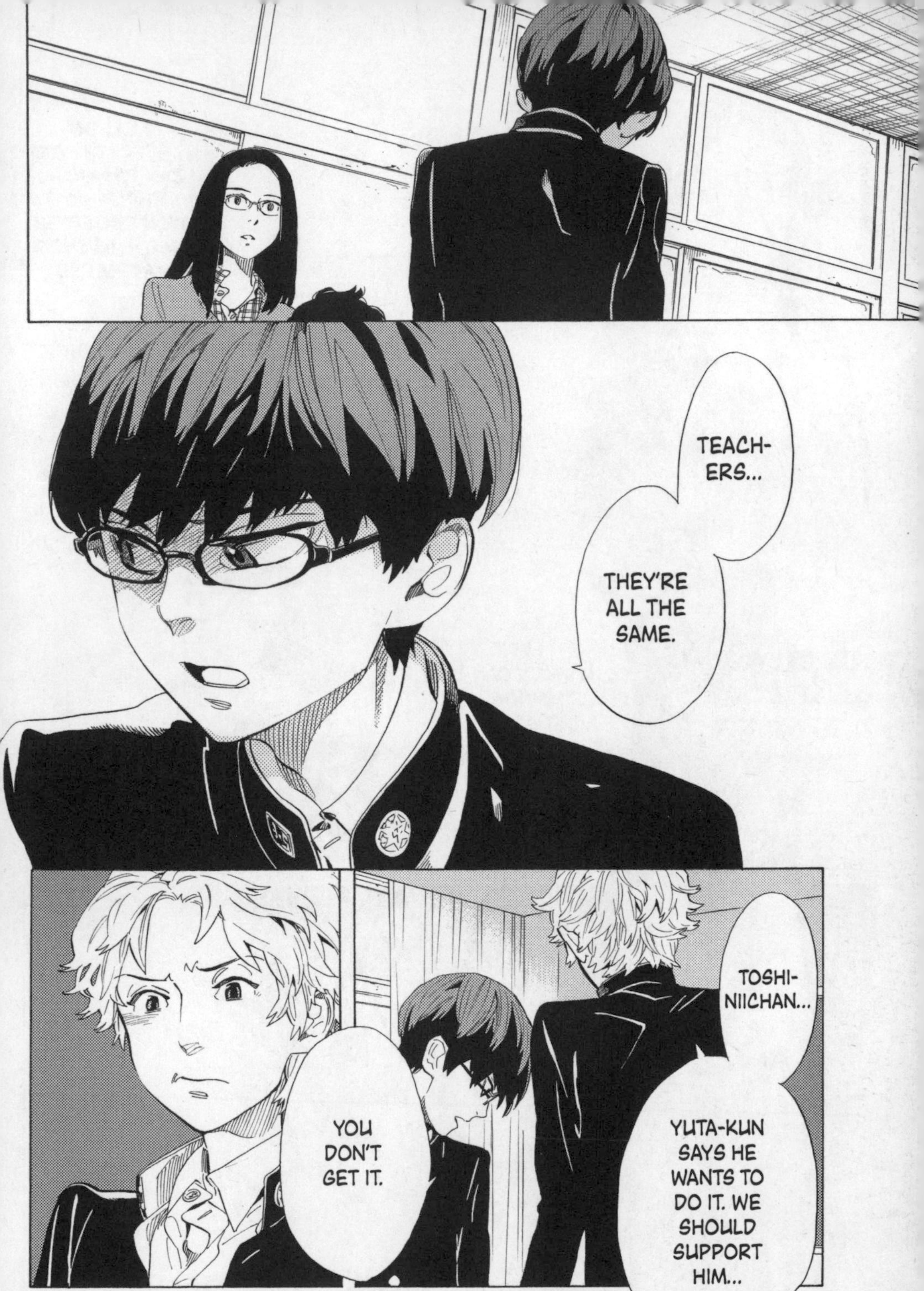
TEACH-
ERS...
THEY'RE ALL THE SAME.
TOSHI-NIICHAN...
YUTA-KUN SAYS HE WANTS TO DO IT. WE SHOULD SUPPORT HIM...
YOU DON'T GET IT.

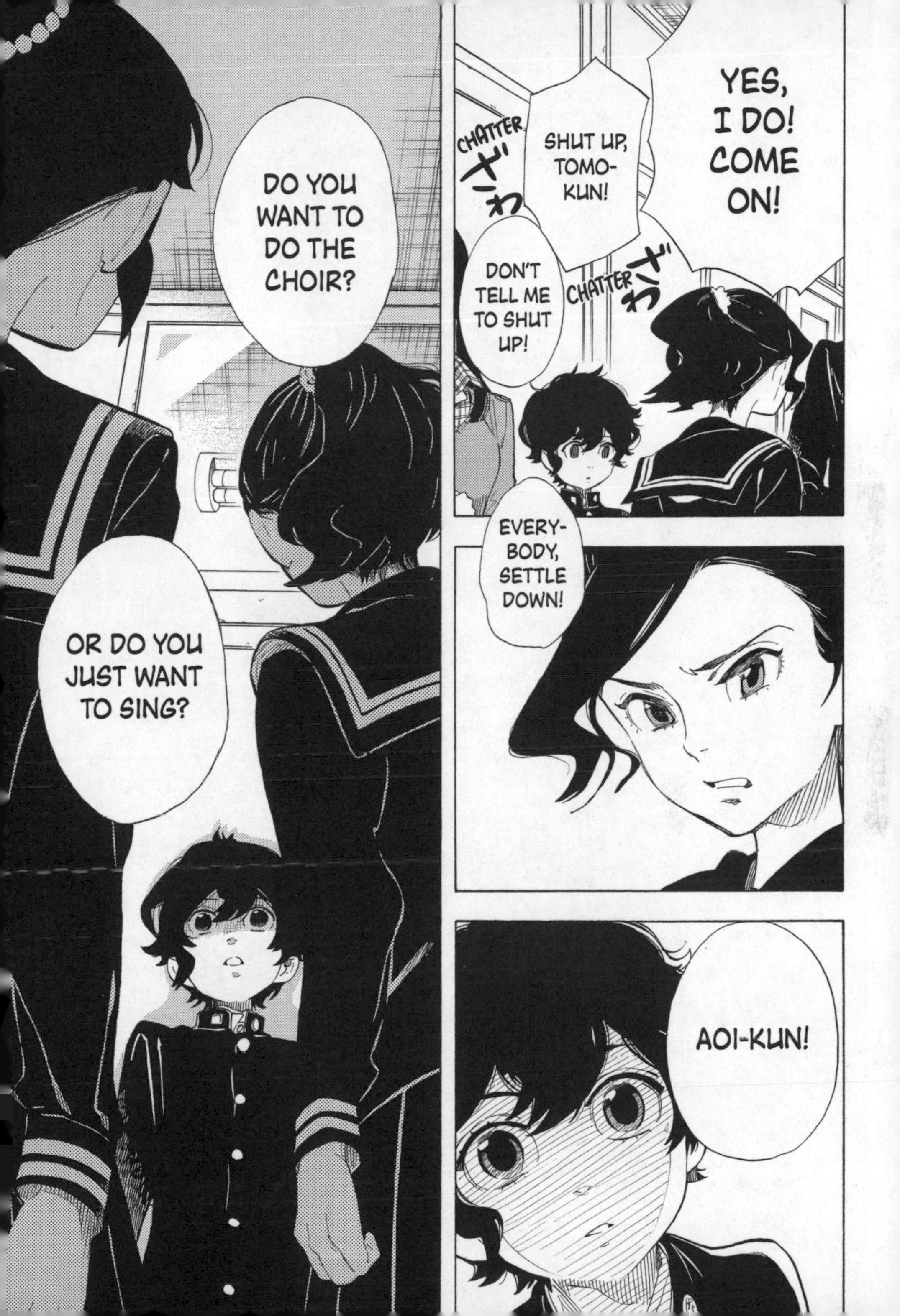
YES, I DO! COME ON!
SHUT UP, TOMO-KUN!
CHATTER ざわ
DON'T TELL ME TO SHUT UP!
CHATTER ざわ
EVERY-BODY, SETTLE DOWN!
AOI-KUN!
DO YOU WANT TO DO THE CHOIR?
OR DO YOU JUST WANT TO SING?

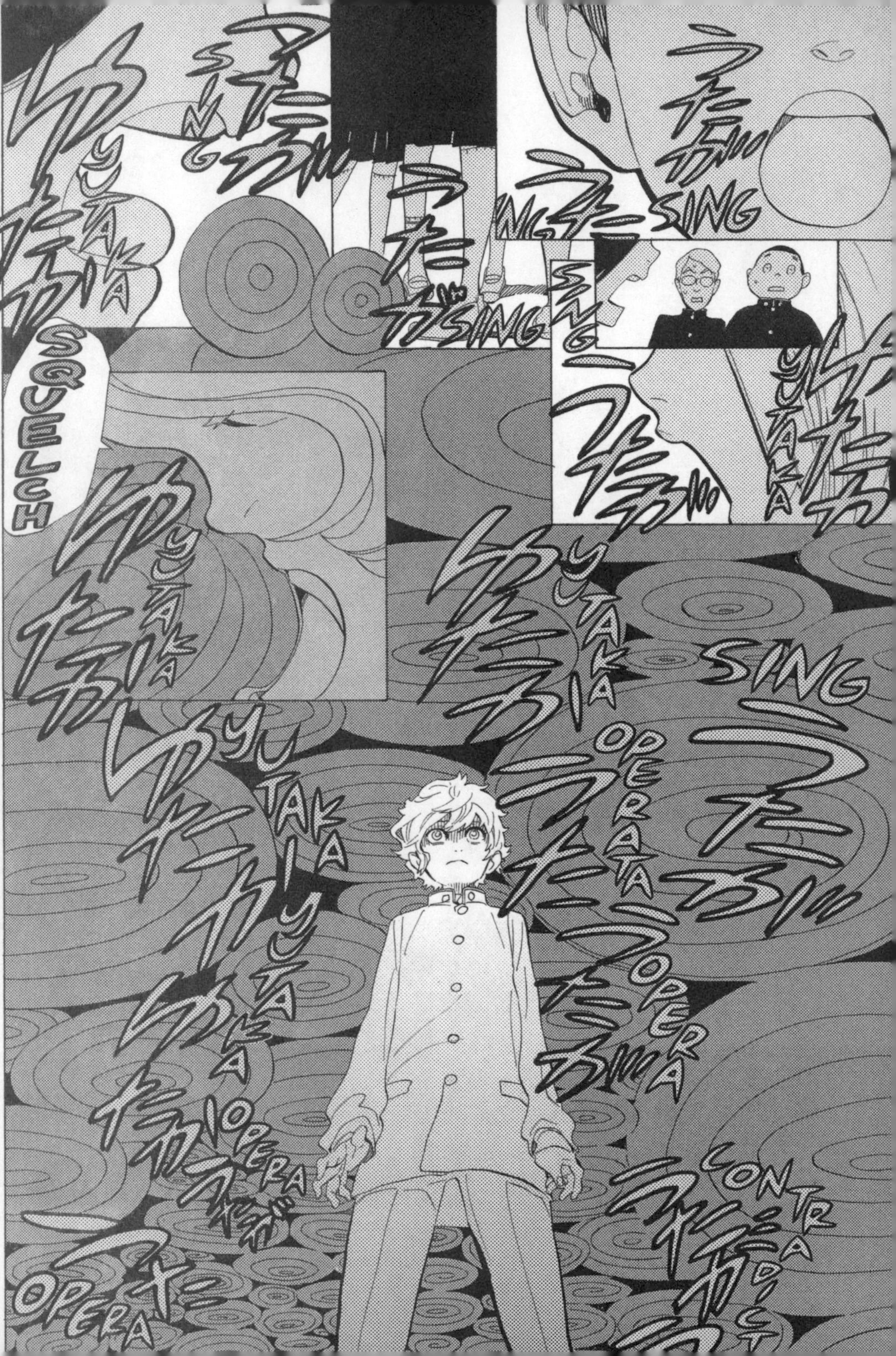
SING
SING
SING
SING
SING
YUTAKA
YUTAKA
SQUELCH
YUTAKA
SING
YUTAKA
OPERA
OPERA
YUTAKA
YUTAKA
OPERA
CONTRADICT
OPERA

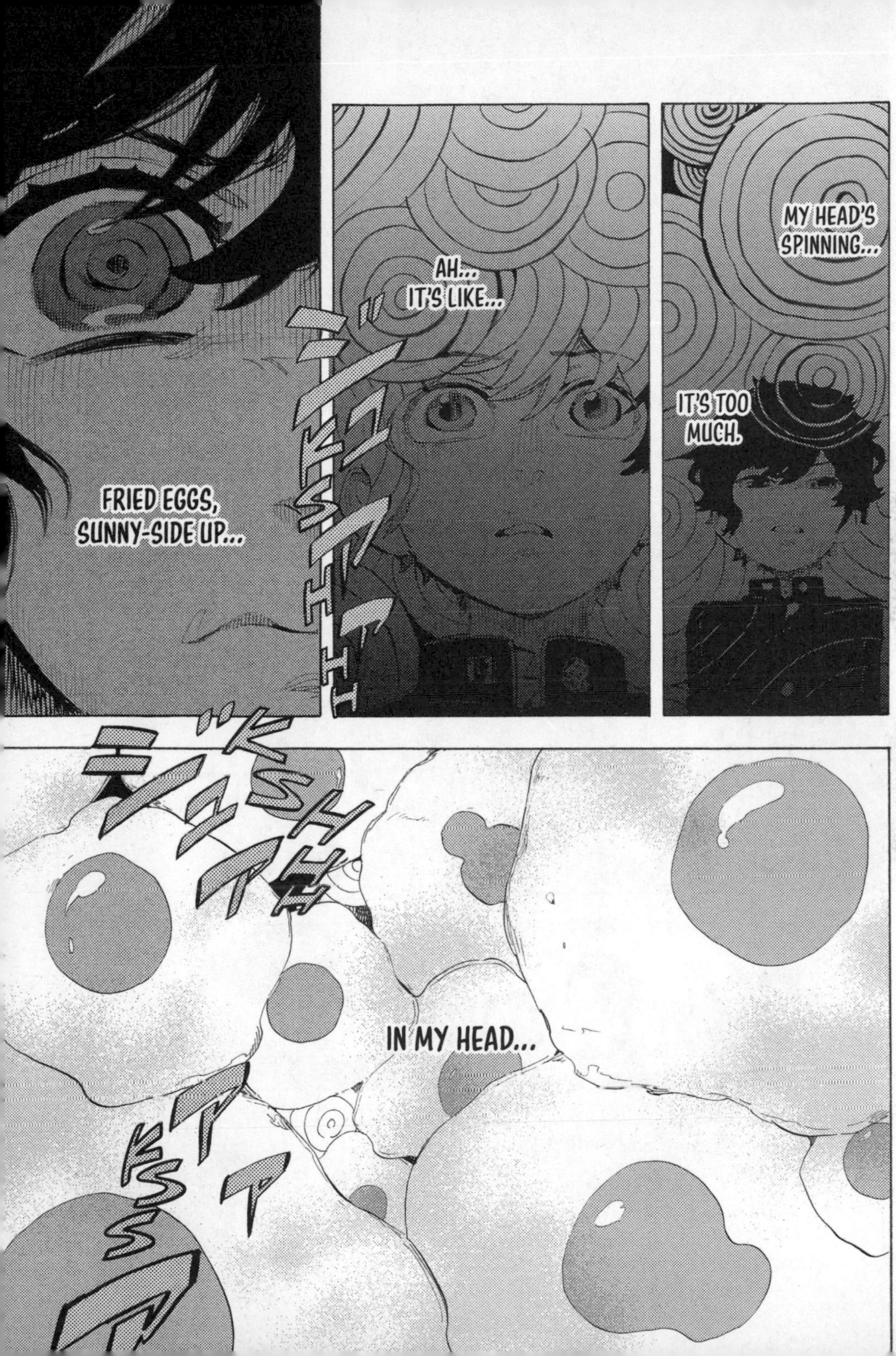
MY HEAD'S SPINNING...
IT'S TOO MUCH.
AH... IT'S LIKE...
FRIED EGGS, SUNNY-SIDE UP...
IN MY HEAD...

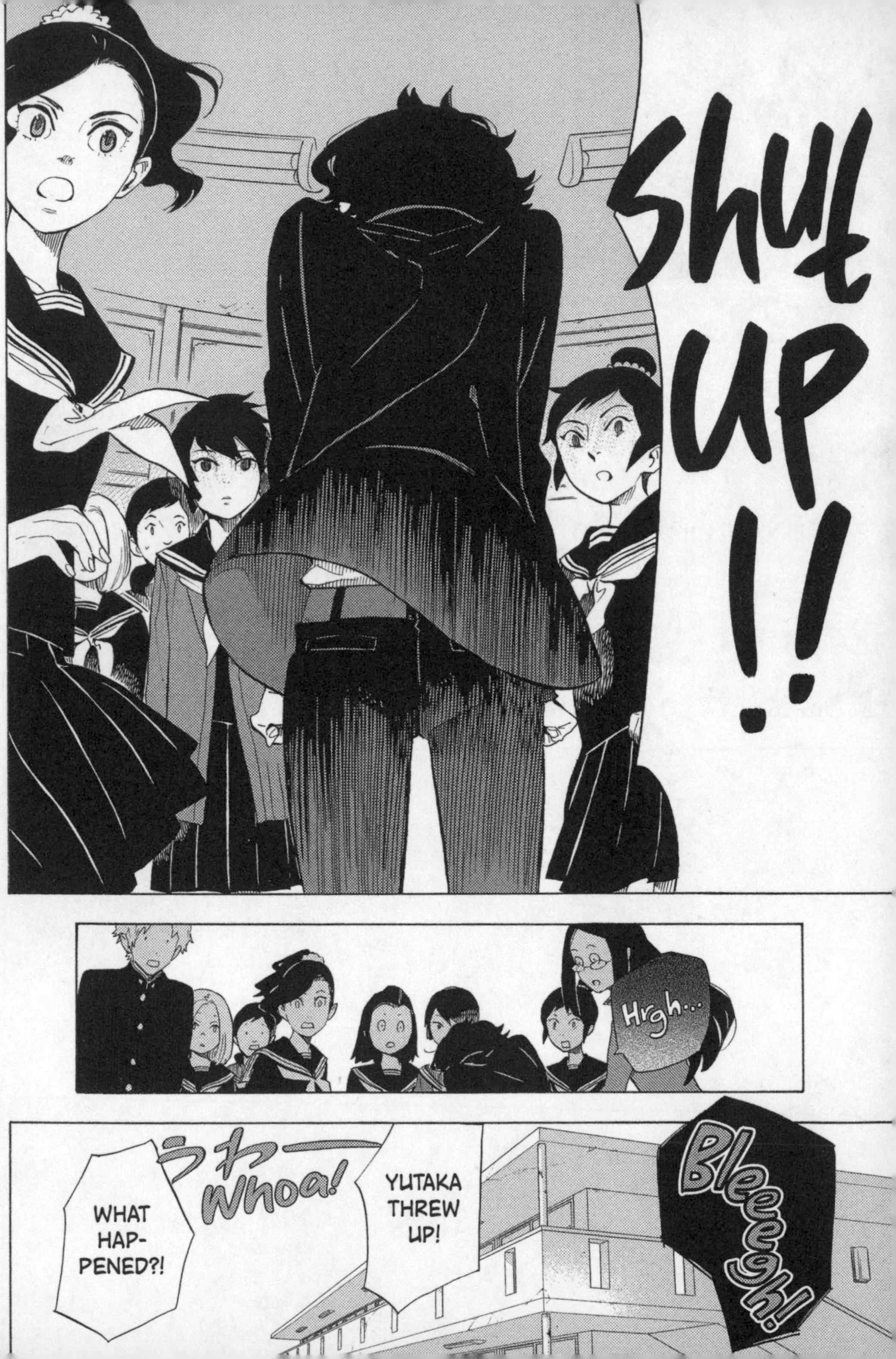
Shut UP!!
Hrgh...
Bleeegh!
YUTAKA THREW UP!
うわー
Whoa!
WHAT HAP-PENED?!

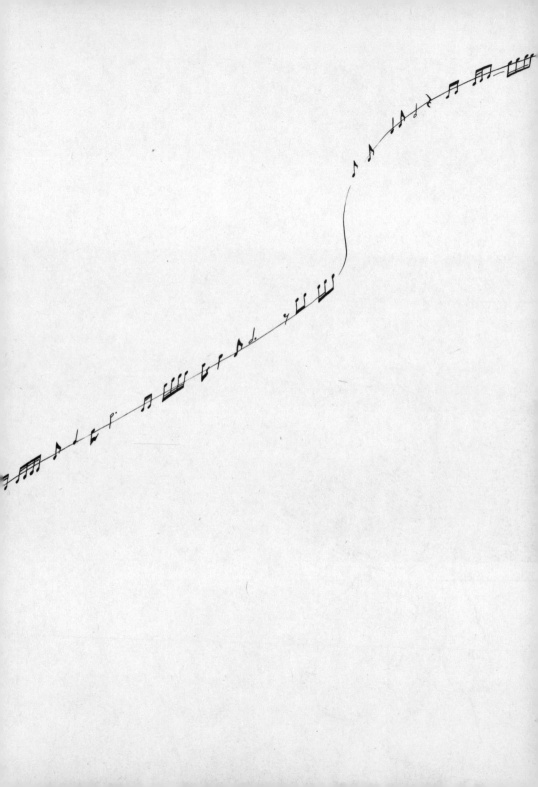

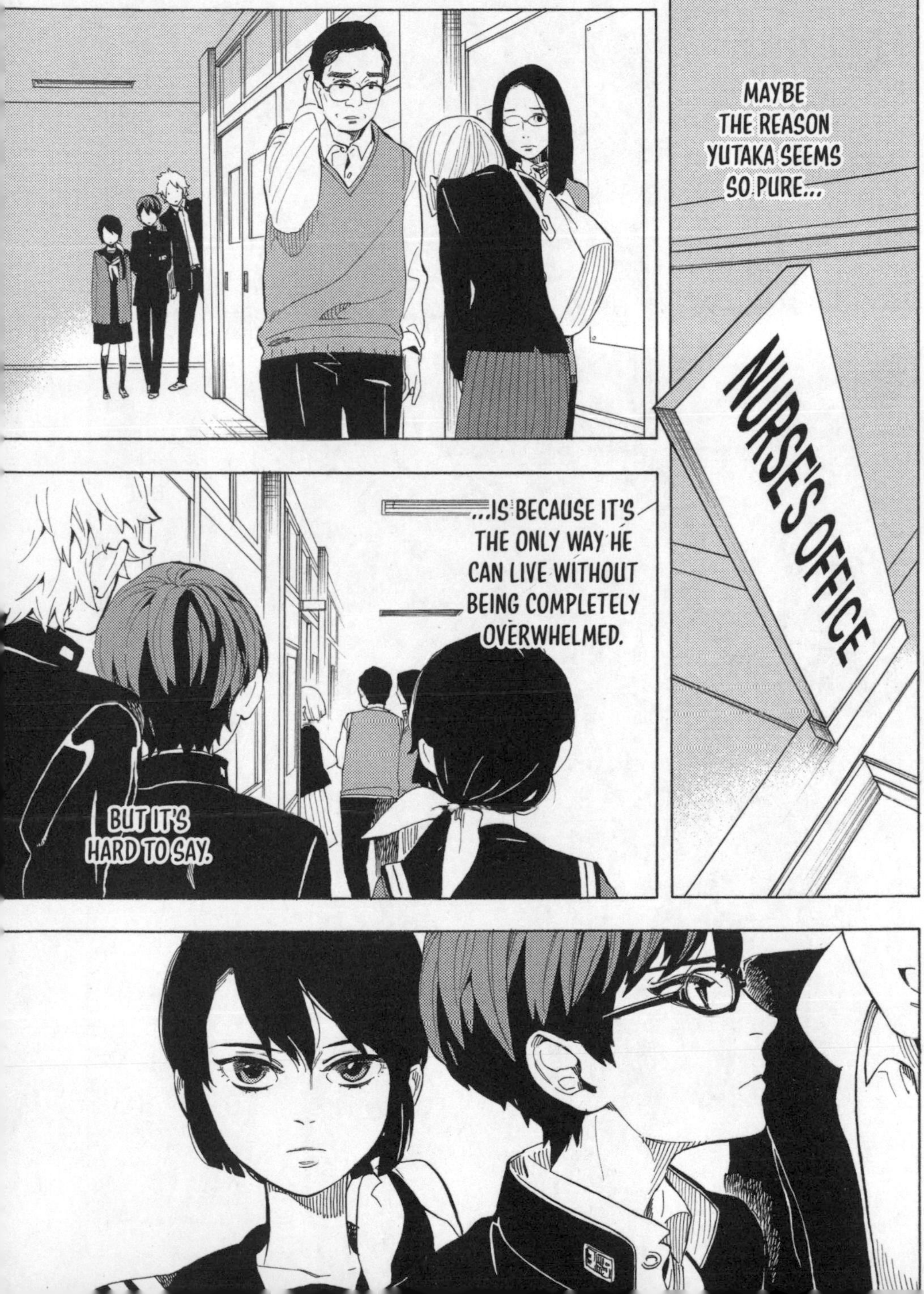
MAYBE THE REASON YUTAKA SEEMS SO PURE...
NURSE'S OFFICE
...IS BECAUSE IT'S THE ONLY WAY HE CAN LIVE WITHOUT BEING COMPLETELY OVERWHELMED.
BUT IT'S HARD TO SAY.

note 𝄢:05

A Reason to Sing

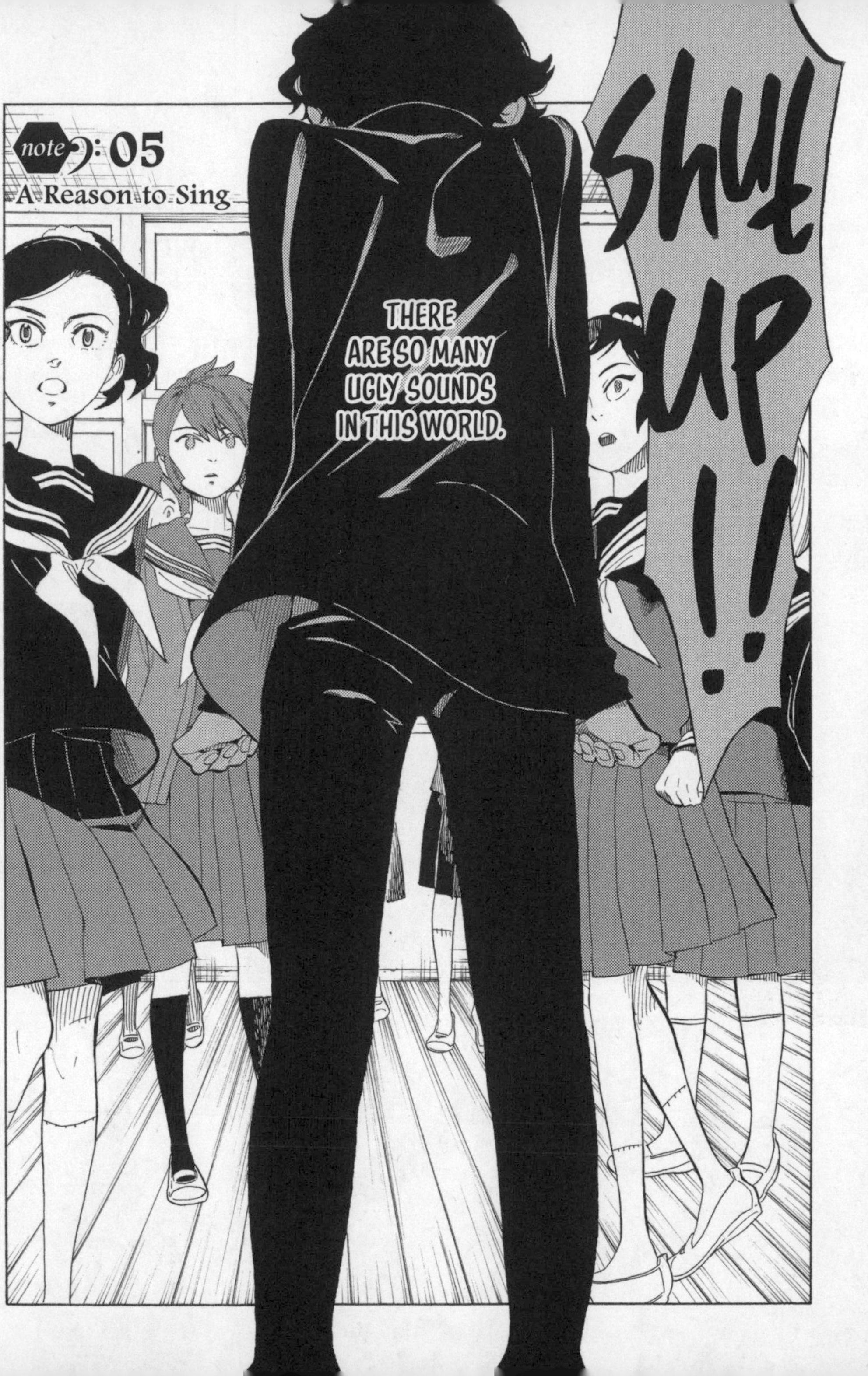
SHUT UP!!
THERE ARE SO MANY UGLY SOUNDS IN THIS WORLD.

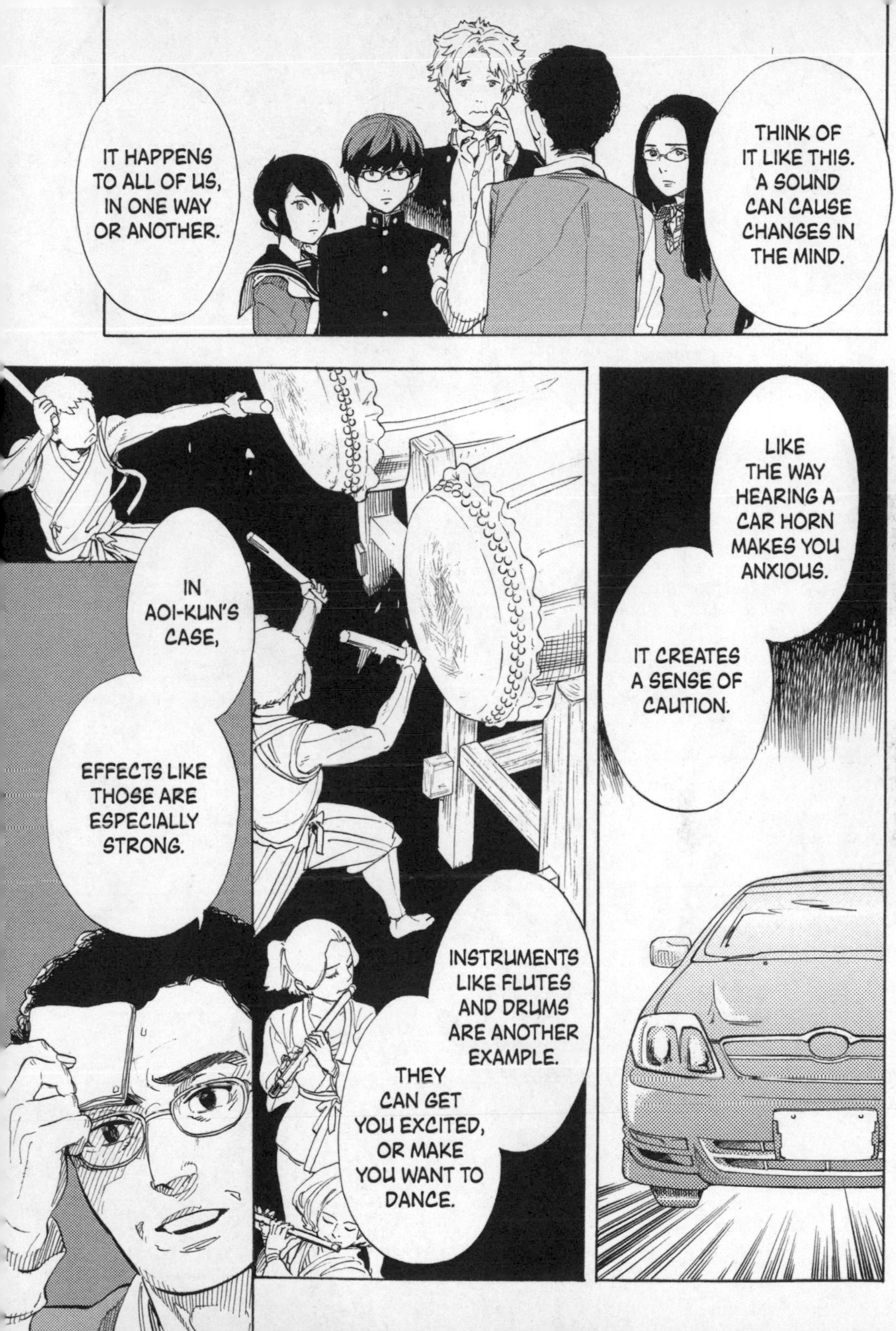
THINK OF IT LIKE THIS. A SOUND CAN CAUSE CHANGES IN THE MIND.
IT HAPPENS TO ALL OF US, IN ONE WAY OR ANOTHER.
LIKE THE WAY HEARING A CAR HORN MAKES YOU ANXIOUS.
IT CREATES A SENSE OF CAUTION.
INSTRUMENTS LIKE FLUTES AND DRUMS ARE ANOTHER EXAMPLE.
THEY CAN GET YOU EXCITED, OR MAKE YOU WANT TO DANCE.
IN AOI-KUN'S CASE,
EFFECTS LIKE THOSE ARE ESPECIALLY STRONG.

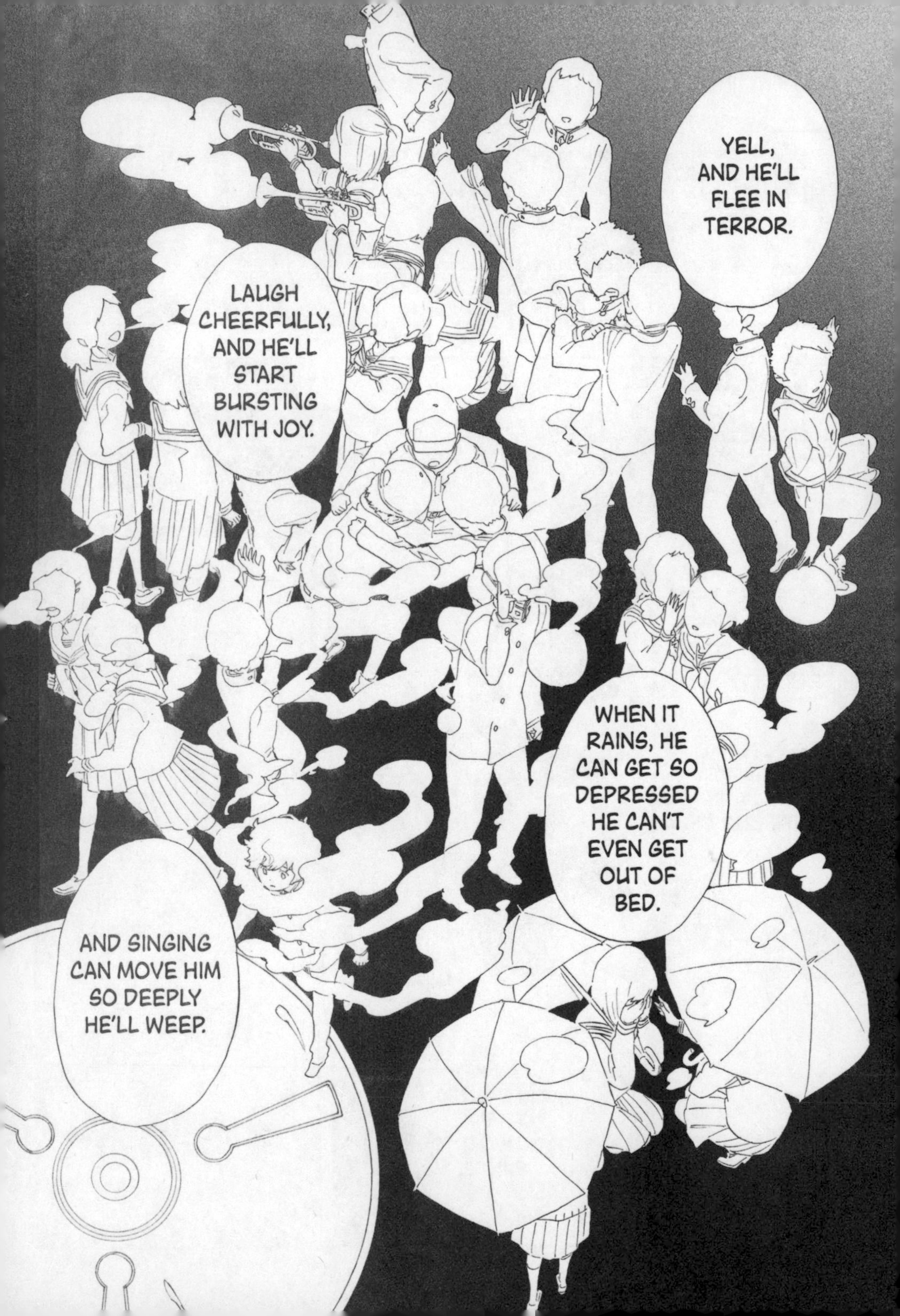
YELL, AND HE'LL FLEE IN TERROR.
LAUGH CHEERFULLY, AND HE'LL START BURSTING WITH JOY.
WHEN IT RAINS, HE CAN GET SO DEPRESSED HE CAN'T EVEN GET OUT OF BED.
AND SINGING CAN MOVE HIM SO DEEPLY HE'LL WEEP.

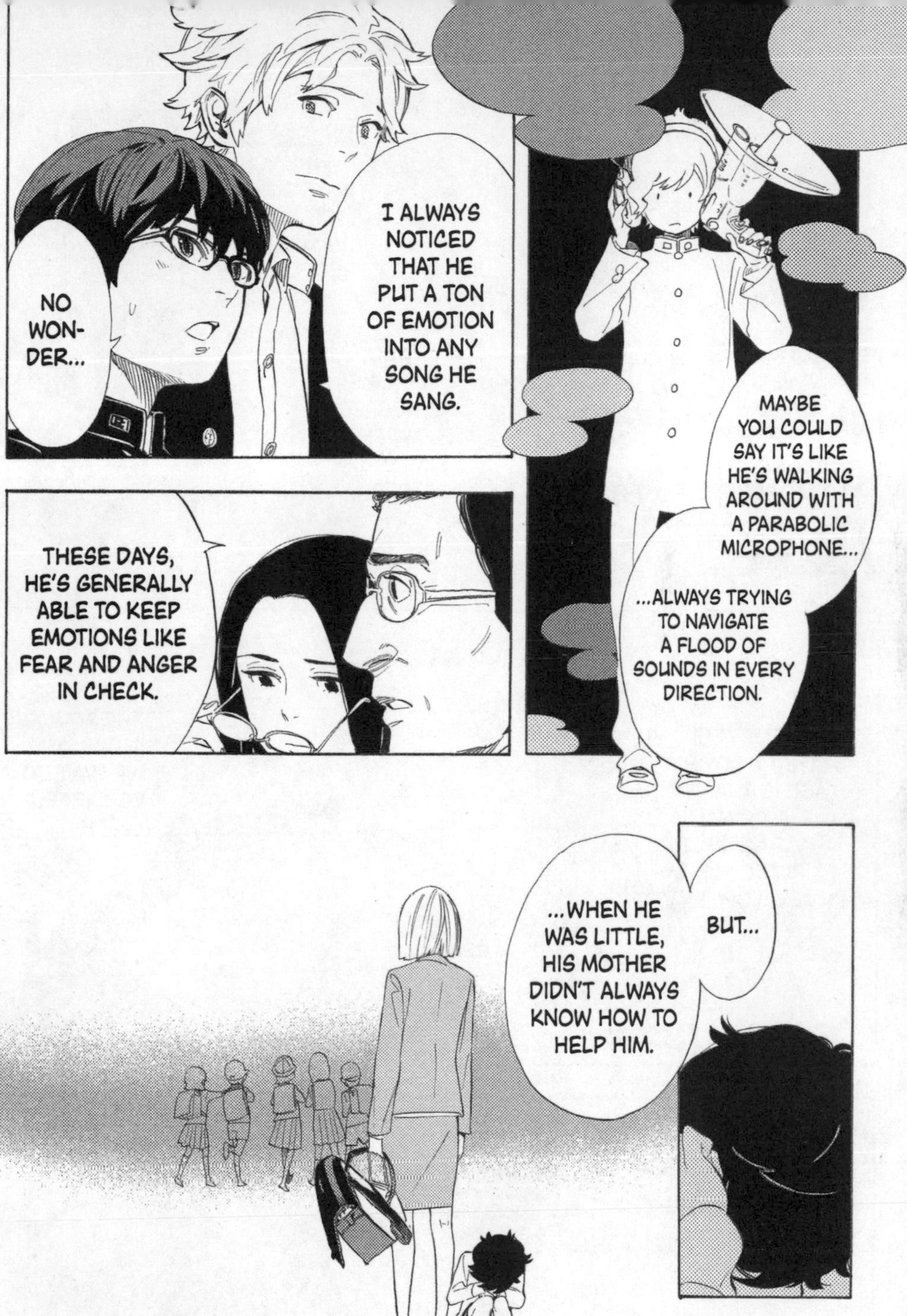
MAYBE YOU COULD SAY IT'S LIKE HE'S WALKING AROUND WITH A PARABOLIC MICROPHONE...
...ALWAYS TRYING TO NAVIGATE A FLOOD OF SOUNDS IN EVERY DIRECTION.
I ALWAYS NOTICED THAT HE PUT A TON OF EMOTION INTO ANY SONG HE SANG.
NO WON-DER...
THESE DAYS, HE'S GENERALLY ABLE TO KEEP EMOTIONS LIKE FEAR AND ANGER IN CHECK.
BUT...
...WHEN HE WAS LITTLE, HIS MOTHER DIDN'T ALWAYS KNOW HOW TO HELP HIM.

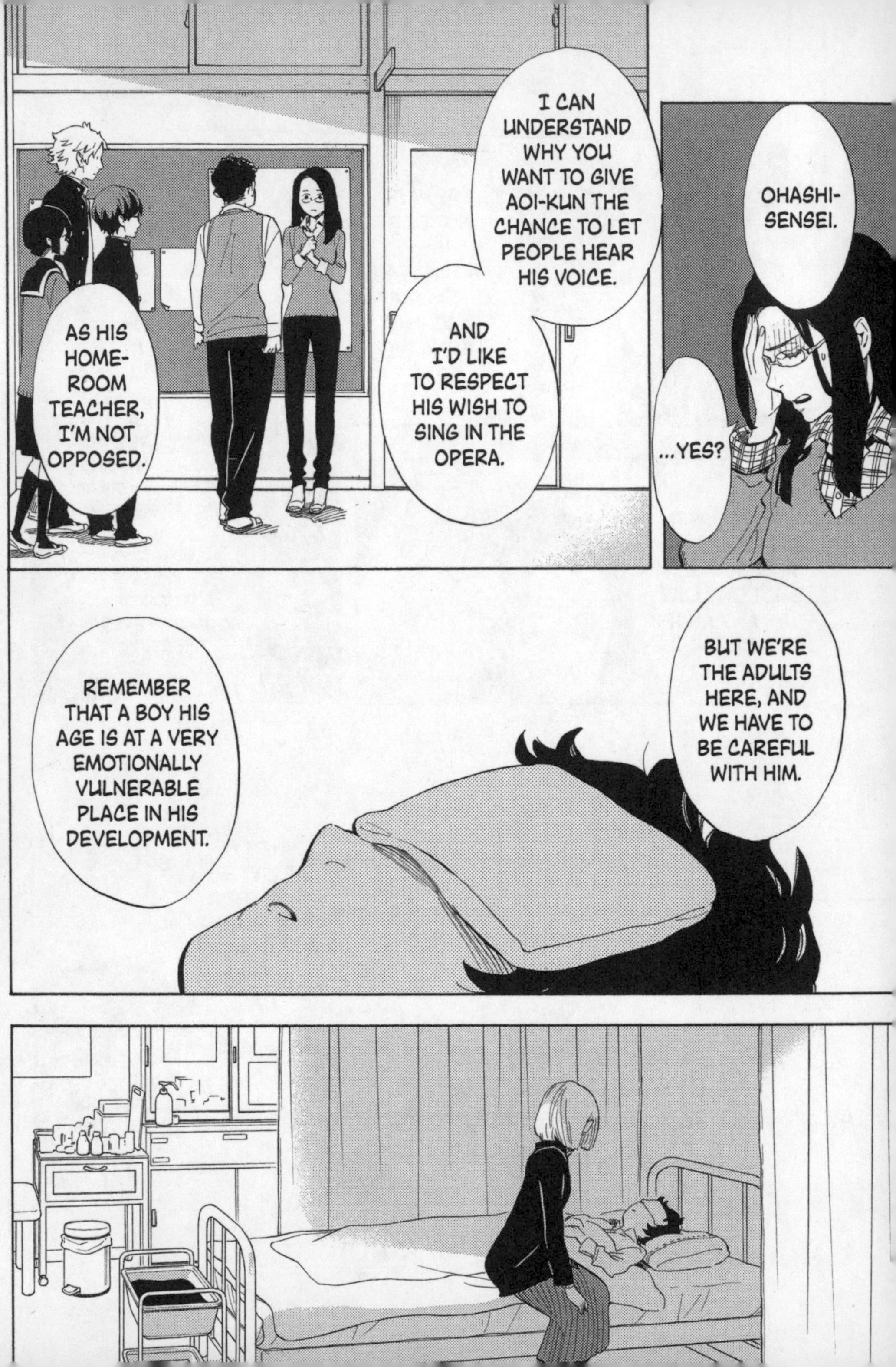
OHASHI-SENSEI.
...YES?
I CAN UNDERSTAND WHY YOU WANT TO GIVE AOI-KUN THE CHANCE TO LET PEOPLE HEAR HIS VOICE.
AND I'D LIKE TO RESPECT HIS WISH TO SING IN THE OPERA.
AS HIS HOME-ROOM TEACHER, I'M NOT OPPOSED.
BUT WE'RE THE ADULTS HERE, AND WE HAVE TO BE CAREFUL WITH HIM.
REMEMBER THAT A BOY HIS AGE IS AT A VERY EMOTIONALLY VULNERABLE PLACE IN HIS DEVELOPMENT.

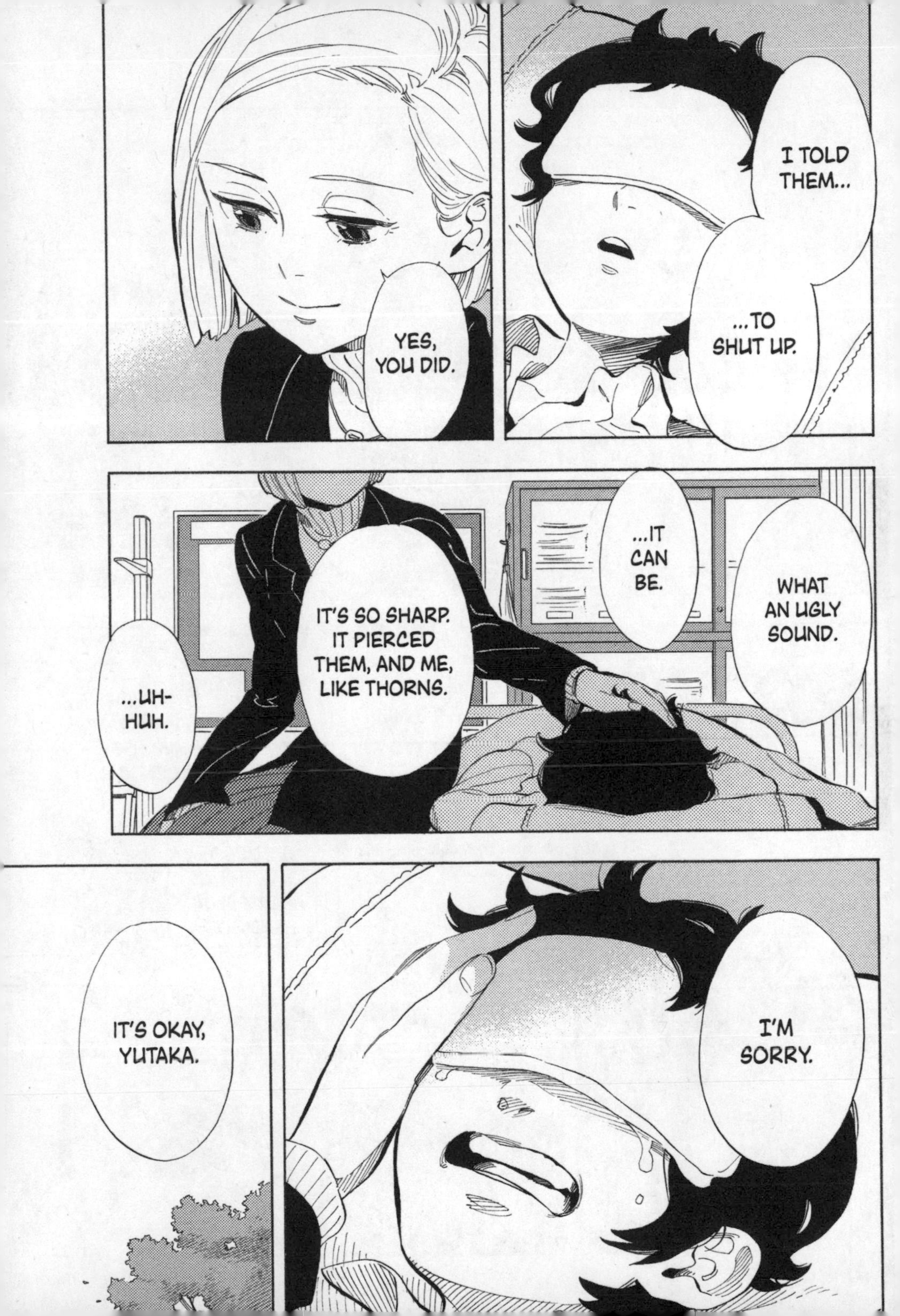
I TOLD THEM...
...TO SHUT UP.
YES, YOU DID.
WHAT AN UGLY SOUND.
...IT CAN BE.
IT'S SO SHARP. IT PIERCED THEM, AND ME, LIKE THORNS.
...UH-HUH.
I'M SORRY.
IT'S OKAY, YUTAKA.

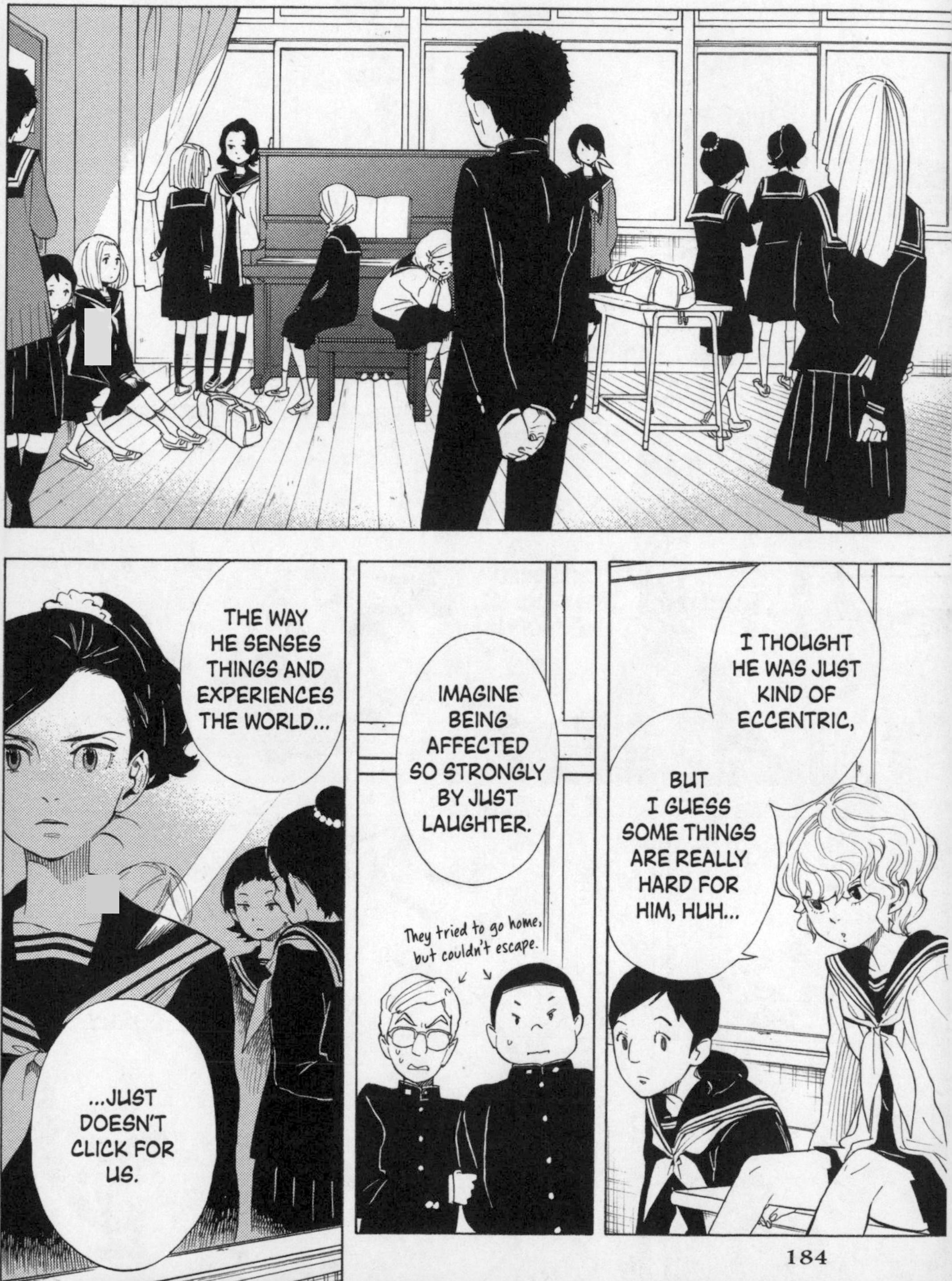
I THOUGHT HE WAS JUST KIND OF ECCENTRIC,
BUT I GUESS SOME THINGS ARE REALLY HARD FOR HIM, HUH...
IMAGINE BEING AFFECTED SO STRONGLY BY JUST LAUGHTER.
They tried to go home, but couldn't escape.
THE WAY HE SENSES THINGS AND EXPERIENCES THE WORLD...
...JUST DOESN'T CLICK FOR US.

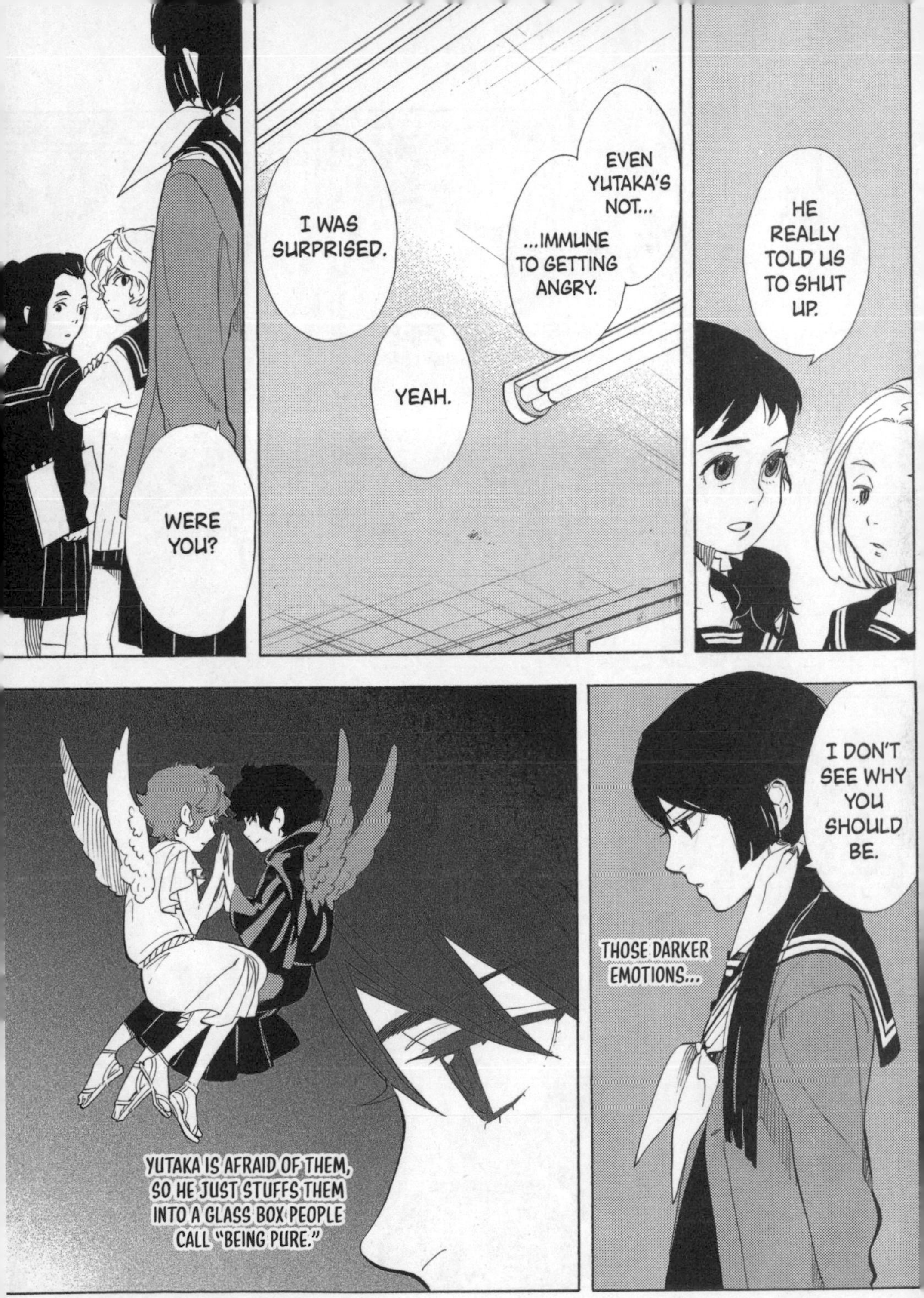
HE REALLY TOLD US TO SHUT UP.
EVEN YUTAKA'S NOT...
...IMMUNE TO GETTING ANGRY.
I WAS SURPRISED.
YEAH.
WERE YOU?
I DON'T SEE WHY YOU SHOULD BE.
THOSE DARKER EMOTIONS...
YUTAKA IS AFRAID OF THEM, SO HE JUST STUFFS THEM INTO A GLASS BOX PEOPLE CALL "BEING PURE."

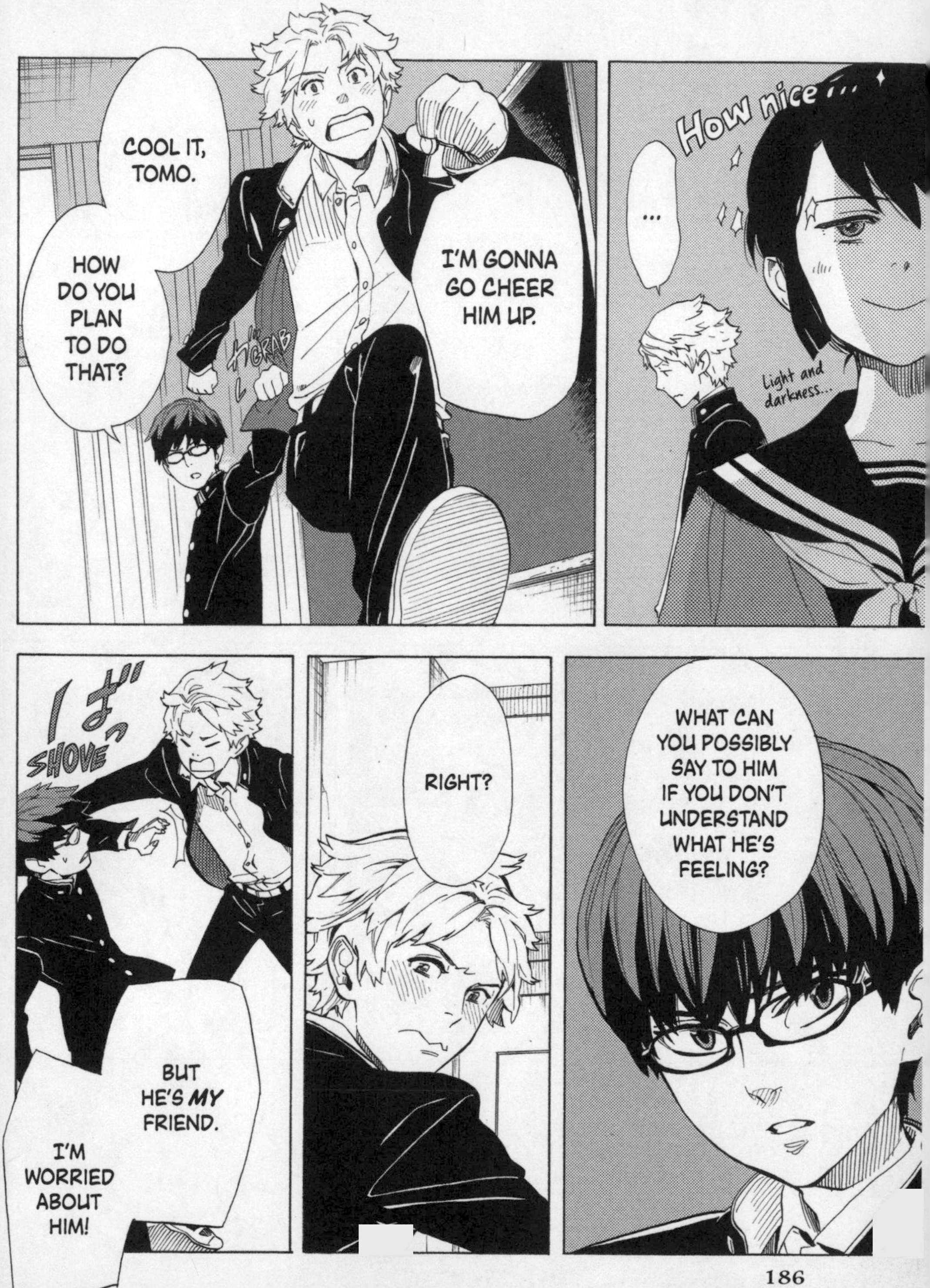
...
How nice...
Light and darkness...
I'M GONNA GO CHEER HIM UP.
COOL IT, TOMO.
HOW DO YOU PLAN TO DO THAT?
GRAB
WHAT CAN YOU POSSIBLY SAY TO HIM IF YOU DON'T UNDERSTAND WHAT HE'S FEELING?
RIGHT?
SHOVE
BUT HE'S *MY* FRIEND.
I'M WORRIED ABOUT HIM!

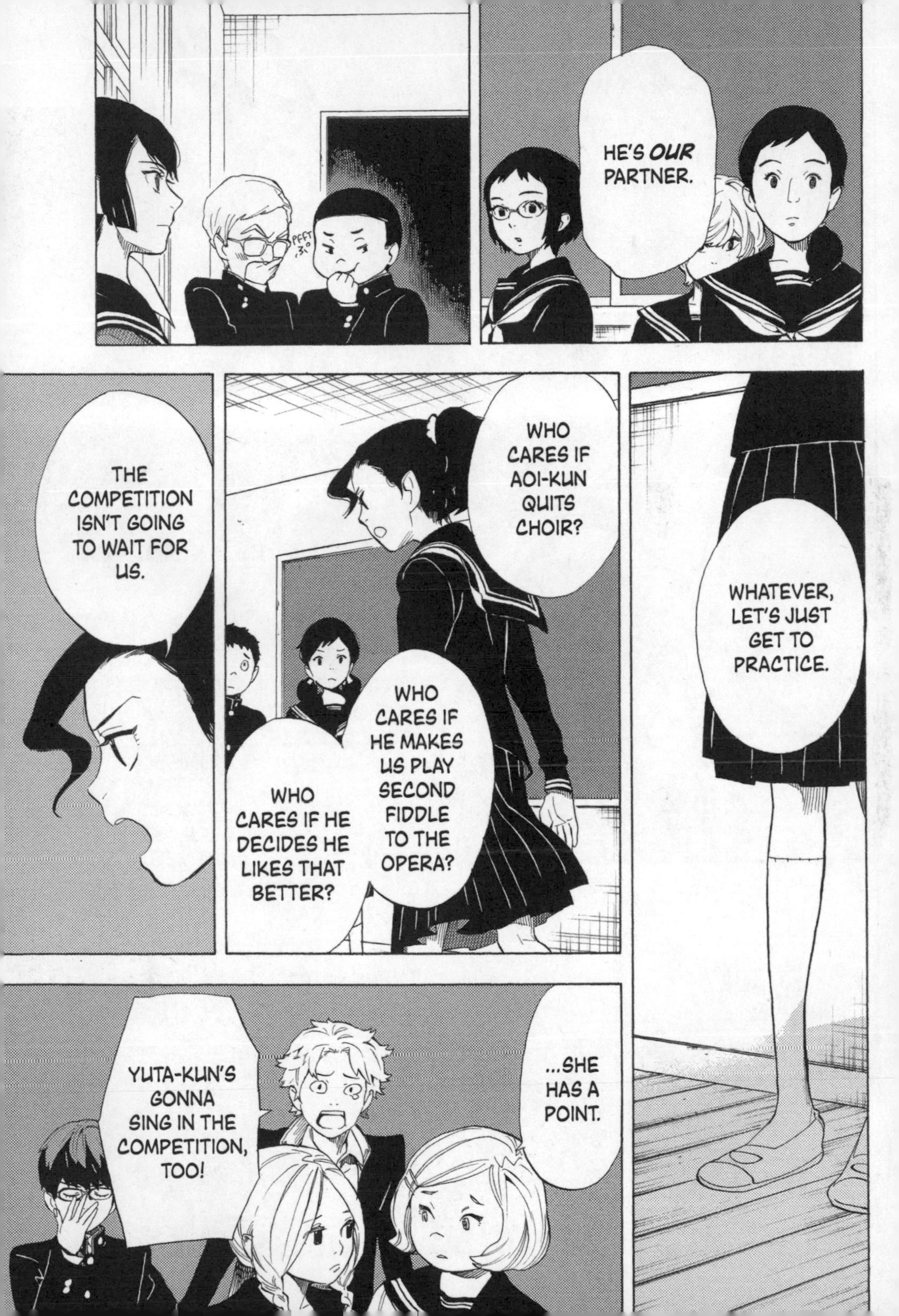
HE'S **OUR** PARTNER.
PFFT
WHATEVER, LET'S JUST GET TO PRACTICE.
WHO CARES IF AOI-KUN QUITS CHOIR?
WHO CARES IF HE MAKES US PLAY SECOND FIDDLE TO THE OPERA?
WHO CARES IF HE DECIDES HE LIKES THAT BETTER?
THE COMPETITION ISN'T GOING TO WAIT FOR US.
...SHE HAS A POINT.
YUTA-KUN'S GONNA SING IN THE COMPETITION, TOO!

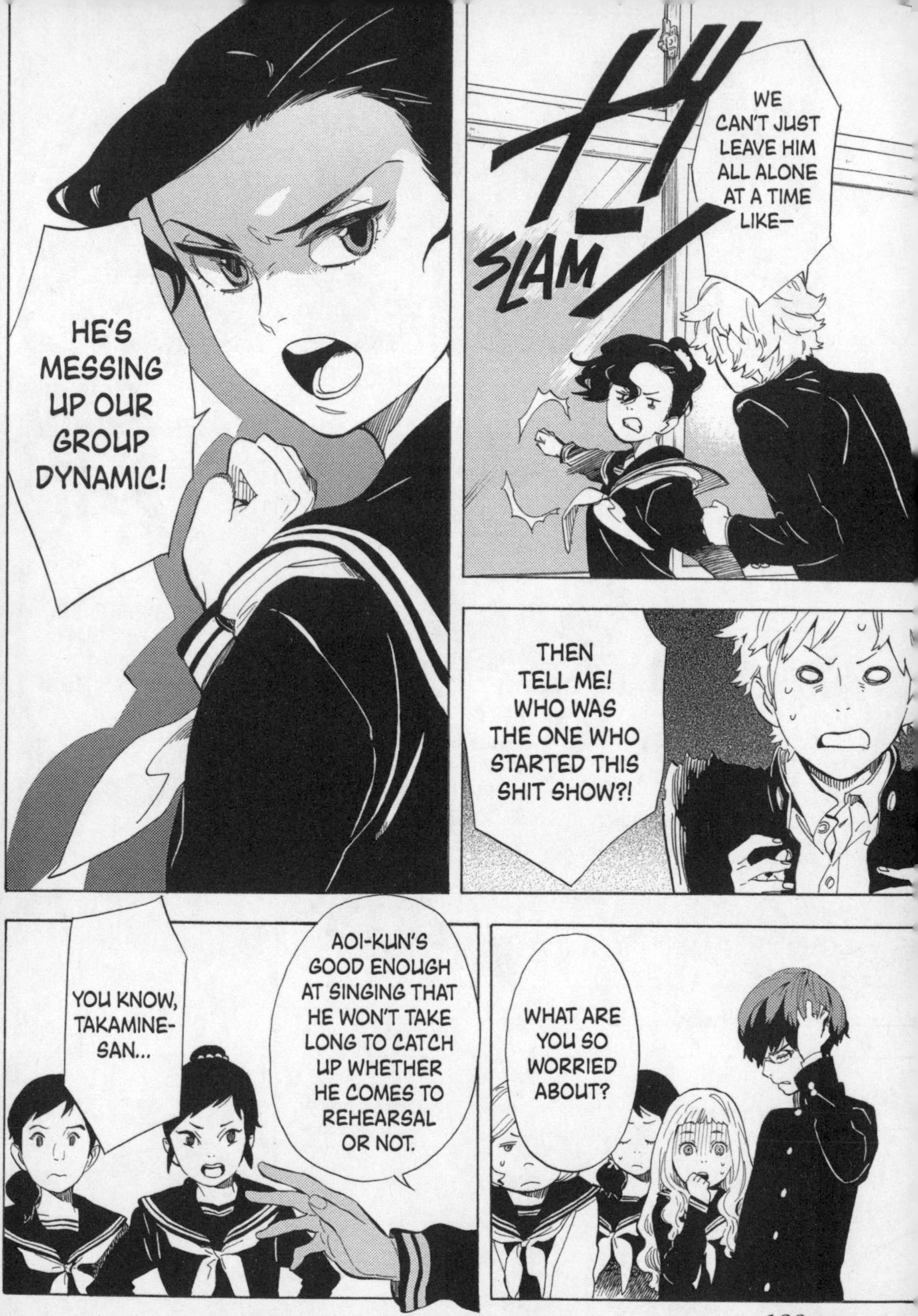
WE CAN'T JUST LEAVE HIM ALL ALONE AT A TIME LIKE—
SLAM
THEN TELL ME! WHO WAS THE ONE WHO STARTED THIS SHIT SHOW?!
HE'S MESSING UP OUR GROUP DYNAMIC!
WHAT ARE YOU SO WORRIED ABOUT?
AOI-KUN'S GOOD ENOUGH AT SINGING THAT HE WON'T TAKE LONG TO CATCH UP WHETHER HE COMES TO REHEARSAL OR NOT.
YOU KNOW, TAKAMINE-SAN...

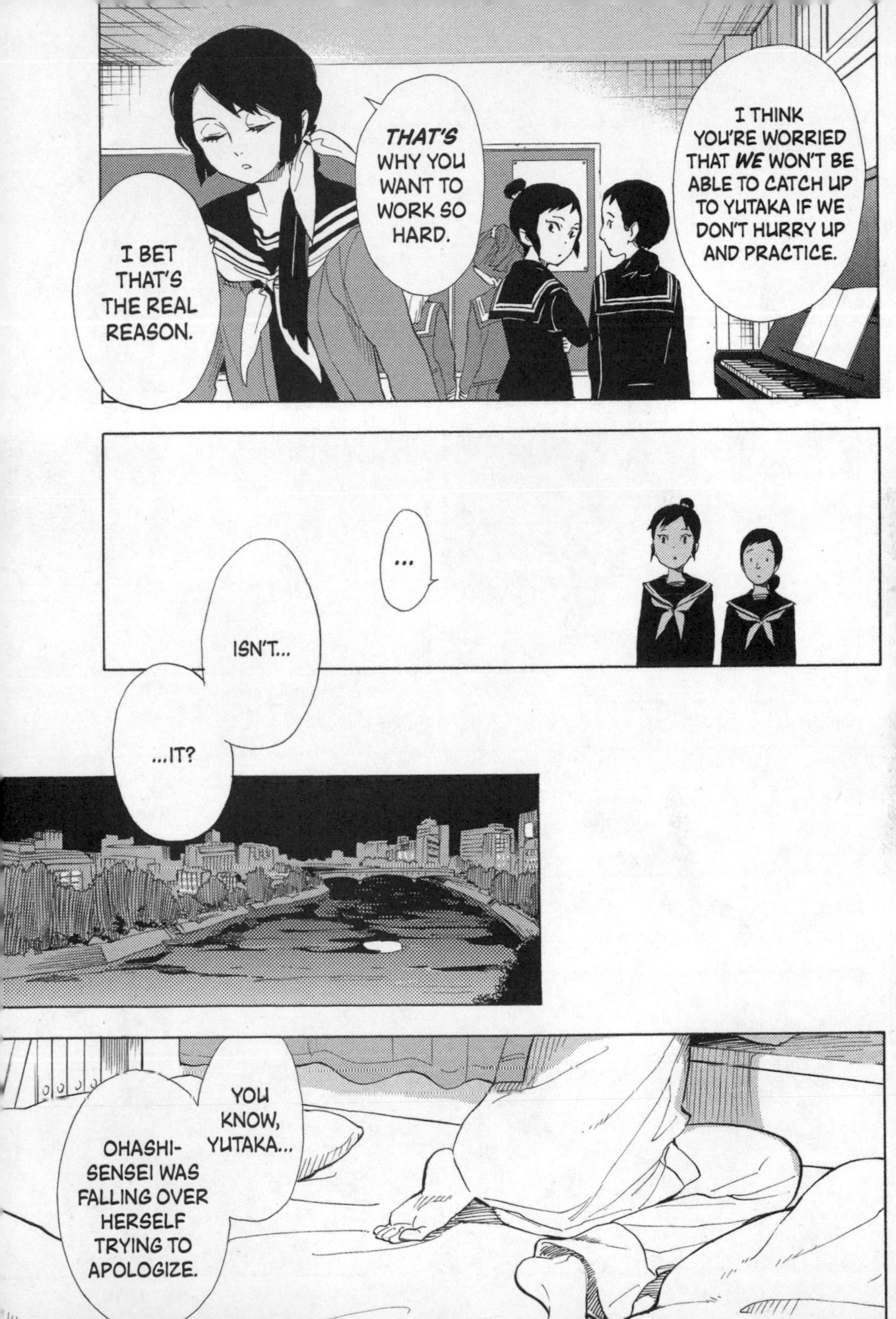
I THINK YOU'RE WORRIED THAT *WE* WON'T BE ABLE TO CATCH UP TO YUTAKA IF WE DON'T HURRY UP AND PRACTICE.
THAT'S WHY YOU WANT TO WORK SO HARD.
I BET THAT'S THE REAL REASON.
...
ISN'T...
...IT?
YOU KNOW, YUTAKA...
OHASHI-SENSEI WAS FALLING OVER HERSELF TRYING TO APOLOGIZE.

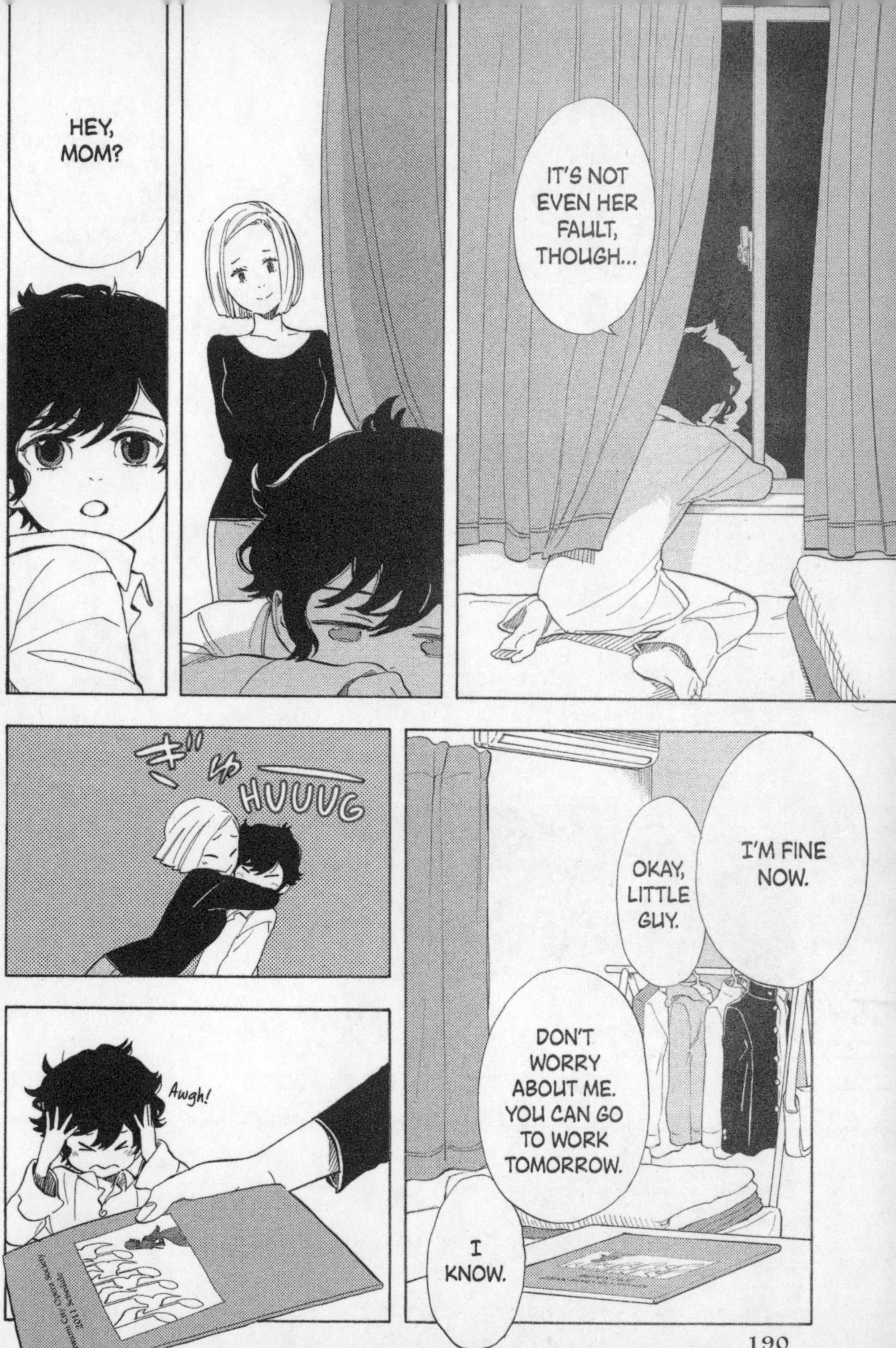

IT'S NOT EVEN HER FAULT, THOUGH...
HEY, MOM?
I'M FINE NOW.
OKAY, LITTLE GUY.
DON'T WORRY ABOUT ME. YOU CAN GO TO WORK TOMORROW.
I KNOW.
HUUUG
Awgh!

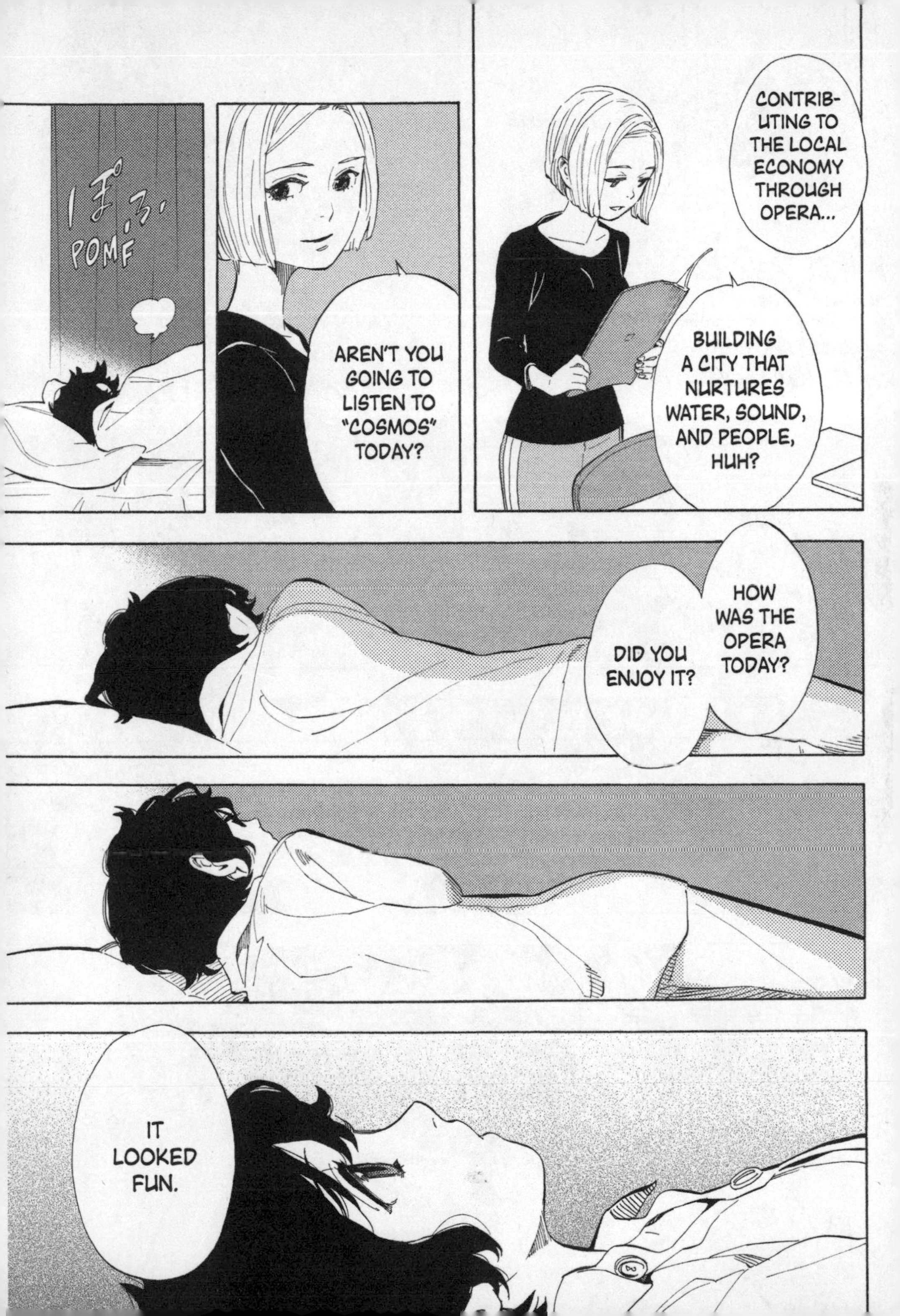
CONTRIB-UTING TO THE LOCAL ECONOMY THROUGH OPERA...
BUILDING A CITY THAT NURTURES WATER, SOUND, AND PEOPLE, HUH?
AREN'T YOU GOING TO LISTEN TO "COSMOS" TODAY?
ぽふ
POMF
HOW WAS THE OPERA TODAY?
DID YOU ENJOY IT?
IT LOOKED FUN.

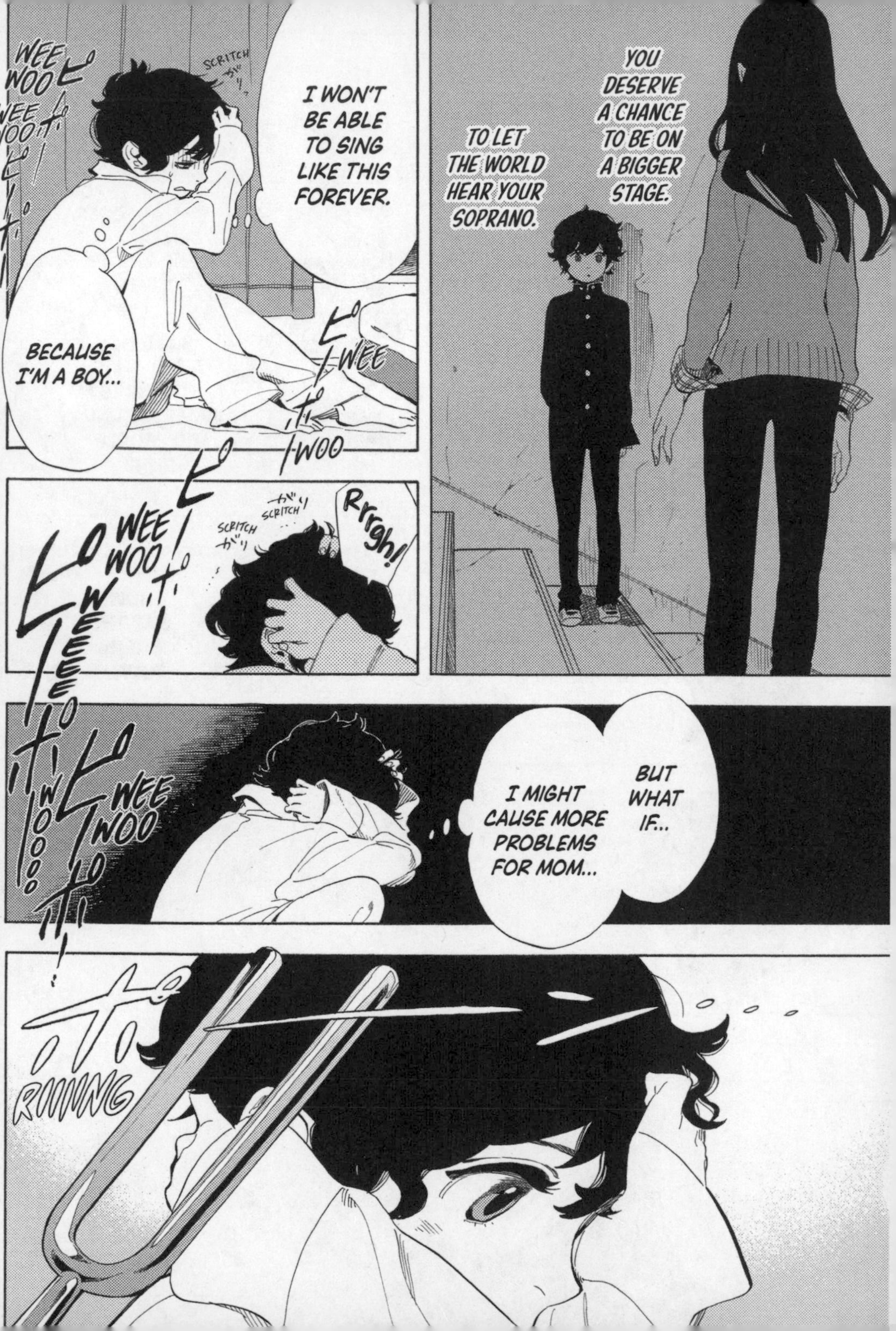
YOU DESERVE A CHANCE TO BE ON A BIGGER STAGE.
TO LET THE WORLD HEAR YOUR SOPRANO.
SCRITCH
WEE WOO WEE WOO
I WON'T BE ABLE TO SING LIKE THIS FOREVER.
BECAUSE I'M A BOY...
WEE
WOO
Rrrgh!
SCRITCH
SCRITCH
WEE WOO
WEEEEE
BUT WHAT IF...
I MIGHT CAUSE MORE PROBLEMS FOR MOM...
WEE WOO
RIIING

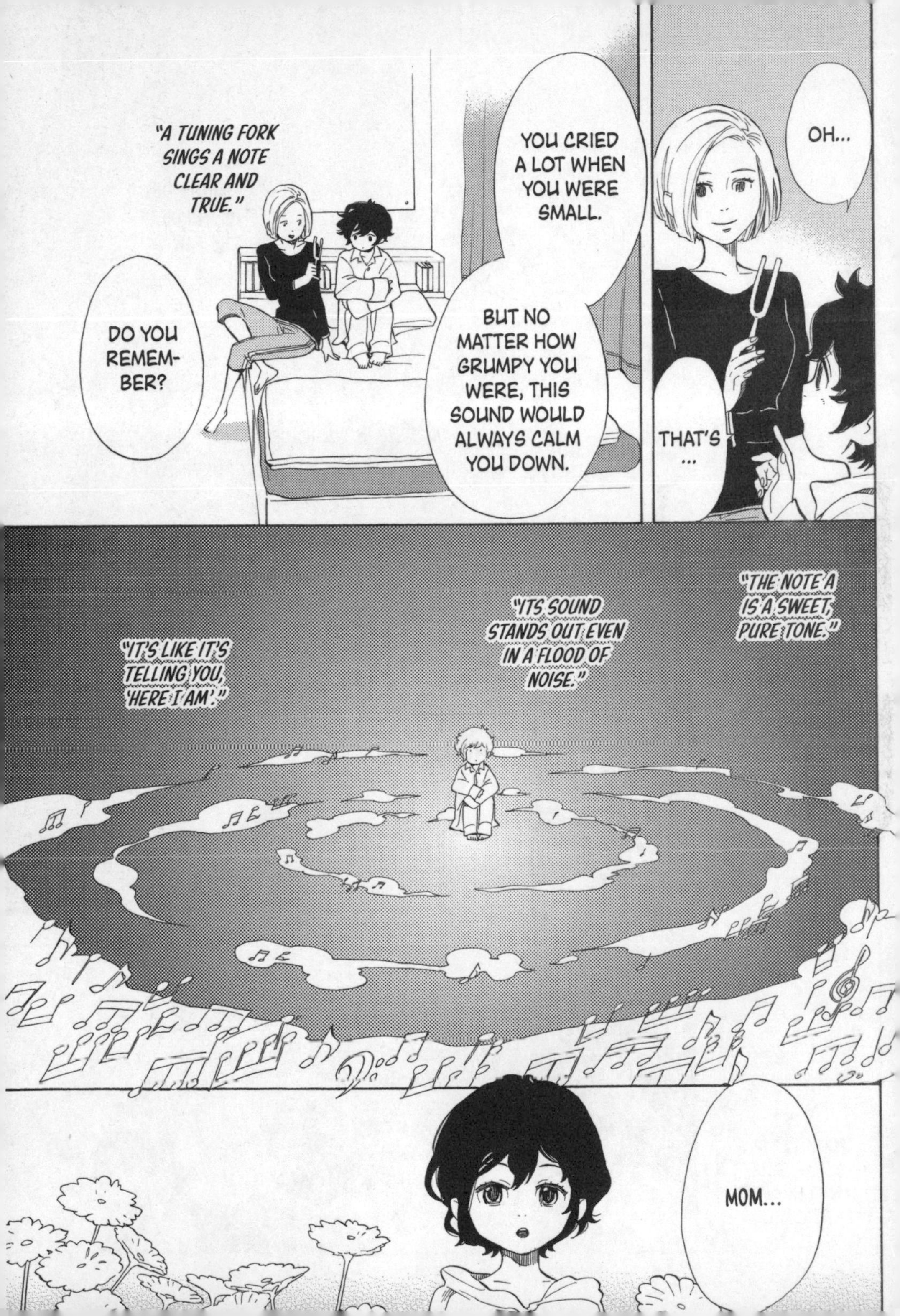
OH...
THAT'S ...
YOU CRIED A LOT WHEN YOU WERE SMALL.
BUT NO MATTER HOW GRUMPY YOU WERE, THIS SOUND WOULD ALWAYS CALM YOU DOWN.
"A TUNING FORK SINGS A NOTE CLEAR AND TRUE."
DO YOU REMEMBER?
"THE NOTE A IS A SWEET, PURE TONE."
"ITS SOUND STANDS OUT EVEN IN A FLOOD OF NOISE."
"IT'S LIKE IT'S TELLING YOU, 'HERE I AM'."
MOM...

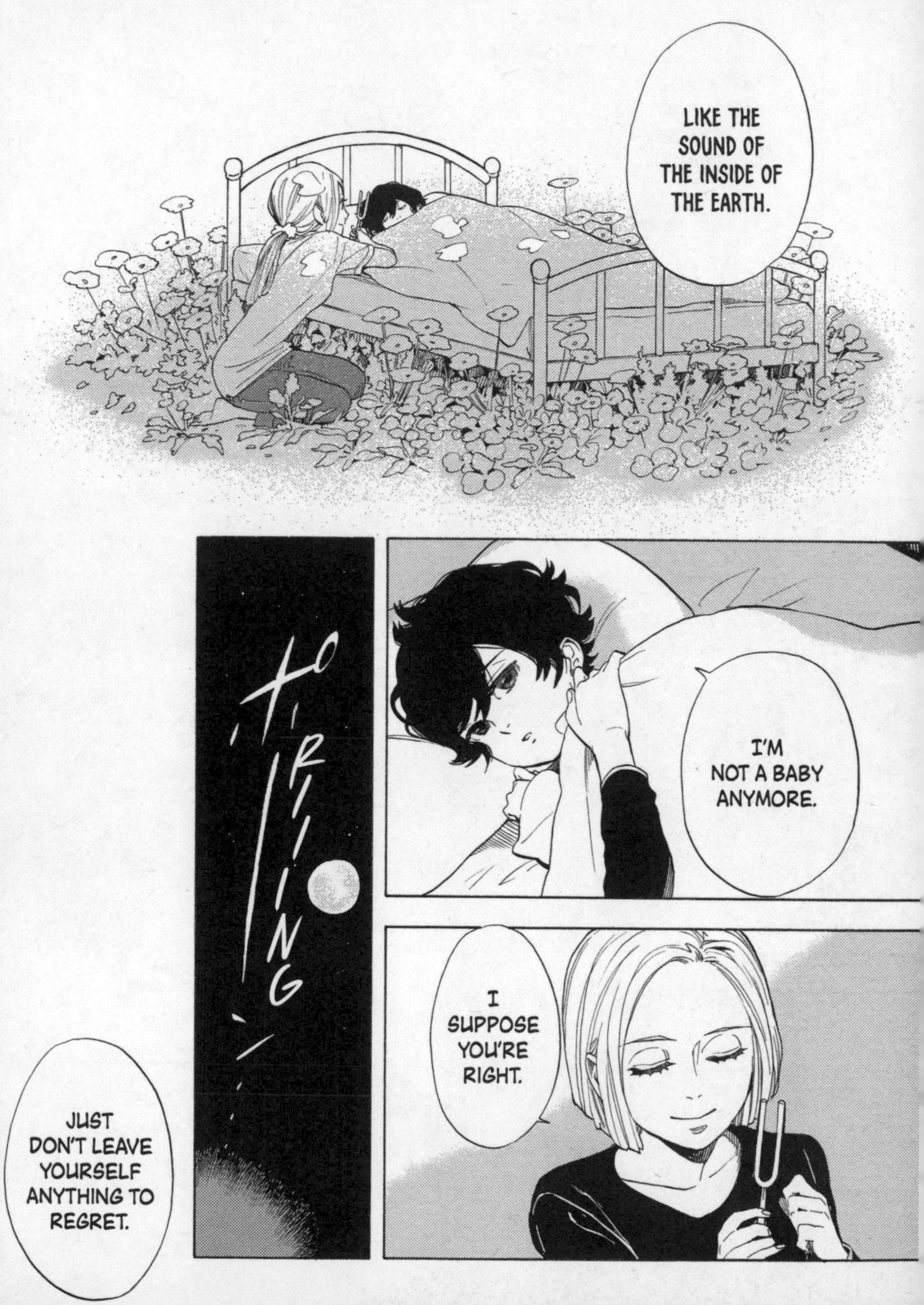
LIKE THE SOUND OF THE INSIDE OF THE EARTH.
I'M NOT A BABY ANYMORE.
I SUPPOSE YOU'RE RIGHT.
TRIIIING
JUST DON'T LEAVE YOURSELF ANYTHING TO REGRET.

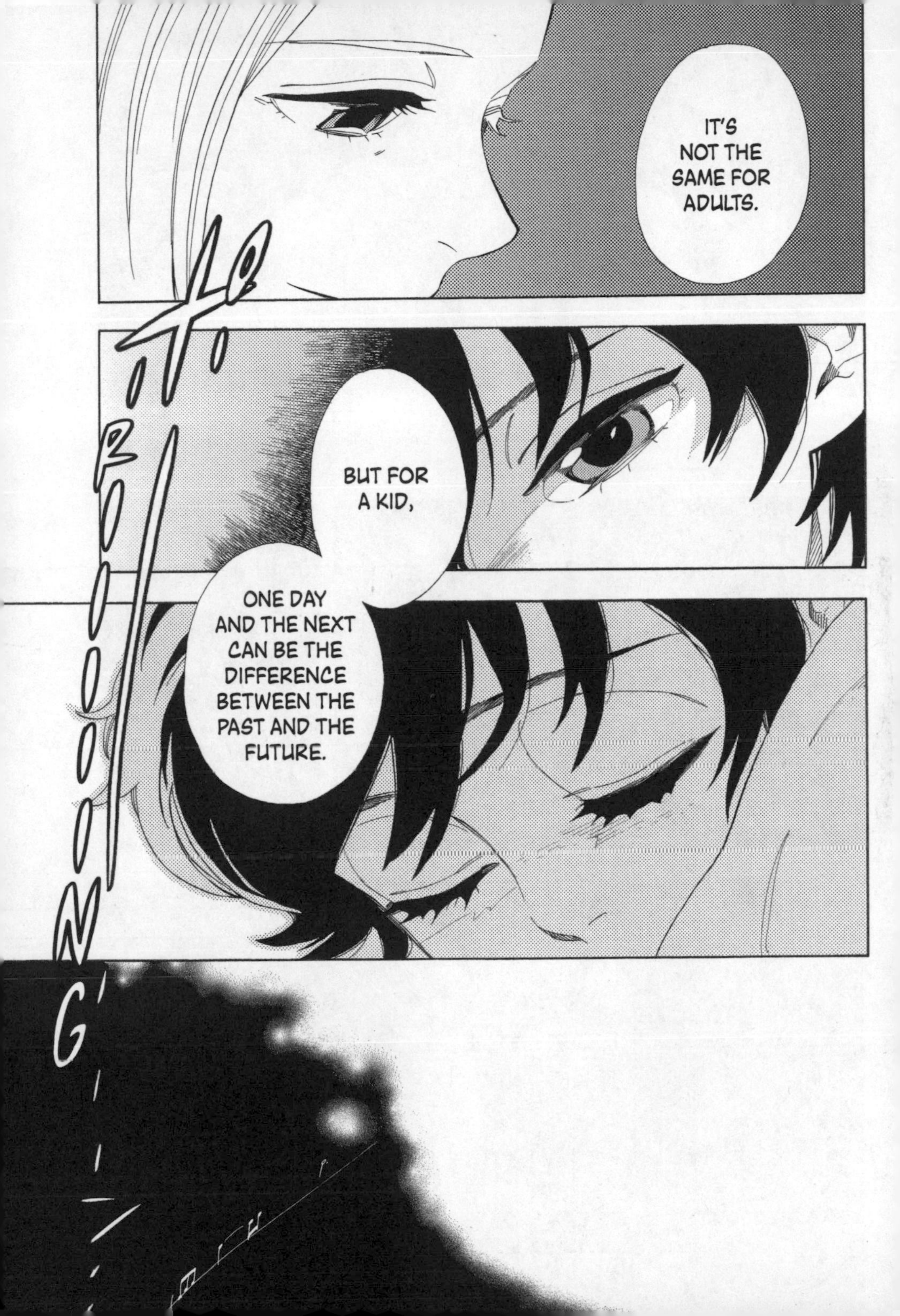
IT'S NOT THE SAME FOR ADULTS.
BUT FOR A KID,
ONE DAY AND THE NEXT CAN BE THE DIFFERENCE BETWEEN THE PAST AND THE FUTURE.

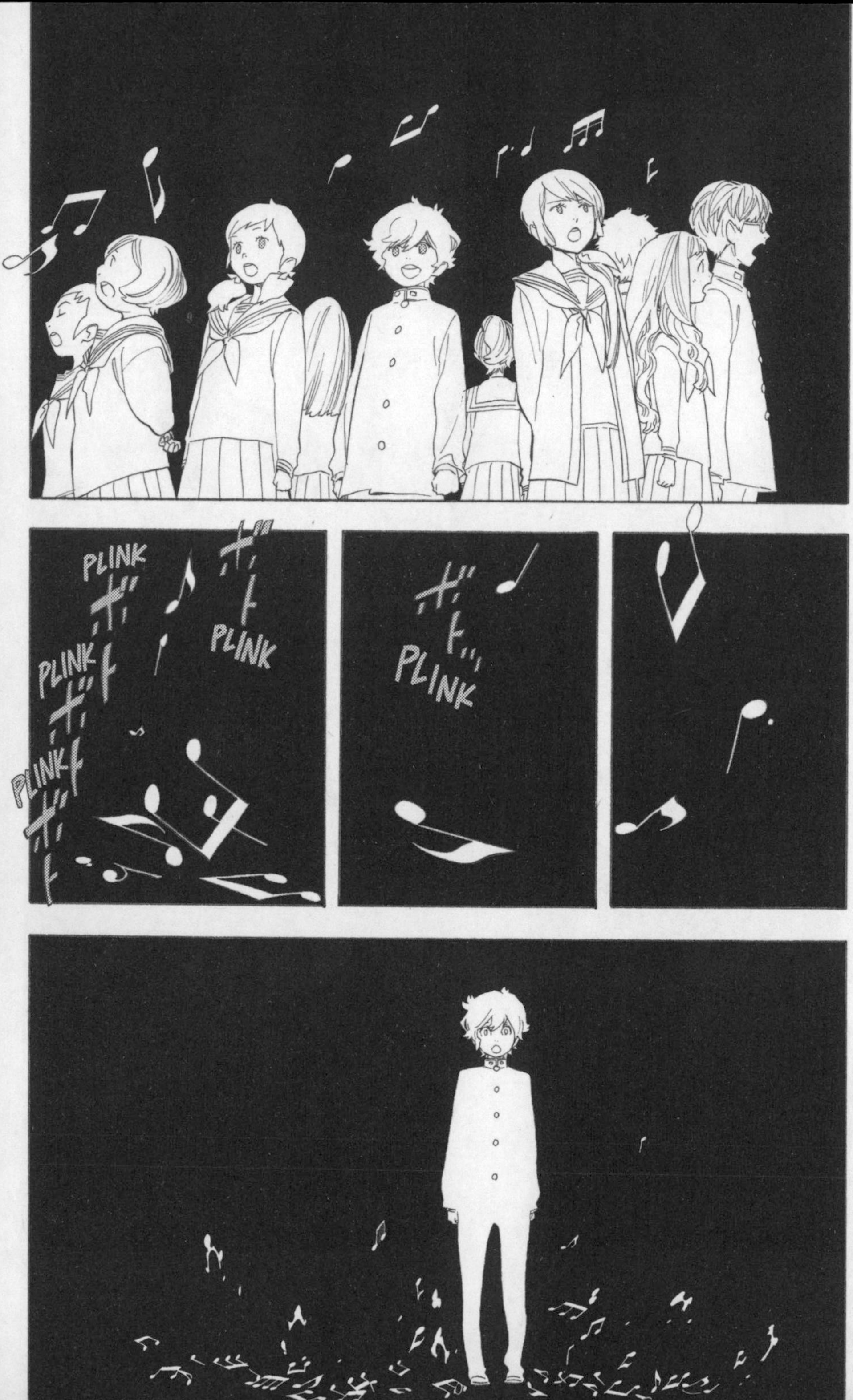
PLINK
PLINK
PLINK
PLINK
PLINK

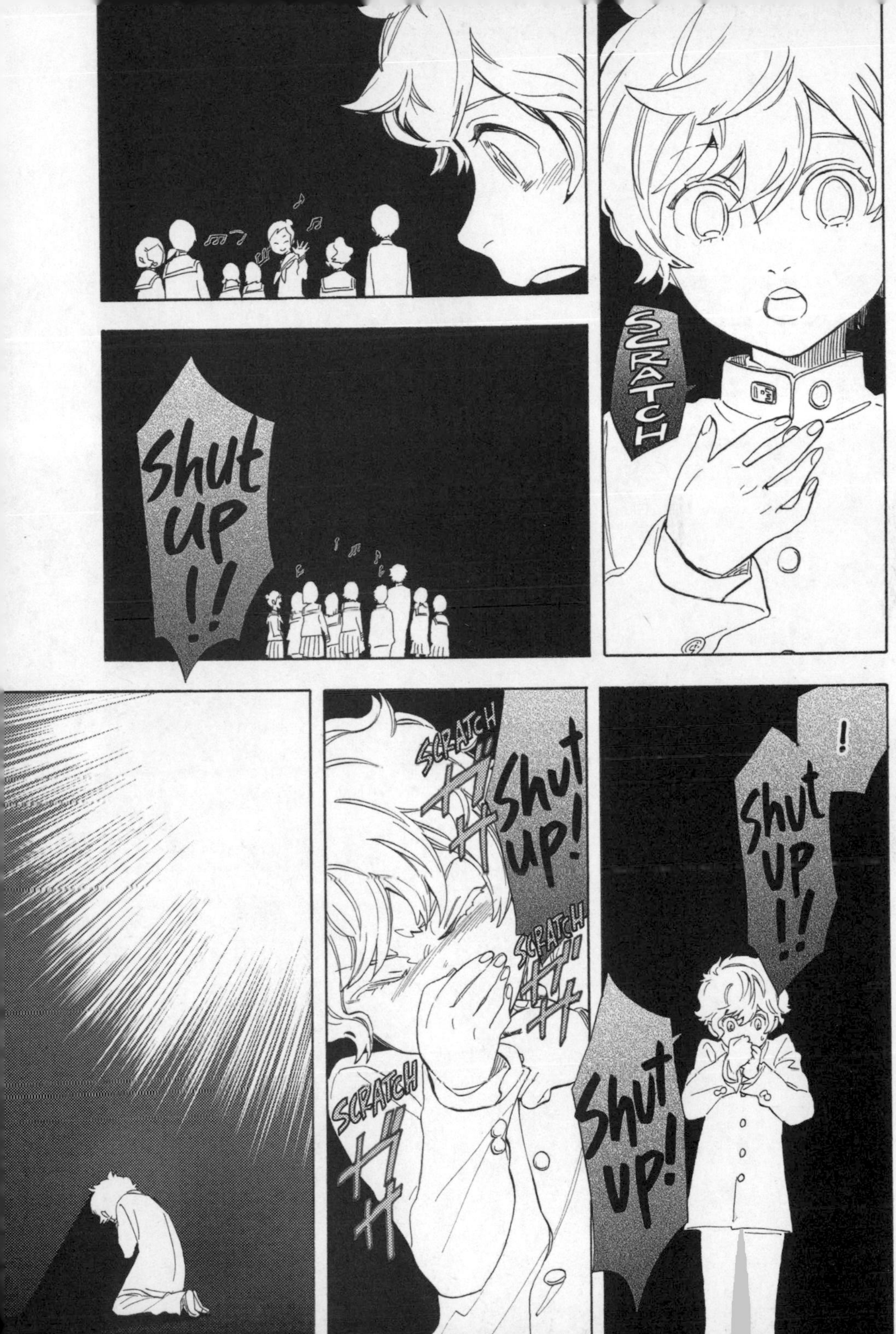
SCRATCH
Shut up!!
!
Shut up!!
Shut up!
SCRATCH
Shut up!
SCRATCH
SCRATCH

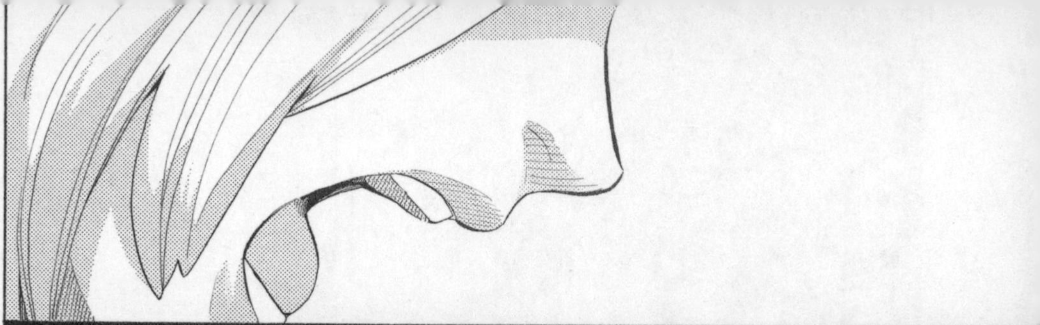
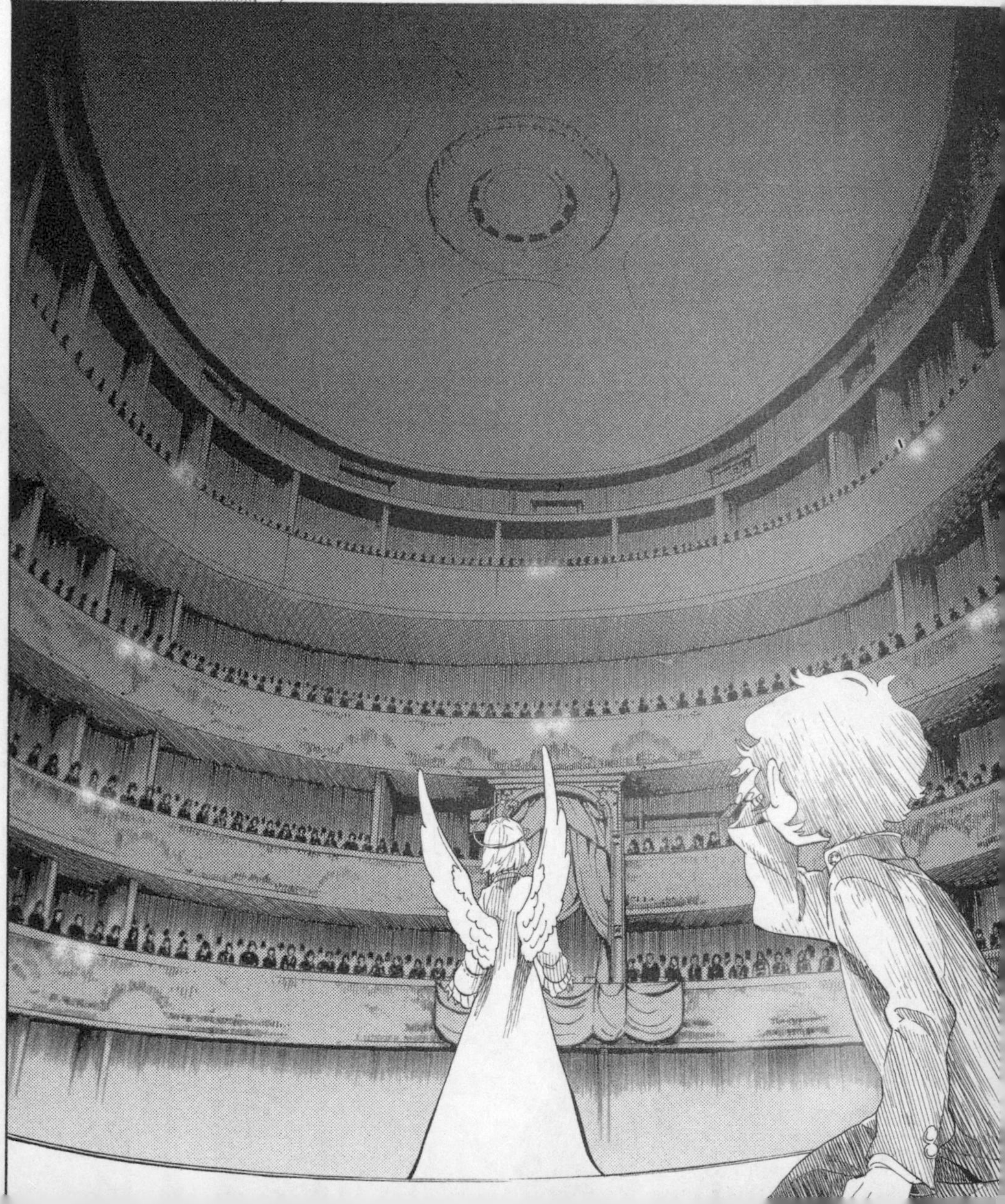

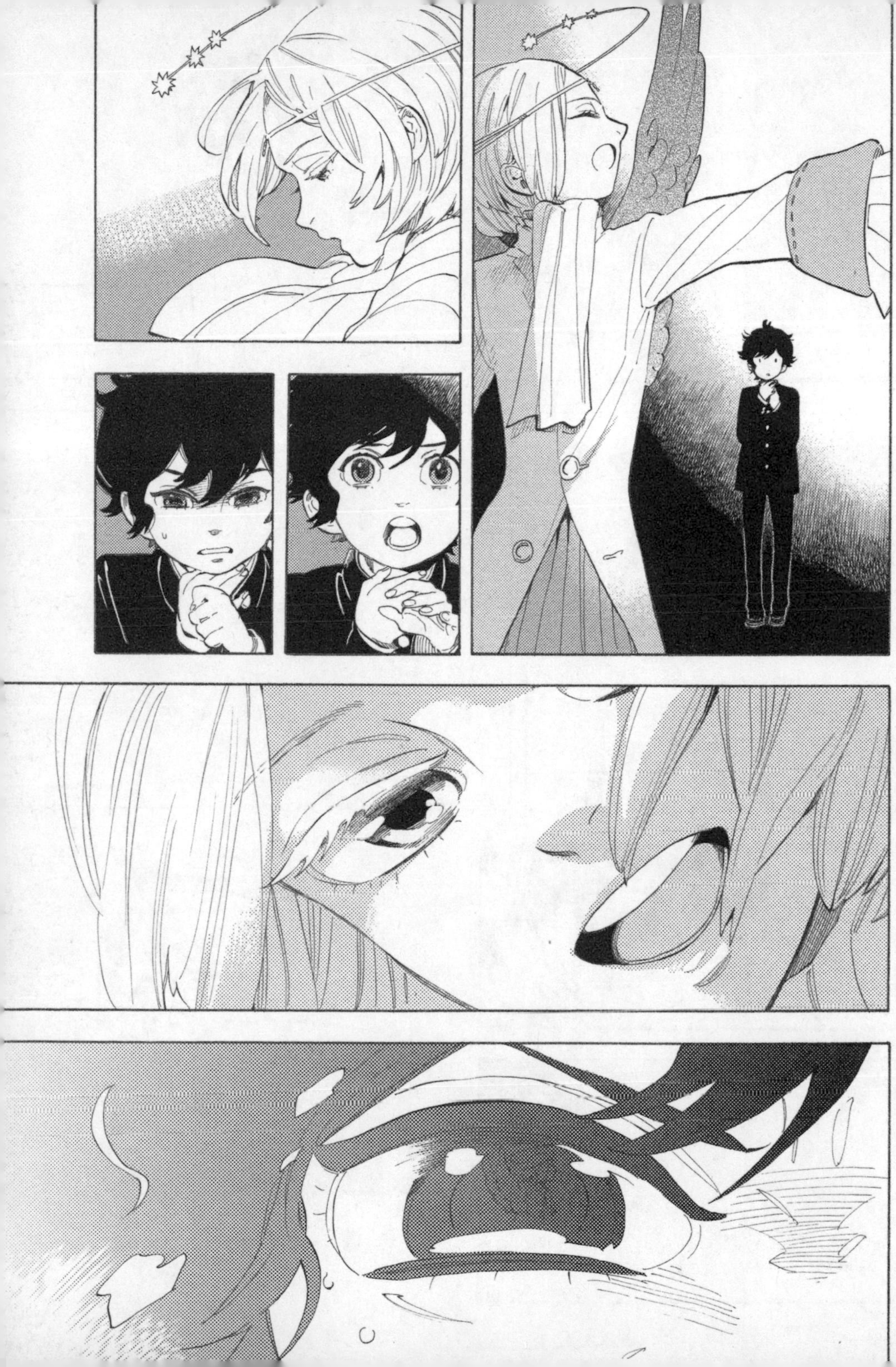

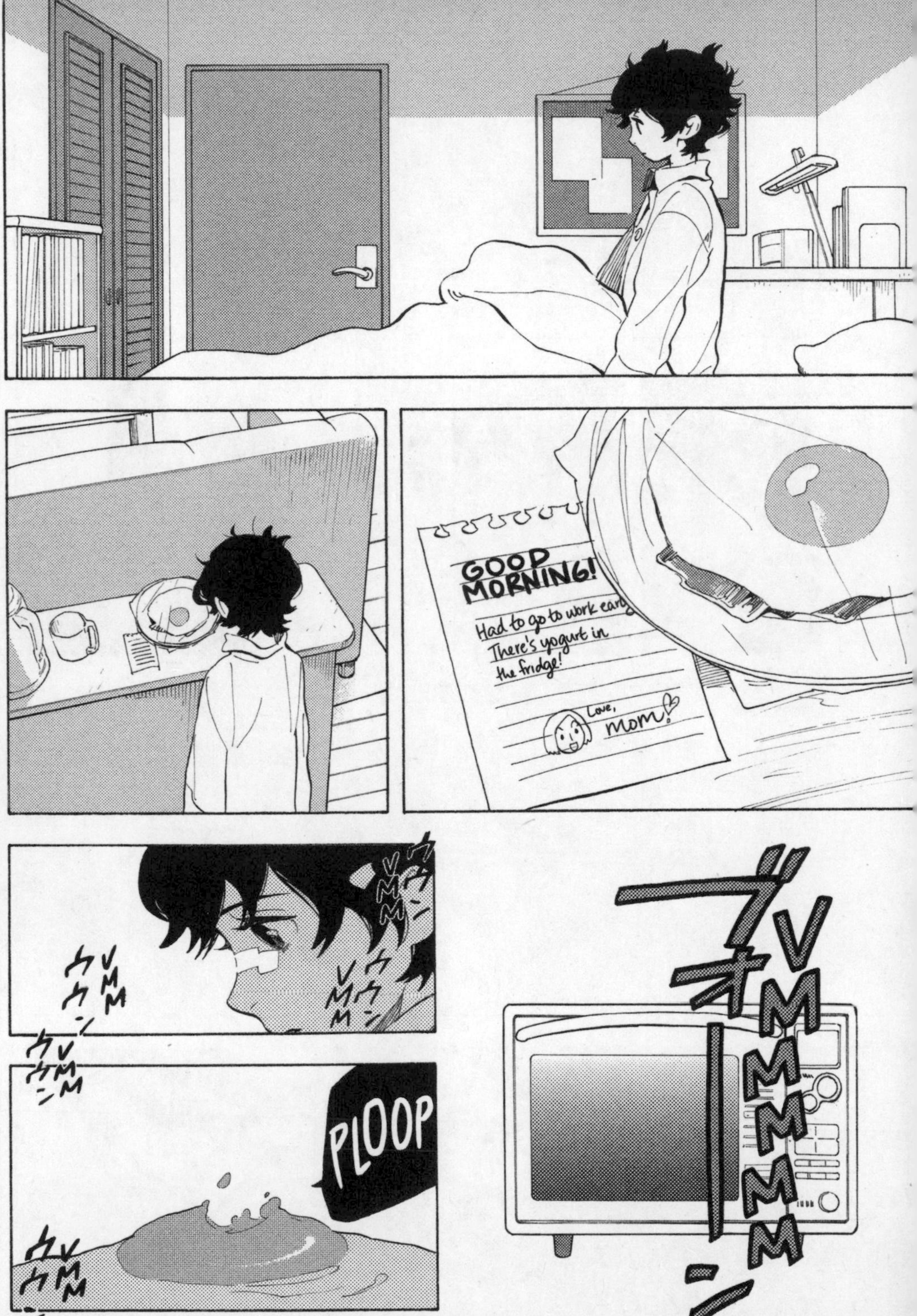
GOOD MORNING!
Had to go to work
There's yogurt in the fridge!
Love, mom
ブオーーン
VMMMMMMM
VMM
VMM
PLOOP
VMM

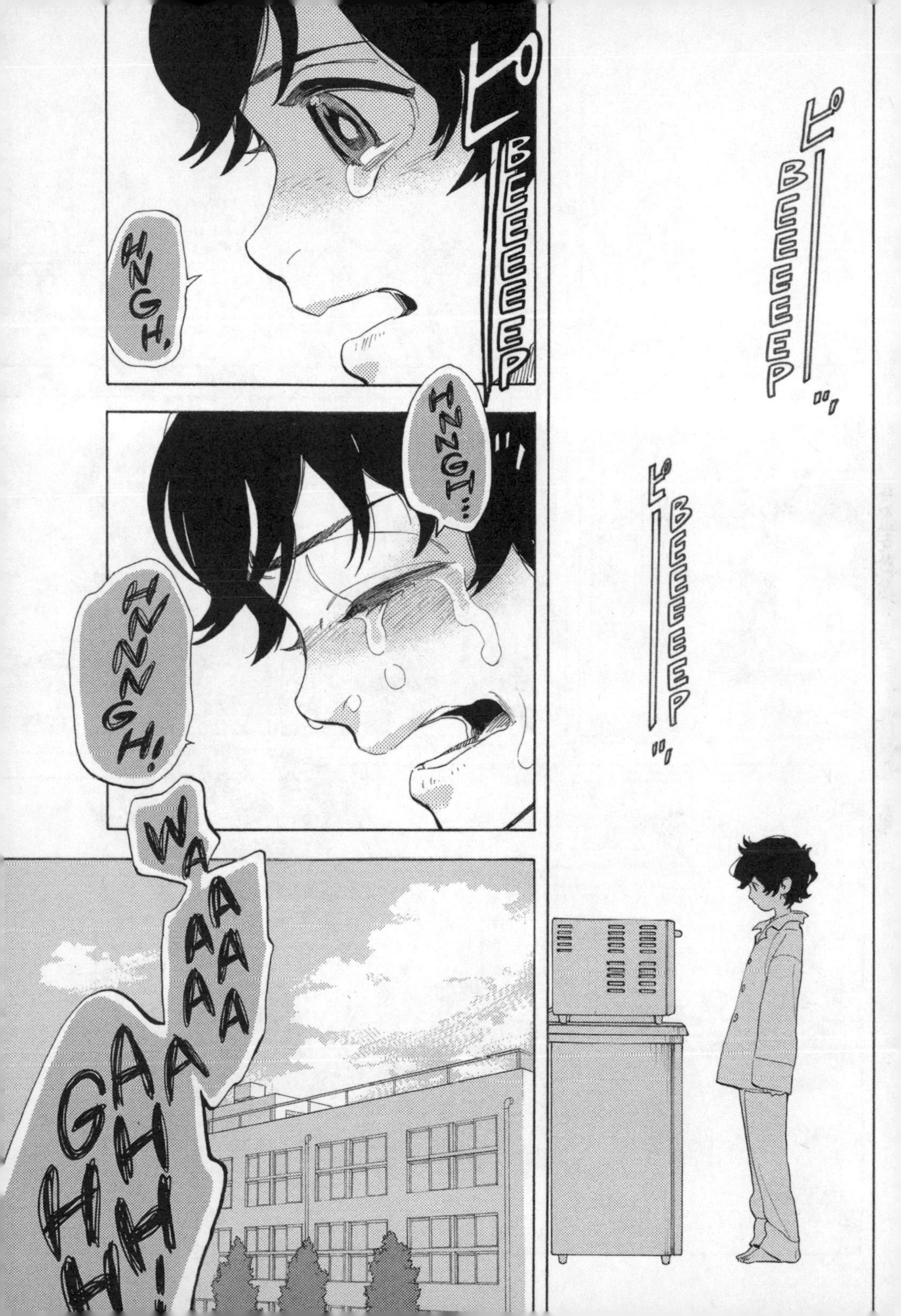
ピ BEEEEEEP…
ピ BEEEEEEP…
ピ BEEEEEEEP
HNGH.
HNNGH…
HNNNNGH!
WAAAAAAA
GAHHHHH!

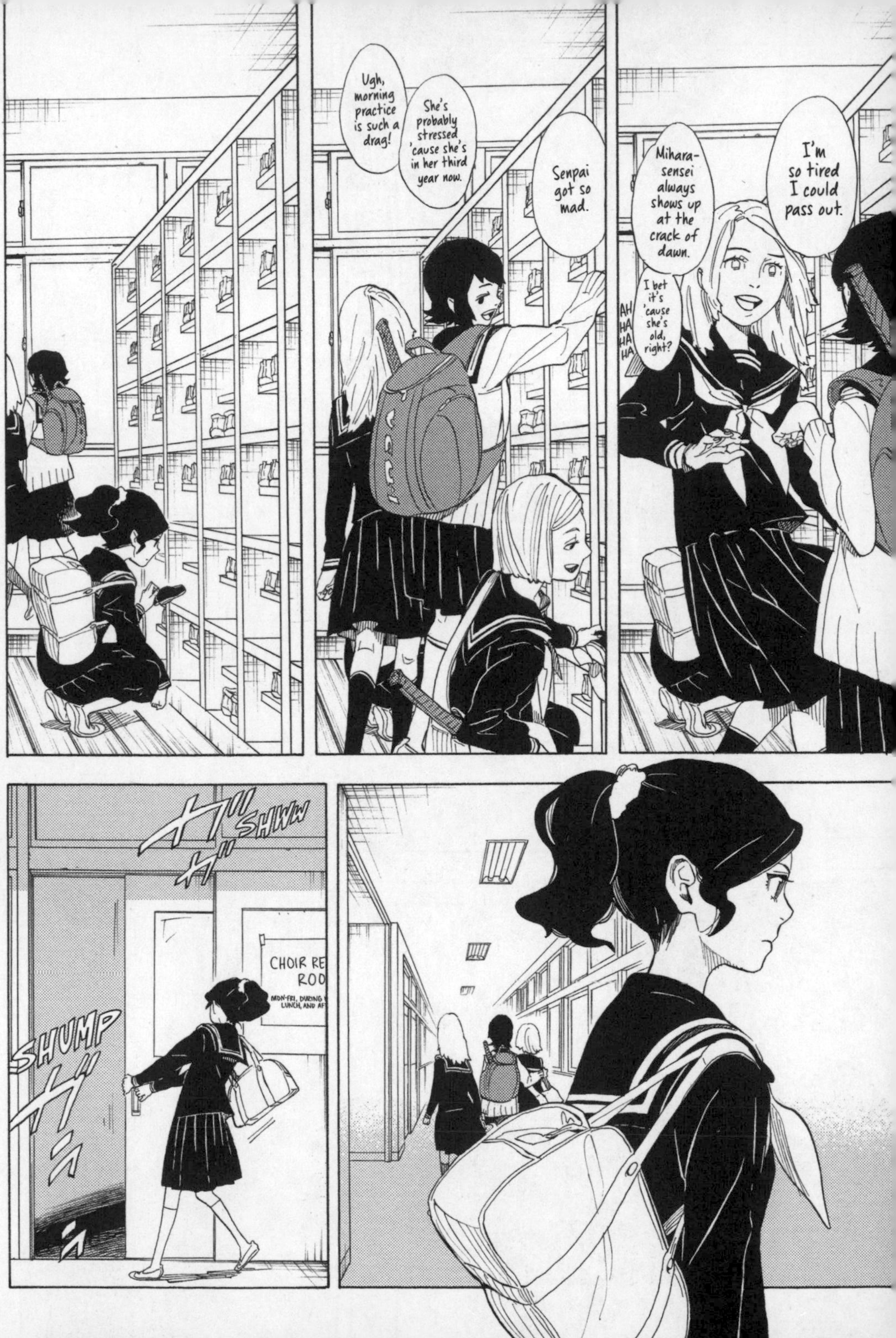
I'm so tired I could pass out.
Mihara-sensei always shows up at the crack of dawn.
I bet it's 'cause she's old, right?
HA HA HA HA
Senpai got so mad.
She's probably stressed 'cause she's in her third year now.
Ugh, morning practice is such a drag!
SHWW
CHOIR RE
ROO
MON-FRI, DURING
LUNCH, AND AFT
SHUMP

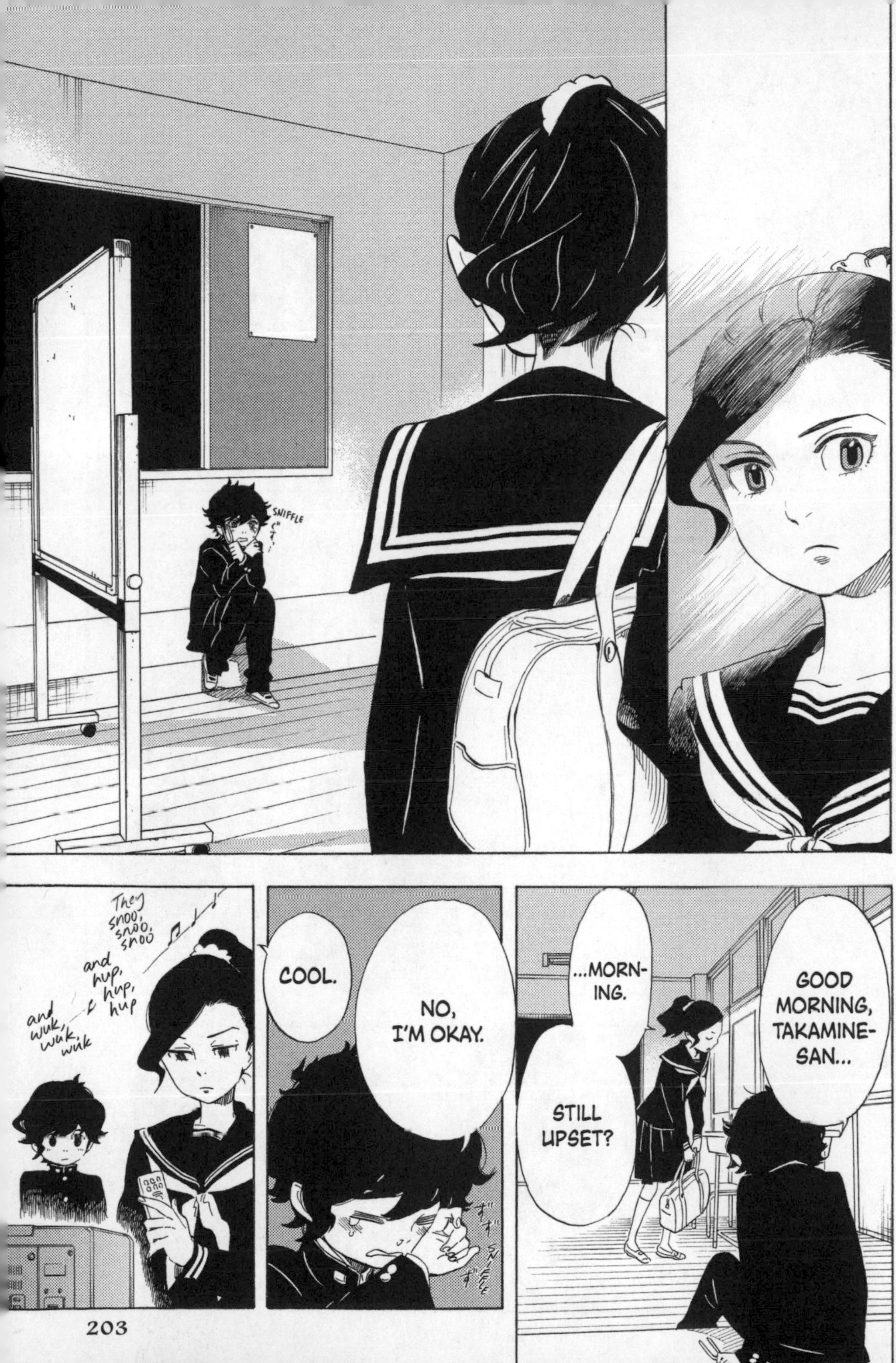
SNIFFLE
GOOD MORNING, TAKAMINE-SAN...
...MORN-ING.
STILL UPSET?
NO, I'M OKAY.
COOL.
SNIFFLE
They snoo, snoo, snoo
and hup, hup, hup
and wuk, wuk, wuk

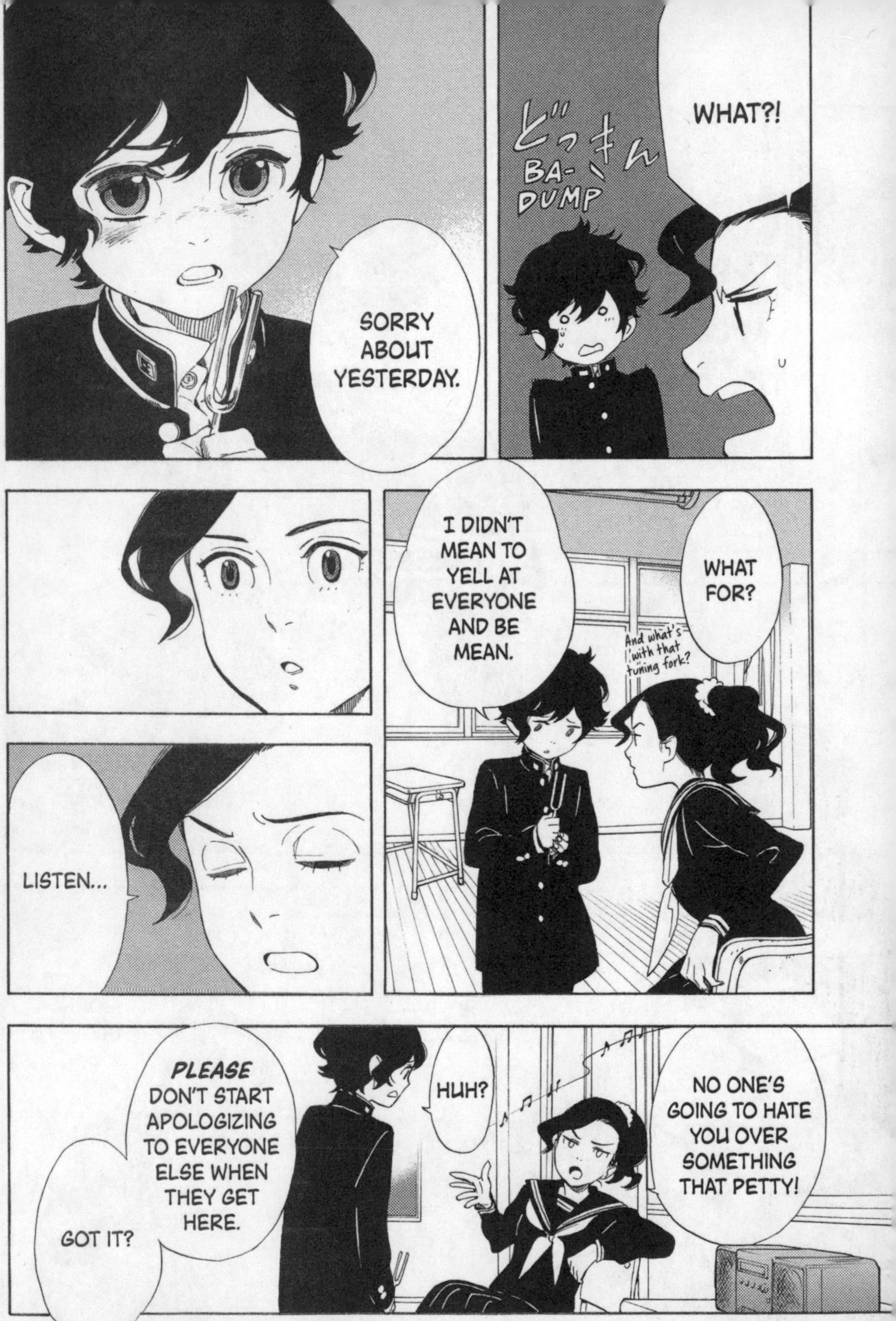
WHAT?!
どっきん
BA-DUMP
SORRY ABOUT YESTERDAY.
I DIDN'T MEAN TO YELL AT EVERYONE AND BE MEAN.
WHAT FOR?
And what's with that tuning fork?
LISTEN...
NO ONE'S GOING TO HATE YOU OVER SOMETHING THAT PETTY!
HUH?
PLEASE DON'T START APOLOGIZING TO EVERYONE ELSE WHEN THEY GET HERE.
GOT IT?

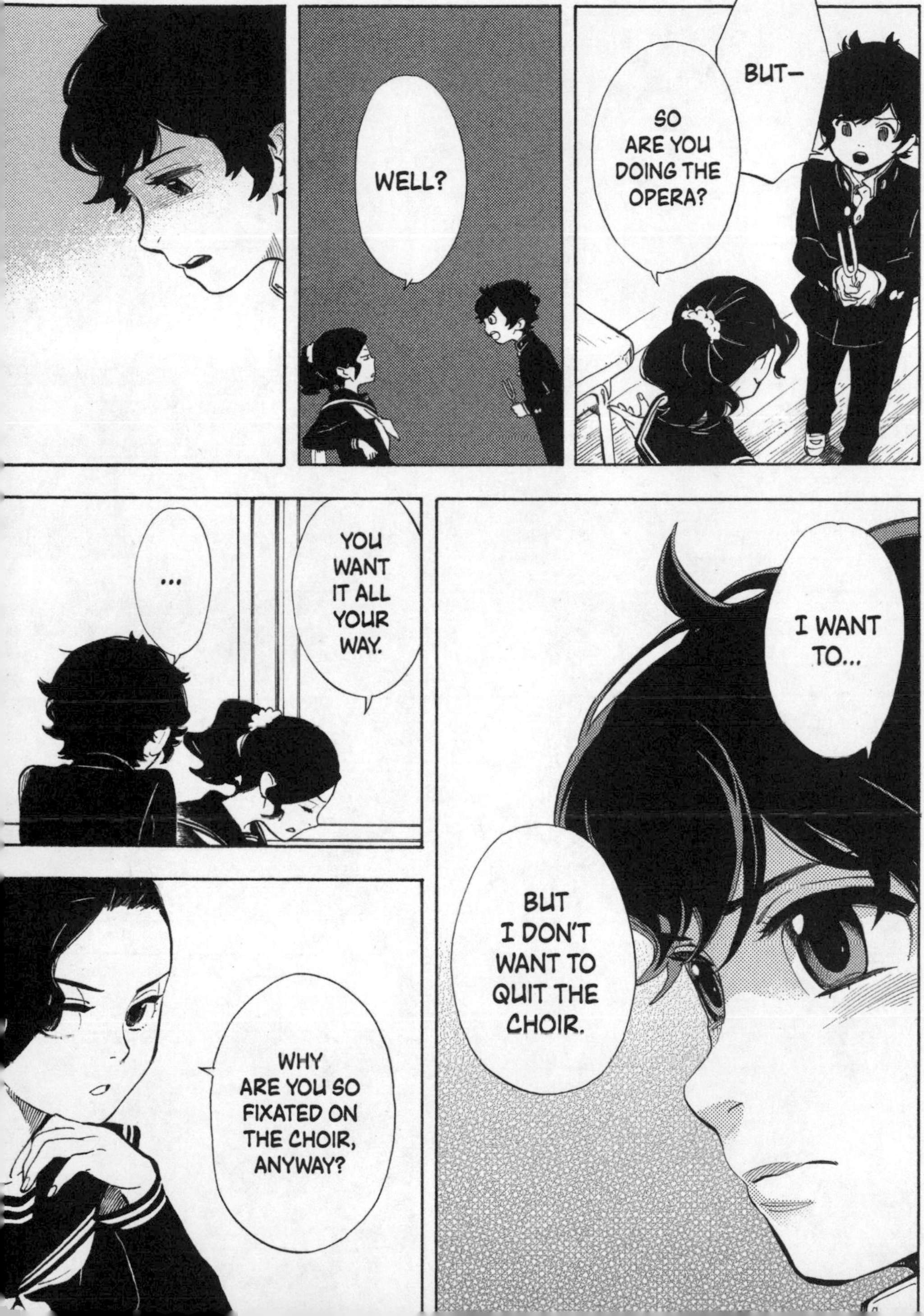
BUT—
SO ARE YOU DOING THE OPERA?
WELL?
I WANT TO...
BUT I DON'T WANT TO QUIT THE CHOIR.
YOU WANT IT ALL YOUR WAY.
...
WHY ARE YOU SO FIXATED ON THE CHOIR, ANYWAY?

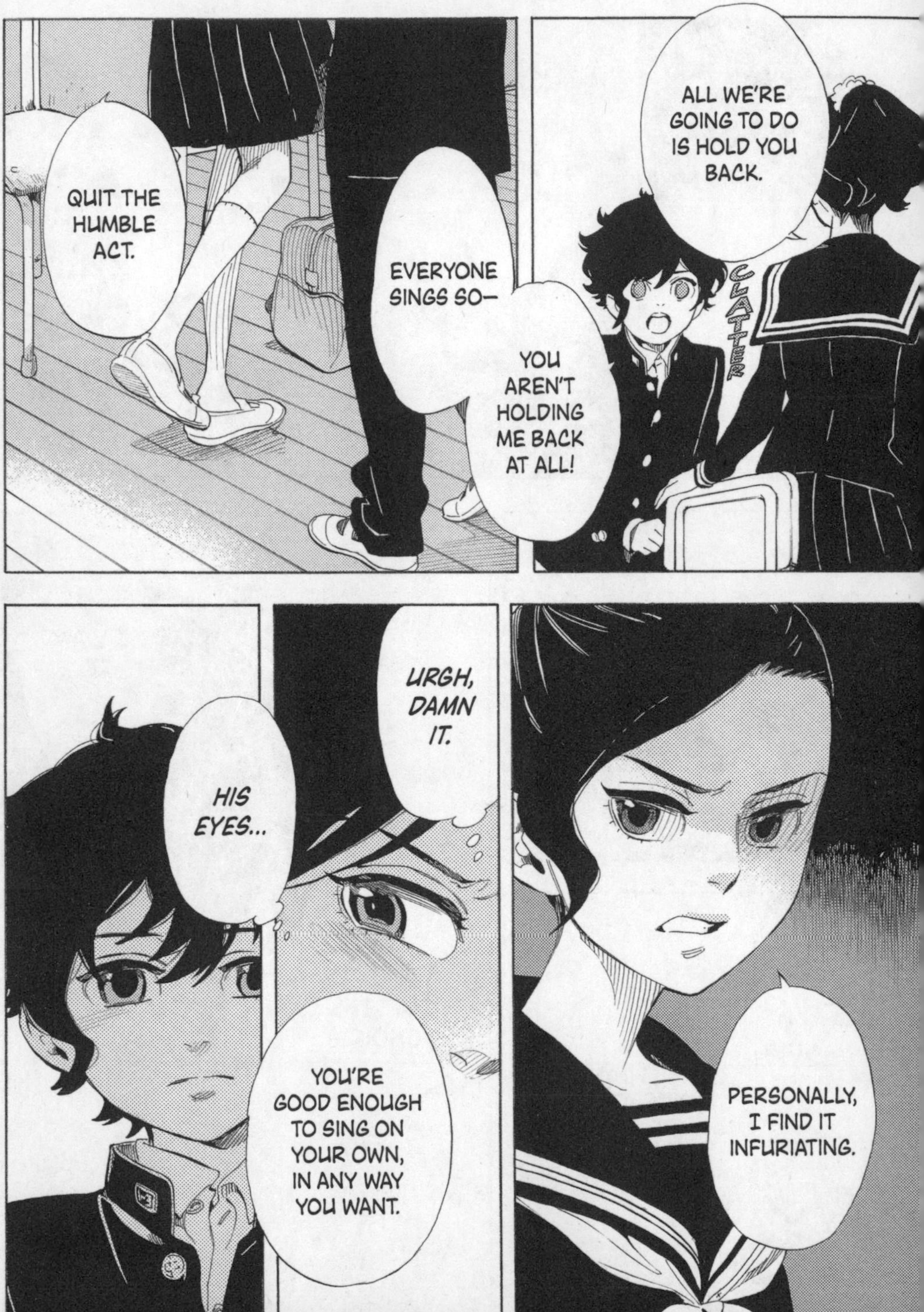
ALL WE'RE GOING TO DO IS HOLD YOU BACK.
CLATTER
YOU AREN'T HOLDING ME BACK AT ALL!
EVERYONE SINGS SO—
QUIT THE HUMBLE ACT.
PERSONALLY, I FIND IT INFURIATING.
URGH, DAMN IT.
YOU'RE GOOD ENOUGH TO SING ON YOUR OWN, IN ANY WAY YOU WANT.
HIS EYES...

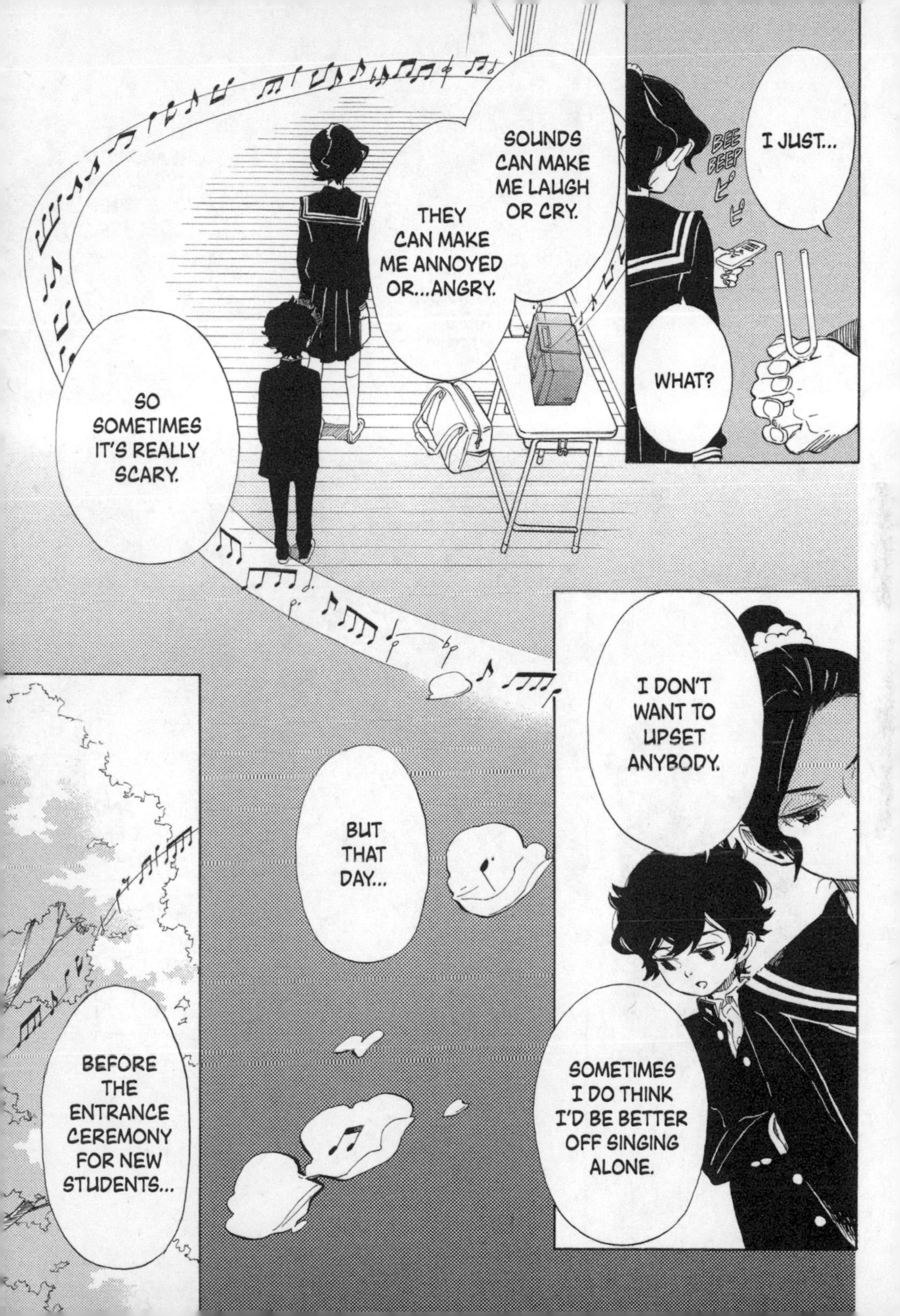
I JUST...
BEE BEEP
ピピ
WHAT?
SOUNDS CAN MAKE ME LAUGH OR CRY.
THEY CAN MAKE ME ANNOYED OR...ANGRY.
SO SOMETIMES IT'S REALLY SCARY.
I DON'T WANT TO UPSET ANYBODY.
SOMETIMES I DO THINK I'D BE BETTER OFF SINGING ALONE.
BUT THAT DAY...
BEFORE THE ENTRANCE CEREMONY FOR NEW STUDENTS...

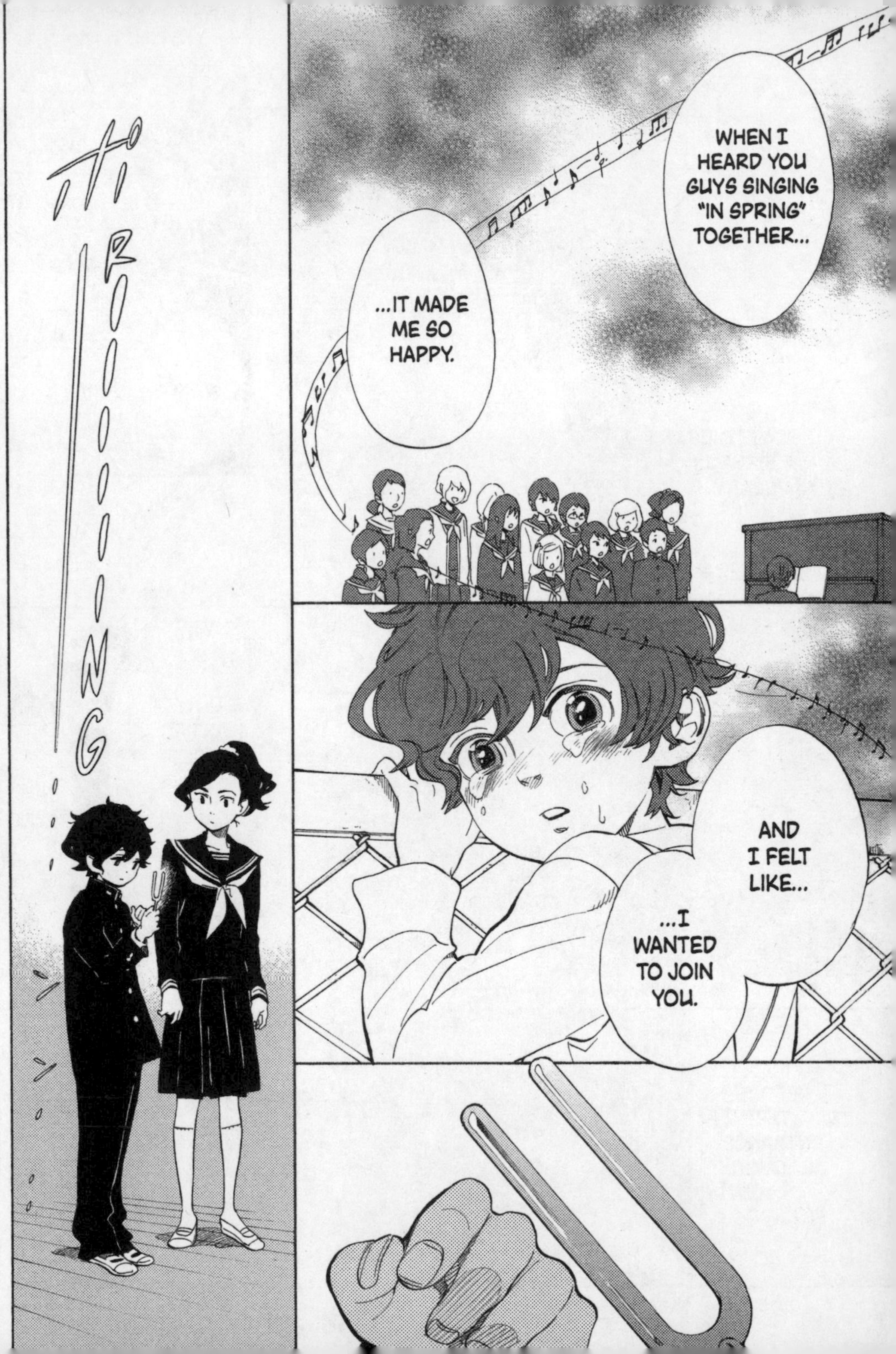
WHEN I HEARD YOU GUYS SINGING "IN SPRING" TOGETHER...
...IT MADE ME SO HAPPY.
AND I FELT LIKE...
...I WANTED TO JOIN YOU.
TIRIIIIIING

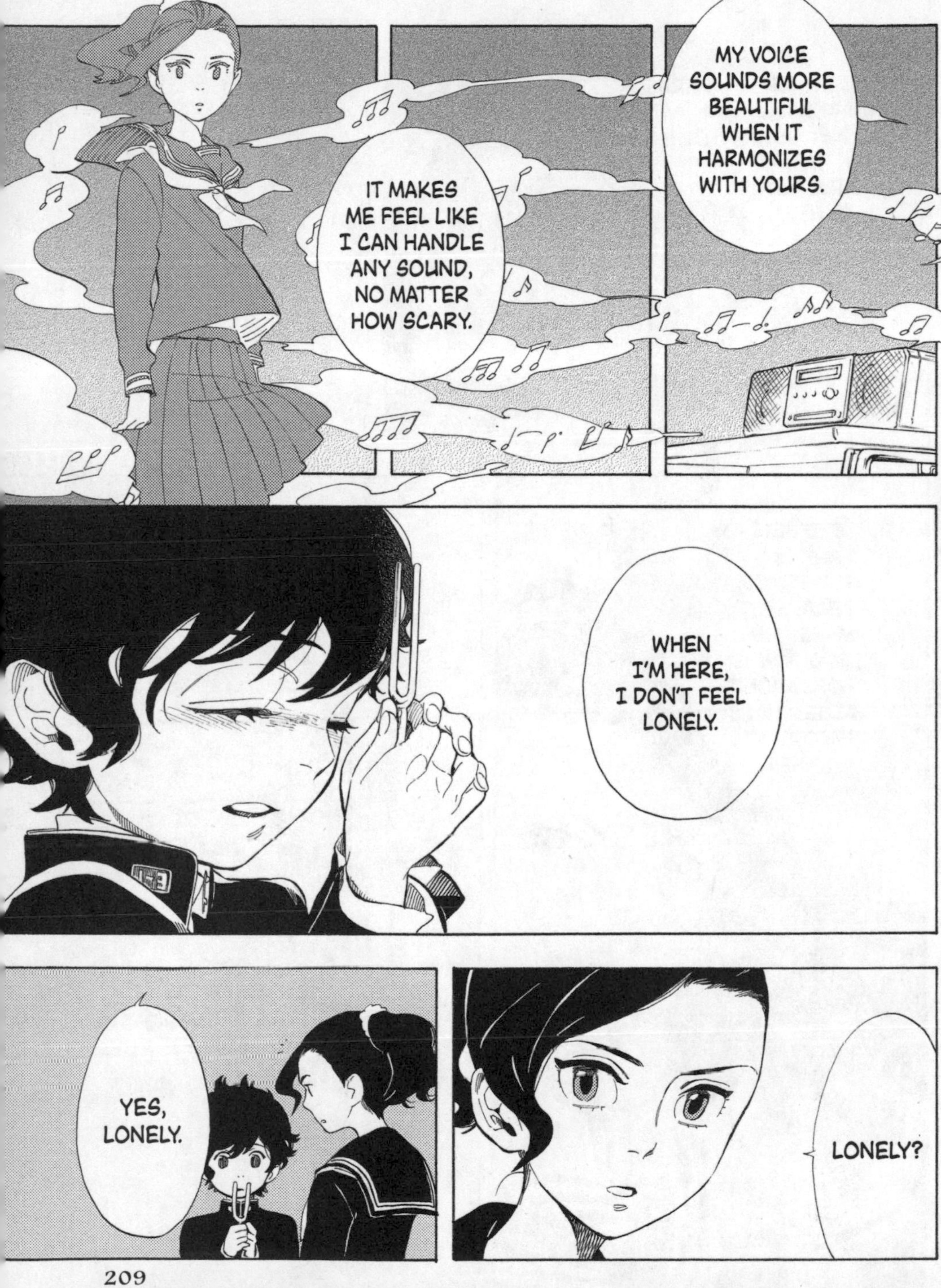
MY VOICE SOUNDS MORE BEAUTIFUL WHEN IT HARMONIZES WITH YOURS.
IT MAKES ME FEEL LIKE I CAN HANDLE ANY SOUND, NO MATTER HOW SCARY.
WHEN I'M HERE, I DON'T FEEL LONELY.
LONELY?
YES, LONELY.

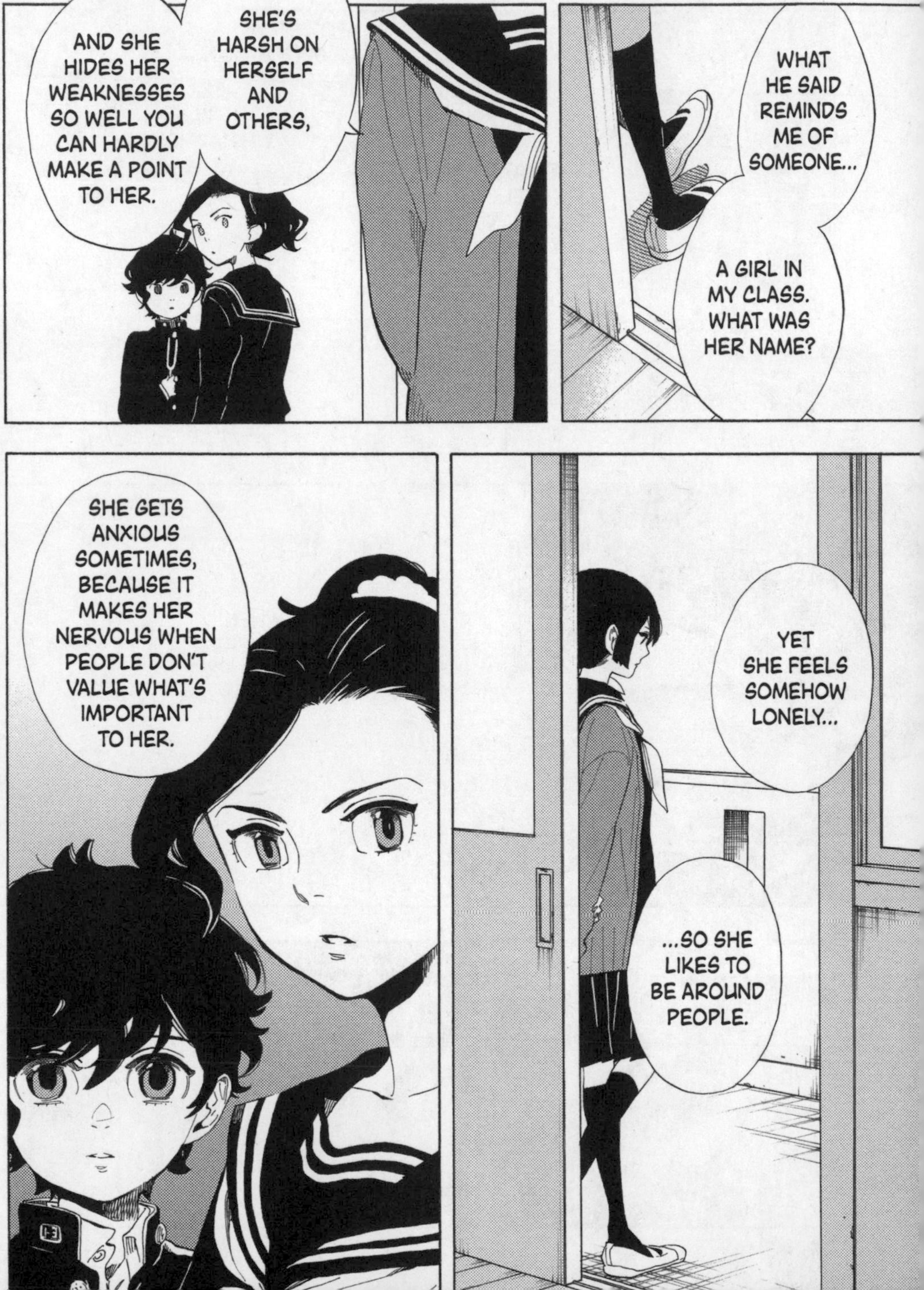
WHAT HE SAID REMINDS ME OF SOMEONE...
A GIRL IN MY CLASS. WHAT WAS HER NAME?
SHE'S HARSH ON HERSELF AND OTHERS,
AND SHE HIDES HER WEAKNESSES SO WELL YOU CAN HARDLY MAKE A POINT TO HER.
YET SHE FEELS SOMEHOW LONELY...
...SO SHE LIKES TO BE AROUND PEOPLE.
SHE GETS ANXIOUS SOMETIMES, BECAUSE IT MAKES HER NERVOUS WHEN PEOPLE DON'T VALUE WHAT'S IMPORTANT TO HER.

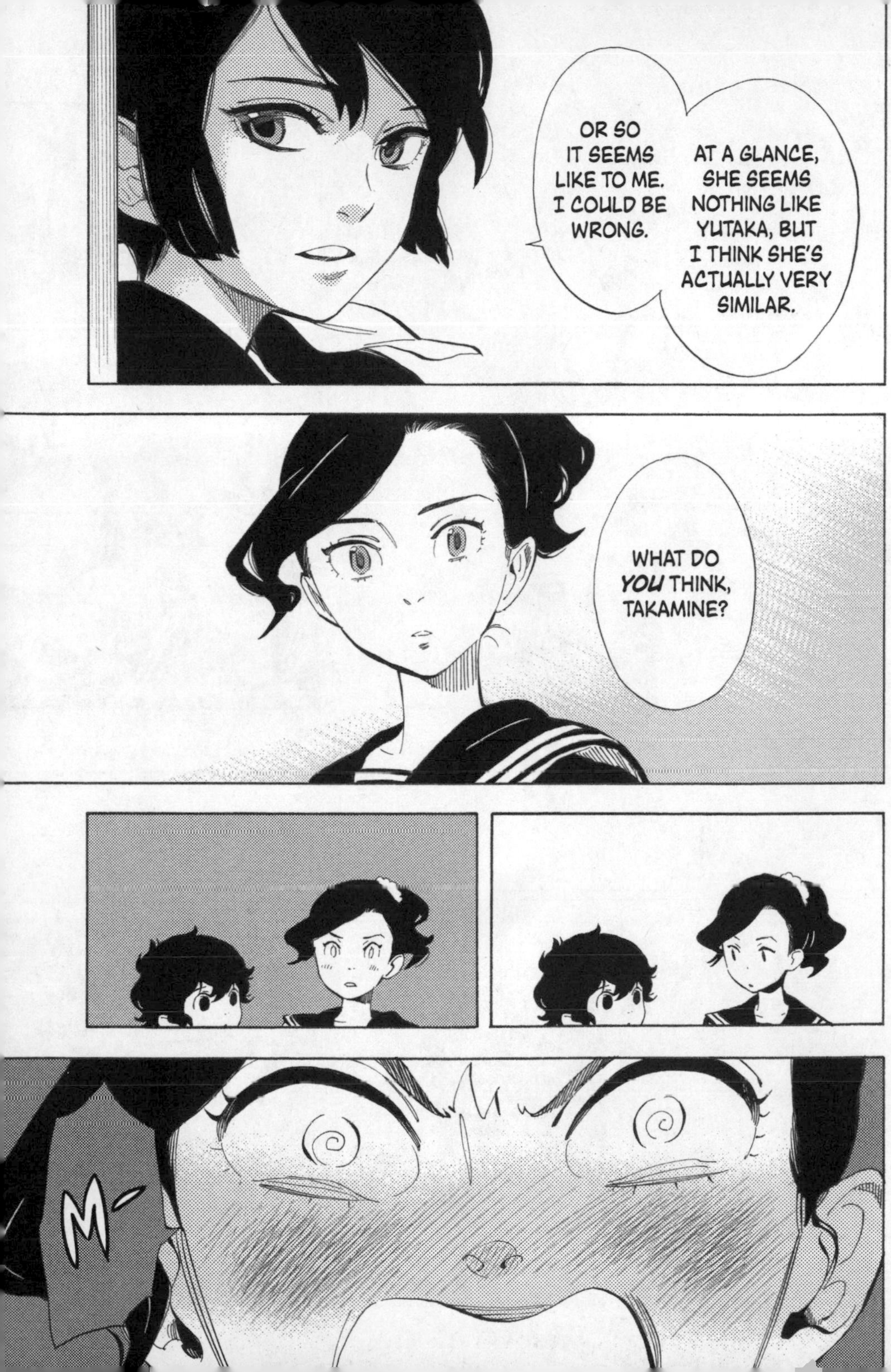
AT A GLANCE, SHE SEEMS NOTHING LIKE YUTAKA, BUT I THINK SHE'S ACTUALLY VERY SIMILAR.
OR SO IT SEEMS LIKE TO ME. I COULD BE WRONG.
WHAT DO *YOU* THINK, TAKAMINE?
M-

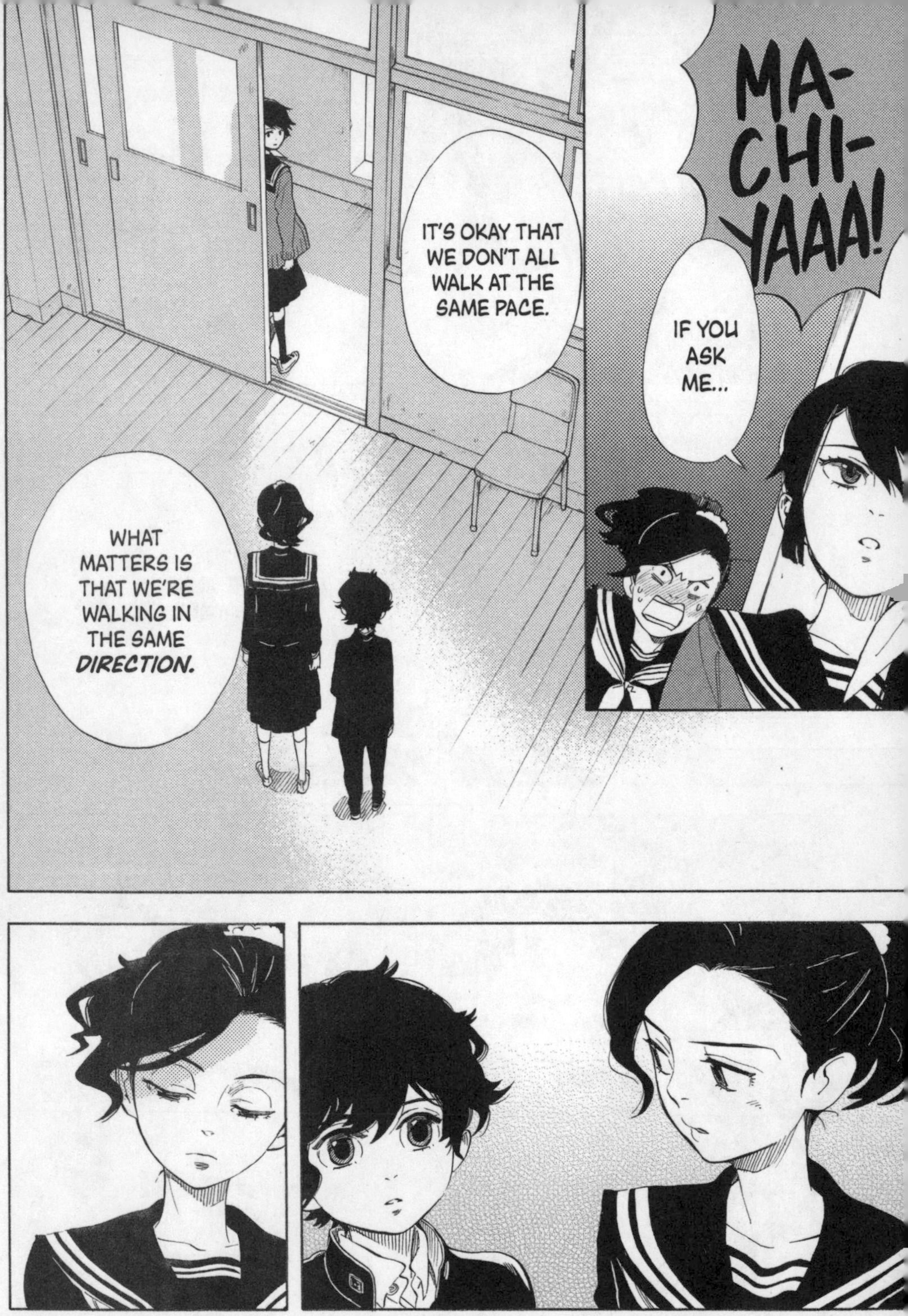
MA-CHI-YAAA!
IF YOU ASK ME...
IT'S OKAY THAT WE DON'T ALL WALK AT THE SAME PACE.
WHAT MATTERS IS THAT WE'RE WALKING IN THE SAME *DIRECTION.*

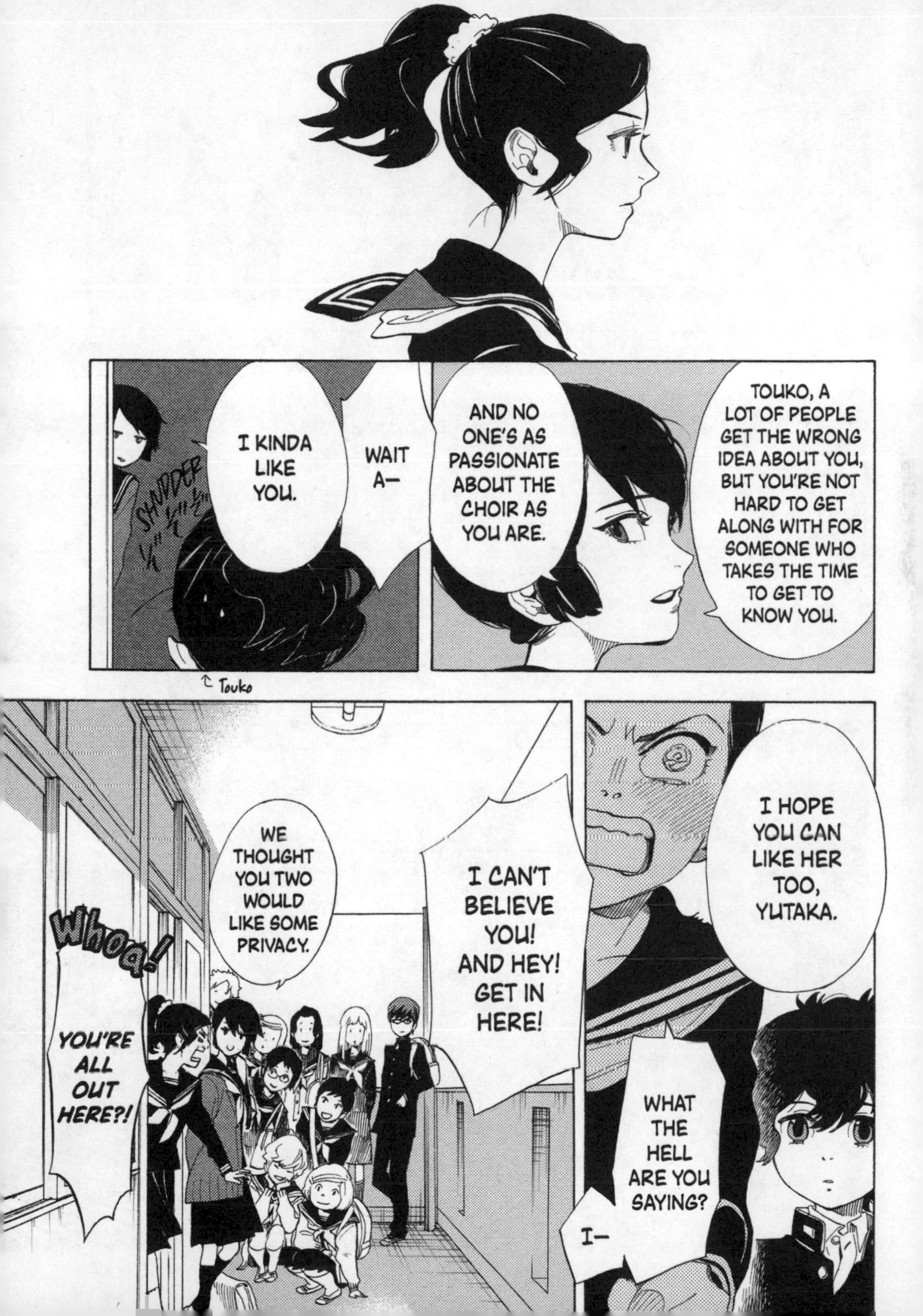
TOUKO, A LOT OF PEOPLE GET THE WRONG IDEA ABOUT YOU, BUT YOU'RE NOT HARD TO GET ALONG WITH FOR SOMEONE WHO TAKES THE TIME TO GET TO KNOW YOU.
AND NO ONE'S AS PASSIONATE ABOUT THE CHOIR AS YOU ARE.
WAIT A—
I KINDA LIKE YOU.
SHUDDER
Touko
I HOPE YOU CAN LIKE HER TOO, YUTAKA.
WHAT THE HELL ARE YOU SAYING?
I—
I CAN'T BELIEVE YOU! AND HEY! GET IN HERE!
Whoa!
WE THOUGHT YOU TWO WOULD LIKE SOME PRIVACY.
YOU'RE ALL OUT HERE?!

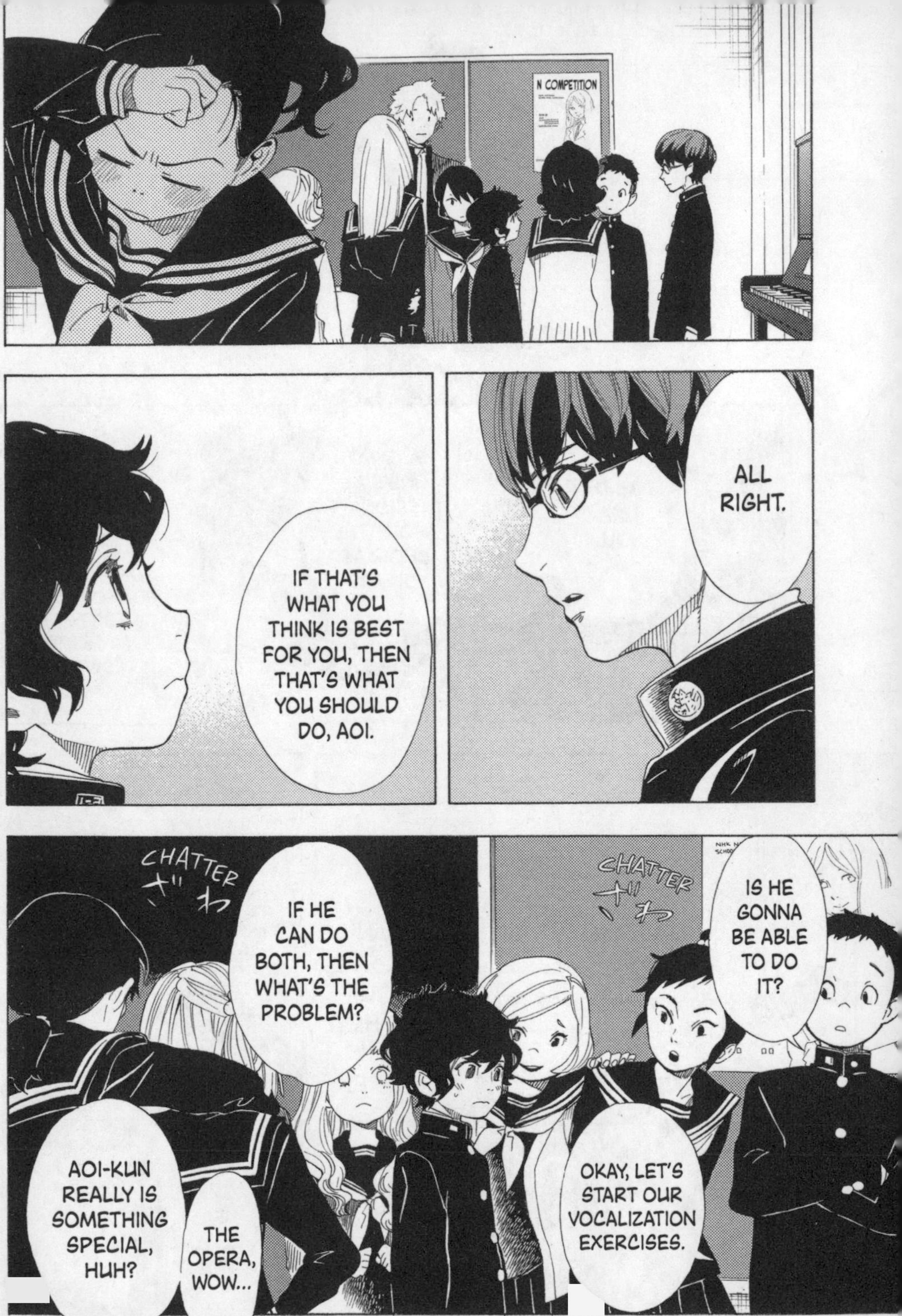
N COMPETITION
ALL RIGHT.
IF THAT'S WHAT YOU THINK IS BEST FOR YOU, THEN THAT'S WHAT YOU SHOULD DO, AOI.
IS HE GONNA BE ABLE TO DO IT?
CHATTER ざわ
IF HE CAN DO BOTH, THEN WHAT'S THE PROBLEM?
CHATTER ざわ
OKAY, LET'S START OUR VOCALIZATION EXERCISES.
THE OPERA, WOW...
AOI-KUN REALLY IS SOMETHING SPECIAL, HUH?

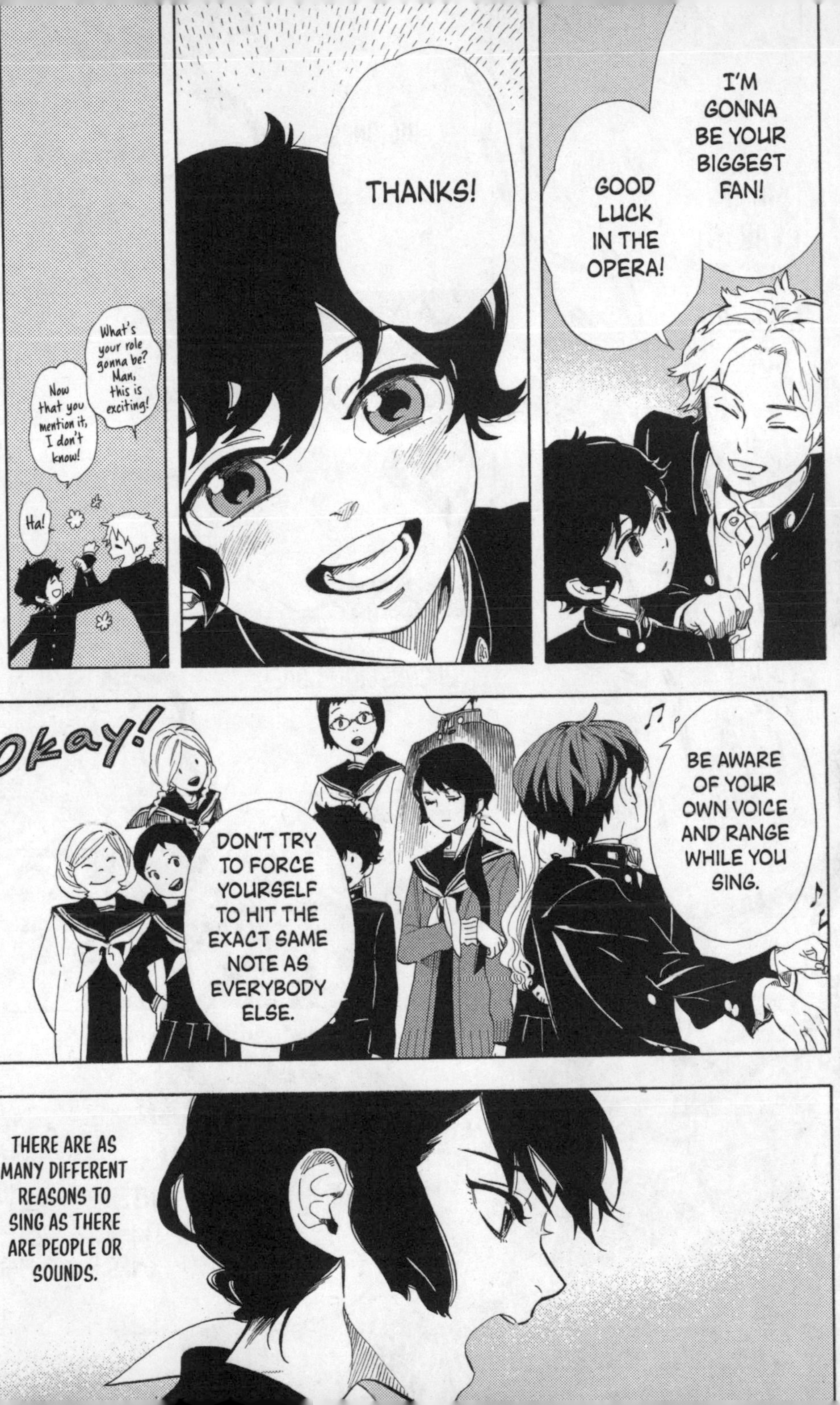
I'M GONNA BE YOUR BIGGEST FAN!
GOOD LUCK IN THE OPERA!
THANKS!
What's your role gonna be? Man, this is exciting!
Now that you mention it, I don't know!
Ha!
BE AWARE OF YOUR OWN VOICE AND RANGE WHILE YOU SING.
DON'T TRY TO FORCE YOURSELF TO HIT THE EXACT SAME NOTE AS EVERYBODY ELSE.
Okay!
THERE ARE AS MANY DIFFERENT REASONS TO SING AS THERE ARE PEOPLE OR SOUNDS.

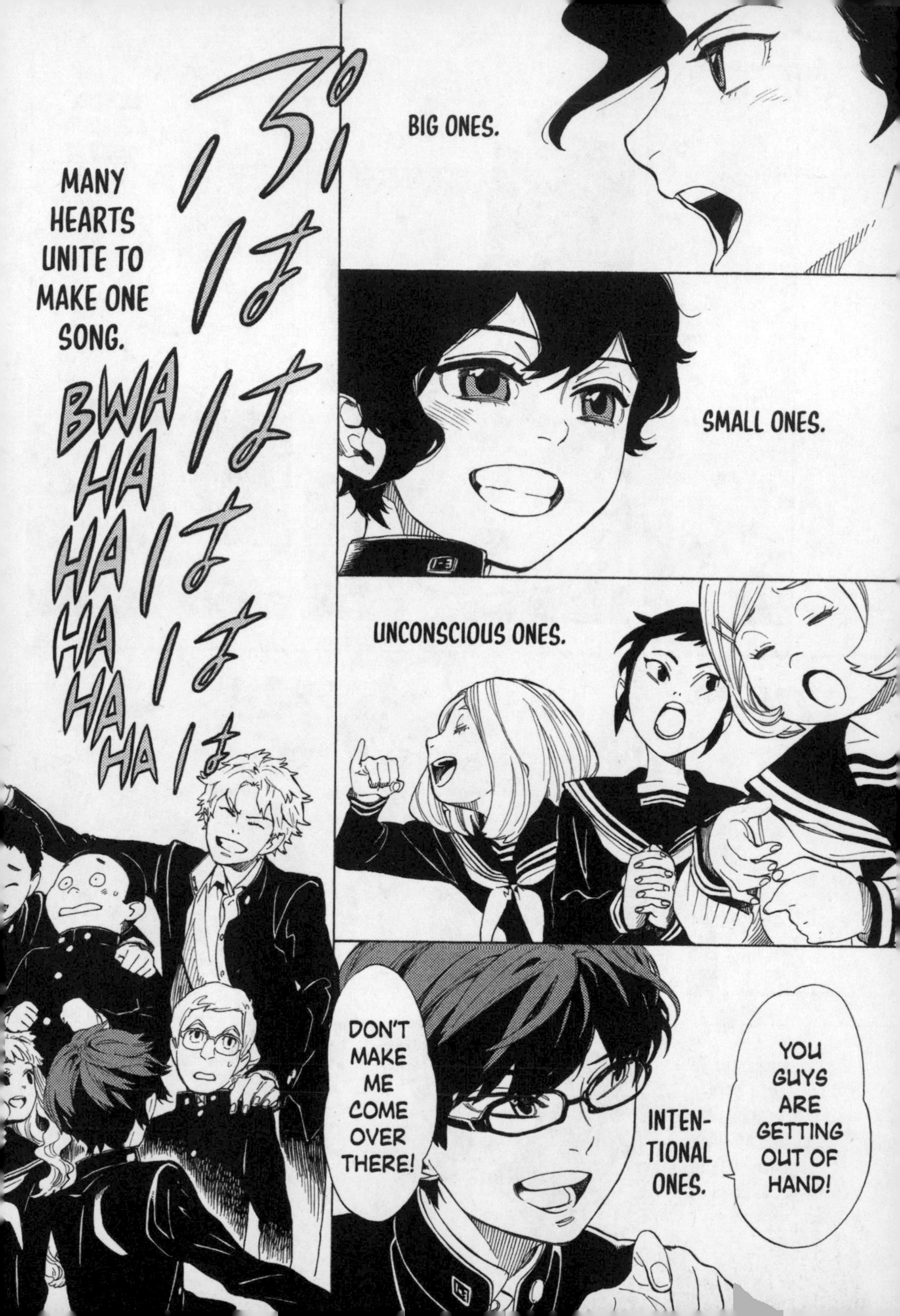
BIG ONES.
SMALL ONES.
UNCONSCIOUS ONES.
YOU GUYS ARE GETTING OUT OF HAND!
INTENTIONAL ONES.
DON'T MAKE ME COME OVER THERE!
MANY HEARTS UNITE TO MAKE ONE SONG.
ぷはははははは
BWA HA HA HA HA HA

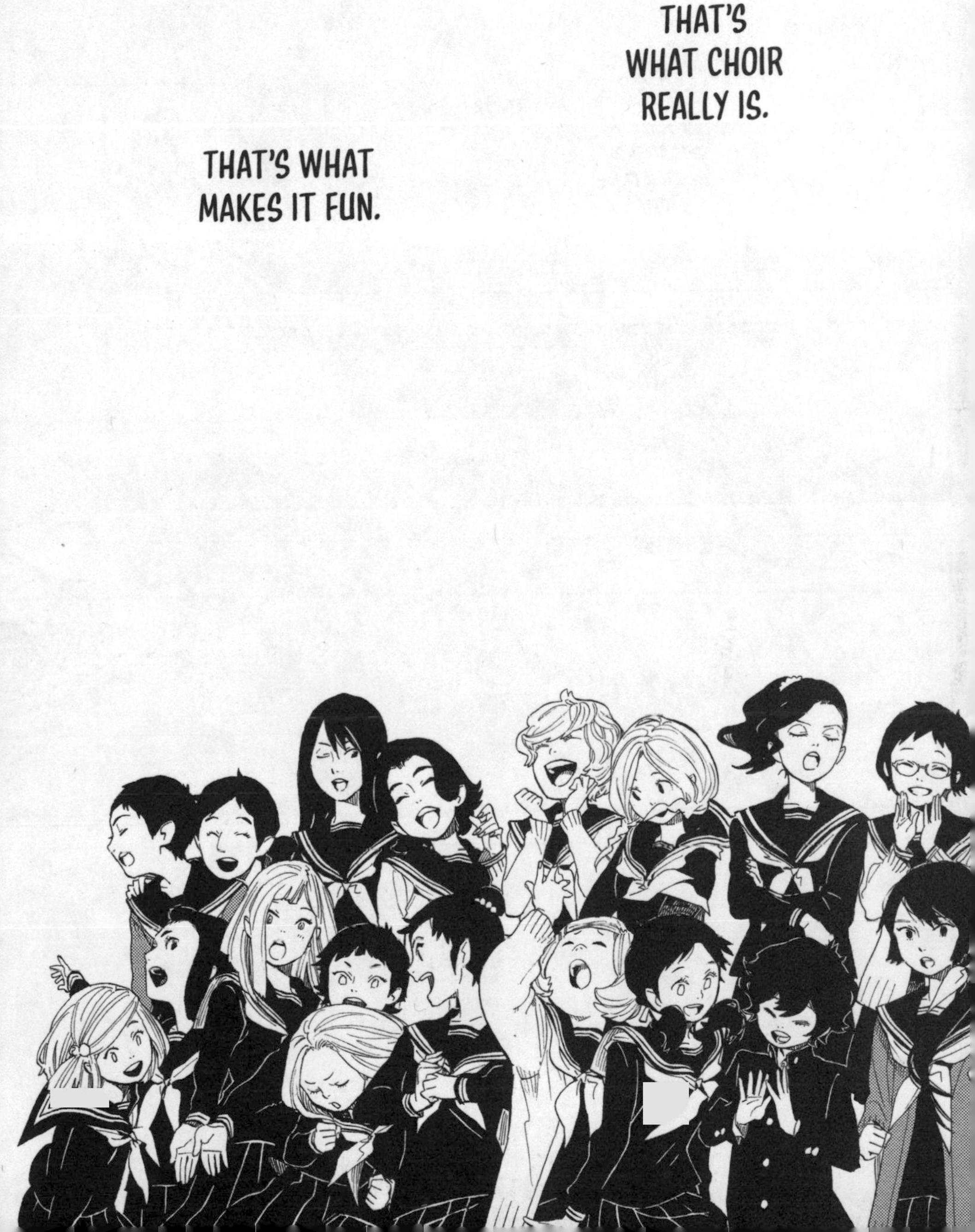
THAT'S WHAT CHOIR REALLY IS.
THAT'S WHAT MAKES IT FUN.

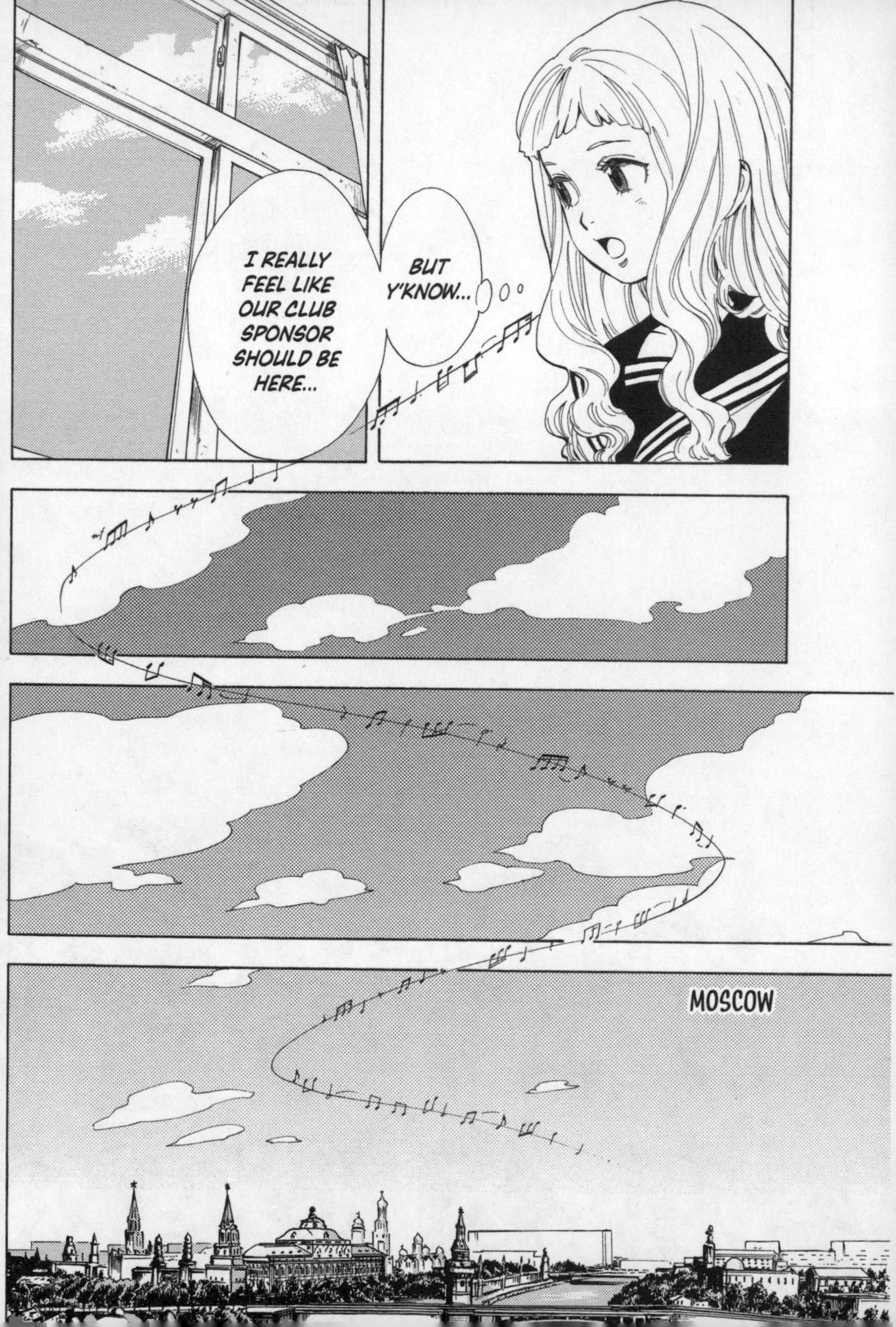
BUT Y'KNOW...
I REALLY FEEL LIKE OUR CLUB SPONSOR SHOULD BE HERE...
MOSCOW

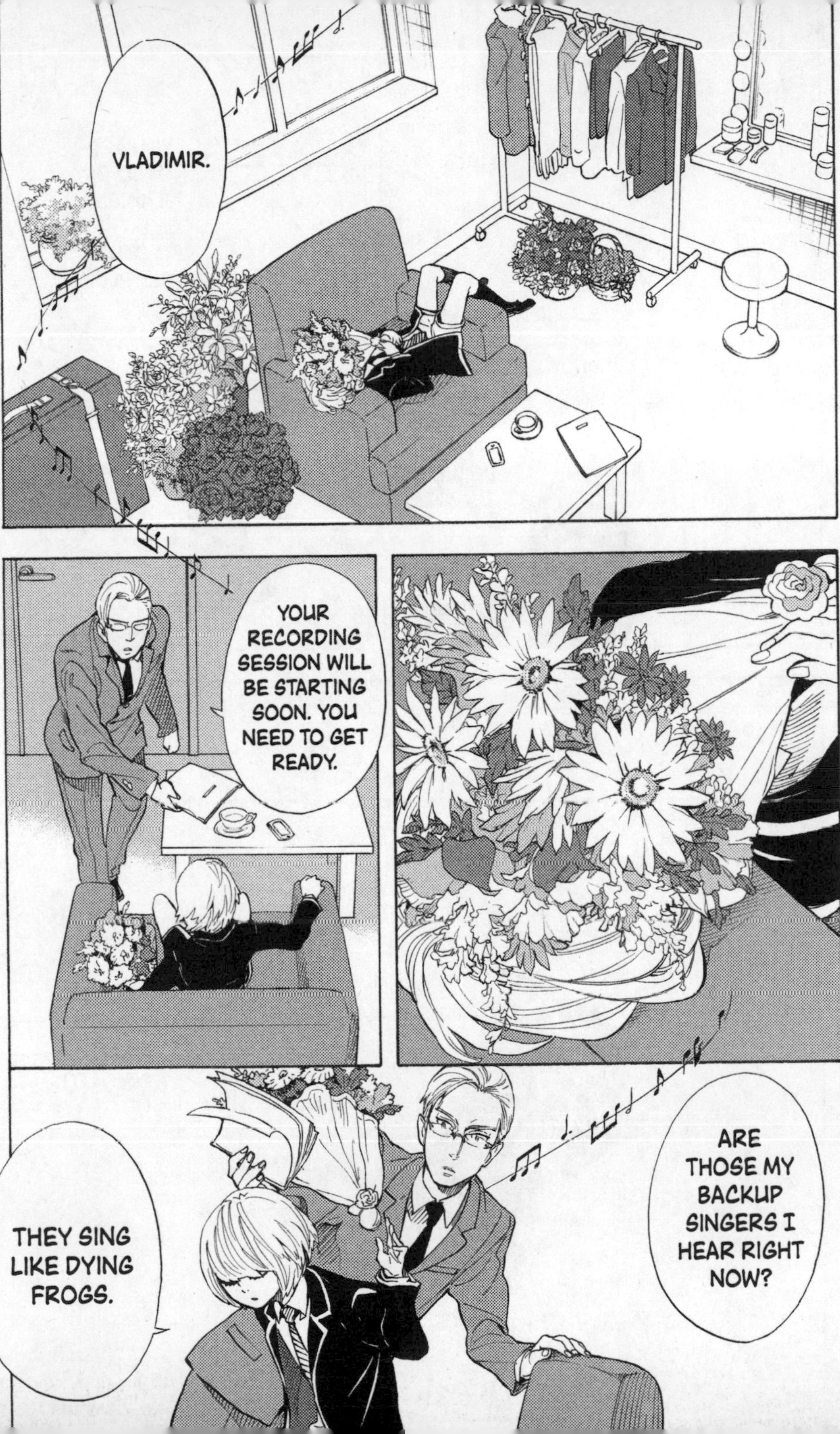
VLADIMIR.
YOUR RECORDING SESSION WILL BE STARTING SOON. YOU NEED TO GET READY.
ARE THOSE MY BACKUP SINGERS I HEAR RIGHT NOW?
THEY SING LIKE DYING FROGS.

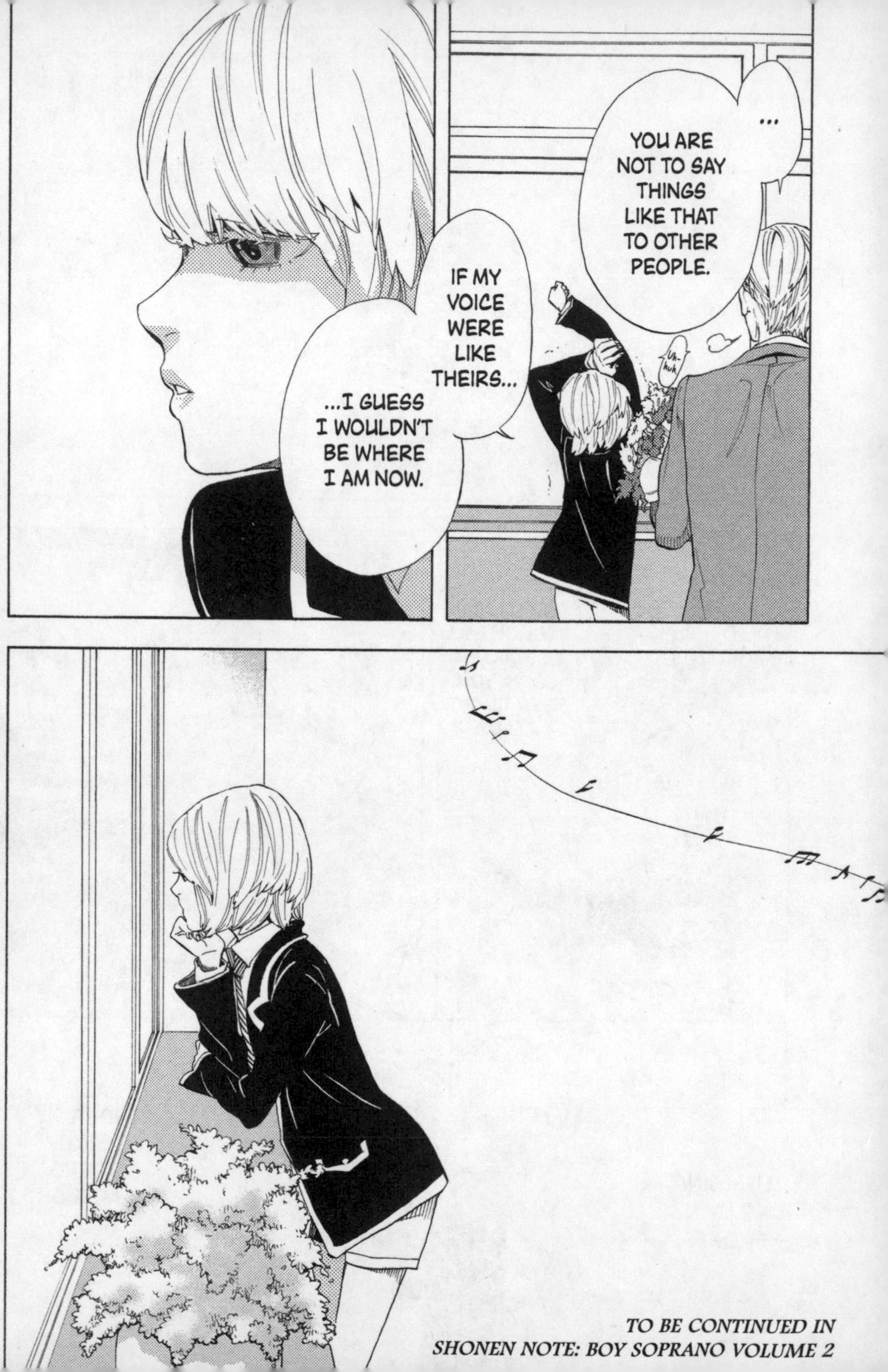
...
YOU ARE NOT TO SAY THINGS LIKE THAT TO OTHER PEOPLE.
Uh-huh
IF MY VOICE WERE LIKE THEIRS...
...I GUESS I WOULDN'T BE WHERE I AM NOW.
TO BE CONTINUED IN SHONEN NOTE: BOY SOPRANO VOLUME 2

Translation Notes

Boy soprano, page 1

While, historically, a boy soprano traditionally refers to a young male singer whose voice falls within a treble or high vocal range, as of April 2021, the Music Library Association updated the wording of their thesaurus regarding the usage of gendered terms to describe one's vocal range, stating "there was a broad consensus among members of the Cataloging and Metadata Committee that we should separate the issue of vocal range from that of gender of the singers, since the accuracy of these terms for contemporary and historical use is questionable. Although there are times when a gendered term may be more appropriate (scores calling for a 'boy soprano', for instance), there was agreement that we should have options for disassociating these concepts in the vocal and choral terms."

"In Spring," page 10

"In Spring" (*"Haru ni"*) is a Japanese choir song by Shuntaro Tanikawa and Makiko Kinoshita.

"Cosmos," page 19

The song Yutaka is singing here is "Cosmos," stylized in Japanese as *"COSMOS (コスモス),"* a popular Japanese choir song often sung in middle schools.

Spring break, page 22

It's worth noting that "spring break" means something very different in Japan than it does in the US, as the Japanese school year, which begins in April, starts immediately after it. (Japanese schools typically operate on a trimester system, with the first running from April to July, the second from September to December, and the last from January to late March.) Since students have breaks in between each trimester, the Japanese spring break would be similar to summer break in American schools, although not as long.

Toshi-niichan, page 56

Here, Tomoya is addressing Betsuyaku with a shortened version of his first name, Akitoshi, coupled with the suffix *~niichan.* While *~niichan,* written with the character 兄, is a suffix often used to address an elder brother, it can also be used when addressing someone, typically male, who's older than oneself. (For example, here, Betsuyaku is a third-year student.)

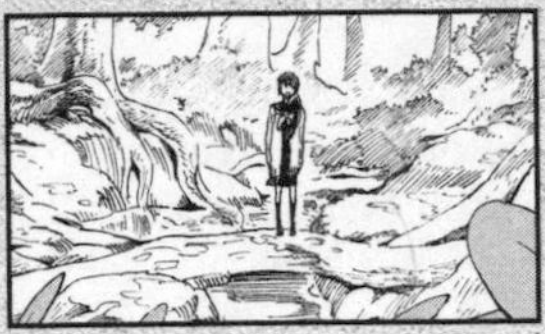

Echo, pages 74–75

The word Yutaka uses to describe the "echo," or reverberating quality, in Machiya's voice is *kodama*, which readers may recognize from the Studio Ghibli movie *Princess Mononoke*. Echoes in Japan's mountainous regions were once attributed to forest spirits called kodama, and, eventually, their name came to mean "echo" in Japanese.

"I sure know how to sound pretentious, don't I?", page 83

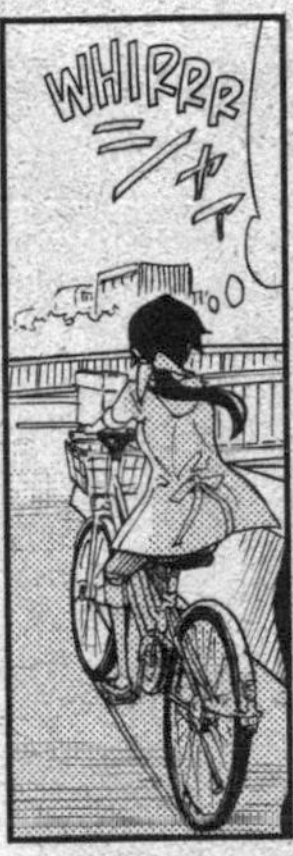
WHIRRR

In the original Japanese, Machiya is calling herself "*chuuni-byou manten*," or "extremely *chuuni-byou*." *Chuuni-byou*, or "second-year middle school sickness", is a joke "condition" (think "senioritis") said to afflict some teenagers in their second year of middle school. Symptoms include delusions of grandeur or a feeling that one is special that members of broader society (or peers not suffering from this malady) might consider pompous in someone so young. Given the remark, Machiya is presumably in her second year of middle school.

"Snoo, hup, wuk," page 99

This little song from Shuntaro Tanikawa's "Two Billion Light Years of Solitude" is about Martians who do these things. The fun of the song is largely in the fact that the verbs are suggestive of meaning without being truly meaningful. If you must know what they mean, please refer to the following glossary, disemvoweled to make it harder to spoil for readers who would rather not have this idea seeded for them: "Thy slp, slp, slp nd gt p, gt p, gt p nd wrk, wrk, wrk." It kind of seems like a depressing way to think about Martian society when you interpret it like that...

"VOICE" by Lyrico, page 104

Lyrico is the former stage name of Harumi Tsuyuzaki, a Japanese pop, R&B, and soul singer-songwriter.

Milky Way, page 132
In Japanese, the word for "galaxy" (*ginga*) used here is written with the kanji for "silver river," reminiscent of the river so prominent in the landscape and name of the town in which Yutaka lives, Kawami (the *kawa* in Kawami means "river").

Sing, sing, sing, page 172
When Yutaka gets overloaded here, the words all around him start to blend together, and all the rhymes and overlapping syllables in the words become extra-prominent. His name, Yutaka, rhymes with the Japanese "*uta ga*" ("the song..."). "*Uta ga*" sounds a lot like "*utagau*" ("to doubt"). "*Takauta ga*" suggests a high-pitched or reverberant song. Unfortunately, there was no way to precisely capture all of these gnomic resemblances in English. Japanese as a language is especially well suited for puns because it features a very small number of vowel sounds, leading to many homophones, and because it uses a mixed ideographic/phonetic writing system. It's enough to make one's head spin!

This English edition of *Shonen Note: Boy Soprano* is
dedicated to the beloved memory of Fall Rose Padgett.

A SMART, NEW ROMANTIC COMEDY FOR FANS OF *SHORTCAKE CAKE* AND *TERRACE HOUSE*!

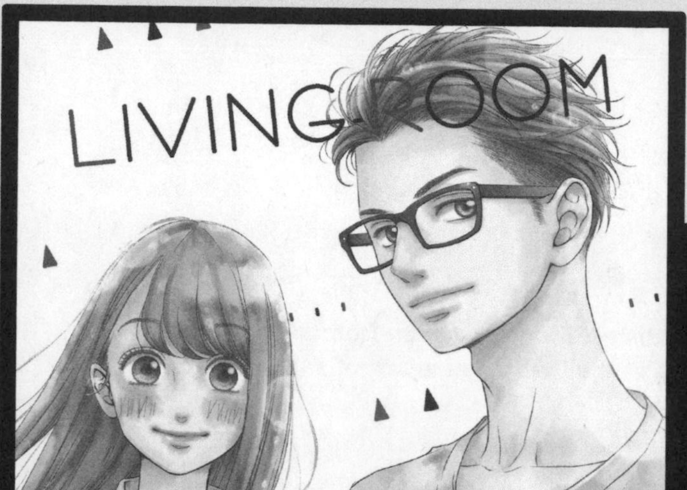
LIVING-ROOM
MATSUNAGA-SAN
1
Keiko Iwashita

A romance manga starring high school girl Meeko, who learns to live on her own in a boarding house whose living room is home to the odd (but handsome) Matsunaga-san. She begins to adjust to her new life away from her parents, but Meeko soon learns that no matter how far away from home she is, she's still a young girl at heart — especially when she finds herself falling for Matsunaga-san.

KC KODANSHA COMICS

Knight of the ICE

Yayoi Ogawa

Knight of the Ice ©Yayoi Ogawa/Kodansha Ltd.

SKATING THRILLS AND ICY CHILLS WITH THIS NEW TINGLY ROMANCE SERIES!

A rom-com on ice, perfect for fans of *Princess Jellyfish* and *Wotakoi*. Kokoro is the talk of the figure-skating world, winning trophies and hearts. But little do they know... he's actually a huge nerd! From the beloved creator of *You're My Pet* (*Tramps Like Us*).

Chitose is a serious young woman, working for the health magazine *SASSO*. Or at least, she would be, if she wasn't constantly getting distracted by her childhood friend, international figure skating star Kokoro Kijinami! In the public eye and on the ice, Kokoro is a gallant, flawless knight, but behind his glittery costumes and breathtaking spins lies a secret: He's actually a hopelessly romantic otaku, who can only land his quad jumps when Chitose is on hand to recite a spell from his favorite magical girl anime!

Young characters and steampunk setting, like *Howl's Moving Castle* and *Battle Angel Alita*

Beyond the Clouds © 2018 Nicke / Ki-oon

A boy with a talent for machines and a mysterious girl whose wings he's fixed will take you beyond the clouds! In the tradition of the high-flying, resonant adventure stories of Studio Ghibli comes a gorgeous tale about the longing of young hearts for adventure and friendship!